World War I on Film

ALSO BY PAUL M. EDWARDS
AND FROM MCFARLAND

*United Nations Participants in the Korean War:
The Contributions of 45 Member Countries* (2013)

*Combat Operations of the Korean War:
Ground, Air, Sea, Special and Covert* (2010)

*Between the Lines of World War II:
Twenty-One Remarkable People and Events* (2010)

*Small United States and United Nations
Warships in the Korean War* (2008)

*The Hill Wars of the Korean Conflict: A Dictionary
of Hills, Outposts and Other Sites of Military Action* (2006)

World War I on Film
English Language Releases through 2014

PAUL M. EDWARDS

McFarland & Company, Inc., Publishers
Jefferson, North Carolina

LIBRARY OF CONGRESS CATALOGUING-IN-PUBLICATION DATA

Names: Edwards, Paul M., author.
Title: World War I on film : English language releases through 2014 / Paul M. Edwards.
Description: Jefferson, N.C. : McFarland & Company, Inc., Publishers, 2016. | Includes bibliographical references and index.
Identifiers: LCCN 2016000595 | ISBN 9780786498666 (softcover : acid free paper) ∞
Subjects: LCSH: World War, 1914–1918—Motion pictures and the war. | War films—United States—History and criticism. | War films—Great Britain—History and criticism.
Classification: LCC D522.23 .E35 2016 | DDC 791.43/658403—dc23
LC record available at http://lccn.loc.gov/2016000595

BRITISH LIBRARY CATALOGUING DATA ARE AVAILABLE

**ISBN (print) 978-0-7864-9866-6
ISBN (ebook) 978-1-4766-2063-3**

© 2016 Paul M. Edwards. All rights reserved

No part of this book may be reproduced or transmitted in any form or by any means, electronic or mechanical, including photocopying or recording, or by any information storage and retrieval system, without permission in writing from the publisher.

On the cover: Lew Ayres in *All Quiet on the Western Front*, 1930 (Photofest)

Printed in the United States of America

*McFarland & Company, Inc., Publishers
Box 611, Jefferson, North Carolina 28640
www.mcfarlandpub.com*

Dedicated to Cora, Vera, Sofia and Samantha.
Awesome all.

Table of Contents

Preface **1**

A Brief History of the Production of Films About World War I **9**

An Introduction to the Films **26**

The Films **32**

Appendix:
Films by Year of Release **217**

Notes **221**

Bibliography **225**

Index **227**

Preface

A good many historians of World War I consider that conflict to be the most significant event in modern history and believe that almost every important thing that has happened since that time is in some way related to it. Despite the fact that the war is not well remembered, particularly in America, this position is hard to dispute. Those years of fighting, a fight that encompassed most of the known world, radically changed the political, economic, and social character of a great percentage of the Western world. Without a doubt it altered the geography of the world, and ignited the fires of nationalism and ethnic diversity. The impact of the war challenged the existing moral codes and put to rest many Victorian ideas including that of the role of women. The conflict opened up to criticism many of the assumptions of Western civilization. Overall it produced a universal disquiet that "saw all gods dead, all heroes humbled, and all causes exhausted."[1]

Many saw both the harsh realities of the war and the unrelenting demands of the Treaty of Versailles as the source of their revulsion to war, and the roots of the new demands for peace and national isolation. There was surprising agreement with Paul Fussell's view that "every war is ironic because every war is worse than expected. Every war constitutes an irony of situation because its means are so melodramatically disproportionate to its presumed ends."

War, like all critical situations humans must deal with, brings out both the worst and best in people. The process of war is so extreme, it provides the defining moments in many people's lives. War personalizes the accumulative fear and puts the individual on the spot as they alone are required to respond. And yet war is also inclined to lay the foundations for comradeship and to cement them with powerful bonds. It is the tendency of these situations to dehumanize the enemy, and yet at the same time combat itself provides a unification of appreciation that non-combatants cannot possibly realize. Literature and the arts do a good job of personalizing these themes but it is in the film that we find the best and most poignant expressions of the events that occurred..

The perceptions we have of the war were, and are still, influenced by films about it. During World War I, all of the movies produced were silent and today, surrounded with vast technological advances and fantastic special effects, we might consider them an inefficient means of communication. But they were surprisingly efficient. In those days before the heyday of radio and without any television at all, the filmed documentaries and the variety of fiction films were the most widely shared public experience available. They were the primary means for informing the movie going audience about what was happening in the world and how it was affecting them.

The films were invaluable in generating an expanded sense of national unity and community that in turn allowed the fledgling industry the chance to play a significant if somewhat unexpected role in defining wartime America. The emergence of the film industry took place during a period that ran from approximately 1870 to 1920, during which time America was reaching the climax of a demographic transition—a move from the vastly isolated communities of rural America to increasingly complex urban settings. New identities, both individual and national, were being forged. Films offered them a whole new field of information and entertainment to fill their increasing hours of leisure.

The war film genre, by definition, includes those films concerned with warfare in most of its phases and focuses either on massive land, sea or air battles or on covert operations. It encompasses military training, the lives of prisoners of war, or in some significant way depicts the effect of the war on the individual and/or a community. They depend on the war for plot or for a situation in which to tell their story. The setting is established by acknowledging the presence of the war and in doing so left the moviemakers free to manipulate the situation for their creative endeavor. The general themes of these films include combat, weapons, equipment, strategy, survival, death, escape, sacrifice, and the very human and moral issues involved in the struggles of life and death.

In the focus on combat coverage, they misrepresent the military as many men and women knew it. That is, they provide little evidence of the military other than the horrors of trench warfare. If we are to let these films serve as our memory of those days, then we will be greatly misinformed: Thousands upon thousands of men served in the armed services doing the work necessary to keep those on the front line supplied. The job was not romantic but was vitally necessary.

These war films are generally historical or semi-historical—sometimes biographical—but also are fictional and in more recent times they even reflect alternative history.[2] This genre also includes what are called anti-war films, which used the medium to focus on the pain and disruption of war and its aftermath and to promote peace and even isolationism.[3] Many believed that films, because they could show the death and destruction as many had never seen it, were the key to establishing some sort of world peace or, at the least, could perhaps keep America out of war.

In the presentation of the genre, however, Hollywood also created, and has continued to create, the concept of combat as exciting and romantically glorifying—an opportunity for a man to challenge death and prove his masculinity. It was seen as a chance to face death in "a socially acceptable manner"; men could emerge scarred but essential unbroken. It was the perfect military recruiting tool.

It is difficult to evaluate war films. In the long run and in terms of artistic merit, the war film is not much different than other films. They are created to entertain and ultimately to make money and they did both of these things very well. But they are also obviously trying to sell something, or push an agenda, and whether they did it well or not often depends of the acceptance of the idea. If it is a matter of entertainment, that is one thing and might be more easily accomplished. However, if the war film is trying to tell us about war—that is, the issues involved in the conflict and the effects it causes—then there are other ways to evaluate them. In general the war film has not done as well as it might in this latter case. The image is as yet primarily unclear.

The gene has been around for a long time. In America we usually claim that it began with the 90-second, Diagraph Company movie *Tearing Down the Spanish Flag* (1898). It was a highly fictionalized account of the American victory at Havana, Cuba. While it was successful and suggested that audiences were attracted to the genre, there were not a lot of war movies produced as filmmakers avoided making them because of the costs involved in providing the necessary extras, weapons, equipment, uniforms, and massive battle sequences. The real potential for such a film emerged with the popular success of D.W. Griffith's *The Birth of a Nation* (1915).

At their best, war films can do little other than to create an illusion of war, but the fact that they remain popular lead most critics to believe that the filmmakers have been able to capture some of the ambience of battle. That is, they have managed to identify the lure as well as the danger of war—the terrible romance of battle. This has been partially accomplished because there has always been a strong symbolic relationship between the armed services and the filmmakers. As the viewers' interest was sparked by watching newsreels, the industry moved on to the creation of dramatic feature films building on the interest. They were creating their own audiences.

This work is designed to provide a look at the films that feature World War I, or "the Great War" as they knew it. It will provide concise technical descriptions of the films produced and take a look at some of the themes of that war. Highly competent authors and film historians Peter C. Rollins and John E. O'Connor in *Why We Fought: America's Wars in Film and History* (2008) and Lawrence Suid's *Guts and Glory: The Making of the American Military Image in Film* (2002) have provided some remarkably detailed analysis of the movies of America's wars. Their coverage of select and significant films is well done and very informative; even though they do not include a lot of minor works. However, for most military and film buffs these scholarly works may well provide far more information than they need. What most viewers seek is a clear, compact generalization by which they can understand and remember the films, and reflect on how they both portrayed the war and were themselves affected by the war.

The book begins with two essays that provide generalized information about the war films. The first takes a look at the history of the development and production of the World War film. It examines how their production followed the activities of the war, and how the flow of these films has been both restricted and generated through time. A second essay discusses the essence of the films of the Great War, including a look at primary and secondary themes and plot productions as well as some coverage of characterization and the questions of realism and authenticity.

The third section is an alphabetical listing of the films. This list identifies the producer-distributor, director, author, cinematographer, musical director, significant stars, running time, sound or silent, etc. Also provided are a short synopsis, comments about the film's background and importance, and interesting trivia.

Film critics suggest that somewhere between 70 and 80 percent of silent films have been lost to us. This includes many war films, yet it is estimated that about 350 features and shorts of the genre are still available.[4] A vast number of these were silent films. The selection of films to be covered depended on their being produced by English-speaking countries or originally released with English intertitles.

There is no reason to make too much of a point of it, but even a casual look at these selected films will show just how much they reflect national agendas. There is no doubt that the government was involved from the very beginning, first in using films to stress the nation's neutrality and then, once the United States entered the war, bringing to bear all the nation's resources toward achieving a victory. A good many historians believe that Hollywood worked as a shill to sell the war to the American people. Others hold that the film industry went the extra mile for the American people, presenting them with information reflecting both jingoistic and anti-war ideas.[5]

But this is too simple an analysis. Perhaps it's more realistic to say that most American films made during and shortly after the war could be considered the results of "pragmatic patriotism." That is, it was of great value to this expanding and budget-restricted industry to have learned its craft while at the same time being of service to the nation. The availability and the popularity of films concerning the Great War came about at a time when the movie industry was in its infancy. Those writing and directing these films were seeking both the method and the message of their films while struggling to establish themselves. And while a good many of them were created as commercial enterprises, they generally came with a message. Most research on the effects of propagandas indicate that it will not generally change someone's mind on a given issue. What it does, however, is reinforce existing shared opinions. It reinforces viewers' existing beliefs. That was its major role. This was what America needed.

The propaganda value of the films was one thing but the impact of their advertisements was something else again. This role, as yet to be studied with the seriousness it deserves, tells a far more powerful story than many of the movies themselves. The production of posters, waybills, trailers, and flyers allowed the distributors to consider their work in two lights, the commercially successfully sale of their films and a powerful involvement in the needs and the expectations of the community. The advertisement of war-related films at some points, even after the war was over, showed the civilians how they needed to be involved at a time of the nation's need. The displays were harsh, stark, and often far more jingoistic than the movies they advertised. For example, the poster for *The Unpardonable Sin* (1919) shows the silhouette of a German soldier approaching a young girl. The text reads "Not a war story, but a story of the sacrilege of womanhood that made any red blooded man fight."

Obviously my selection of the movies covered in this book was subjective. While it was made carefully, there are bound to be some missing. Some films were released under several titles and these have been identified along with their other titles in the description. Some films were titled but never released and the titles used later. Just how much of the war has to be involved for it to be considered a "war movie" is also very subjective, and efforts have been made to come down on the side of inclusion. Therefore the list includes such films as *Lieutenant Pimple and the Stolen Submarine* (1914) but not *Crashing Through to Berlin* (1918).

In the identification of directors, producers, music directors, cinematographers, stars, and writers, the effort has been made to include all that are possible, realizing that for a long time this information was not considered important enough to record. There are a surprising number of individuals who first appeared in small bit parts in these early films and then went on to later stardom.

While aware that many of these early movies were produced in places other than Hollywood (in New York, for example), the term Hollywood has been used as a synonym for the film industry. Release dates provided are taken, when possible, from the films themselves, the Library of Congress National Registry or the British Film Institute Catalogue or National Registry. But it should be kept in mind that the dating is often unrealistic. For example, some productions were designed to be released on special days like *The Littlest Scout* (1919) on National Scouting Day; it did not make it in time but is still recorded it being released at that time.

The commentary available on the films is of necessity uneven. This results first of all from the limits of information often available; in some cases, little is known other than the title, and because some films are simply not worth much notation. However, it is good to keep in mind that the popularity of a movie does not necessarily reflect its value, and some films deserve more discussion than others. This of course is a judgment call and thus is the sole responsibility of the author.

Sources of Films

Unfortunately only a relatively small percentage of these early film can be located today. At the time of their production, most were considered "quickies." Certainly there were no film historians around taking notes. The problems of time and film decay, along with arbitrary disposals done by unthinking individuals, have greatly reduced what is available. There is no one to blame and yet everyone is to blame. There are many fine collections of films and their curators have been unstinting in their willingness to help me.

The more significant preservation and research centers include the National Archives and Records Administrations, Archives Record Group (RG) 111, located at College Park, Maryland. It collects and preserves the films that have helped shape American life since the development of the film industry. Another is the J. Paul Getty, Jr., Conservation Centre in Berkhamsted, Hertfordshire, England. Highly unstable nitrate films are held at Gaydon in Warwickshire. The National Film Registry is maintained by the United States National Film Preservation Board of the Library of Congress. The only known film of the 1915 Gallipoli campaign is listed in Australia's Documentary Heritage. Also significant is the Cecil B. DeMille Collection at the Brigham Young University Archives in Utah; the George Klein Collection, Library of Congress; George Eastman House in Rochester, New York; the British Film Institute Movie and Television Archives; the Imperial War Museum, London; Chief of the Signals Office, RG 11, National Archives, College Park; Film Archives, University of California at Los Angeles; Lawrence Suid Collection, Georgetown University Library; Special Collections Division; the Academy of Motion Picture Arts and Sciences, Beverly Hills; the Museum of Broadcasting; the Marine Corps Film Archives; the University of Southern California Cinema-Television Library, Los Angeles; the University of Wyoming, Library Division of Rare Books and Special Collection, Laramie, Wyoming; Wisconsin Center for Film and Theater Research at the University of Wisconsin Library (Madison); and the Thanhauser Film Preservation Center.

All film historians owe a great debt to Philip W. Stewart whose *Battle Film. U.S. Army Signal Corps Motion Pictures of the Great War* details 467 films that deal with America's involvement in World War I. It is an indexing of the film documentary films stored in Record Group 111 in the U.S. National Archives. Jack Bauer's Special List Number 14, List of World War I Signal Corps Films, provides a most definitive listing. A significant number of these World War I films made before 1939 are available for purchase or, sometimes, screening. The best sources appear to be World War I Movies (www.war-movies.com/world-war-one) or World War-1.Net (www.worldwar-1.net/world-war-1-on-film/world-war-1). Songs, music, and interviews with World War I soldiers are available at the Flanders House in Glasgow, Scotland (www.glasgowstories.com).

Wide use has been made of the archives of *Motion Picture World* and *Official Film News* (published by the Committee on Public Information, Division of Films), the *New York Times, The Chicago Tribune* and the *Exhibitor's Trade Review*. On the other hand, virtually all my inquiries to persons involved in the production of films have remained unanswered. Nevertheless, the number of persons who helped in this compilation are numerous. Certainly those keepers of the film at the National Film Preservation unit of the Library of Congress and British Film Institute deserve a great deal of credit, as do the hundreds of reviewers of these war films whose reviews are sometimes still available in newspaper files.

On a more personal level, my sincere thanks for institutional support from the Center for the Study of the Korean War; to friends and colleagues who not only put up with the quest but assisted in it: Gregg Smith, Tom Peterman, Cindy Easter, Greg Edwards, and my wife Carolynn.

A Brief History of the Production of Films About World War I

Film historians John E. O'Connor and Peter C. Rollins have suggested a four-pronged method to analyze war films. They are aware that much can be learned about a film by knowing the intent behind the production. They suggest that one method of consideration is found in looking at the moving document as a representative of history; that is, the interpretation of a historical event. A second way of looking at a film is as an image that is seen as evidence for social or cultural history; that is, an event that evokes the values the producer wants to create. The third represents the moving image as evidence of a historical fact; actual footage of something that has taken place in real time. And, last, that the movie is an image that tells the history of the film itself.[1] While this view is most helpful in trying to tie the film to the culture of the nation, and it has been widely used, it is not that valuable when trying to identify the themes of the movies themselves. I believe the presentation of the film is best determined from the story and the context and how the film relates to the subject matter that it addresses. That is how they are presented here. Very little effort has been made to judge the films as historical pieces.

The history of films that focus on the Great War runs approximately from *The Invaders* (1909) to *The Water Diviner* (2014). Considering the impact of the war, and the dramatic growth of the film industry, there were surprisingly few of them produced. This is especially true in the period following the war. There are about 350 feature films.[2] World War I films appear to come and go depending on the mood of the nation and the wavering conflict that has been continuously waged between the isolationists and the interventionist; between the militarists and the pacifists. The outbreak of World War I was rather fortunately well timed for the film industry with its ability to respond to the opportunity. The flow of movies about the war expanded during the war, then slowed down, then grew, then dissipated, and then grew again. The production of these films pale in comparison to films that were produced, and continue to be produced, about World War II or even Vietnam.

After the Civil War, the nation's military activity consisted of skirmishes against the Plains Indians and eventually the Spanish American War. That war provided us with the first fictionalized account of the American victory at Havana, Cuba. Called *Tearing Down the Spanish Flag*, it was filmed in 1898 and directed by J. Stuart Blackton. As an example of what was to become a pattern in moviemaking, this film about the war in Cuba was filmed in the Morse Building in Brooklyn, New York. It was a novelty and well received, but it was hardly history.

In general, however, early filmmakers avoided war pictures because of the costs involved. This attitude changed as the potential for a market was identified following the popular success of D.W. Griffith's *The Birth of a Nation* (1915). The darkening clouds and political tensions felt in Europe led Hollywood to make some early efforts at prevention propaganda as made evident in the filming of *The Perils of the Fleet* (1909). From the very beginning of the war, the British and the French as well as the Central Powers produced documentary films to be used as propaganda pieces at home and abroad. Many of these were seen in America. Significant among these, for it set a standard, was Albert K. Dawson's *The Battle and Fall of Przemysl* (1915), shot by the official German war photographer.[3]

Considering the strict neutrality of the United States the government urged film makers to avoid partisanship in their films. Nevertheless, with some considerable forethought and right from the beginning, the federal government found a way to be involved in movie production. The desires of the government cannot be discounted when considering the themes of movies produced.[4] It was not the government, however, but the prevalence of anti-war sentiment in the country that welcomed films like *Civilization* (1916) that played to a highly isolationist audience. In this case, the deep concerns about war was expressed by Christ himself in a very heavy scene. Before America's entry into the war, *The Battle Cry of Peace* (1915) depicted a foreign power's disastrous invasion of America and called on the country to prepare for war. It was during this time that the industry acknowledged that it could promote films for its own best interests while at the same time acknowledging the need to create good relations with the government, public opinion, local business, and the ever-expanding film-going public.[5]

In just about every way possible, the war—first in Europe and then after America's late entry—provided an easy, popular, understandable and often predictable plot to be used.

Following the United States' entry into the war, all restrictions were gone and anti-war films became a thing of the past. The rapid and serious nature of the change might well be marked by Robert Goldstein's ten-year jail sentence for making a pro-peace movie, *The Spirit of '76* (1917). There is little evidence that the film industry moved immediately to alter its film production just to honor the commercial potential that the war provided, and war films would not be a significant part of their production schedule until 1918. But the groundwork was being laid. By 1917 the narrative conventions of the classic Hollywood feature film and the characteristics of the star system were becoming standardized, and film production went into high gear. Along with some B features,[6] highly sophisticated works appeared—such as *The Slacker's Heart* (1917), *The Little American* (1917), and *The Hun Within* (1918)[7] as well as some well-directed comedies like *Shoulder Arms* (1918)—that quickly identified the evil Huns and beastly Germans.[8]

From the beginning of the war until late 1919, government involvement, public opinion, the media, and literature allowed few attitudes to be expressed other than those that supported the war effort and the defeat of the Hun. Yet, if there was a golden age of films depicting the Great War, it would have centered in 1918. Among other things that happened at this time is that the filmmaking industry became respectable. Moviemakers were welcome on Wall Street, movie stars were celebrities, and even presidents watched movies. In the 1920s the stage performers coined the phrase "legitimate theater" as an insult but also, if nothing else, to identify themselves apart from the movie industry. In the industry itself, economic power was collected in large interrelated companies with the first traces of a later oligopoly becoming visible as studios combined and theater chains formed.

But, even with this patriotic fever, a somewhat significant debate was developing. It came to a head in the June 1917 issue of *The Moving Picture World*, when they announced that they were no longer going to print depressing stories. The reason behind this announcement was much more serious than it might appear. The argument was over whether the film industry was there to provide entertainment for its customers and relief from the harsh realities of the world, or obligated to display the realities of contemporary problems for the information and enlightenment of its viewers. In this case, how much of the war did the American people need to know about? The majority of producers seemed to believe the latter. The significance of contemporary consideration became the selling point for most film companies that wanted to inform as well as entertain. People wanted to know what the war was like and the movies could tell them. It was more than an opportunity, it was a duty.

But there was more to it than that. The war film not only conveyed the cultural meaning of patriotism and national pride, but also provided reasons why the country was at war and why the people should participate in it. It was to provide much of the justification for the nation to fight a people with whom they have had no serous quarrel. And, in time, the films were to provide the means of remembering why the nation was involved. Michael T. Isenberg concedes that war films were not particular popular in the years immediately following World War I, and discounts the traditional wisdom that Americans in the 1920s rejected war and were overly embittered by the experience and extremes of World War I. The soldiers portrayed in *The Big Parade* (1925) sought the blessings of peace but they were also committed civilians who were aroused when the nation was in danger.

Millions of Americans were interested in what was happening in Europe and stories of the war still had an attraction even for those who disagreed with war in general. The argument was not solved and did not diminish, but wars played out among the producers and directors as they followed their own agendas. Keep in mind, however, that while the war films were being produced and given wide distribution, they never dominated the studios' other offerings of feature films. The comment of Kevin Brownlow, film historian, "Hate-the-Hun films poured into the theaters like poison gas," is clever but not true.[9] Hundreds of totally unrelated films were also being produced. The lack of historical and critical writing that links World War I to the movie business leaves the mistaken idea that only war-related films were produced. As it was, only about 14 percent of the 568 films released during the war were war films. The height of the war, for example, saw the distribution of *Mickey* (1918), *Bound for Morocco* (1918) and *Tarzan of the Apes* (1918), all of which did very well at the box-office.

Nevertheless, once involved, directors like D. W. Griffith went all the way to identify the enemy and to take them to task. Significant among the films produced was *Hearts of the World* (1918) with Lillian Gish, and dozens of documentaries that he produced that showed scenes of British troops going "over the top" in such strange places as Scotland and Los Angeles. *The Kaiser, the Beast of Berlin* (1918) served to mark the high point in the excess of the "hate-the Hun" films. But as soon as the Armistice was signed, this sort of film was almost immediately dropped and those available were viewed as being ludicrous. The hatred expressed toward Germany and its people quickly diminished, at least in the immediate post-war films.

During the war, the American neutrality had given them an edge in the world market. When the war finally ended, most European filmmakers had suffered great losses and were primarily out of business, again aiding the American movie industry. They picked up the slack and responded with some eighty percent of the films being made. War films took on a new life. *The Big Parade* (1925) was able to better portray the realistic horrors of battle and the struggles for survival, while at the same time portraying characters who were less interested in killing Germans and more interested in seeking the blessings of peace. A spectacular success, it made more money than any other film MGM had yet produced. The studio tried to repeat its success with Lon Chaney in *Tell It to the Marines* (1926) that was profitable but not nearly as successful.

Between 1918 and 1920 more than thirty war films were produced but following that there was an overall industry decline in all features films, including war drama. This was in some respect due to a lessening interest in the war but more realistically a fear of large crowds created by the spread of the Spanish flu. Interestingly there was, at the same time, an increase in the number of independent film producers, perhaps to take up some of the slack, some created by the stars themselves. There was also a growing attitude of regret about the war and bitterness about its human and commercial costs. Before 1920 there had been the feeling that war, with all its problems, was necessary and was undergone in order to save the nation's honor, protect the chastity of women, and to make the world safe for democracy. After 1920 or so it was really not all that clear why we had gone to war.

In the 1920s there was an increase in, but little success in, efforts by American and international agencies to outlaw war itself. The best example was the idealistic Kellogg-Briand Pact of 1928 and its anticipation of anti-war conservatism. There were a few war films produced. Among them was *The Four Horsemen of the Apocalypse* (1921) that made Rudolph Valentino a star. But it did not do a lot for the genre, with the *Morning Telegraph*'s review suggesting that it "helped prompt Americans into keeping the war in mind."[10] Besides, the growing number of pacifists wanted the movies to use their newfound sound, to bring mass attention to a better, more peaceful and humanitarian world.

Audiences were beginning to prefer simple adventure stories and mysteries, not recounts or condemnations of the war. A strong sense of renewed isolationism was cutting into the demand. In the main the studios began producing movies that appealed to audiences who had grown profoundly disillusioned with the war. Nevertheless, for reasons that are not all that clear, the number of war-related features began to increase between 1922 and 1926. And their messages were mixed. The now classic film *What Price Glory?* (1926) was received at the time with considerable criticism, some even giving strength to the belief, now held by more and more Americans, that the government's wartime propaganda had been misleading,[11] and that the films placed the American soldier outside the culture and defaced the reality of war.

While not all were aware of what had happened, some were and the reaction carried over into criticism of the film industry. C. Hartly Grattin suggested that honest, unbiased news reporting simply disappeared from the pages of American newspapers about the middle of August 1914. The truth that seemed to be so much a part of the goals of the war had been immediately sacrificed by those promoting involvement. George Creel's efforts to make the films promote the government agenda meant that he and his committee lied; victories were routinely manufactured and failures routinely covered up. Propaganda was successful and those who recognized it were both delighted and afraid. Many were aware that the methods invented and tried out during the war were far too valuable for governments to forget, and much of the intellectual community was aware of the possibility of regimenting the American mind. And while the movies were not the motivation behind the selling of national agendas, they were most certainly a significant media.

In the Fall of 1927 the war once again begins to prove a rich heritage for stories and settings and the war film regained some popularity spurred on by American's fascination with the air. The frail aircraft and their magnificent pilots were a great attraction. Films like *Wings* (1927) and *Hell's Angels* (1930) depicted massive aerial battle scenes. The public was so enamored with them that one critic warned of an "air war flood." *Photoplay Magazine* suggested the coming demise of the cowboy movie unless they took to the air. Movies like *The Legion of the Condemned* that united John Monk Saunders, William Wellman and Gary Cooper were well received. *Lilac Time* (1928) and *The Sky Hawk* (1929) followed the well-worn theme to good advantage.

The year 1927 also saw much change in Hollywood as the first of the sound pictures were released. While many considered it a wonder, many critics and viewers felt that the sound of voices and background noises ruined the dramatic nature of films. Also, a significant number of actors and actresses discovered that while they had the looks for Hollywood, they did not have the voices. This change in technology, as well as the dawning days of the Depression, would hamper Hollywood a good deal.

The 1930s brought a brief return of the war film with such powerful movies as *The Dawn Patrol* (1930) and *A Farewell to Arms* (1932). But the 1930s also brought *All Quiet on the Western Front* (1930) that showed in theaters all over the nation. A special showing was even provided for the United States Senate. German-language copies of the film distributed overseas set off riots in Berlin and Bavaria.[12]

The times were quickly changing, however. The outbreak of the Spanish Civil War in 1936, the British-German naval arms race, and the growing awareness of Germany's rearmament did a great deal to counter the anti-war movement and some of the isolationist sentiment; war seemed to be a renewable topic.[13] *The Fighting 69th* (1940) and *Sergeant York* (1941) were surely preparedness films. Films like Hitchcock's *Foreign Correspondent* (1940) were produced to warn the world of like Germany's national ambitions.

The threats and then the fighting of World War II brought an end to most movies about the Great War with only six produced in a dozen years. The same was basically true during the period of the Korean War (1950–1953) with only three movies dealing with the Great War. From 1960 until today, there have been only one or two movies a year about World War I. Somewhere about 1970 Hollywood seems to have turned away from the conventional war film although they are still open to the spectacular. Nevertheless there is plenty of war to be found on TV. The interest in World War I as a topic or situation started increasing again about 2001. Surely the one hundredth anniversary of the war has some effect on these productions and more will come. As late at 2014 the tabloids tell us that actor-director Russell Crowe is producing a movie about the Battle of Gallipoli in 1915, called *The Water Diviner*.

The Essence of the Films of the Great War

As the movie studios developed their talents and extended their abilities, they were also forming traditions, character traits, scene expectations, and production concepts that would remain a significant part of the industry up to and including today. This was especially true of the war film since any attempt to present such a film was offset by the reality of what they were attempting to present. While certainly not all the basic themes adopted by war movies were developed during these early productions, a surprising number of today's movies take advantage of what was created in feature films made between 1914 and 1940. The more modern war films that appeared during and after World War II are certainly better produced, more technically accurate, and generally more subtle than the earlier films, but they are not that much different.

Between the years 1914 and 1917, producers and distributors created and developed the business practices that would sustain them through the 1920s and beyond as the consolidation of production and the emergence of nationwide distribution promised them success. The same is true of the narrative conventions of the Hollywood cinema and the characteristics of the star system that had become standardized. The same is true of theme and character and the early characteristics and emotions presented on the silver screen with such stark exaggeration have proven relevant to the long haul. There are several that are worth considering and they are easily divided into what are generally called situational themes and those identified as character themes.

SITUATIONAL

The lack of sound (at least the absence of dialogue) and the need for exaggerated movement and facial expression in order to carry the message, partic-

British troops carry a wounded man through the mud at Loos (courtesy Center for the Study of the Korean War, Independence, Missouri).

ularly any emotional one, as well as the dark tones and persistent flickering on the screen, all contributed to the harshness of these early films. Whatever the producers and directors were trying to convey, subtlety was not a prime characteristic found in these efforts. Whether the intent was to horrify and thus reduce the chance of America's entry into the war, or if they were designed to warn America of the danger of being unprepared, the message itself was brutally clear. Some of the more prevalent themes are considered here.

The Clarity of Moral Issues: Both during the First World War and in movies made long after the fighting had stopped, the basic issues of right and wrong were very carefully identified and addressed. There are few gray areas in these films. While the human conflict involved in the participation in war was seen as a dichotomy, the role of participation in the war itself was not. Events and persons involved were presented in such a way as to acknowledge the morality of their situation and, in time, it was necessary to suffer the moral results of their involvement. Those who were in the right, as well as those identified as emotional patriots, either survived the ordeal of war to enjoy the blessings of the peace they had earned, or they died while making the grand gesture in recognition of their principles. Those in the wrong, the evildoer and the unrepentant sinner, the enemy, even the coward who was discovered on the field of battle, was without lasting merit and even a shadow of goodness was denied to most of them. Sooner or later they got what they deserved, often by the hands of those they had violated or by a moral universe applying the final fate of judgment; they often died in shame and dishonor. Or, for some, the final act was one of conversion, seeing the evilness of their ways, and performing some act to set things right. But the dastardly deeds of men could not be hidden, especially in the violent conditions provided by war where death and danger made all things clear.

The source of this moral authority is hard to pin down because the outbreak of war was the cause of both an increased dependence on God and an increase in the number of those who felt God had deserted the world. Apart from the war, but certainly affected by it, the religious climate in America was further dividing between conservative and liberal persons who were both disappointed in religion's failure to meet the changing needs of society and who saw the religious community as America's only hope. The moral crusade was generally assumed but not explained; the movies—like the communities from which they emerged—did not question the source of the moral reality they presented, they simply accepted it as being true. The evaluation of those decisions would be argued long after.

Fate: The individuals upon whom these films focused were, regardless of whether they served in the trenches on the front lines, or on the high seas, or in the air, or as spies for their mother country, were but pawns in the massive hands of fate. The mindless movements, the gigantic weapons, the inhuman behavior, the leaderless political implications and the vast disillusionment were all part of the seemingly unreasoned maneuvering on the part of small men and unprepared leaders with little or no direction in mind. From the beginning, the individual had little control over his or her life as the tide of events swept over them. Previous accomplishment or status made no difference now. Once circumstances had drawn the individual into the river of events, they were no longer individuals and were soon molded by phenomenon that always seemed out of control. Men and sometimes even women were pushed along by the system, mistreated by the events, and endangered by vast misconceptions. The existential absurdity, the abyss of the human predicament, though not well articulated until a later war, was closely and clearly identified in many of these films.

Later analysis suggested a temporary but nevertheless an identifiable sweep of Fatalism, an attitude that is so easily expressed in the belief that if your number is up, you are going to get hit. It is an attitude born of the understanding that things happen without apparent reason, that what is normally understandable is no longer understandable. It is not defeatism as was reflected in the mutiny of French soldiers, but rather the belief that all activity is predetermined by events over which the individual has no control. Thus you are unable to do anything but what you are doing. It is a feeling of resignation, the acceptance of the inevitable, the acknowledgment that you are a pawn controlled by massive and undeniable energies.

Waste: Equally as common in the production of films depicting the war is an awareness of the senseless misuse of men in battle.[14] Even while the war was going on and every effort was being made to portray the military in the best light possible as requested by the government, it is obvious that those producing these early films were well aware of the waste. Some producers and directors had already been involved in the war and had firsthand knowledge of just how bad it was. And what most seemed to know, but could not seem to do anything about, was that massive battles, perhaps best identified by *The Battle of the Somme* (1916), were not only a disastrous waste of men, but they were simply not going to work. There seemed to be an understanding among producers and directors, that was lacking in officers in the field, that the appearance of new weapons and the lack of adequate training were making fodder out of the men sent into battle.

The Assumption of National Responsibility: There does not appear to be a single film that promotes the idea that a man or woman should not go to war when the nation calls. Some of these war films have characters who are at first expressing this idea, but they are quickly dispelled and their arguments never presented in a believable fashion. The Socratic assumption that men, having lived under the protection of the state all their lives, are obligated to defend the state when called, was on display. The nation has the right to ask its citizens to repay their responsibility to the state. This does not have to be explained, it is a given. Many of the films are against the war and suggest that America should not be involved, but even the most dramatic of these do not make any effort to avoid individual participation if and when the nation makes that decision to fight.

Desolation: The land over which the war was fought was denuded, the savagery of war compounded by dark photography and ghostly images. There were no images of limited warfare for there was none envisioned. There seemed to be no in-between; either the land and the buildings were intact or it was barren. The films focused on long distance shots, often taken from the air or by the use of a crane, exaggerating the massive scope of the field of battle, the ghastly pockmarked land, huge holes, broken buildings, dead animals, damaged and discarded equipment, and miles and miles of barbed wire. Dark foreboding shots of trenches, mud, and bodies thrown about by exploding shells, were standard. The message was clear: Those lands on which such fierce fighting took place would never be the same again. Perhaps no film did this so well as *All Quiet on the Western Front* (1930) though *Wings* (1927) provided masterful shots taken by early planes.

Anti-war: To one degree or another all films carried something of an anti-war message. Producers and directors were aware that any movie about the war had the potential of turning off those who saw it as unnecessary and unwanted. A good many of these films were, of course, created primarily for that purpose. Even the most patriotic of the directors appeared to have been touched by the horror of it all and felt some need to warn the viewers as well as tantalizing them. Many of the early directors were themselves veterans of the war and had a deep and often emotional understanding that they tried to put into their films. War was allowed to be glorious, even romantic, and the theme of patriotism and courage was always present. War was almost always portrayed as being necessary in the light of the evil Hun who faced us. But if the films were realistic, and most tried to be, they conveyed the sense of horror found in war. War was, as many films suggest, a valued place for men to test their mettle, but it was nevertheless a horrifying experience.

Democratic: Freedom meant many things during this period and for many it was the universal dream of equality. That is, the value and expectation of equality. Many of films proclaimed this message. The class system was much more obvious in, but not limited to, Great Britain, and the British-produced films often had this as a significant subplot. The class difference was stressed in *Blighty* (1926) and *Doughboys* (1930). They portrayed persons of unequal rank in the society who found themselves incredibly equal once they were on the field of battle. The message was loud and clear: "All men are equal on the battlefield; death knows no class structure." In several films this plot is addressed head-on with the wealthy employer and the working-class employee ending up in the same small trench where they are dependent on one another. Interestingly, in many of these films the newfound equality was rewarded by entry into an advanced class. At the end 'the poor chauffeur finds out that he is really an earl. This theme is well played out in such films as *The Showdown* (1917).

Military Ignorance: This question of equality did not stretch into the army itself and particularly the officer corps as much. Some films, most obviously the air movies, used the aristocracy of the officers to raise the question of class structure. The lieutenants and captains who were highlighted were almost always acceptable, even if harsh, and kindly portrayed. But the higher commands appeared to be above, or perhaps only unaware of, the terror of the war. These general officers appeared to be far more concerned with their engagement in small political battles among themselves than they were in understanding and directing the war. This is perhaps best illustrated in Stanley Kubrick's powerful *Paths of Glory* (1957), a movie well designed to portray the intense hardships for soldiers and the massive toll of casualties brought on by national pride and military arrogance. The injustice that resulted from misguided officers whose ambition clashed with the needs of his men, is focused in this line uttered by General Broulard after the execution of a man accused of cowardice: "There are few things more fundamentally encouraging and stimulating than seeing someone else die."[15]

Hatred: Using the term Hun, which had been a derogatory term since the Revolutionary War, America set out to hate the Hun with a passion that has been unequaled even during the darkest days of the war against Japan (1941–1945). Lacking a scapegoat like the Nazi to separate the evil ones from the rest of the population, in World War I the whole German nation had to be castigated for their cruel, albeit insane, behavior. By nature German soldiers apparently drooled at the mouth while raping simple peasant girls, ran their bayonets through babies, crucified soldiers on barn doors, violated nuns, and destroyed all good things that got in their way. There was no halfway measure and the film industry bought into this image.

Absurdity: Again, borrowing an existential term before it was available, many of these early films set the stage for the acknowledgement of the total absurdity and brutality of war. Sooner or later, the incredible paradox of killing for peace and the violent participation of those involved, bring most of those who experience it to the point of utter disbelief. Well over half the movies considered in this guide had plots that included the desperate human paradox that usually results from the fact that most men are more afraid of killing another man than they are of dying themselves. Despite the political or international implications of their actions, the fact that two human beings face off to kill one another, when they have no particular issues between them, is seen in all its absurdity. In such a setting the degree of brutality that emerges adds to the anguish, and the lack of answers evolves into disillusionment.

Gender Consciousness: It would be hard to overestimate the impact these early war films had on the world's attitude toward women. The screen heroine was something else again and both directors and actresses made the most of the shock value of treating a women like a man. While taking advantage of the feminine attraction, creating exaggerated sexual situations, and well aware of the sexy lady sulking in the background, Hollywood also introduced the brash young woman who served as a nurse, or followed her man into war, or spied for the nation. The women who went to war were not all that innocent, nor did they claim to be, nor were they inclined to be afraid. In fact, many films used the courage of the wife to counter the evil deeds of the disloyal husband. These women were brash and adventurous and more than capable of dealing with the world. The presence of a young woman was necessary for the story and the films got them involved by a wide variety of means.

It needs to be noted that the role played was never too far away from the tradition of *The Birth of a Nation* (1915) in which sexual threats to "little sister" was a key theme. In the World War I vintage, the worst thing that the Hun could do was rape, or threaten to rape, the innocent young peasant girls at their mercy. These films eliminated or at least greatly reduced the role of woman as causal agents. Realizing that the films were primarily for entertainment and not historical studies, it is still important to acknowledge that the easy manner in which the female lead was injected into the plot by means of being a nurse or USO entertainer does a significant disservice to the thousands of women who served in these capacities, and who lived with the horror, danger, and discomfort of the situation. Unfortunately many a movie patron came away from these early films with some serious misconceptions of the role of women.

Pain: In considering the transition between situational and character traits, it seems important to mention an interesting aspect about these films: the portrayal of the pain of the wounded. It has to do with how the filmmakers understood and thus how they displayed pain. British historian Joanna Bourke makes a very interesting observation that is illustrated in the films of this early period: The pain and suffering associated with war wounds is portrayed differently when covering different wars. This is not a science, certainly, but it can be a significant insight into the cultural context. In the American Civil War, for example, the severity of the wound and the acuteness of the pain did not correlate. The fact of the wound was recorded but there was little to indicate if it was fatal or a mere scratch; little to suggest what amount of pain was involved. The dialogue at the moment of death was not about the wound but about family, or the outcome of the battle. In World War I, however, the wound was almost always seen in terms of patriotic service, as evidence that one had paid the price demanded by honor. The primary concern of the wounded seemed to be the fear that the wound would mean leaving their buddies behind.[16] The response to wounds changed with time, as did the general public attitude toward the wounds, and by World War II and Korea the response to wounds was expressed in nihilistic individualism and almost always in anger.[17]

CHARACTER

Heroism: From the beginning—and little has changed—the hero is the center of the war movie. The hero is a real man or a woman who stands up when duty calls and accepts the challenges, however absurd, imposed by the situation. No matter what is called for, they perform their duty well, often magnificently. These men and women are not only fearless, they are often foolhardy. They are strong, bright, capable, dedicated and willing to confront danger and the unknown with courage and a brave heart. This characteristic often puts them ahead of other men and women and they become the model for the behavior of others, the standard for action, even the goal for the nation. This heroism is often localized, that is, it is acted out in a mission or responsibility so designed to show that the individual's actions go way beyond the call of duty. The hero in *Captain Swagger* (1914) is such a man, but even with the rare anti-hero film, nearly all films about the military adopt this stance.

Loner: In a typical World War I film, the primary character is basically a loner (a lone wolf). Generally humble, he or she, while often boisterous on social occasions, is basically quiet and mild-mannered. This person acts alone primarily because others cannot match his or her speed and endurance. They work alone because that is the way they can always be in charge. Because they are always right, others just get in the way. They move fast and without justification, often against prevailing orders or authority. When with a partner, they are secretive and disdaining. Such a character is seen in *False Face* (1919). With high moral principles guiding them, they are often self-critical and think too harshly of themselves, thus they easily take on the burdens of others.

Hardboiled/Smart Ass: The hero often exhibits these characteristics as if they were hand in hand with heroics. The snappy one-liners, the antics, the exaggerated and sometimes outrageous behavior, the total lack of respect for authority, reflects their uncommon quick wit and independence. Sometimes the films use this as the theme for a subplot character to keep the plot moving, but the characteristic is almost always present. Obnoxious and overbearing, the characters are usually likable but not lovable and sooner or later they get what is coming to them. These characteristics are usually provided to hide feelings of fear or regret. Often they play the second man in the love triangle during which their true but unexpressed nature is betrayed.

Cowardice: Where there are heroes, there are also cowards. Most persons involved in war are concerned at one time or another if they will be brave enough to deal with what they encounter. Most are, but some are not. Anyone who says they are not afraid when in combat is lying or deeply sick. The fear and weakness that leads men to turn their backs on their comrades and run from the fight is a theme often present as a subplot in even the strongest propaganda films. In a good many of these early war films, and it became standard fare, the cowardly character comes to his senses at some point and realizes in some dramatic way "that a hero dies only once, a coward dies a thousand deaths."

Underdog: In most war movies the story takes on a David and Goliath situation with the individuals we are concerned with fighting insurmountable odds. In the reality of warfare this is rarely the case. Therefore the World War I hero had to be separated from the larger battle in some way—a small skirmish, a patrol, a mission behind enemy lines, an escape from a prison camp—that would allow the hero to meet his nearly insurmountable challenges. The odds are always against the hero, he or she is almost always outnumbered (but never outsmarted), the options for survival vastly limited. The rugged individualism emerges when the odds were the greatest, thus the heroic nature of the action performed becomes even more astounding. To provide this scene, many war films focus on the activities of a small unit. One excellent example of this effort is found in *The Lost Patrol* (1929 and 1934) and Humphrey Bogart's World War II drama *Sahara* (1943).

Achilles' heel: Most of the men and women who enter the field of battle in war films do so with some personal conflict or burden they are carrying. It is often the reason for their involvement in the larger conflict. Sometimes it is simply the average person's concern about the demands being put on them. Or, as in the case with *Sergeant York* (1941), it can be a fairly serious clash of religious convictions and patriotic beliefs. Often this concern is hidden from the movie fan and then is exposed and worked out during the course of the movie. Whatever it is that detracts from the hero is brought to a head by the tension and dangers involved. This soul-searching, burden-carrying effort is often at odds with their military assignment and is an added challenge that must be dealt with before the end of the movie.

Moral weakness: A good many World War I movies set the stage for a moral weakness subplot. In these cases the soon-to-be-hero is presented as an arrogant rich man, or maybe racist, a man or woman stifled by a sense of class consciousness, or sometimes even greater problems like not believing in God, violence toward women, an unwanted child, a failed marriage, or even criminal behavior. During the course of the movie these weaknesses are beaten out of them "on the anvil iron of pain" as the horror (as well as the equality) of war teach them the error of their ways and they find peace in democracy or religion, or self-confidence, repentance, or forgiveness.

Character Variance: By the time World War II war films began to come out, the cast of characters was pretty much identified. Just about every film, and the unit about which the film was made, has its representative members: the hero (tough-talking, quick-witted, loner and take-charge type); the coward (who hides it well but sooner or later betrays them all); the intellectual (usually a struggling writer who records their actions for his great American novel, and often gives the final statement of victory and morality); the nice guy (who never makes it to the end of the film, usually killed in some paradoxical situation); the foreigner, often a Swede (just trying to get along with the rest of them[18]) , the religious enthusiast (whose God is never quite close enough); and the smart-talking not-very-smart man almost always from Brooklyn.

Authenticity

Partly because the medium was new, but to a large extent because viewers were seeing the material "with their own eyes," movie patrons were inclined to believe what they saw on the silver screen. The "it has to be true because we saw it on the screen" mentality carried over from the newspapers. In the case of combat footage, this was even more likely as the essential horror of what they were seeing made disbelief difficult. The newsreel burst upon the scene with pictures of the Kaiser opening the Kiel Canal in 1895, and by 1906 London had available almost daily coverage through *Day by Day*. But even these early battle reports were faked or restaged after the battle.[19]

Newsreels provided pictures of marching troops, flying planes, tanks, and vast fields of trenches and barbed wire. Because so many were influenced by them, the general assumption has been that the films were authentic and were portraying some actual event. The unfortunate truth is that a great deal of the footage that came out during the war, and even after it, contained combat film that was faked. That is, they had not been taken during the fighting that is pictured, nor were the camera persons in any danger when they were taking it.

The gray, bombarded landscape, the exploding shells, the endless miles of barbed wire, the long lines of mud trenches, ancient tanks creeping along over barren ridges, machine-guns firing into massed troops, were the images that most appeared on the screen. What was available for photographing, however, were marching bands, nurses in hospitals, men on maneuvers, ships sailing out to sea. The images of the war itself were, to a large degree, fakes. It can long be argued if these episodes were deliberately presented out of a feeling of benign concern or perhaps with malice aforethought. It does not really matter now. But they were faked and the public was rarely told.

Film critics as well as military historians of the period have become more aware, as they investigate much of the "stock" footage that is still available, that what they are seeing was not filmed during the combat of the war. On the contrary the amount of film that is, in fact, combat coverage, is very small indeed. It has been estimated by film specialists that only 12 to 20 percent of the motion picture materials that is available on film, and that is identified as having been filmed in the field during World War I, is what it claims to be.

The rest of this very realistic appearing material was created by re-enactments. Sometimes it was filmed by the real soldiers paid to recreate a battle they had recently fought.[20] Often the whole battle was staged in an area that looked like, but was remote from, the action it was suppose to portray. It is important to remember that this is not only the case for those works of fiction—feature films that included "combat footage"—but also for a significant number of documentary and newsreel films presented to the public as reports on the war.

Certainly it is understandable that procuring actual combat footage would be very hard given the dangers and the difficulties. The European War was the first such conflict to be fought after the movie camera had come into its own. Yet, the camera was large, heavy, and difficult to transport, and operating it required considerable training. It is hard to conceive of an efficient way to take them into combat. Those studios who sent brave cameramen into combat for footage soon found that most of what was taken by them was generally uninteresting because it was just too dangerous to get too close to the action. The faking of these films, however, does a considerable disservice to those who were involved and who brought back film at great risk to themselves.

W.F. Jury's *The Battle of the Somme* (1916) mixed film taken during the titular battle with a significant number of reenacts safely shot at a nearby mortar training school. The distributors made no mention of this. A few movie critics, while not condoning the practice, have suggested that the fake scenes were more realistic (more like the actual war being fought) than those shot in combat because the faked scenes always allowed the cameraman to be in the right place at the right time.

In a few of the cases, the fakes were identified by the producer. Without the identification, however, it is not hard to pick out the staged scenes. Most reconstructions are typically close-ups with the action being shown as moving toward, and away from, the cameras. Famed director D.W. Griffith, who used the technique, made no bones about it and even suggested that "some events are too colossal to be dramatic. No one can describe it. You might as well try to describe the ocean or the Milky Way ... no one saw a thousandth part of it."[21]

An Introduction to the Films

The movie began to grow in the United States following the impact of the British innovations of the Industrial Revolution. It can generally be said that while most of the world was considering movies in terms of artistic and inventive characteristics, in the United States the movies were an industry, a commercial venture right from the very beginning. When the time came for the film to make its mark, America was ready.[1]

The American reaction to war in Europe was largely designed to keep the United States from becoming involved. The general feeling of the American people was as much isolationism as it was anti-war. President Wilson had won re-election on the promise that there would be no involvement and he appeared to reflect the national mood. While many films reflected this position and were blatantly anti-war, this was not the case elsewhere. European propaganda pieces like Albert K. Dawson's *The Battle and Fall of Przemysl* (1915), released by the American Correspondent Film Company, widely seen in the United States There were directors and filmmakers who wanted to warn the United States of the dangers of being unprepared for what they saw coming. As the United States drew closer to war, the mood began to change and propagandistic films began to appear and to serve, among other things, as recruitment tools. D.W. Griffith's *Hearts of the World* (1918) was a sentimental film designed to support America's entry into the war and included some actual battle scenes filmed in 1917 that displayed the beastly behavior of the Hun.

The early war films also reflected a point of view about war, perhaps best called a mood, that prevailed during most of the war years and for some time after. The mood seemed to change with the rising threats posed by Hitler and the reawakening of Germany. The poet soldier Rupert Brooks, after his death in 1915, became the common reference for the merging of the political, cultural and social disposition of the British people. And in a good many respects this carried over into American society. Sometimes referred to as the "poetic feel" to the war, it served as the perfect symbol of volunteerism and commemoration that allowed for the individualization of the experience of war. In a manner not experienced before, people became personally involved with the emotions of war as it was portrayed in the writing and reading of poetry, articles, even obituaries. The impact of these images provided a significant relevance to the poet-heroes who went way beyond any legitimate justification. They became the source of national memory not only of the war itself but of the emotions of war. The films became a part of this and the gut-wrenching nature of the Great War, a seminal experience for many, provided inspiration right from the beginning and for many decades afterwards. Some of Hollywood's early efforts to tell the story of this war resulted in many of the best war movies ever made. Since then the movie industry became more sophisticated and technically polished and few have returned to this event. When they have, it has not been done nearly so well.

It is hard to determine from existing records if the viewing audiences preferred the comedy films over the more serious and sometimes gut-wrenching melodrama being produced by men like Griffith and Chester Withey. The authorities were aware that actual footage of the carnage of war could turn audiences off, and cameramen on the field were few. Nevertheless, as production plummeted in Europe, the output of production and the themes including comedies quickly picked up.

Television, seeking new backgrounds for stories, has sometimes returned to World War I, but not all that often. This is evident, for example, in *The Young Indiana Jones Chronicles* (1992–1996), whose young hero visited many of the more famous battlefields and war theaters. Television has also brought the war back in modern adaptations of classic works. For example, director Julian Jarrold's 1999 version of *All the King's Men* retells the story of the Sandringham Company. There is also the Russell Mulcahy adaptation of *The Lost Battalion* (2001) and Brian Kirk's adaptation of *My Boy Jack* (2007).

Keys to Using This Guide

List of Films: Forging a list of films to include in this volume was harder than anticipated. Many films have all but disappeared and some drew so little attention when they came out that I could find no reviews.

Order: Films are listed in alphabetical order by title. A good many of these films also came out under alternate titles, especially when distributed in a non–English speaking country. Some of these alternate titles are included in the index for easy location.

Selection: In the main, films selected are those in which combat was shown to some degree and the characters were directly affected by the events of the war. I have included some short films since during the early years they were about the only films being made. The films were made in France, Australia,

Poland, Russia, Canada, Italy, Great Britain and the United States. I have not included films in which the war is used only as an explanation as in *The Stolen Ranch* (1926), a melodrama about two veterans who fight through the trauma of their experience. In it, the war is always in the abstract.

Time: In silent film days, the speed at which the film was projected varied between fourteen and eighteen frames per second. Sometimes the rate was varied for creative purposes. There was no standard speed for the projectors but most ran at one of two extremes, twenty-four frames a second for sound and sixteen frames per second for silent.

When sound became popular, the industry developed a standard of twenty-four frames per second. In many cases the length of the film is listed here at a somewhat higher figure than the actual projection time, since that is what was generally reported. Standard reels were 900 to 1000 feet.

Cinematographers: For many of the early films, there was a single location camera that rarely moved. The actors played in front of a camera that was positioned primarily by the director. When new and more developed photoplay techniques were devised, more cinematographers began receiving screen credit. There was considerable adjustment necessary as photo techniques improved and directors discovered cameramen who were willing and able to intensify the film by the injection of distance and angles. There was some early criticism of those directors who moved cameras, believing that it dispelled the sense of realism when the audience watched rather than participated.

Directors: Many of the early directors were also actors and writers but by 1916 or so the art of direction was becoming increasingly specialized and the number of directors diminished. As they took on styles, films were often best known for the ability of their director. This was certainly the case with D.W. Griffith. In many cases these silent films had more than one director as up-and-coming directors learned the trade through involvement. When listening to critics, most directors seem to be divided into two camps: one, the innovators who included Griffith, von Stroheim, King, Vidor, Murnau, and Flaherty) and a second group who were often identified as "traffic cops," meaning that ran a good tight film but they tended to let the films run themselves.

Genre: Some critics identify war films as westerns in disguise and list and treat them similarly. The same is often true of the relation between war films and gangster movies. But in the main, the genre has gained its own identity. It is interesting and somewhat astounding that William K. Everson's extremely valuable and well-written *American Silent Film* (Da Capo Press, 1998) does not acknowledge war films as a genre when discussing the silent film.

Writers: As might be expected, a good number of silent films were based on books or plays. This is equally true of war films written by young men (and occasionally women) who had been involved in the war. The well-received *What Price Glory?* (1926) was written primarily by Laurence Stallings who, as a captain of Marines, had lost his leg in the Battle of Belleau Woods. By the same token the screenplays of these films were generally written by established Hollywood types. It is worth noting the significant number of women who were writing for the movie industry.

Music: Almost all films were accompanied by sheet music for songs to be sung either before or after by the audience or for a local musician to play at appropriate times. Many of these were complicated compositions rendered by rather large orchestras. A good many were super-patriotic and some quickly gave rise to renditions that were less than socially acceptable; for example, "Over There" became "Underwear." Laurence Stallings referred to them as "yawping patriotism" and panned Tin Pan Alley for their lack of conviction. An essayist writing in *The Independent* pointed out that most lyrics "did not merely lack conviction; they denied reality." The inclusion of sound was not easy, however, because besides it being seen as a "stylized and unrealistic device," the musicians were in constant battle with the dialogue. The scoring was usually done live on the sets and with their use of mixes and remixes, they often forced the actors to pitch their voice to overcome the musical competition.

Credits: For decades, the listing of major contributors to a film was usually seen at the beginning. Both the number of persons involved and the number of them wanting recognition led to the listing of more and more names. In 1942 the industry made an effort to limit the number of persons who could be credited, but they failed. *Superman* (1978) listed 457 credits.

Sound: Silent movies were not necessarily silent. The lack of voiced dialogue did not prevent theaters from providing accompanying appropriate sounds to follow along with the movie. Certainly the organ played, but there were clashes, explosions, the sound of marching men and whatever could be provided to make the film appear more realistic. One drawback to the intertitles system: Actors could say whatever was inspired by the moment and then lip readers in the audiences could tell that the "darn" on the intertitles was not what the actor had said. Sound, which appeared in short segments and then in the whole film, was greatly improved by the development of the Dolby system, a noise reduction procedure. Many top directors (Borzage, Ford, von Stroheim, von Sternberg, Vidor) saw the rush to sound as sad for the industry and felt that it would destroy much of the unique art form and even lessen the commercial value. One obvious result was that since dialogue was itself a novelty, audiences did not expect wit or sophistication to emerge. Many of the early talkies had dialogue that was so casual and unpolished as to be honest and spontaneous—but also very dull.

Length: The length of the film at first was primarily determined by budget and available equipment and, to some degree, the belief that short films were all that was needed. But as the industry realized the popularity of the films, they started to expand in length. At first many of these films simply did not have enough narrative to excuse their continuation and they got by with the public basically on the uniqueness of the process. To give length to film with limited plots, Edison wrote lengthy footage-eating titles into the narrative. Detective films were especially welcome since they provided their own logical excuse for long questions and complicated answers. By 1919 or so, many of the films took on a specific look that we now identify as a lack of pacing, but simply means they slowed down to lengthen the time involved; films moved at a snail's pace by the end of the silent era, in contrast to the early fast pace of films. Some producers believed that the prestige of the film was to be linked to its length. The big pictures were long ones; *The Patent Leather Kid* (1925) and *What Price Glory?* (1926) ran twelve reels. The films of the twenties are skilled but they are slick and quite often somewhat lifeless. Twenties movies invariably seem overwhelming for the artistry, the size, the variety, and the determination on the part of the industry to entertain and give the customers their money's worth.

Special Effects: As the movies became increasing complex, more and more excitement was created by the staging of scenes with models or in some cases string puppets. This was particularly true with air combat scenes. The ability to make cardboard tanks look real and broomstick barrels appear to fire was adding a great deal to the early films.

Bloopers: The making of a film can be a highly complex business and sometimes mistakes reached the screen. One of the best known is in John Wayne's *The Green Berets* (1968) which ends with Wayne and a little Vietnam child looking out to sea at the sun setting in the east.

"Warnography": Sex has always been a significant part of movies. In 1896's *Le Coucher de la Mariée* a bride undresses before her new husband and in doing so gave birth to a whole new industry, the licentious film. Hundreds of short subjects were made for this purpose alone. Audrey Munsun, a model, appeared naked in *Inspiration* (1915). War and sex seem to be natural companions. The war film is so prone to sexual exposure that there is even a word for it, "warnography," which means highly sexualized and stylized depictions of women in war as expressed by the media. When the Hays committee showed up in 1921, some very strict rules appeared.

Military Correlation: An attempt has been made to evaluate the film in terms of its contribution to an understanding or appreciation of the events of the First World War. The following indicators are used:

- Excellent: The film focuses on the war, giving it a prime role, and deals with it openly with consideration to both the physical and emotional costs.
- Good: The conflict plays a significant role in the film and is carefully and reasonably considered in a meaningful context.
- Spotty: War is an important part of the story, but distorts and or exaggerates to the point of misdirection.
- Helpful: The fighting of the war has a limited role but the film provides some insights or introspection about the conflict.
- Bad: Presents the war in such a manner as to ignore the significance of the event, or exploits the situation for the sake of narrative.
- None: The film made no contribution to understanding the war and uses it only as a backdrop for the narrative.
- Unknown: Unable to screen the film.

The Films

Aces High (1976)

Produced-distributed by Jacques Roitfeld, S. Benjamin Fitz Productions (United Kingdom), Cine Artists Pictures, EMI (United States). Directed by Jack Gold; written by Howard Barker; based on a play by R.C. Sherriff. Cinematography by Gerry Fisher. Music by Richard Hartley and Carlos Rustichell. This 114-minute Technicolor film starred Malcolm McDowell, Christopher Plummer, Simon Ward, Giles Behat, Elliott Cooper, David Daker, Jaces Maury, Peter Firth, Christopher Blake, David Wood, John Gielgud, Trevor Howard, Richard Johnson, Ray Milland, Tim Pigutt, Gilles Benat, Elliot Cooper, Jeanne Patou, Pascale Christophe, John Serret, Gerard Paquis, Jean Driant, Judy Buxton, Trica Newy, Penny Irving, Roland Viner, Steven Pacey Kim Lotis, Jane Anthony, Evelyn Corraeau, Paul Henley, Paul Rosebury, James Cormack, and Barry Jackson.

Story: An inexperienced officer appears at the Western front to fight in the air war where the life expectancy was about two weeks. The commanding officer (Malcolm McDowell), while himself very brave, is nevertheless deeply troubled and concerned about his men and dies a little when one of them is killed. To deal with this he soon turns to drink and in time this affects his abilities in the air. The film focuses on the hardening of the men so that in time they will be able to send others out to be killed, just as their officers are now sending them. His commanding officer and friend (Christopher Plummer) is required to interfere.

Military Correlation: Excellent

Comment: This film is reported to be a remake of *Journey's End*, a 1930 movie that was based on a play by R. C. Sherriff, and some additional materials from *Sagittarius Rising* by Cecil Lewis. A few of the scenes have been taken directly from *The Blue Max* (1966), including the view of the observer parachuting out of a balloon. Most of its original reviewers tended to call it a somewhat heavy-handed anti-war film but later critics were kinder, reflecting on the accuracy of the content and the realism of the dogfights. This is one of the films recommended to teachers for American history classes. When the movie was not focusing on the pious elitism of the British aristocracy, it manages to show the war as a somewhat "tongue-in-cheek" performance.

The air war was popular in films far in excess of its influence on the outcome of the war. Even the most generous of historians are reluctant to suggest that air power—fighters and bombers in combat—had played a significant role in World

War I. If anything, the less romantic and equally dangerous work of the reconnaissance pilot was more significant. But the lonesome one-on-one clashes between two pilots high in the sky had the same attraction as two gunfighters meeting at high noon.

Bloopers: During one of the dogfights, the Avro 504 suddenly becomes a Cauldron Luciole. This is not a mistake that will bother most viewers but the purist will be turned off by the substitution. While the aerial fight scenes are well done, the technical realism of the planes themselves is very poor.

The African Queen (1951)

Produced-distributed by Sam Spiegel. Released by United Artists. Directed by John Huston and written by Peter Viertel and James Agee, it was based on a book with the same name by C. S. Forester. Cinematography by Jack Cafrdiff. This 105-minute Technicolor film starred Humphrey Bogart, Katharine Hepburn, Walter Gotell, Peter Bull, Richard Marner, Theodore Bikel, and Robert Morley.

Story: Charlie Allnut (Humphrey Bogart), a gin-swilling boat operator in German East Africa delivers supplies to missionaries along the river. He warns the pietistic and somewhat snobbish brother and sister missionaries (Katharine Hepburn and Robert Morley) of the advancing Germans but they decide to stay. On his return he discovers the wreckage of a missionary village that the Germans had destroyed; the sole survivor is Rose the missionary. After he takes the moralistic Rose on board his boat, she is able to convince him to head down river to attack a German gunboat that is patrolling the lake. While maintaining an interesting and delightful romantic theme, the two fight the troubles created by the treacherous river and the ancient boat. In time the two go from isolated characters determined not to like each other into deep human beings. After their long journey, Charlie and Rose are captured by the Germans gunboat crew and, after being married by the sympathetic German captain, are about to be hanged. The gunboat sails into the wreckage of Charlie's boat—and her makeshift torpedo—and is destroyed. Charlie and Rose swim to safety.

Military Correlation: Helpful

Comment: During the location filming, most of the cast was ill with the exception of Bogart, who swore he drank only whiskey and thus avoided disease. Bogart originally spoke his lines with a heavy Cockney dialect but the actor was unable to make it work and the accent was dropped. The film provides an excellent look at the impact of World War I on the vast colonial empires affected by it. Bogart received the Academy Award for Best Actor, beating out Marlon Brando. The director was nominated, as was Katharine Hepburn for the Best Actress. It was listed on the National Film Registry in 1994.

It was one of the few movies that took the war out of Europe. As far as Hollywood was concerned, the war was being fought in France and Belgium, primarily ignoring the fact that it was in all ways a world war, involving more than a hundred nations.

Special effects were well done, especially the shots of the *African Queen* shooting over the rapids that was done with miniature models including tiny likenesses of the stars. Charles Laughton and Elsa Lanchester, David Niven and Bette Davis, and John Mills and Deborah Kerr all declined roles in the film.

All Quiet on the Western Front (1930)

Produced by Carl Laemmie, Jr. Released by Universal. Directed by Lewis Milestone. Based on Erich Maria Remarque's German novel of the same name. The screenplay was written by Maxwell Anderson and George Abbott. Cinematography by Arthur Edeson. This film is 103 minutes long, black and white, and starred Louis Wolheim, Lew Ayers, John Wray, Slim Summerville, Scott Kolk, Harold Goodwin, William Bakewell, Ben Alexander, Owen Davis, Jr., Arnold Lucy, Walter Browne Rogers, Russell Gleason, G. Pat Collins, Richard Alexander, Edmund Breese, Marion Clayton Anderson, Heinie Conklin, Raymond Griffith, Bertha Mann, William Irving, Arthur Gardner, and Beryl Mercer.

Story: A German high school teacher talks his students into enlisting in the infantry, believing they will bring glory to themselves and to the nation. The young men move off en masse to fight. In a series of vignettes narrated by the young recruits, the story follows the day-by-day growth of their disillusionment as it is worked out against the background of debilitating horror in trench warfare, artillery bombardments, and machine-gun fire. Strongly anti-war, *All Quiet* is also strongly humanitarian as it counters the demands of human needs against the brutality of the war itself.

Military Correlation: Excellent

Commentary: After film studios in Germany declined to make the film, Universal Studios in Hollywood took it on. A lot of changes were made before the German-dubbed version premiered in Berlin in December 1930.[1] Despite these efforts it was met with raucous protests in the streets of Berlin, Saxony, Brunswick, and Wurttembery. In America it played to packed houses. It was re-released in 1934 during the "merchant of death hearing in Congress."[2] It was released again in 1939 as war clouds gathered in Europe. A shortened version was released in 1950 during the Korean War. In the 1970s there was a color remake in the wake of the Vietnam War.

Seen as the first anti-war movie with sound, it takes full advantage of the effects of exploding shells and the rhythmic pounding of the machine-gun. The film featured some beautifully natural performances and is still popular today. Many film critics claim that its depiction of war has never been equaled. Hitler believed it showed German in a bad light and banned it when he came to power. Lew Ayres was so moved by his experience during the filming of the movie that he declared himself a conscientious objector in World War II; result, more than one hundred Chicago theaters refused to show his films. During World War II Ayres served in combat with valor as a medical corpsman. *All Quiet* received an Academy Award for Best Picture and Lewis Milestone was voted Best Director. Considered to be the best World War I film, it was filmed again in 1979 as a TV presentation. The film was placed on the National Film Registry in 1990.

Zasu Pitts, a noted comedienne, was signed to play Paul's mother and was filmed in the part. Preview audiences were so aware of her as a comedienne that they laughed when she came on screen. The director reshot the scene with Beryl Mercer.

All Quiet on the Western Front (1979)

Film: Produced by Norman Rosemont Productions, ITC Entertainment (United States). Directed by Delbert Mann and written by Paul Monash, based on a book by Erich Marie Remarque, the 131-minute film starred Richard Thomas, Ernest Borgnine, Donald Pleasence, Ian Holm, Patricia Neal, George Winter, Mark Drewry, Ian Hastings, Paul Mark Elliott, Dai Bradley, Matthew Williams, Dominic Jephcott, Colin Mayes, Michael Sheard, Mary Miller, and Katherina Lirova.

Story: An update of the earlier (1930) movie version, it tells the story of the lives of ordinary German soldiers who enlist to fight in France. It focuses on the experiences of Paul Brennan (Richard Thomas), who enlisted with his school chums at the encouragement of their schoolmaster who promises them adventure and glory in the defense of Germany. Under the direction of an old timer they learn about war and realize that it is not so much about glory as it is about gore, that the expectations of the nation that sent them are soon lost in the growing disillusionment and distrust they feel. Despair and a growing distance from hope eats at the men as they survive the ravages of the war and the conditions in which they must live. Eventually most of the young men are dead. Fairly well received, the film left a sense of desolation, hardship and waste but that of course was the author's intention.

Military Correlation: Excellent

Comment: The German translation reads "In the West Nothing New" but the English version is the one remembered. Tom Courtenay was offered the part eventually played by Ian Holm. It won the Golden Globe Award for Best Picture. It might have been expected that the advances in techniques would have made this a better picture than the earlier version, but that does not appear to be the case.

Bloopers: In one scene, this movie about World War I features trucks that were made after 1930.

All the King's Men (1999)

Produced by Gareth Neame and Ruth Mauruas, and the British Broadcasting Company (United Kingdom). It was directed by Julian Jarrold and written by Alma Cullen, based on the book of the same title by Nigel McCrery. Cinematography was by David Odd. Music by Adrian Johnson. This 110-minute color film starred David Jason, Maggie Smith, William Ash, Tom Burke, Jo Stone-Fewings, Gaye Brown, Ian McDiarmid, Roland Oliver, Sonya Walger, Stuart Bunce, James Murray, Ed Waters, Tom Burke, Ben Crompton, Eamon Boland, Jo Stone-Fewings, James Hillier, Emma Cunniffe, Adam Kotz, Patreick Malahide, Gaye Brown, Phyllis

Logan, Ian McDiarmid, Danny Worters, Laurence Dobiesz, Roland Oliver and Jamie Beddard, and David Throughton.

Story: The Royal Army Sandringham Company, led by Captain Frank Beck, was a Pals Battalion[3] composed primarily of servants and land keepers who worked on King George V's Norfolk Estates. They enlisted together, trained together and then marched together into battle against the Turks at Gallipoli in April 1915. The myth immediately grew that as they had marched forward, a great mist formed out of nowhere. By the time the mist lifted, the entire unit had vanished. They were never seen or heard from again. They had, it was reported at length, simply advanced into what looked like a low-hanging cloud and disappeared. For a long time the event was considered one of the great mysteries of the war. While the book written about the event follows the more mystical myths that accompany the story, the film gives far more credit to a realistic account that shows the English soldiers overwhelmed by the Turks, captured, and then massacred. Only one survivor is left to tell the tale: Private Arthur Webber of Yarmough county was wounded and claimed to have witnessed the whole thing.

Military Correlation: Spotty

Comment: The film claimed to tell the true story of what happened, but many historians are more inclined to believe that most of the Englishmen died in the heavy fighting. The book on which it is based relies a good deal on the account of the Reverend Pierrepoint Edwards who discovered the mass grave. The title is taken from the Humpty Dumpty nursery rhyme and expressed the idea that they are gone, never to be reconstructed. The film exaggerates the situation by making the number of men involved in the execution far in excess of those actually killed. The film is brilliantly acted and gives an inside picture to one kind of outfit, the Pals battalions, that few know about. It tells both an emotional and bittersweet story. The Turkish Ambassador in London criticized the film as being unsupported by evidence, and the descendants of the central character, Captain Beck, were not supportive for it was too practical an account. Folks from Norfolk reported that the dialect was poorly presented. David Jason, as Captain Beck who was the Sandringham manager, won Best Actor in the TV Quick Awards.

An American Home (1915)
see *The Battle Cry of Peace* (1915)

An Honest Man (1918)

Produced and distributed by Triangle Film Corporation (United States). Directed by Frank Borzage and written by Henry Payson Dowst and George Elwood Jenks, it was based on a short story by Dowst. Cinematography by Pliny Horne. This five-reel, silent, black and white film, with English intertitles, stars William Desmond, Mary Warren, Ann Forrest, and Graham Pettie.

Story: When Benny Boggs (William Desmond), a hobo traveling around

America, hears about the war, he goes to the enlistment office thinking it's expected of him. But he goes drunk, and realizes that he was hoping to be rejected—which he was. So he goes back on the road planning to ignore the war. In his travels he meets an old farmer who seems to see right through him. In one of their conversations, the farmer describes the young Boggs as "an honest man." Touched by the event, Boggs decides to try and live up to the description. He cleans up and returns to the recruitment office and is accepted as A-1. Thus he wins back the love of his dismayed sweetheart Beatrice Burnett (Mary Warren) as she watches him march proudly off to war.

Military Correlation: None

Comment: This is an example of the "real men enlist" films that came out, as well as some of the late redemption films that Hollywood seemed to like so well. Despite its formula presentation, it is still a pretty good story that avoids too much sentimentality. It provides a good look at rural America at the time of the war. The Triangle Company soon went out of business, primarily because they failed to provide any showmanship to its advertising. They adopted the theme "Clean pictures for clean people" that was soon transplanted by the viewers to "Dull pictures for dull people."

Anzacs, the War Down Under (1985) / *aka* **ANZACS**

Produced by Geoff Borrows, Burrows-Dixon Company, Nine Network, Celebrity Home Entertainment (Australia). Directed by John Dixon and George Miller. Written by John Clarke and John Mitchello. Cinematography by Keith Wagstaff. This (five-episode film) starred Paul Hogan, Megan Williams, Noel Travarthen, Michael Edgar, Rod Hewitt, Edmund Pegge, Jim Holt, David Bradshap, Rhys McConnochie, Mark Hembrow, Jim Blake, Christopher Cummins, Tony Bonner, Alec Wilson, Peter Stratford, Vivean Gray, Francis Bell, Meradith Rodgers, Nick Waters, Bill Kerr, Diana Greentree, Tony Bonner, Howard Bell, Vincent Ball, Michael Adams, David Lynch, David Allardice, Patrick Ward, Peter Finley, and Andrew Clarke.

Story: This five-part made-for-TV movie dramatizes the Australian and New Zealand Army Corps during World War I as it fought from Gallipoli to the Armistice. The film focuses on three members of this volunteer unit: rich aristocrat Martin Barrington (Andrew Clarke), his best friend (Mark Hembrow) and his friend's lovely sister (Megan Williams). The two men engage in a variety of battles at the front. Barrington is wounded and sent home where he is nursed by to health by Megan. The rest of the film follows the thinning of the unit as more men are killed and morale suffers.

Military Correlation: Excellent

Comment: A lively action mini-sized with plenty going on. It has its fair share of British bashing, but is not as hard on the English officers as other renditions. The Australian took their participation in World War I very seriously and this type of patriotic film always does well in Australia.

Arms and the Girl (1917) / aka Delicate Situation; Red Salute; Runaway Daughter

Produced and distributed by Famous Players Lasky Corporation, Paramount (United States). Directed by Joseph Kaufman. Written by Robert Bakers, Charles Whittaker and Grant Stewart. Cinematography by William Marshall. This silent black and white film, with English intertitles, stars Billie Burke, Thomas Meighan, Louise Bates, Malcolm James Dunn, Arthur Bauer, William David, George S. Trimble, Harry Lee, and May De Lacy.

Story: Seeking a reunion with her fiancé, a young American girl (Billie Burke) travels to Europe. There she discovers that her sweetheart (Malcolm Dunn) has been two-timing her. War breaks out all over the world. Left in Europe without resources, she is at the mercy of events until she finds, and falls in love with, a hardworking American engineer (Thomas Meighan) who takes her under his wing and they both survive.

Military Correlation: None

Comments: Director Joseph Kaufman died in 1918 of Spanish Influenza shortly after making this film. It was Burke's second film. Best known for her role in the Ziegfeld Follies (she was married to Florenz Ziegfeld), she gave a serious and credible performance.

As in a Looking Glass (1916)

Produced and distributed by Shubert Film Company, World Film (United States). Directed by Frank Hall Crane (as Frank Crane). Written by Francis Charles Philips, based on his novel. Cinematography by Edward Lord. This 50-minute, silent, black and white film with English intertitles stars Lillian Cook, Charles Eldridge, Frank Goldsmith, Kelly Gordon, Lumsden Hare, Teddy Sampson, Gladden James, Eugenie Woodward, George Maeroni and Philip W. Masi.

Story: A British stage star (Lillian Cook) makes her American appearance as a sexy agent working for an unnamed enemy. She is very good at what she does until she meets a handsome American (Lumsden Hare) and eventually falls in love. After that she changes loyalties and betrays her former colleagues.

Military Correlation: Helpful

Comment: American audiences loved spies and fascinated by the idea that hundreds of presumably German-Americans were planning the nation's demise. This film, produced prior to America's entry into the war, does not identify the nationality of the country involved, but there is no doubt that it is Germany. Some critics have wondered why it is always the heroine's father and not her mother who is the German spy. Dozens of films use the divided loyalty between father and daughter but none with that role played by the mother.

At the Front (1918)

Produced and distributed by American Pathe, B. F. Production Company (United States). Directed by Harry Conway "Bud" Fisher, Raoul Barre and Charles Bowers, it was written by Fisher based on the "Mutt and Jeff" comic series. The short (seven minutes), silent, black and white film was animated by Dick Huemer.

Story: The film focus on the antics of the "two mismatched tinhorns" Augustus J. Mutt, an incurable gambler, and his dimwitted friend Edgar Horace Jeffries (always called Jeff), who join the Army and work together to fight the Kaiser. The Mutt and Jeff comedies play an interesting role in that they redirect the war, and the movie public's understanding of the war, from the technical to the personal. These two characters attacked at the personal level and bombarded the Kaiser as if he were any other citizen. They were extremely crude but the public appeared to love them.

Military Correlation: None

Comment: This was one of more than 300 such films made by Fisher's company between 1913 and 1926 and one of the few that focuses on World War I.

Austeria (1982) / aka *The Inn*

Produced and distributed by Zespol Filmowy "Kadr" (Poland), Afra Films (United States). Directed by Jerzy Kawalerowicz, it was written by Kawalerowicz, Tadeusz Konwicki and Jan Szuremie, based on a novel by Julian Stryjkowski. Cinematography by Zygmunt Samoslui. Music arrangements by Anna Izykowska. This 105-minute color film stars Seweryn Dazecki, Zofia Bajuk, Marek Wilk, Syzmon Sandello, Wojciech Standelus, Ewa Domanska, Wojciech Pszoniak, Franciszek Pieczka, Golda Tencer, Izabela Wieczorek, Jan Szurmiej, Zofia Saretok, Stanislaw Igor, and Miroslawa Lombardo.

Story: In Polish Galicia in 1914, three men are living in a small inn managed by Tag, an old Jewish man (Franciszek Piecka). They are facing the advance of the Cossacks. One man is a Pole, one a Ukrainian, and one a Jew. They are accompanied by an Austrian baroness (Zofia Saretok) and a Hungarian Hussar who has been cut off from his command. The story is primarily one of their rather nostalgic, poetic and even cruel vision of the beliefs, traditions, legends and even the humor of their lives. One reviewer said it was an "earthy and touching expression of the eastern European world that perished in time."

Military Correlation: None

Comment: The story deals not so much with their interaction in the face of the coming enemy, but with the emergence of their own personalities during these moments of frustrating anticipation. The set and production leaves something to be desired but the acting is excellent and the story is well paced.

Back to the Primitive (1917)
see *The Showdown* (1917)

The Battle Cry of Peace (1915) /
aka *The Battle Cry of War;*
Call to Arms Against War; An American Home

Produced and distributed by Vitagraph-Lubin-Selig-Essanay Company of America (United States). It was directed by J. Stuart Blackton and Wilfrid North and written by Blackton, based on a book by Hudson Maxim. Cinematography by Arthur T. Quinn and Leonard Smith. Music by S.L. Rothafel. This 90-minute, silent, black and white film, with English intertitles, starred Charles Richman, L. Rogers Lytton, Mary Morrison, Mary Maurice, Louise Beaudet, Harold Hubert, Jack Crawford, Charles Kent, Julia Swayne Gordon, Evart Overton, Belle Bruce, Norma Talmadge, George Stevens, Thais Lawton, Lucie Hamilton, Joseph Kilgour, Paul Scardon, William J. Ferguson, Hudson Maxin, Tefft Johnson, and James Morrison.

Story: Enemy agents in the United States under the leadership of someone named Emanon ("no name" spelled backwards) have organized the nation's anti-war movement in an effort to defeat any attempt to promote and develop American defenses. Sure enough, the nation is invaded by an unidentified enemy that looks very much like the World War I German soldier, and in the process New York, Washington and many other American cities are destroyed. At last the patriots, who had actually stored weapons, are able to defeat the enemy.

Military Correlation: Spotty

Comment: This film, made before the United States got involved in the war, was criticized for being such a strong call to arms. The military was so impressed with the script that they loaned a regiment of Marines to act as extras, and then Admiral Dewey appeared in the film. President Roosevelt was a strong supporter of its production. There was also a rumor that Russian revolutionary Leon Trotsky (then in exile) was among the extras.[4] One reel of the film is believed to have survived; the film is considered lost.

Battle Cry of War (1915) see *Battle Cry of Peace* (1915)

The Battle of Gallipoli (1931) see *Tell England* (1931)

Battleground (2013) see *Forbidden Ground* (2013)

Battling Jane (1918)

Produced and distributed by New Arts Film Company, Paramount Pictures (United States). Directed by Elmer Clifton, it was written by Arnold Bernot. Cinematography by Karl Brown. This five-reel silent, black and white film, with English intertitles, starred Dorothy Gish, May Hall, Katherine MacDonald, Ernest Marion, Bertram Grassby, Adolph Lestina, Kate Toncray and George Nichols.

Story: A small town waitress, Jane (Dorothy Gish), assumes the guardianship of a baby whose mother has died and left it alone. When the child wins a prize, her unscrupulous father Dr. Sheldon makes an effort to steal the prize money. Jane manages to fight off the doctor and his hated followers. The money is used to buy Liberty Bonds and to make a donation to the Red Cross. The movie moved rather arbitrarily between pure comedy and pure melodrama without warning.

Military Correlation: None

Comment: A limited comedy, it used the war as a backdrop to give credibility to the gift that Jane was protecting. It was one of the most financially successful of the movies made by Dorothy Gish for Paramount films. On May 9, 1919, the *Wellington Evening Post* wrote, "[T]here are hundreds of Janes in the world, no doubt. Ms. Gish portrays the character realistically," and the *Toronto World* though Gish was "a marvel of cleverness."

A Bear Named Winnie (2004) / aka *Winnie the Bear*

Produced and distributed by Original Pictures, Powercorp (Canada). Directed by John Kent Harrison and written by Simon Vaughan and John Goldsmith. This 90-minute color film starred Michael Fassbender, Gil Bellows, David Suchet, Jonathon Young, Aaron Ashmore, Stephen Fry, Robert Gauvin, Joshua J. Ballard, Ted Atherton, Miriam Smith, Arne MacPherson, Nathan Valente, Chris Sigurdson, Carson Nattrass, and Stan Lesk.

Story: At the beginning of World War I, Lieutenant Harry Colebourn (Michael Fassbender) of the Canadian Army Veterinary Corps saves a black bear from being killed by a hunter that had killed its mother. He takes her back to his military camp at White River, Ontario, as the mascot for the unit, naming her Winnie for Winnipeg. The men in camp come to love the bear and bond with her as they train for war. The head of the veterinary division does not approve but, while he is tough, he is also fair and tries to work it out. Nevertheless, he is being pressured by the commanding officer who is busy trying to use the military to further his own agenda.

Military Correlation: Good

Comments: Most reviewers found this movie to be an excellent expression of hope and the respect for the values of life at a time when war was questioning all that. The humanitarian nature of the event sparked something in the men despite their situation. One aspect of this film worth mentioning is that it provide some evidence about the nature of military life other than the horrors of trench warfare. If we are to let these films serve as our memory of those days, then we will be greatly misinformed. Thousands upon thousands of men served in the armed services doing the totally unromantic but absolutely essential work necessary to keep those on the front line supplied.

These events are considered to be the source of A.A. Milne's *Winnie the Pooh* stories and there is a park and large monument to the bear on the shore of Lake Superior. Out of deference to Disney Studios, the name Winnie the Pooh is never mentioned. *A Bear Named Winnie* won the Chrystal Heart Award.

Bloopers: Some critics noted that the CPR engines pulling the troop train are green rather than the more realistic maroon.

The Beast of Berlin (1918) see *Kaiser, the Beast of Berlin* (1918)

Behind the Door (1919)

Produced and distributed by Thomas H. Ince Corporation (United States). It was directed by Irvin V. Willet and written by Gouverneur Morris and Luther Reed, based on a short story by Morris. This 75-minute silent, black and white film, with English intertitles, starred Jane Novak, Wallace Beery, Hobart Bosworth, James Gordon, Richard Wayne, J.P. Lockney, Gibson Gowland, Otto Hoffman, and Tom Ashton.

Story: It was assumed, because of his name, that Oscar King (Hobart Bosworth) was a German sympathizer. In order to prove his loyalty to the United States he joins the armed services and is assigned to a merchant marine vessel. The night before he leaves, he secretly marries his long-time sweetheart, Alice Moore (Jane Novak). In order to go along with him as he heads out to war, she disguises herself as a Red Cross nurse. The ship on which they sails is sunk by a submarine and the German U-boat commander brutalizes the wife. King gets revenge by killing the U-boat captain.

Military Correlation: Poor

Comment: The production company altered the outline of the American submarine USS H-8 and it was seen in this movie as the German U-boat U-98. The message of the amoral submarine commander and the need for revenge is delivered harshly in what one critic called a "kickass" film. In many of these films the easy manner in which the female lead was injected into the plot by means of being a nurse or USO entertainer does a significant disservice to the thousands of women who served in these capacities. These women should be better remembered than they would be if these films were taken seriously.

Behind the Front (1926)

Produced and distributed by Famous Players Lasky productions, Paramount Pictures (United States). Directed by A. Edward Sutherland and written by Monte

Brice, Ralph Spenser, Hugh Wiley and Ethel Doherty from the story "The Spoils of War" by Wiley. Cinematography by Charles Bonce. This 60-minute, silent, black and white film, with English intertitles, starred Wallace Beery, Raymond Hatton, Mary Brian, Richard Arlen, Hayden Stevenson, Chester Conklin, Tom Kennedy, Francis Raymond, Melbourne MacDowell, Jerry Mandy, Charles Sullivan, and Gertrude Astor.

Story: In this well filmed comedy set in the early days of World War I, myopic detective Riff Swanson (Wallace Beery) chases crook Shorty McKee (Raymond Hatton) into an enlistment party being put on by wealthy socialite Betty Bartlett Cooper (Mary Brian). The two men, attracted to the lady, sign up. The men, direct opposites, end up in France where they get in trouble with the military police and harass a French girl. Assigned a desperate mission, they nearly destroy the Armistice.

Military Correlation: Poor

Comment. This movie, a series of gags with wisecracking subtitles, ends with an attack on the man who is responsible for the creation of the hated K rations. Some of the gags were repeated by the comedy team of Laurel and Hardy in their film *Pack Up Your Troubles*.

Behind the Lines (1997) / *aka* **Regeneration**

Produced by Art House and International Drama, British Broadcasting Company, Famous Players, Norstar Entertainment Company (Canada). Directed by Gillies Mackinnon and written by Allan Scott, based on the novel of the same name by Pat Barker. This 95-minute Dolby sound color film starred Jonathan Pryce, James Wilby, Jonny Lee Miller, Stuart Bunce, David Hayman, Dougray Scott, John Neville, Paul Young, Alastair Galbraith, Eileen Nicholas, Julian Fellowes, David Robb, Kevin McKidd, Rupert Proctor, and Tanya Allen.

Story: In 1917, famed poet Siegfried Sassoon writes a statement against the war that is read at the House of Parliament. Because of the position it takes, they decide the author must either be court martialed or cured of shell shock. They send him to Craiglockart, a Scottish castle where the shell-shocked are treated by Freudian methods. A psychiatrist in the respected Scottish asylum, Dr. Rivers (Jonathan Pryce), heals shell-shocked soldiers so they can go back to the trenches. But he encounters a different kind of patient when he meets Sassoon. The poet was considered ill because he published outspoken criticism and anti-war pamphlets, but he has an insightful view of the war. As they work together the line between the two men, and their positions, begins to blur. Another individual we meet there is Wilfred Owens (Stuart Bunce), one of England's most important poets. Sassoon finally returns to combat but survived the war.

Military Correlation: Good

Comment: This movie takes on a very sore subject for those involved in the war. While shell shock was identified early in the war, there was a debate between the military men and medical men as to whether it was a form of mental illness (a wound) or just a form of cowardice. Suicides, primarily caused by shell shock and fear on the battlefield, were considered wounds and the dead listed among those killed in action The film is on the National Film Registrar.

Bloopers: Some of the early shots of the battlefield are taken from a crane and you can see the reflection of the crane in pools of water.

Beneath Hill 60 (2010)

Produced and distributed by Lucky Country Productions (New South Wales), Pacific Film and TV Committee (Australia) Directed by Jeremy Sims (as Jeremy Hartley Simms) and written by David Roach. This 122-minute color film starred Brenden Cowell, Harrison Gilbertson, Steve Le Marqand, Warwick Young, Mark Coles Smith, Oliver Leimbach, Martin Thomas, Alan Dukes, Fletcher Illidge, Morgan Illidge, Duncan Young, Gyton Grantley, Anthony Hayes, Alex Thompson, Harrison Gilbertson, and Leon Ford.

Story: This movie was based on a true story. In 1916, Queensland miner Oliver Woodward (Brenden Cowell) leaves his newly acquired love and finds himself at the front where he and his crew of Australians dig a tunnel deep under enemy lines. During the course of the film they dig, repair, defend, and expand the tunnel and pack it with enough explosives to change the course of the battle, and eventually the war. The film provided a somewhat detailed account of the awful conditions of those working hundreds of hours underground in constant danger from cave-ins and German countermines. The tension of the work exacerbated the tensions of the war going on around them.

Military Correlation: Good

Comment: The film depicts the mining efforts of Australian troops at Flanders near Ypres, and draws attention to a little-known activity of the war. Like in the American Civil War, the strategy of undermining the enemy works was almost always employed when possible.

Bloopers: At the grave site, late in the film when it has been raining for two days, the dirt at the grave is dry. At the church celebration they are all wearing their medals, some of which were not awarded until after the war was over.

The Better 'Ole (1926)

Produced and distributed by Vitaphone Corporation, Warner Brothers (United States). Directed by Charles Reisner. Written by Arthur Eliot, Robert Hopkins, Charles Reisner and Darryl Zanuck, based on a play by Bruce Bairnsfather. This 95-minute silent black and white film starred Syd Chaplin, Harold Goodwin, Jack Ackroyd, Edgar Kennedy, Charles K. Gerrard, Theodore Lorch, Tom McGuire, Arthur Clayton, Doris Hill, Olaf Hytten, Tom Kennedy, Hank Mann, and Kewpie Morgan.

Story: While putting on a stage play, the actors are suddenly attacked by the Germans and must get away wearing whatever disguise they had on. Our hero was disguised as a horse. Thirty-year veteran Old Bill (Syd Chaplin) and his friend Alf

(Jack Ackroyd) go from the trenches to a French town where they cause a great amount of trouble. The plot, such as it is, is simply a vehicle for the slapstick comedy.

Military Correlation: Poor

Comment: In order to understand any of this film, one needs to know that just as World War II had Bill Maudlin's doughboys "Willie and Joe," old pros stoically enduring the dangers and difficulties of military service, World War I also had such a comic character, a Tommy Atkins; "Ole" was the tough old bird who knew the answers and thus became the butt of cartoonist Bruce Bairnsfather's wit. This film was the second effort at developing a synchronized music and sound system and while it was an improvement, it was still hard to follow some skits.

The Big Parade (1925)

Produced by Irving Thalberg (Metro-Goldwyn-Mayer) (United States). It was directed by King Vidor and George W. Hill, the latter not credited. It was written by Laurence Stallings, King Vidor, Harry Behn and Irving Thalberg. Photography by John Arnold. This 140-minute silent black and white movie, with English intertitles, starred John Gilbert, Renee Adoree, Hobart Bosworth, Claire McDowell, Claire Adams, Robert Ober, Tom O'Brien, Karl Dane, Rosita Marstini, and George Beranger.

Story: The film portrays the lives of the ordinary soldier on the line trying to survive in a very hostile environment. It focuses on a committed citizen who, when he became aroused to injustice, becomes a magnificent warrior. The three principal characters are steelworker Slim (Karl Dane), Mike "Bull" O'Hara (Tom O'Brian) and James Apperson (John Gilbert). The son of a rich businessman enlists and is sent to France. There he meets and becomes friends with two working class soldiers. He also falls in love with a Frenchwoman (Renee Adoree) but has to leave her behind when he is sent to the front. His increased democratization is led by a desire for the blessings of peace and humanitarian. He returns to find his girl has fallen in love with his brother and he goes back to France to find the girl he left there. The politics of the film are muted.

Military Correlation: Excellent

Comment: While it is not as obvious here, there is some reason to believe that author Stallings and his companions could never really admit the possibility that the whole thing was unnecessary, meaningless, and disastrous. It was filmed with the help of the Second Infantry Division and Air Services units at Kelly Field and the titles acknowledge them. It is believed to be the first film in which the word "damn" is uttered by a character albeit by intertitles. The film is listed as 17th out of 100 on the Silent Era Film List.

It is considered one of the best films about World War I and is praised by most critics. It replaced Griffith's *Hearts of the World* (1918) as the quintessential World War I film. In it the war is perceived not only as a democratic one but also as a moral one in that it portrays the American soldier in a most appealing way. These new films showed muddy life in the trenches, basic training, mail call, soldiers going over the top and the before and after moments of big battles. It stressed the fact that war is an intense leveler of the classes—the big boss at the plant and the common steelworker all come out the same in the end. The film also viewed the war not only as a democratic war and a righteous cause, but also an intrinsic leveler of class differences. and the affirmation of a simpler, un-ostentatious existence. The soldier is a committed civilian who when aroused becomes a dominant warrior, only to yearn for the blessing of peace.

The film reflects a different viewpoint. The hero enters the war but not out of any patriotic sense of duty. He meets a French girl but is not really serious about her. The only time he gets really invested in what is going on is when a friend is killed. The appeal of the war was more a human one than a patriotic one. Nothing about the episodes were new, but there was a somewhat different package. This democratic yet somewhat apathetic sense was also reflected in *Unbeliever* (1918) and *The Lost Battalion* (1919). Critics Peter C. Rollins and John E. O'Connor suggested that it "is flawed as an anti-war statement by the very individualism Thalberg regarded as of primary value." It was the result of "dramatic conventionalism, and judging from its reception, so was its audience."[5]

For the sequence of the advance in *The Big Parade*, theaters stopped the music and played only a muffled brass drum keeping cadence with the advancing soldiers on the screen. The film was placed on the National Film Registry in 1992. Dane was promoted from stage carpenter to actor just before the filming began.

Bloopers: The parade line of march is reported to be in New York City but one will note the palm trees lining the walks; obviously it was shot in Los Angeles. Most of the sets and costumes are of the period when the film was made, not the years depicted.

The Big Shot (1930) see *Doughboys* (1930)

Big Time (1942) see *For Me and My Gal* (1942)

Billy Bishop Goes to War (1918) see *The Kid Who Couldn't Miss* (1918)

The Birth of Patriotism (1917)

Produced and distributed by Universal Film Manufacturing Company (United States). Directed by E. Magnus Ingleton and written by Ingleton and I.A.R. Wylie. Photography by Lucie Brown. This silent, black and white film with English intertitles, starred Irene Hunt, Ann Forrest, Leo Pierson, Ernest Shields, Frank Caffray, Lydia Yeamans Titus, Neal Hart, and J. Edwin Brown.

Story: Johnny Roberts (Leo Pierson), a Cockney worker, marries schoolteacher Mary (Ann Forrest). After a terrible fight, Johnny goes off to the pub where he meets Anna (Irene Hunt), a barmaid who takes him in. He remains with her until he goes into the army. After some time Anna learns that Mary and her child, which Johnny has never seen, are starving and she comes to their aid. They have received word that Johnny has died in combat but it is not true as he was only blinded by gas. When he finally comes home, Anna realizes that the family belongs together and withdraws from the picture.

Military Correlation: Spotty

Comment: This plot was well-worn even by 1917 and there was nothing about the acting or production that made this outstanding. It comes across as a flat, cliché-ridden comment about the evils of war and what it does to families. Hollywood was making a major stretch trying to get as many of its production to work toward the war effort (to influence one way or the other) and often manipulated the titles so that they appeared to be more about national pride than they were. This was one of those cases.

Blighty (1927)

Produced by Carlyle Blackwell and Michael Balcon, Gainsborugh Pictures, Woolf & Freedman Film Service (United Kingdom). Directed by Adrian Brunel and written by Eliot Stannard, Charles McEvoy, Adrian Brunel, and Ivor Montagu. Cinematography by Jack E. Cox. This silent, black and white film, with English intertitles, starred Ellaline Terriss, Lillian Hall-Davis, Jameson Thomas, Godfrey-Winn, Nadia Sibirskaia, Annesley Healey, Wally Patch, Dino Galvani, Renee Houston, Seymour Hicks, and Billie Houston.

Story: The son of a wealthy family and the family chauffeur go off to the war at the same time. Robin (Godfrey Winn) falls in love and marries a local girl (Lillian Hall-Davis) but then loses his life in action in France. David, the chauffeur (Jameson Thomas), is promoted and returns to England. After the war the romance between David and Ann emerges but has to conquer class bias. All is overcome and the family accepts the situation and makes peace. The class-conscious son and the chauffeur theme is found in several movies produced at this time.

Military Correlation: Spotty

Comment. The director did not want to make a war film and objected to the genre on moral grounds but, on the other hand, he wanted to go to work for Gainsborough. He agreed to the film if there was no direct depicting of the conflict or jingoistic appeal. The film's title comes from a term the British troops used to mean home (England) It came originally from a Hindustani word that meant foreigner.

Blockheads (1938) / aka **Just a Jiffy**

Produced by Stan Laurel and Hal Roach Studio (United States). Directed by John G. Blystone and written by Charles Rogers and Felix Adler. This 57-minute, black and white film starred Stan Laurel, Oliver Hardy, Patricia Ellis, Minna Gombell, Billy Gilbert, James Finlayson and Zeffie Tilbury.

Story: Placed on guard and forgotten, Stan, who does not know in 1938 that the war is over, shoots down a French aviator. Oliver, seeing his friend's picture in the paper, goes to the veteran's home to visit him. Taking pity on him he invites him home to his apartment (located thirteen flights of stairs up) for a meal. Oliver's wife say no and leaves it to Oliver. Helped by his neighbor Mrs. Gilbert (Patricia Ellis) they all get along well until her husband (Billy Gilbert) returns from a hunting trip with a shotgun. Many of the eras sacred cows are attacked, including religion, politics, public offices, homosexuality, drugs, old age and even death.

Military Correlation: None

Comment: A much-edited version of this film was shown under the title *Do It Yourself* as part of a TV series. It is considered to be the comedy team's last good film together. All in all the film is more a series of slapstick situations than it is a story. The humor of the movies of Laurel and Hardy—known in Germany as Dick and Doof—could easily be transferred from the silent to the sound stage. They remain popular today with a variety of followers who feel that no current comedy team has captured, or equaled, their high standards of performance.

Bloopers: The newspapers in which the two see their picture is a different paper each time.

The Blue Max (1966)

Produced by Christian Ferry, Twentieth Century–Fox Film Corporation. It was directed by John Gullermin and written by Jack Hunter, David Pursall, Jack Seddon, Gerald Hanley and Ben Barzman, based on a novel by Hunter. Cinematography by Douglas Slocombe This 158-minute Deluxe color CinemaScope movie starred George Peppard, James Mason, Ursula Andress, Jerry Kemp, Karl Michael Vogler, Anton Diffring, Harry Towb, Peter Woodthorpe, Derek Newark, Derren Nesbitt, Loni von Friedl, Friedrich von Ledebur, Carl Schell, Hugo Schuster, Alex Scott and Roger Ostime.

Story: Stachel, a German officer (George Peppard), leaves the infantry for the air and sets his sight on winning Imperial Germany's highest decoration, the Pour le Merite.. To do so, he must shoot down twenty enemy aircraft. The success of this World War I ace is offensive to his aristocratic comrades who feel he has forgotten his place. General von Klugermann (James Mason) sees the potential in Stachel. As the flyer carries on a discreet affair with Kaeti (Ursula Andress), the German high command, after awarding him the highest decoration for twenty kills, finds a final use for him: the testing of an untried plane. This results in his death. The war scenes are excellent and moving but they are not matched by the same sort of sensitivity when it comes to the romance, either the prime love affair, or any of the associated ones. After saving Manfred von Richthofen (Carl Schell), the Red Baron, Stachel is offered a position in the flying circus but turns it down, seeking his own fame. After considerable combat, Stachel, who was also claiming the victories scored by Willis before his death, receives the Blue Max.

Military Correlation: Spotty

Comment: While the movie provides some breathtaking scenes, the reality of the World War I combat is questionable. Peppard is hard to accept as a German and Andress' performance is dry and colorless. Some critics pointed out the total lack of expression on the faces of the characters. On the other hand some critics call this film a classic and it certainly is one of the better films about the Great War. The Fokker Dr 1 tri-planes used were replicas but beautifully done. Many of the dogfight scenes were recreated by pilots from the Irish Air Corps. For the scene in which the planes fly under the bridge, Derek Piggot was the only one willing to try. The director placed a flock of sheep near the bridge so they would scatter, thus showing it was a real scene. But they practiced it so many times that when they finally shot it, the sheep took no notice. Peppard learned to fly in preparation for the making of this film, and actually flew in some of the scenes.

Historical accuracy was not of paramount interest. Jack D. Hunter, one of the authors, later wrote that he asked why the D-7 had curved-sided crosses rather than the more accurate straight ones, and he was told they photographed better. The same was true of the machine guns with no ammo racks that just kept firing. Many suggested that the film was really designed as to a modern lesson on the evils of the military-industrial complex.[6] Film critic Pauline Kael remarked, "[T]he monophonic planes and biplanes can't smash or burn fast enough."[7] It does seem to contain somewhat too much righteous jingoism for its own good.

Blooper: In both of the scenes of planes crashing, the wires suspending the aircraft can be seen. While Heidemann is listed as a colonel in the credits, he is addressed in the film as Hauptmann, Captain.

The Bond (1917)

Produced and distributed by Chaplin Studios (United States). This five-minute silent, black and white comedy starred Charlie Chaplin, Sydney Chaplin, Edna Purviance and Henry Bergman.

Story: The storyline illustrates a variety of bonds that humans make between themselves and with the things that they cherish, and focuses on the liberty bonds that will administer the knockout to the Kaiser. The film includes a scene in which Charlie actually does that.

Military Correlation: None

Comment: *The Bond* was produced and distributed at Chaplin's own expense in support of a Liberty bond drive. Chaplin is obviously deserving of all the credit he received. But most critics agree that this film is not up to the standards that fans had come to expect from him. This is not one of his best.

Bonnie Annie Laurie (1918)

Production and distributed by Fox Film Company (United States). Directed by Harry F. Millarde. Written by Lela Rogers and Hamilton Thompson. This silent black and white film, with English intertitles, starred Peggy Hyland, Henry Halliam, William Bailey, Sidney Mason, and Marlow Singer.

Story: A Scottish lass is about to lose her boyfriend Donald McGregor (William Bailey) who is headed for the front lines, so old man Sandy Laurie (Henry Halliam) sets it up to be sure his daughter Annie (Peggy Hyland) is engaged to Donald before he leaves. While he is at the front, Annie finds a man (Sidney Mason) unconscious on the beach and takes care of him. The man has lost his memory but nevertheless they fall in love. Sandy is determined that Annie will keep her promise to Donald and sends the man away. In London the mysterious man remembers that he is Lieutenant Hathaway, an American officer whose ship had been sunk. Recovered, he goes to France where he meets and becomes friends with McGregor. McGregor, blinded in combat, is in a hospital where Annie is working as a nurse. She is torn by her love for the both of them. When McGregor heals and returns to Scotland, she goes with him.

Military Correlation: Spotty

Comment: As a technique for getting a character into the story, "I found him on the beach" seems to be very popular. Before being too critical, however, it is good to remember the vast number of ship losses during the U-boat campaigns meant that a lot of persons, as well as bodies, washed ashore. The title comes from the poem by Robert Burns and the song "Maxwelton Braes" but it has little to do with the film other than the Scottish nationality of the heroine.

Boom Boom (1936)

Produced by Leo Schlesinger of Warner Brothers Looney Tunes (United States). Directed by Jack King. It features the voices of King, Billy Bletcher, and Joe Dougherty. A seven-minute film with music by Norman Spencer.

Story: This is an animated short film where Porky Pig (voice of Billy Bletcher) and Beans (voice of Joe Dougherty) are soldiers hiding in the ruins of an underground bunker. While they are having a meal they receive a note via a dove that says their general is being held hostage by the enemy force. Beans and Porky go on their motorcycle across enemy lines where they find their general being tortured. They rescue the officer and try and leave in an airplane, but they are shot down. All three survive and while in the hospital injured they are honored by the general for their bravery.

Military Correlation: None

Comment: The animated cartoon format seems somewhat out of place as it is staged in World War I, with the evidence of the war available, but it provides one giggle after another. Information about the short is very limited, and there apparently are no copies of the film known to exist.

Born for Glory (1934)
see *Brown on Resolution* (1934)

Broken Lullaby (1932) / aka The Man I Killed; The Fifth Commandment

Produced and distributed by Paramount Pictures (United States). Directed by Bertrand Tavernier (Ernst Lubitsch). Written by Ernest Vajda and Samson Raphaelson, from the story by Maurice Rostand and adapted by Reginald Berkeley from the play *The Man I Killed*. Cinematography by Victor Milner. This 82-minute black and white film starred Lionel Barrymore, Nancy Carroll, Phillips Holmes, Louise Carter, Lucien Littlefield, Tom Douglas, Zasu Pitts, Frank Sheridan, George Bickel, Reinhold Pasch, Emma Dunn, and George Davis.

Story: A highly sensitive French soldier (Phillips Holmes) is overcome with guilt when he kills a German soldier who was a musician like he is. As young men the two soldiers attended the same music academy in France and had been friends. Despite the fact that it was done in the heat of battle during a war, he is not able to forgive himself. After the war he returns to Germany to see the victim's family. While there, he confesses his crime to the boy's father and receives a limited but generally unaccepted forgiveness. When he also falls in love with Carroll, the man's sweetheart, the villagers are upset.

Military Correlation: Good

Comment: The Women's International League for Peace and Freedom (WILPF) promoted the making and distribution of films supporting peace, or at least anti-war activities. They endorsed *Broken Lullaby* as promoting an "antimilitaristic nature or any picture which would create a better understanding between nations."

It is unashamedly a pull for empathy and the star, Phillips Holmes, goes overboard, giving a performance that reminds the viewer of Montgomery Cliff in *A Place in the Sun*. The *Times of London* reported, "The acting is overwrought; the dialogue is uniformly on the nose. Yet 'purity' is the word that comes to mind. The movie is a nakedly sincere ode to the power of sympathy, and it's not to be missed."[8]

Brother Officers (1915)

Produced by Paul H. Cromelin of London (United Kingdom). Directed by Harold M. Shaw and written by Bannister Merwin, based on a play by Leo Trover. This film stars Henry Ainley, Lettice Fairfax, Gerald Ames, Charles Rock. George Bellamy, Wyndham Glise, and Gwynne Herbert.

Story: The very rich Playdell (Gerald Ames) and the very poor Hinds (Henry Ainley) become close friends while serving in the army. In time Hinds saves Playdell's life and the latter invites him into his home after the war to learn how to become a gentleman. The plot thickens when both fall in love with the same girl, who is perfectly willing to play one off the other. When Hinds realized that Playdell is in deep trouble with a gambler (Charles Rock), he realizes that he has a chance to steal the girl. But his love for the girl, plus whatever he has learned about being a gentleman, drives him to confront the gambler, thus saving his friend and his relationship with the girl.

Military Correlation: Spotty

Comment: The very rich and very poor getting together on the battlefield is standard fare and "two men for the same girl" is as old. The premise of the film is based on the rather large assumption that Hinds wants to be a gentleman. In many of these stories of World War I a romantic triangle is played out and it is hard to know if this was simply seen as a way to include more men and fewer women, or if there was an assumed glamour to that situation. The one thing that seems to be consistent is that the woman involved is too fickle (a word from the period) to make up her mind and allows the winds of fate to determine her future. But this one has a certain flair that make it worth watching and makes a case, albeit an old one, for equality.

Brown on Resolution (1934) / aka *Born for Glory; Forever England*

Produced by Michael Bolton, Gaumont British Picture Corporation (United Kingdom). Directed by Walter Forde and Anthony Asquith, written by Gerard Fairlie and Michael Hogan, based on C.S. Forester's *Brown on Resolution*. Cinematography by Bernard Knowles. This 80-minute black and white film starred Betty Balfour, John Mills, Barry MacKay, Jimmy Hanley, Howard Marion-Crawford, H.G. Stoker, Percy Walsh, George Merritt and Cyril Smith.

Story: The movie is focused on the life of a illegitimate boy, Albert Brown, the son of Elizabeth Brown (Betty Balfour). The boy always loved the sea and, reaching age, joins the navy. He is marooned on the island of Resolution when the HMS *Rutland*, his ship, is sunk. He is taken prisoner on board a German battle cruiser, the factious ship SMS *Ziethen*, which after a battle with an inferior British force retreats to an isolated bay where the crew can make repairs to the vessel. Brown escapes with a rifle and heads to the hills from which he can fire on the crew. The big ship is unable to lower its guns enough to blast him out and he is well hidden among the rocks and scrubs of the island. He is eventually killed but has delayed them long enough for the British pursuers to arrive. As the situation is being worked out, the British commander comes to realize that this young hero is his long-unseen illegitimate son. He claims him as his boy and expresses his pride in him.

Military Correlation: Good

Comment: The illegitimate son who proves he is really a man seems to be some hangover from an earlier day when bastards were generally unacceptable. The HMS *Curacoca*, which sank in October 1942 after being hit by the *Queen Mary*, was used in the film. It was the first film to actually use Royal Navy ships. This movie was remade in 1953, updated to a World War II setting.

Bud's Recruits (1918)

Produced by Boy City Film Company (United States). Directed by King Vidor and written by Judge Willis Brown and Vidor. This 26-minute silent black and white film, with English intertitles, starred Ruth Hampton, Thomas Belamy, Earnest Butterworth, Wallace Brennan, Robert Gordon and Mildred Davis.

Story: In this short comedy, a little boy, Bud (Budlong Thomas Gilbert), can't wait to get in the army and fight the Kaiser. His mother and older brother are members of the local pacifist association. To compensate, he set himself up as the unrelenting and militaristic example for his draft age, somewhat feminized brother and his peace-loving mother who wants to keep her boy home and safe. In desperation the young man poses as his brother and signs up for the army. Mother, sweetheart, and the townsfolk are all impressed. But it does not end there.

Military Correlation: Helpful

Comment: This was one of King Vidor's first efforts before moving on to films like *The Big Parade*. He was known as a man exactly for his times, a "traffic cop" sort of director, more administrative than creative. The unnamed and unmentioned father seems to play a role in this but the director has not made it clear to the viewer. This was one of the films in the Judge Brown Series, and while it appears to have been well received, it came too late to be of any value to the war effort.

The Bugler of Algiers (1916) / aka We Are French

Production and distributed by Blue Bird Inc., Universal Film Manufacturing Company (United States). Directed by Rupert Julian and written by Elliot J. Clawson and Robert Hobart Davis, based on the novel *We Are French* by Davis and Perley Poore Sheehan. Cinematography by Stephen Rounds. This silent, black and white movie, with English intertitles, stars Kingsley Benedict, Ella Hall, Harry Carter, Charles K. French, Zoe Rae, and Rupert Julian.

Story: Two lovers live in a French village, Gabrielle (Ella Hall) and Pierre (Rupert Julian). Gabrielle's brother Anatole (Kingsley Benedict) is called into the service with Pierre and they are sent to Algiers. Anatol becomes the bugler and in the heat of battle, when called on to blow retreat, he blows charge instead and saves the day. They are heroes but when they return home they find it ransacked and their friend Gabrielle gone without a trace. They are determined to find her, but after years of trying they fail to do so. Later, Anatole is called to Paris to receive honors for his earlier heroism. In their seventies the two old men start out to walk to Paris but on the trip Anatol dies of exhaustion. When Pierre arrives he finds that the committee has located Gabrielle and she is there. The two lovers deliver the medal to Anatol by placing it on his grave and head home together.

Military Correlation: Spotty

Comment: Fun and totally unrealistic, this was made for the emotional appeal and used the war to provide a ready-made background for separation. It was nicely produced but it was not one of Julian's better films.

Burgomaster of Stilemonde (1929)

Produced and distributed by Woolfe & Freedman Film Service, British Filmcraft (United Kingdom). Directed by George Banfield and written by Maurice Maeterlinck, based on his 1918 play *La Borgmestre de Stilemonde*. This eight-reel, silent, black and white film stars John Martin Harvey, Fern Andra, Robert Andrews, John F. Hamilton, Fred Raynham, Wilfred Shine, A.B. Imeson, Oswald Lingard, Kinsey Peile, Mickey Brantford, Adeline Hayden Coffin, and C.V. France.

Story: As far as we know from existing pieces of the film, it portrays the harsh nature of German atrocities during the occupation of Belgium. The vicious German Uhlans orders the burgomaster's (John Martin Harvey) son-in-law to shoot him.

Military Correlation: Unknown

Comment: C.V. France was in reality the British actor Gerrards Cross. Fern Andra, who played the lead, was a retired circus tightrope walker.

By the Kaiser's Orders (1914)

Produced and distributed by Barker Production Corporation (United Kingdom). Directed by F. Martin Thorton and written by Rowland Talbot. This was a three-reel silent, black and white film with English intertitles.

Story: An unemployed chemist who is also a spy, intends to use a stolen secret weapon, the F-Ray, to ignite explosives and destroy supplies.

Military Correlation: None

Comment: This is all that is known about this film, which is listed in production catalogues but cannot be located. The natural format of silent black and white films is such that they provide a formidable setting for the spy and espionage drama. With weak lights and long shadows, hazy focuses, fixed cameras and the like, they easily provide the atmosphere of skullduggery and evil intent. The dramas were a perfect match for the studio looking for quick and fairly inexpensive productions that could keep their contract stars and crews busy and the theaters satisfied. The plots of most of these films were simple and often formula productions with studio screenwriters producing different dialogue but generally the same story. Very few of them are deserving much credit but there were some directors able to create suspense and tensions power enough to carry the weak plots.

Cafe Moscow (1936) / aka Only One Night

Produced and distributed by Istvan Sekely (aka Steve Sekely), Patria Films (Hungary). Directed by Steve Sekely and written by Sekely, Istvan Tamas, Gyula Csortos, Ferene Kiss, and Lajos Vertes. Cinematography by Willy Goldberger and Rudolf Icsey This 84-minute anti-war film with Hungarian and English intertitles starred Anna Tokes, Gyula Csortos, Ferenc Kiss, Lajos Vertes, Manyi Kiss, Jozsef Juhasz, Nusi Somogyi, Jozsef Timar, Lajos Gardonyi, Bela Balini, Ilona Erdos, Istvan Berend, Istvan Barsony, Guyla Szoreghy, Audor Sarossy, Lazzlo Keleti, and Gero Maly.

Story: On the Eastern Front, in a small Galician town, the wife of a Russian general (Anna Tokes) hopes to avoid imprisonment by posing as a café singer. In her struggles she seeks the aid of a handsome Hungarian (Lajos Vertes) but he determines that she is a woman of loose morals and refuses to help her. As circumstance develop, the lieutenant himself needs to be saved and after Anna comes to the rescue he determines she is okay, and love prevails.

Military Correlation: Poor

Comment: The movie seems unnecessarily dark, depressing and slow-moving. It is also hard to follow. Director Istvan Sekely had a long and successful career in Hollywood using the name Steve Sekely.

Call to Arms Against War (1915) see *The Battle Cry of Peace* (1915)

Captain Conan (1996)

Produced by Canal + Les Films Alain Sarde, Little Bear (France). Directed by Bertrand Tavernier and written by Jean Cosmos, based on a novel by Roger Vercel. This 130-minute film starred Philippe Torreton, Samuel Le Bihan, Bernard Le Cog, Catherine Rich, Claude Rich, Francois Berleand, Andre Falcon, Claude Brosset, Crina Muresan, Cecile Vassort, Francois Levantal, Pierre Val, Roger Knobelspiess, Frederic Pierott, and Jean-Clude Calon.

Story: A dedicated career soldier, Conan (Philippe Torret) served with a band of 50 French irregulars known for being unnecessarily ruthless. As the war ends they go to Bucharest where Conan makes the effort to keep them out of trouble. He finds that he is unsuited for the peaceful life. When his friend Norbert (Samuel Le Bihan) is facing military charges, he accepts a job as court-martial prosecutor to get him off. Eventually they are sent to the Russian border to fight Bolsheviks and he finds his true calling. His friend Norbert is let go.

Military Correlation: Spotty

Comments: The motto of Conon's force is "We forgot to take prisoners." This is one of the very few films dealing with the period between the Armistice and when the troops were sent home. During this period an almost unknown war existed between men of several nations and the Red Army because many of the Western nations believed Communism would spill over into the rest of Europe. The film dealt with the reality that after having lived through the war, many of the young men were unable to adjust to it being over. They did not know what to do with themselves and could not, in fact *did* not want to adjust to peacetime.

Captain Swagger (1928)

Produced and distributed by Hector Turnbull and Pathe Exchange Film (United States). Directed by Edward H. Griffith and written by Adelaide Heilbron,

Paul Perez and Leonard Praskins. This 70-minute, silent, black and white film, with English intertitles, stars Rod La Rocque, Sue Carol, Victor Potel, Maurice Black, Ulrich Haupt, and Richard Tucker.

Story: Hugh Drummond (Rod La Rocque), an American aviator during the war, was so fearless his men gave him the nickname Captain Swagger. Assigned to a French flying squadron, he takes on the challenge of fighting Von Stahl (Ulrich Haupt), a German air ace. He wins the battle but manages to rescue the German officer from his burning plane. After the war, unable to find work, Drummond turns to crime. A young girl (Sue Carol) turns him straight and they become a dance team. While working they are held up by none other than Von Stahl, who has turned to crime. Seeing who is involved, he returns the favor and lets them go.

Military Correlation: Poor

Comment: This was basically a silent film with some music and synchronized sound. The best review of the film in the 1920s suggested that while it was not great entertainment, the acting was good. The plot certainly tests the limits of belief.

The Case of Sergeant Grischa (1930)

Produced by William LeBaron for RKO Radio Pictures (United States). Directed by Herbert Brenon and written by Elizabeth Meehan, based on the novel by Arnold Zweigh. Cinematography by J. Roy Hunt. This 82-minute film starred Chester Morris, Betty Compson, Jean Hersholt, Alec B. Francis, Gustav von Seyffertitz, Leyland Hodgson, Paul McAllister, Raymond Whitaker, Bernard Siegel, Frank McCormack, Percy Barbette and Hal Davis.

Story: A Russian Army sergeant, Grischa Papotkin (Chester Morris), is captured and put in a POW camp. He escapes and ends up hiding with a young Russian refugee named Babka (Betty Compson). When he wishes to return home, Babka, who is in love with him, agrees to help in his escape. She gets forged credentials off a dead Russian soldier, Bjuscheff. In their escape they stop at a friend's house in Mervinsk but he is captured when a German soldiers spies his hat. Babka is captured after they realize the identity that they have stolen is that of a Russian spy who was being hunted. While in captivity, his true identity is determined but for reasons not explained the German authorities refuse to consider this and he is sentenced to be executed. General von Lychow (Alec B. Francis) decides to intervene on his behalf but the hardnosed General Schieffenzahn (Gustav von Seyffertitz) fights back. Again without a lot of explanation, Schieffenzahn changes his mind and decides to call to stop the execution. But a storm has caused the wires to go down and the message never gets through. Grischa is executed.

Military Correlation: Spotty

Comment: John E. Tribby received a Best Sound Oscar nomination for this film. The movie moves quickly and hold together in most places. The twist on the identity could be seen coming but it was well played out. The lack of explanation for unreasonable behavior made it difficult to appreciate, however.

The Cavell Case (1918)
see *The Woman the Germans Shot* (1918)

Chunuk Bair (1992)

Produced by Dale G. Bradley and David Arnell, with Daybreak Pictures in association with Avalon National Film Unit (New Zealand). Directed by Dale G. Bradley. Written by Grant Hinden-Miller and based on the play *Once on Chunuk Bair* by Maurice Shadbolt. Cinematography by Warrick Attewell. Music by Stephen Bell-Booth. This 110-minute film stars Robert Powell, Kevin Wilson, John Leigh, Murray Keane, Danny Mulheron, Richard Hanna, Lewis Rowe, Norman Forsey, Darryl Beattie, John Wraight, Donald Holder, Tim Bray, Peter Kaa and Stephen Ure.

Story: This is the story of the 7th Wellington Regiment of the New Zealand Expeditionary Force that was involved in the tragic events at Gallipoli in 1915. On August 8 1915, the regiment took and held Chunuk Bair, one of the Turkish strong points, but at the cost of 645 men out of 700. It was considered a suicide mission and the stronghold was known to be of no military value. Many of these soldiers, and the commanding officer, were killed by misdirected British naval fire. Numerous New Zealanders felt the British had sacrificed their nation's soldiers to save British troops, and that attitude is reflected in this movie.

Military Correlation: Excellent

Comment: Focused on the character of Sergeant Major Frank South (Robert Powell) who is paradoxically anti-war and glory-seeking, this movie stresses the incompetence of the British officers. Obviously studio-bound, it is nevertheless remarkably realistic. There was considerable tension between the English and the Colonial forces, particularly Australia and New Zealand, and the English were often blamed for misusing them.

Civilization (1916)

Produced by Thomas H. Ince, Thomas H. Ince Production Corporation, Triangle Distribution (United States). It was directed by Reginald Barker, Thomas H. Ince, and Raymond B. West. Written by C. Gardner Sullivan. Cinematography: Joseph August, Dal Clawson, Clyde DeVinna, Otis M. Gove, and DeVereaux Jennings. Music by Hugo Riesenfeld and Victor Schertzinger. This 88-minute silent black and white film, with English intertitles, starred Howard C. Hickman, Enid Markey, George Fisher, Kage Bruce, J. Frank Burke, Claire Du Brey, George Fisher, Charles K. French, Thomas H. Ince (as himself), Herschel Mayall, Fanny Midgley, J. Barny Sherre, Jerome Strom, Ethal Ullman and Woodrow Wilson (as himself).

Story: This allegorical drama depicts a pacifist German submarine commander (Howard C. Hickman) who refuses to fire at an ocean liner that, according to his intelligence, is carrying war supplies. When the king of this unidentified country (Hershel Mayall) orders him to sink the liner *ProPatria*, he refuses. Citing orders from a "higher power," he fights with his crew and eventually sinks his own submarine. The film opens with a depiction of Civilization kneeling at the feet of the God of War and pleading for peace. Set in a mythical country, the film features large battle scenes, naval battles and aerial warfare scenes. After his death the hero descends into Hell where Jesus Christ offers him the chance to return to life if he will preach the word of peace. He returns but discovers that he is "stoned" and reviled and after being found guilty of some charge, is tried, and executed. Jesus then appears at the stage of royalty and takes the count on a tour of the battlefields showing him the cost of wars. After that the armies lay down their arms and peace is restored.

Military Correlation: Good

Comment: This film, released prior to America's entry into the war, is unashamedly a strong appeal for pacifism. Author, C. Gardner Sullivan claimed to have written the outline in a matter of minutes on Easter Sunday morning in 1915. He called it *Mother of Men*. He showed it to producer Ince who was willing to invest a million dollars in its creation. The film paints a vivid portrait of the destruction caused by war and displays images of the inevitable results. Ships from the United States Navy were used in the filming. An ocean liner was actually sunk. The Democratic National Committee credited the film with helping to re-elect Woodrow Wilson in 1926.[9] It was also the first film to depict Jesus Christ as a character. The producer had Billie Burke faint in the audience at the premiere in order to create publicity.

While most reviews were kind to the film, some also acknowledged that the appearance of Jesus was overdone; the first was acceptable but the second was, even by the standards for the time, silly. Henry Christen Wasrnack of the *Los Angeles Times* felt the depiction of Christ was in poor taste, "offensive to Christians, Jews and Atheists alike."[10] One contemporary viewer said it "reeked of a message no one was listening to." A Fairbanks, Alaska, reviewer wrote that if the film had been shown to the people in Europe prior to the war, there would have *been* no war. It was Ince's last film as director; he soon died a mysterious death aboard a yacht owned by William Randolph Hearst. *Civilazation* was placed on the National Film Registry in 1990. It was selected for preservation in the United States National Film Registry by the Library of Congress in 1999. Only a preservation copy is available.

The Claws of the Hun (1918) / aka *The Hands of the Hun*

Produced and distributed by Thomas H. Ince Film Corporation (United States). Directed by Victor Schertzinger and written by Ella Stuart Carson and R. Cecil Smith. This silent black and white film, with English intertitles, starred Charles Ray, Jane Novak, Robert McKim, Dorcus Matthews, Melbourne MacDonald, Mollie McConnell, and Henry A. Barrow.

Story: John Stauton has been asked to help his father run the ammunition factory that is essential to the war effort. Many people who don't understanding his position accuse him of being a draft dodger. Torn between his loyalty and his personal reputation he is able to redeem himself in the eyes of the village when he uncovers a group of Germans saboteurs who are planning on destroying the munitions factory. He is able to save the day and his reputation.

Military Correlation: Poor

Comment: This film seems to be a Hollywood response to the impact of the Overman Act of 1918, which primarily gave the president the power to make men and corporations "work or fight" and showed that those who maintained the industrial power to create weapons were also participating in the war effort.

Colonel Blimp (1943)
see *The Life and Death of Colonel Blimp* (1943)

Colton, U.S.N. (1916)
see *The Hero of Submarine D-2* (1916)

Company K (2004)

Produced and distributed by Waterfront Picture Corp. (United States). Directed by Robert Clem, written by Clem and William March based on the novel by March. This 102-minute CinemaScope film starred Ari Fliakos, Terry Serpico, Steve Cuiffo, Joe Delafield, Rik Alan Walter, Daniel Stewart Sherman, P.J. Sosko, Cosmos Pfell, Adam Grover, Matt Seidman, Ian Pfister, James Nardella, Tina Benko, Thomas Sadoski, and Hilary Keegin.

Story: Joe Delaney, a young man living in America in 1933 and struggling to put his service years during World War I in perspective, decides to write a history of the Marine company he served with. In the film each man in the company is defined by a singular event during the war that reflected his true character. Key to the film is Delaney's need to confront the appearance of a dead German that keeps haunting his dreams.

Military Correlation: Spotty

Comment: The film is really a combination of 113 vignettes tied together by the author's often confused memory. Most found the movie to be anti-war at a time when war clouds were gathering again and did not appreciate its message. Reviewers generally found it to be well made but there is a rather universal opinion that the acting was very poor, primarily by the "real" personalities that provided "uneven" performances, often overcome with emotion. The book on which it is based appeared to have had a profound effect.

Comradeship (1919)

Produced by Maurice Elvey of the Stoll Film Company (United Kingdom). Directed by Maurice Elvey and written by Louis N. Parker and Jeffrey Bernerd.

Cinematography by Paul Burger. This 6000-foot silent black and white film, with English intertitles, starred Lily Elsie, Gerald Ames, Guy Newall, Teddy Arundell, Peggy Carlisle, Dallas Carins and Kate Gurney.

Story: The film covered the entire span of the war and is very complicated. The hero, pacifist John Armstrong (Gerald Ames), works with assistant Peggy (Peggy Carlisle) and German-born Otto (Dallas Carins). Otto, whose loyalty lies with his homeland, leaves to protect Germany after first impregnating Peggy. When war breaks out, John defies his pacifist leanings and enlists. While in training, he becomes good friends with Ginger (Teddy Arundell). John goes off to fight in the war; Peggy has a miscarriage; and on the battlefield Otto is killed by Ginger. John, blinded in the war, returns to establish a network of Comrades Clubs for ex-servicemen. Ginger and Peggy re-establish their relationship and overcome any concern that she might pity him for his blindness, and are married. Medical science gives hope his sight may return.

Military Correlation: Spotty

Comment: This was the first film of the Stoll Film Company. Stoll was a philanthropist who aided disabled World War I soldiers and worked to make the country aware of the plight of blinded soldiers. It was considered the first film to discuss the social impact the war had on Great Britain, particularly providing a challenge to the class-based society. Filmed just after the war ended, the movie was the first to use some footage taken at the victory celebrations in London.

Conflict (1933) see *Hell Below* (1933)

Conscription (1918) see *Her Boy* (1918)

The Court Martial of Billy Mitchell (1955) / aka *One Man Mutiny*

Produced by Milton Sperling, Warner Brothers (United States). Directed by Otto Preminger and written by Ernest Lavdery and Milton Sperling. Cinematography by Sam Leavitt. This 100-minute CinemaScope film starred Gary Cooper, Chales Bickford, Ralph Bellamy, Rod Steiger, Elizabeth Montgomery, James Daly, Darren McGavin, Jack Lord, Fred Clark, Peter Graves, Robert Simon, Charles Dingle, Dayton Lummis, and Adam Kennedy.

Story: General William Lendrum "Billy" Mitchell (Gary Cooper), commander of the air forces in the American Expeditionary Force during World War I, was a powerful proponent of the fighter plane and a believer in the value in long-range bombing. He fought to establish some sense of awareness among the Navy brass, but seemed only to upset them. Because of his outspokenness he was court-martialed and found guilty of "conduct prejudicial to good order and military discipline." The life of the general is portrayed in a series of flashbacks during the trial.

One showed that even the dramatic sinking of an "unsinkable" German battleship by bombardment from the air had not changed any minds. President Calvin Coolidge orders a swift end to the trials to avoid further embarrassment and the officer is found guilty and demoted to colonel. He leaves the court as a civilian.

Military Correlation: Spotty

Comment: Many, including Mitchell's wife, felt that Gary Cooper was not a good choice for the role. David Shipman said that Cooper displayed too many "effeminate mannerisms." It is hard to be very objective when you know just how right Mitchell was, and how the thickness of the military mind at that time pretty much failed to prepare America's air defenses. Since that time, Mitchell was proven to be prophetic and is now regarded as the founding father of the Air Force. The film was released at the opening of the U.S. Air Force Academy in Colorado.

Cooper won the applause of several peace groups for his refusal to join the Hollywood Hussars, a quasi-military unit started by the highly jingoistic Victor McLaglen.

Blooper: There were a lot of goofs in the movie. Mitchell first arrives in 1921 flying a Grumman JC "Duck" that was not available for service until 1932; the suitcase he is carrying was obviously so light that it must have been empty.

Coward (1915)

Produced by Martin Codyre and Neil Corbould, Different Productions (Ireland). Directed by David Roddham and written by Roddham, Terry Donnelly, Mark O'Halloran, and Steve Handley. Cinematography by Stephen Murray. Music by Haim Frank Ilfman. This 28-minute color film starred Martin McCann, Sean Steward, Charlotte Bradley, Nick Moran, Cillian Roache, Charlie Clements, Joe Van Moyland, Karl Sullivan, Paul McNeilly, Rupert Mason, Michael Parle, Brian Markey, Gareth Stewart, and James Hicks.

Story: The film takes us from the peaceful villages of Ireland to the muddy trenches of World War I where Private Patterson (Martin McCann) had taken on a family promise to care for his young cousin. The assignment proves to be impossible as they face the conflict and confusion in Belgium of 1917. Soon he is faced with a situation that placed courage and commitment on a collision course. He learns the hard way that he cannot keep his promises and that one of the major casualties of war, is justice itself.

Military Correlation: Good

Comment: This appears to be an awfully heavy load for the film's simple plot to carry. The concern over cowardice, real and/or imagined, was heavy on the minds of the military and was reflected by many film producers. The problem was just what constituted being a coward and what were the other causes for questionable behavior. The promise to care for another was, of course, totally unrealistic and just why that is was well shown here.

The Cradle of Souls (1916)
see *The Greatest Thing in Life* (1918)

Crimson Romance (1934)

Produced by Nat Levine, Mascot Pictures (United States). Directed by David Howard and written by Milton Grimes and Sherman L. Lowe. Cinematography by Ernest Miller. Music by Lee Zahler. This 71-minute black and white film starred Ben Lyon, Sari Maritza, Erich von Stroheim, James Bush, Hardle Albright, William Bakewell, Herman Bing, Bodil Rosing, Vince Barnett, Arthur Claton, Oscar Apfel, Jason Robards, Sr, Wilhelm von Brincken, Brandon Hurst, and Crauford Kent.

Story: The fact that he is a German immigrant means that Fred Von Bergen (James Bush) is forced to leave his job as a test pilot. His friend Bob Wilson (Ben Lyon) goes with him. Anti-German hysteria is running high and the two men decide to return to Germany and join the air force where they will find acceptance. Before long, both of them have fallen in love with a pretty ambulance driver and things get even worse when America enters the war. With his loyalty tested, Bob feels that he must join the Americans against Germany, but to do so would put Fred in danger. The two split up with Fred remaining loyal to Germany. Soon after, the German is shot down and Wilson moves in quickly to console his girl friend (Sari Maritza). In a short time they fall in love and marry. At the fallen airman's funeral his mother gives a long and impassioned anti-war speech.

Military Correlation: Good

Comment: Strong on the theme of friendship and loyalty in the face of crisis, the film addresses the question of which is more important, friendship or country. This question is realistic since a large percentage of the American people were first or second generation German. Von Stroheim is cast once again as the brutal German commanding officer but he does so this time with a somewhat morbid sense of humor that makes him almost likable. The understated was not a part of his character, however, and von Stroheim used villainous makeup, eye patches and the like to make himself look vicious. And he overacted outrageously. Overall the sympathies of the producer are not clear. It is, most of all, a good tale.

Crimson Wing (1915)

Produced and distributed by Essanay Film Manufacturing (United States). Directed by E.H. Calvert and written by Hobert Chatfield-Taylor, based on a novel of the same name. This silent, black and white film, with English intertitles, stars E.H. Calvert, John Cossar, Ruth Stonehouse, Beverly Bayne, Betty Scott, Bryant Washburn, Harry Dunkinson, Grant Foreman, and Harard McCormick.

Story: When Count von Leun-Walram (E.H. Calvert) finds himself in love with two different women, he decides to go off to war. While he is fighting in France he learns that one of his girlfriends has taken her own life. Only temporarily concerned, if at all, he quickly begins to daydream about living in domestic bliss with the other woman he left behind. The film ends there amidst his dreams of marriage, leaving the audience totally uninformed about whatever point is being made if, in fact, there is one. Really an awful movie.

Military Correlation: Poor

Comment: While there are some scenes of combat, only by a huge stretch of the imagination can this be considered a legitimate war film, as there is little to no action, and no point being made. The hero is such a shallow, even dimwitted character that one must wonder why anyone would really care what happened to him. The attitude he expresses is very unusual for films of this period. Anyone who was expecting an exciting war drama would have been terribly disappointed with this meaningless melodrama.

Elisha Helm Calvert, who played the count, completed a distinguished military career before he entered acting.

The Dark Angel (1925)

Produced and distributed by First National Pictures and Samuel Goldwyn Productions (United States). Directed by George Fitzmaurice and written by Frances Marion and Guy Bolton, based on *The Dark Angel, a Play of Yesterday and To-day* by H.B. Trevelyan [Guy Bolton]. Cinematography by George Barnes. The 80-minute silent black and white film stars Ronald Colman, Vilma Banky, Frank Elliott, Charles Willis Lane, Florence Turner, Helen Jerome Eddy, Wyndham Standing, Billy Butts, Roger Byrne, Virginia Davis, Billy "Red" Jones, George Noisom, and Lassie Lou Ahern.

Story: Captain Alan Trent (Ronald Colman), recalled to the front, must leave his fiancée Kitty Vane (Vilma Banky) behind. Unable to get a marriage license, they spend the night in a hotel. Once in combat, Alan is blinded and captured by the Germans and everyone back home thinks he is dead. His friend Captain Gerald Shannon (Wyndham Standing) moves in on Kitty, hoping to provide some gentle love to soothe her grief. When the war ends, Gerald discovers that Alan is still alive and in England. With his sense of friendship overcoming his passion, he notifies Kitty. She goes to find him but Alan, not wanting to hurt her, hides his blindness and tells her he no longer loves her. She sees through his efforts, however, and they are reunited with Gerald's blessing.

Military Correlation: Spotty

Comment: *The Dark Angel* is considered lost. This film, where they do not pity the blind man and she joins up with the friend who is really a cad, suggests this is a formula film. Ronald Colman is his usual sophisticated tower of strength and Vilma Banky is great both in her grief and her romance.

The Dark Angel (1935)

Produced by Samuel Goldwyn (United States). Directed by Sidney A. Franklin. It was adopted by Lillian Hellman and Mordaunt Shairp from a play by Guy Bolton (aka H.B. Trevelyan). The cinematography was by Gregg Toland. This 110-minute film stars Fredric March, Merle Oberon, Carl Voss, Charles Tannen, David Torrence, Herbert Marshall, Janet Beecher, John Halliday, Henrietta Crosman, Frieda Inescort, Claud Allister, Cora Sue Collins and C. Montague Shaw.

Story: Friends since childhood, Alan (Fredric March), Kitty (Merle Oberon), and Trent (Herbert Marshall) are still together. Trent has been in love with Kitty for years, but it is Alan who wins her hand. Called off to war, Alan is blinded and gallantly pretends to have been killed in order to save Kitty from a life of hardship. Trent moves in, hoping to fill the void in Kitty's life. Then he discovers that Alan is alive and living in England. When Kitty arrives at Alan's, he tries to hide his blindness in order to save Kitty's feelings, but it does not work and they come together again with the support of Trent.

Military Correlation: None

Comment: This is a remake of Goldwyn's 1925 movie of the same name, considered by many reviewers to be somewhat sappy. The ten years between the two films perhaps made a difference in what the viewer expected. One reviewer identified it as a sumptuously produced soap opera. Another called it "a tear-stained melodrama from another age." Merle Oberon received her only Oscar nomination for her performance.

Dark Invasion (2015)

Produced by John Leesher, La Grisbi Productions, Warner Brothers (United States). Directed and written by Taylor Sheridan, based on the non-fiction book by Howard Blum. The film will star Bradley Cooper.

Story: This movie takes place in the New York of 1915 and focus on German secret service agents sent to America to stop them from helping the Allies. The Kaiser plans to bombard factories, sabotage ships, shoot the financier J. P. Morgan, bomb the United States capitol and establish an anthrax lab six miles from the White House. Captain Tom Tunney (Bradley Cooper) is given the task of creating a team to halt the spies.

Military Correlation: Not known.

Comment: If the film is based on the book as it says, then, as one critic has suggested, "the narrative is the enemy of reality."

Bloopers: The author's chronology is a little messed up. For example, the Stokes Mortar appears in the narrative before it was invented.

The Dark Road (1917) / aka *The Road to Honor*

Produced and distributed by Kay-Bee Pictures, New York Movie Picture Corporation (United States). Directed by Charles Miller and written by J.G. Hawks and John Lynch. This silent, black and white film, with English intertitles, stars Dorothy Dalton, Robert McKim, Jack Livingston, John Gilvert, Walt Whitman and Lydia Knott.

Story: Cleo is a beautiful woman with no moral standards married to a naively devoted military officer. She uses seduction to steal secrets to pay for whatever she wants. When war breaks out and the husband goes to France to fight, she takes up with the master of the house where she is staying. When he also leaves for war, she gives him a good luck charm her husband had given her, and a torrid love letter. Her next lover turns out to be a German spy who convinces her to go to London and spy for him. On the battlefield, the local lover is killed and Cleo's husband goes through his belongings and finds the charm and the letter. With the husband's help the German's spy is arrested. Cleo is left to the angry response from her husband and tragedy follows.

Military Correlation: Helpful

Comment: Silent films fit easily into the spy atmosphere. With their weak lights and long shadows, hazy focuses, fixed cameras and the like, they easily provide the atmosphere of skullduggery and evil intent.

Darling Lili (1970) / aka *Where Were You the Night I Shot Down Baron Von Richthofen?*

Produced and distributed by Geoffrey Production, Paramount (United States). Directed by Blake Edwards and written by Edwards and William Peter Blatty. Cinematography by Russell Harlan and Richard Wellman. The 107-minute (director's cut) film stars Julie Andrews, Rock Hudson, Jeremy Kemp, Gloria Paul, Bernard Kay, Lance Percival, Michael Witney, Andre Maranne, and Jacques Martin.

Story: This is the story of a beautiful British lady, based on the infamous Mata Hari legend, who is asked by the Germans to spy for them. It uses the well-worn female spy masquerading as a cabaret singer for a plot. She becomes involved with British Major Larrabee and ends up "giving secrets to one man and her love to another." As a spoof, it is not well done.

Military Correlation: Poor

Comment: This is somewhat typical Blake Edwards productions. The music appears to have saved the movie. Even then, many considered it to be Rock Hudson's worst film. While a serious attempt to deal with serious topics, they simply could not keep from including a series of unnecessary gags of the *Pink Panther* variety.

Daughter of France (1914)

Produced and distributed by Crusade Films, Lift (United Kingdom). A short silent black and white film. This film is listed in production catalogues but no copy has been found nor have any reviews of the film been located.

Story: From the *British Film Institute Catalogue*: "A wounded soldier gives his life to save that of a young French girl who in turn calls on the Highlanders to save her village."

Military Correlation: Unknown

A Daughter of France (1918)

Produced and distributed by Fix Film (United States). Directed by Edmund Lawrence and written by Beta Breuil, Adrian Johnson and Benjamin S. Kutler. Cinematography by Frank Kruger and William Zollinger. This 2000-foot silent, black and white film, with English intertitles, stars Virginia Pearson, Hugh Thompson, Herbert Evans, George Moss, Ethel Kauffman, Tony Merlo, Maude Hill, and Nadia Gray.

Story: The remarkably beautiful Louise de Ciron (Virginia Pearson) is a loyal Frenchwoman who remains behind at her home when the Germans invade. The Germans use her home for their headquarters and soon the two officers stationed there, Rudolph von Knorr (Hugh Thompson) and Fritz von Meyring (Herbert Evans), begin to lust over her. Rudolph corners her and tries to rape her but suddenly changes his mind and leaves. Then Fritz comes in and tries the same thing; Rudolph, who has returned, stops it and finally kills him. The Germans believe she has done it and charge her with the murder and demand her execution. Rudolph steps in and prevents her death, but still the very concerned Louise is not sure of his motives and stabs him. In time she comes to believe him and so she talks him into defecting with her. After they have escaped, Rudolph confesses that he is really a member of the French Secret Service.

Military Correlation: Poor

Comment: A good story well set up and delivered. However, the ending is so abrupt that one wonders if the producers knew ahead of time how to end it. Or perhaps they just ran over budget. But as far as it goes, it is completely far-fetched but nevertheless well done.

Dawn (1928)

Produced and distributed by Herbert Wilcox Productions, British & Dominions Film Corporation and Woolf & Freedman Film Service (United Kingdom). Directed by Herbert Wilcox and written by Wilcox, Reginald Berkeley and Robert Cullen; based on a play by Berkeley. Cinematography by Bernard Knowles. This 90-minute silent, black and white film, with English intertitles, stars Sybil Thorndike, Ada Bodart, Gordon Craig, Michey Brantford, Mary Brough, Richard Worth, Colin

Bell, Dacia Deane, Cecil Barry, Frank Perfitt, Haddon Mason, Maurice Braddell, Edward O'Neill, Griffith Humphreys, Edward Sorley, and Marie Ault.

Story: It is based on the experience of Edith Cavell (Sybil Thorndike), a nurse who risked her life to save more than two hundred Allied soldiers escaping from Belgium during World War I. This unassuming heroine not only provided nursing to the wounded but also organized escape routes for soldiers fleeing occupied territory. Captured, she was found guilty of treason and espionage and was sentenced to be executed by a firing squad. When the execution is carried, it creates an international outrage.

Father Gahan, who was involved with her, at the end said, "Her stoicism was seen as remarkable for a woman and brought her even greater renown than a man under similar circumstances would have received." It is interesting to note that much of her fame was dependent on her propaganda value. With no dishonor to Nurse Cavell, there was not much response at all to the fact that the Germans executed Gabrielle Petit, a Belgian nurse who was sentenced in 1916 for treason.

Military Correlation: Good

Comment: The film was heavily censored because its objectors felt that the brutal depiction of the German behavior during the war and its inherent anti–German position would cause trouble, especially after both the German ambassador and the British Foreign Secretary moved to prevent its exhibition. The movie was banned in Great Britain but had reasonable success in the United States. Herbert Wilcox was not done with the story and in 1939 remade the film under the title *Nurse Edith Cavell*

The Dawn of Reckoning (1918) see *Heart of Humanity* (1918)

The Dawn Patrol (1930) / aka *Flight Commander*

Produced and distributed by Rupert North, First National Films, Warner Brothers (United States). Directed by Howard Hawks and written by John Monk Saunders, Dan Totheroh, Seton I. Miller. Cinematography by Ernest Hallier. This 108-minute film starred Richard Barthelmess, Douglas Fairbanks, Jr., Frank McHugh, Clyde Cook, Neil Hamilton, James Finlayson, Gardner James, William Janney and Edmund Breon.

Story: Courtney (Richard Barthelmess) and Scott (Douglas Fairbanks, Jr.) come together and become friends in a British Royal Flying Corps squadron under the command of Bond, who they think takes unreasonable risks with them. In the course of the war they learn the demands of leadership and eventually end up in positions where they must deal with problems in the same fashion as their hated commander.

Military Correlation: Good

Comments: Howard Hawks was a veteran pilot of the war and played a German pilot in the film. The film received the Academy Award for Best Writing. Actor Richard Barthelmess embodied all the good things (humility, integrity and honesty) and at the same time had that boyish charm and good looks that women liked.

This was his last major role. *Variety* commented: "No women, few laughs."

The Dawn Patrol (1938)

Produced by Jack Warner, Hal B. Wallis, and Robert Lord and distributed by Warner Brothers (United States) Directed by Edmund Goulding. Written by John Monk Saunders, Seton I. Miller, and Don Totheroh, based on the short story "The Flight Commander" by Saunders.[11] Cinematography by Tony Gaudio. Music by Max Steiner. This 103-minute black and white film starred Errol Flynn, Basil Rathbone, David Niven, Donald Crisp, Melville Cooper, Barry Fitzgerald, Carl Esmond, Peter Willes, Morton Lowry, Michael Brooke, James Burke, Stuart Hall, Herbert Evans, Sidney Bracey, John Rodion and Leo Nomis.

Story: Set in France, *The Dawn Patrol* tells the story of a British airplane squadron and depicts not only the wonder of the new machines but the dangers involved in flying them. Two British fighter pilots, Captain Courtney (Errol Flynn) and Scott (David Niven), face the grim realities of war and learn some lessons in friendship. heroism, and patriotism. In 1915 they wait at the Royal Flying Corps 59th Squadron airfield seeking the return of the dawn patrol from dangerous missions on the for side of the enemy line. Major Brand (Basil Rathbone) is near despair having lost 16 young replacement pilots. Then he must order what amounts to a suicide mission. After the death of two more replacements, Courtney and Scott violate orders not to attack Von Richter's German airfield. Courtney becomes the commander and finds himself dealing with the same problems as Brand, including sending Scott's younger brother Donnie (Morton Lowry) on a mission; Donnie is shot down. When assigned a suicide mission, Courtney takes it on himself, destroying an ammo dump. In an air fight with Von Richter, whom he defeats, he is shot down by a third plane. Command of the decimated squadron falls to Scott, who ends the movie with the stoic call to the squadron to be ready for the dawn patrol.

Military Correlation: Good

Comment: The idea was to present a professional group of men living by a code, backed up with bravado and camaraderie. It comes closer to being a romanticized look at World War I with all sorts of old clichés and the "birth" of traditions like hard-drinking fatalism and chivalry between combatants. John Rodion, playing the role of a replacement sent out to die, was Basil Rathbone's son. It is believed that the decision to remake the 1930 film version came from an awareness of the impending war brought on by the German annexation of Austria. The film was one of the few to have an all-male cast. They used rebuilt Nieuport 28s for the British planes and Air 4000s for the German ones. The director used a good deal of film from the original movie to offset costs. Leo Nomis, a movie stunt pilot, was killed while filming a scene for *The Sky Bridge*; he had been air supervisor for this film, and when it was released they included his name in the on-screen credits.

Bloopers: The Royal Flying Corps had a unit identified as the 59th Squadron but it did not arrive at the front until 1917. There is also no explanation given for the markings on the German planes, none of which reflect any known patterns. Also the Nieuports were not used by the Royal Flying Club but were so familiar to the audience that no one seemed to notice.

Delicate Situation (1917)
see *Arms and the Girl* (1917)

The Devil at His Elbow (1916)

Produced and distributed by Popular Plays and Players (United States). Directed by Burton L. King and written by Wallace Clifton and Aaron Hofman. Photography is credited to Neil Bergman. This 90-minute, silent, black and white film, with English intertitles, starred Clifford Bruce, Dorothy Green, John K. Roberts (aka J.K. Roberts), Francis McDonald, Mary Sandway, Adolphe Menjou, and Edward Martindel.

Story: Designer-engineer John Ashton (Adolphe Menjou) was preparing new submarines to be used against the enemy when the war finally broke out. He gets way behind and in order to stay awake starts drinking. His girlfriend Grace (Mary Sandway) urges him not to, but he does. In a drunken dream, Ashton believes Grace had broken off their engagement because of his drinking, that he has been shanghaied by a freighter captain, that he has met and married prostitute Meg (Dorothy Green), and that he has finished the submarine but that it sunk on its first trials. He dreamed that he believed Meg was responsible because she kept him drunk thinking it was only then that he loved her. He is just about to kill Meg for what she has done when he awakens to reality. Happy that all is well, he finishes the submarine, gives up drinking, and marries Grace.

Military Correlation: Poor

Comment: A fun film that takes full use of the "it's a dream" plot. It is spurred on by the war but has little to do with it. Menjou had served as a driver for the American Ambulance Service in France during the war.

Devil Dogs of the Air (1935)

Produced by Edmund Grainger for Warner Brothers (United States). Directed by Lloyd Bacon, written by Malcolm Stuart Boylan and Earl Baldwin, based on a novel by John Monk Saunders. Cinematography by Arthur Edeson. Music by Jacques Offenbach. This 85-minutes black and white film starred James Cagney, Pat O'Brien, Margaret Lindsay, Frank McHugh, John Arledge, Helen Lowell, Robert Barrat, Russell Hicks, Ward Bond, Edward Brophy, and William B. Davidson.

Story: Marine pilots Tommy (James Cagney) and William (Pat O'Brien), once friends, break up their friendship over their mutual love of a pretty young waitress (Margaret Lindsay). The two engage in a variety of pursuits, always in competition and usually with a girl involved. The film is just an excuse to show air scenes.

Military Correlation: Spotty

Comments: The air scenes saved the movie, especially the one in which both men are on a plane that has caught fire. The role pretty much established Cagney's smart-aleck character who makes a mockery of danger and an enemy of authority. While there was no war involved, it does include a highly dramatic war games scene which shows why the film was supported by both the Navy and Marines. The movie is one of seven in which Cagney and O'Brien worked together. It is the same storyline (but with serious intent) as the Universal film *Keep 'em Flying* (1941) that starred the comedy team Abbott and Costello. Many of the props and themes became clichés: hard-drinking fatalism, chivalry in the air, white scarves, short life expectancy, etc. At the same time it does a good job of illustrating the emotion scarring faced by a commander who must send men into battle.

Bloopers: The handwriting on the check that they keep passing around changes from shot to shot.

Poster for Warner Brothers *Devil Dogs of the Air* (courtesy Center for the Study of the Korean War, Independence, Missouri).

Dishonored (1931)

Produced and distributed by Paramount Pictures (United States). Directed by Josef von Sternberg, it was written by Daniel Rubun and von Sternberg. Cinematography by Lee Garmes. This 91-minute black and white film starred Marlene Dietrich, Victor McLaglen, Warren Oland, Lew Cody, Wilfred Lucas, Barry Norton and Gustav von Seyffertitz.

Story: Marlene plays a Viennese officer's widow who has turned to prostitution. She offers her services to her country during World War I as a spy. During the course of the film she manages to seduce and betray a whole series of Russian officers and becomes an invaluable asset to her superiors. However, she falls in love with one of the officers, Lieutenant Kranau (Victor McLaglen), and after a night of lovemaking she allows him to escape. When it is discovered what she has done, she is tried and ordered executed by firing squad. It is hard to know which of the characters is considered to be dishonored and by what.

Military Correlation: Poor

Comment: The plot is so predictable, it is hard to believe it worked up any tension or excitement whatsoever, but certainly Marlene Dietrich livened it up somewhat. The lack of plot may explain the long pauses that seemed to be designed to do little but kill time. The director appears to know the story so well that he does not feel the need to explain it to the audience and some explanation is needed. This sort of film was based on a formula plot with studio screenwriters producing different dialogue but generally the same story. Very few of them deserve much credit but there were some directors able to create suspense and tensions powerful enough to carry the weak plot. If we were to let these films serve as our memory of the war, we would be left with the idea that American men went into battle with courage and determination and a patriotic if fatalistic attitude, while the women became seductive spies or sexual vamps plying their trade under the disguise of nurses or entertainers.

Gary Cooper was offered the starring role but turned it down as he did not want to work with von Sternberg. Cooper was applauded by the peace groups for refusing to join the Hollywood Hussars, a quasi-military unit started by the highly jingoistic Victor McLaglen, who started in several war films.

Doomed Battalion (1932)

Produced and distributed by Paul Kohner and Carl Laemmle, Jr., Universal Pictures (United States). Directed by Cyril Gardner and Karl Harti and written by Luis Trenker and Patrick Kearney. Cinematography by Charles J. Stumar. Music by Giuseppe Becce. This 81-minute black and white film stars Luis Trenker, Tala Birell, Albert Conti, Victor Varconi, Henry Armetta, Gustav von Seyffertitz, C. Henry Gordon and Gibson Gowland.

Story: Well-worn account of Australian troops set in an outpost in the Tyrolean Pass. They are aware that the enemy is digging a tunnel under their position in order to capture them, but the Italian commander will not allow them to move. One man (Luis Trenker) tries to learn of the enemy's timetable in order for the Austrians to move in time to avoid being destroyed.

Military Correlation: Good

Comment: This movie of frustration and self-created tension was remade in 1940 as *Ski Patrol* and was updated to have the storyline follow a Finnish outfit fighting the Russians at the beginning of World War II.

Doorway to Destruction (1915)

Produced and distributed by Bison, Motion Pictures, Universal Film Company (United States). Directed by Francis Ford and written by Grace Cunard and John Ford (as Jack Ford). This 20-minute two-reel silent black and white film starred Francis Ford, Mina Cunard, Howard Daniels, Harry Schumm, and John Ford.

Story: This film is listed as a John Ford production. No copies are known to exist.

Military Correlation: Unknown

Comment: Francis Ford's younger brother John would go on to direct some of the very best films about World War II including *They Were Expendable* (1942) and *The Battle of Midway* (1945).

The Doughboy (1918)

Produced and distributed by American Pathe, B. F. Production Company (United States). Directed by Harry Conway "Bud" Fisher, Raoul Barre and Charles Bowers, it was written by Fisher, based on the Mutt and Jeff Comic Series.[12] Animation was by Dick Huemer. This silent seven-minute black and white film starred Augustus J. Mutt and Edgar Horace Jeff. The first actors to play these parts were Sam D. Drane and Gus Alexander.

Story: The film focuses on the antics of the "two mismatched tinhorns" Augustus J. Mutt, an incurable gambler, and his dimwitted friend Edgar Horace Jeffries (always called Jeff). They join the Army and join together to fight the Kaiser. These half-reelers were extremely crude but the public loved them.

Military Correlation: Poor

Comment: The short films were extremely popular. The producers developed a system where the dialogue was carried on the bottom of the screen rather than on intertitles and the films were billed as "talking." Mutt and Jeff were also the names given to two highly successful Norwegian spies who worked for the United Kingdom in World War II under the Double Cross System.

Doughboys (1930) / aka *The Big Shot; Forward March*

Produced and distributed by Metro-Goldwin-Mayer (United States). Directed by Edward Sedgwick and written by Richard Schayer, Sidney Lazarus, and Al Boasberg. Cinematography by Leonard Smith. This 79-minute black and white film stars Buster Keaton, Sally Ellers, Victor Potel, Frank Mayo, William Steele, Pitzy Katz, Frank Map, Arnold Korff, Cliff Edwards, Ann Sothern, Tiny Sanford, Edward Brophy, John Carroll, and Ann Dvorak.

Story: A rich high society man named Elmer (Buster Keaton) falls in love with Mary (Sally Eilers), a poor working girl, but she wants nothing to do with him. He wants to impress her and mistakenly signs up for the military. Mary is anxious to do her part and has signed up to entertain troops. The plot thickens when Elmer's sergeant falls in love with Mary. It all climaxes when they are shipped out together. The film carries over the Keaton vaudeville style of always following a big comedy scene with a smaller, less funny one so that the audience can catch its breath.

Military Correlation: Helpful

Comments: Critics seemed hard on the film, saying that the moviemakers had not adapted well to sound and still used many old silent movie techniques as well as a lot of Keaton's old army routines, Keaton felt it was his best film (it was his first talkie). He claimed that it was loosely based on his own experiences. The majority of film criticisms play it down and suggest that he comes nowhere close to his usual abilities. The movie was released in English, Spanish, French and German versions, which meant that Keaton had to phonetically form the dialogue in four languages. It's a pre-code film and the "skirt dance" is certainly sexy and in some respects a high point. In this movie, Keaton sings along with Cliff Edwards. Director Edward Sedgwick plays the role of the cook. Keaton, who had entertained troops during the war, was kept in Europe after the Armistice in order to entertain those still on duty.

Draft 258 (1917)

Produced and distribution by Metro Picture Corporation (United States). Directed by Christy Cabanne (as William Christy Cabanne) and written by Cabanne and June Mathis. Cinematography by William Fildew. This seven-reel silent black and white film starred Mabel Taliaterro, Walter Miller, Earl Brunswick, Eugene Borden, Sue Balfour, Eric Von Stroheim, William H. Tooker, Camille Dalberg, Baby Ivy Ward, Sidney D'Albrook, Joseph Weber, M.J. Slaven, Lewis Sealy, and Fred Kalgren.

Story: Mary Alden (Mabel Taliaterro), a highly patriotic woman, works alongside her pacifist brother Matthew (Earl Brunswick) and her sweetheart John Graham (Walter Miller) in a department store. German agents conspire to use Matthew for their own purposes and ask him to speak to a peace meeting. Mary also insists on making a speech at the meeting and in her speech she traces the history of American young men volunteering in support of the nation. She is defended by her younger brother George (Eugene Borden) who has been drafted. The head of the spy ring Amiel van Blerman is not going to let this happen and sends his men to overpower George and kidnap Mary. Matthew has become aware that he is being used, and he rebels only to be overpowered and tied up. George escapes and collects soldiers from the local base to come to the rescue. Matthew enlists and, now in uniform, he frees Mary.

Military Correlation: Helpful

Comment: Much like the previous films *The Slacker* (1917) and *Mrs. Slacker* (1918), this was designed to raise the fighting spirit of the American man and build support for the idea of conscription. The title comes from the fact that the first number called by the Selective Service Conscription lottery was 258.[13]

The Eagle and the Hawk (1933)

Produced and distributed by Paramount Pictures (United States). Directed by Stuart Walker and written by Seton I. Miller and Bogart Rogers, based on a story by John Monk Saunders. Cinematography by Harry Fischbeck. This 68-minute black and white film stars Fredric March, Cary Grant, Jack Oakie, Carol Lombard, Adrienne D'Ambricourt, Leyland Hodgson, Virginia Hammond, Douglas Scott, Robert Seiter (credited as Robert Manning) Forrester Harvey, and Guy Standing.

Story: American pilots Jerry Young (Fredric March) and Mike Richards (Jack Oakie) are flying with the British Flying Club (Royal Air Force) where they face considerable physical danger and mental strain. Jerry slowly loses contact with the real world as the pressure gets to him. He regains control when he has a very discreet affair with Carole Lombard. But, returning to action, he can't take it and kills himself. In an effort to save Jerry's reputation, Mike flies Jerry's body to the front where he fakes a crash, bringing back the news that Jerry died a heroic death at the hands of the enemy.

Military Correlation: Good

Comment: This movie appears to have been inspired by *The Dawn Patrol* (1930) and it is often hard to tell them apart. The mental hardships, particularly of those in the air service, came as something of a surprise and the military did not know how to deal with it. This film does a good job of showing why it happened.

Bloopers: All the planes used with the exception of the De Havilland were of a later vintage, including the DH-4 which was not out until 1933.

East Lynne on the Western Front (1931)

Produced and distributed by T. A. Welsh Gaumont British Picture (United Kingdom). It was directed by George Pearson and written by Mary and Donovan Parsons, based on a novel by Ellen Woods. Photography by Percy Strong. The 85-minute, black and white film starred Herbert Mundin, Mark Daly, Alf Goddard, Hugh E. Wright, Edwin Ellis, Harold French, Adele Blanche, Wilfred Lawson, Escott Davies, Philip Godfrey, Norman Shelley, and Roger Livesey.

Story: A group of bored soldiers, waiting behind the lines during World War I, decides to fight the boredom and to improve camp morale by putting on their version of the highly popular vaudeville musical *East Lynne* with an all-male cast. The production becomes a farce when one of the participants (Wilfred Lawson), an actor in civilian life, becomes serious about it and tries to take over.

Military Correlation: Helpful

Comment: Harold Frank, who plays one of the GIs, later became a prolific director. The vaudeville musical they were trying to stage was based on an 1861 novel by Ellen Woods; first appearing in serial form in *New Monthly Magazine*, it was very popular and became known for its implausible plot based on infidelity and double identities. A number of stage plays were based on it, as was this serious film produced in 1931 that was nominated for best film at the Academy Awards.

Edith Cavell (1916) / aka *Nurse Cavell*

Produced by J.C. Williamson (Australia). Directed and written by W.J. Lincoln. Cinematography by Bruce Berter. This silent film with English intertitles starred Margaret Linden, Arthur Styan, Agnes Keogh, and Stewart Garner.

Story: In 1916 English nurse (Margaret Linden) the, matron in a private hospital in Belgium, finds herself in German occupied territory. She willingly nurses both wounded German and Belgian soldiers and soon becomes involved in an organization that provides safe escapes for French and English soldiers heading for the neutral borders. She co-directs a rather large underground movement supported by the local townspeople. After some amazing success getting young men across the border, she is betrayed to the Germans by one of the local people, and quickly tried. Found guilty she is executed by firing squad.

Military Correlation: Good

Comment: Edith Cavell's death caused an outrage among the Allies and did considerable harm to the German war effort. It was a gruesome story and the British people have had a hard time forgetting it. She was memorialized by a service at Westminster and a statue that stands at Charing Cross. There were several silent films made in relation to her execution: *La Revanche* (1916), *The Woman the German Shot* (1918), *Great Victory* (1919), and *Dawn* (1928). There was also a war-preparedness film in 1939.

There is no doubt that Cavell met her death with poise and dignity. But there is something both sexist about the interpretation made by the British at the time of her death. Her stoicism, they assumed, was remarkable for a woman. It brought her even more renown that such behavior would have, if she had been a man.[14]

The Enemy (1928)

Produced and distributed by Metro-Goldwyn-Mayer (United States) Directed by Fred Niblo. Written by John Colton, Agnes Christine Johnson and Willis Goldbeck, based on a novel of the same name by Charles Pollick. Cinematography by Oliver March. This 96-minute film starred Lillian Gish, Frank Currier, Karl Dane, Polly Moran, George Fawcett, Ralph Forbes, Billy Kent Schaefer, and Joel McCrea.

Story: An Australian couple, Carl Bernard (Ralph Forbes) and his wife Pauli (Lillian Gish), are living the good life when war breaks out. Carl is the son of a rich man and Pauli the daughter of a pacifist university professor. Shortly after Carl is drafted, Pauli's father is fired for his outspoken teaching against the war. Then word comes that Carl has died in an accident while on leave, and their baby dies.

Reduced to prostitution Pauli is degraded and in despair. In time Carl (not dead after all), returns and her father is reinstated at the university. Pauli is forgiven and all ends well.

Military Correlation: Helpful

Comment: Many critics suggested that this would be regarded as one of *the* major silent films if the final reel had not been lost. Recently the reel was found at the MGM library. Lillian Gish gives one of her better performances, moving from blushing bride to desperate mother to woman of the street. One critic felt inclined to write, "Gish is no longer playing the virgin." Later a well-known actor, Joel McCrea debuts in *The Enemy* in an uncredited part.

The Enemy Within (1918) see *Hun Within* (1918)

England Expects (1914)

Produced and distributed by London Film Production. (United Kingdom). Directed and written by George Loane Tucker. This silent black and white film, with English intertitles, starred Jane Gall, Charles Rock, George Bellamy, and Arthur Collins.

Story: The cowardly son of a large military family is not willing to face the dangers of service. He is finally shown the error of his ways by the faith and patriotism of his affectionate wife.

Military Correlation: Helpful

Comment: The movie, like the famed enlistment poster, is keyed to Lord Nelson's quote "England expects every man to do his duty." The expectation to do one's duty appears to be a given for moviemakers with the opposite point of view only rarely discussed (and even then, poorly done). Despite a high level of volunteer enlistments, England was not able to find the number of men it needed for this war of high attrition and launched massive enlistment campaigns. This film was a part of that movement.

Ever in My Heart (1933)

Produced by Hal B. Wallis for Warner Brothers (United States). Directed by Archie Mayo, it was written by Bertram Millhauser and Beulah Marie Dix. Cinematography by Arthur L. Todd. This 68-minute black and white film stars Barbara Stanwyck, Ottto Kruger, Ralph Bellamy, Laura Hope Crews, Frank Albertson, Ronnie Cosby, Ruth Donnelly, Nella Walker, Harry Beresford, Huey White, Pat Wing, Henry Otto, Clara Blandick, Willard Robertson, Virginia Howell, and Ethel Wales.

Story: Mary Archer (Barbara Stanwyck), a bright but inexperienced woman from New England, marries a German citizen (Otto Kruger), a chemist. His friend Jeff (Ralph Bellamy) also loves Mary. They are both pro–American but as anti–German propaganda expands the sentiment in the town drives Hugo from his university job. They have hard times during which their son dies. Hugo talks Mary into returning to her parent's home and he sends her a letter saying he is going back to Germany and will fight the Germans. Later, Mary joins with the USO to entertain troops and goes to France.

While the Allies gather for the Meuse-Argonne offensive, there are rumors of a German spy collecting information. Mary recognizes Hugo dressed in a United States Army uniform but she acknowledges at the same time that she still loves him and urges him to escape. He leaves just as Jeff, now in the military, arrives to arrest him. Mary and Hugo spend the night together and she is torn between her love for him and her duty to protect the American soldiers. Soon they are sharing a glass of wine into which she had put poison. In a final gesture they toast their love as the troops march off outside the window.

Military Correlation: Good

Comment: Barbara Stanwyck referred to films like this as "weepers" or "women's programmers" and did not generally speak well of them though they were instrumental in making her famous. These spy melodramas were a perfect answer to the movie studio seeking quick and fairly inexpensive productions to keep their contract stars and crews busy. While there were hundreds of women involved in World War I as everything from USO entertainers to army nurses, ambulance drivers and even veterinarians, these jobs required professional training and were not easy to fill. "Red Cross Nurse" was a calling, not just an identity.

Every Mother's Son (1918)

Produced by William Fox, Fox Film Corporation (United States). Directed and written by Raoul Walsh. This five-reel black and white film starred Charlotte Walker, Percy Standing, Edwin Stanley, Ray Howard, Gareth Hughes, Corona Paynter, and Bernard Thornton.

Story: This is the simple story of a mother (Charlotte Walker) who does not want her sons to go off to war. The oldest son (Edwin Stanley) enlists and is reported killed in action the day the second son (Ray Howard) heads for Europe. When he is wounded, the mother clings to her one remaining son (Gareth Hughes); despite the anger of his patriotic father (Percy Standing) she takes him off to their beach home to hide. In the midst of this argument, survivors from a torpedoed boat are brought into town. When she sees their suffering, she has a change of heart and decides to let her last son go. On Christmas Day, all her sons return. The oldest is now a captain and married to a young Frenchwoman who saved him from the Germans.

Military Correlation: Helpful

Comment: This was released after the end of the war when many Americans were tired of such films. This one, however, was exceptional in that it does not bash the Germans or portray them as monsters. The director managed to make it emotional and patriotic without being too sloppy.

Everything Is Thunder (1936)

Produced by Gaumont British Picture Corporation (United Kingdom). Directed by Milton Rosmer and written by Marion Dix and J.B. Hardy from a novel by Hardy. Cinematography by Gunther Kramf. This 76-minute black and white film stars Constance Bennett, Douglass Montgomery, Oskar Homolka, Roy Emerton, Frederick Lloyd, Peggy Simpson, George Merritt, Terence Downing, Clifford Bartlett, Albert Chevalier, H.F. Maltby, Norman Pierce, Frederick Piper, Virginia Isham and Robert Atkins.

Story: Canadian soldier Hugh McGrath (Douglass Montgomery) manages to escape from a German POW camp. In the process he killed a guard and the Germans launch a nationwide search for him. He finds shelter in the Berlin home of Anna (Constance Bennett), a German national who is nevertheless apolitical. He hides in her home while the German detective Schenck Gotz (Oskar Homolka) is close behind him. The hero falls in love with Anna and marries her, and they make a break for it. Eventually the Canadian finds his way back to Allied lines.

Military Correlation: Helpful

Comment: This highly simplistic film was definitively sympathetic to the German cause at a time when it was in question. It had very limited distribution. Shortly after 1939 the film suddenly disappeared from distribution and has not reappeared.

Bloopers: While the story takes place in 1917, all the styles, including hair styles, are 1936. This was a problem in maintaining the sense of reality for many early films.

Exploits of the Emden (1928)

Produced by Ken G. Hall, First National Pictures (Australia). Directed by Ken G. Hall and Louis Ralph and written by Ken G. Hall. Cinematography by Ray Vaughn and Claude Carter. This silent black and white film, with English intertitles, starred the Officers and Men of the Royal Australian Navy as well as Louis Ralph, Fritz Greiner, Jack Mylong-Munz, Charles Willy Kayser, Maria Mizenti, and Kapitanleutnant von Mucke.

Story: A German officer in China, assigned to the SMS *Emden*, sends for his wife just as war is declared. He is later reunited with her when his ship, the *Emden*, takes on survivors from a passenger ships, the *Diplomat,* on which she was sailing and which he had sunk. Later the *Emden* fights with the Australian ship *Sydney* and is destroyed but the German officer survives with his wife.

Military Correlation: Excellent

Comment: The same story was made in Germany in 1926 (as *Unsere Emden*) with the German captain offering to surrender at the end but the Australians' Captain Glossop refusing. The film was purchased for production by the Weimar Republic and they were worried about casting Germans to play Australians. The cooperation of the Australian navy allowed them to use sailors and to shoot on the

HMS *Sydney* while the crew were in training. The director Ken G. Hall shared duties with the German director, Louis Ralph, whom he didn't meet until after the film was completed. In 1915 a fine documentary film, *How We Fought the Emden*, was released by Alfred Rolfe about the Battle of Cocos.[15]

F-4 (1918) see *The Hun Within* (1918)

Face Value (1927)

Production and distributed by Sterling Pictures (United States). Directed by Robert Florey and written by Frances Guihan. This 50-minute silent black and white film, with English intertitles, starred Fritzi Ridgeway, Gene Gowing, Betty Baker, Paddy O'Flynn, Jack Mower, Edwards Davis, and Joe Bonner.

Story: Wounded and facially disfigured, young hero Howard Crandall, Jr. (Gene Gowing) returns to his home. His father accepts him tearfully but his sweetheart Muriel Stanley (Fritzi Ridgeway) is revolted by the sight of him. When she finds another lover, he goes on a wild spree with an old army buddy (Paddy O'Flynn). In time he reconsiders his plight, sobers up, and realizes that he has to get his life in order. Understanding that he has no reason to stay at home, he returns to Paris and opens a club for disfigured veterans. His true love has a change of heart as the result of the aid of an old friend (Betty Barker) and travels to Paris where the lovers are reunited.

Military Correlation: Good

Comment: A somewhat muddled melodrama, this touched on a very sore subject at the time, the wounded and disfigured veteran. It is notable for its carefully constructed and visual expressions of the narrative. Florey was upset both with the number of disfigured men and the small amount of attention they received. He again addressed disfigurement in his later movie *The Face Behind the Mask* (1941). A good number of critics suggested that the ending was wrong and that Gowing should have married and dropped the fickle Ridgeway.

The False Face (1919) / aka *The Lone Wolf*

Produced by Thomas H. Ince, Paramount Pictures, Artcraft Picture Company (United States). It was directed by Irvin Willat and written by Willat and Louis Joseph Vance. Cinematography by Paul Eagler and Edwin W. Willat. Music by Pete Wending. This 76-minute (97 in some versions), silent black and white movie starred Lon Chaney, Bert Lytell, Henry B. Walhall, Mary Anderson, Thornton Edwards, William Bowman, Gary McGarry, Ernest Pasque, Steve Murphy, W.H. Brainbridge, and Milton Ross.

Story: During World War I, Michael Lanyard (Henry B. Walhall), also known as the Lone Wolf, a reformed gentleman crook, joins the Secret Service. At their request, and despite the fact that he was determined to go straight, he agrees to pull one last heist. His assignment is to steal a cylinder that contains highly significant military information from the Germans and return it to the Allies. The man with the document is an old adversary, Karl Ecksrom (Lon Chaney); he was also somehow responsible for the death of Lanyard's wife and daughter. When Karl moves to bring the documents to America, Lanyard follows and meet Brooke (Mary Anderson) who, unbeknownst to him, is also a spy for the Allies. During the voyage the documents are destroyed and thrown overboard, an enemy submarine sunk, and Karl gets what's coming to him. Lanyard and Brooke head into a long romance.

Military Correlation: Helpful

Comments: Critics were very hard on director Willat because of his derisive portrayals of French politicians, all of whom seemed to be acting inappropriately considering the events of the war. While it was little more than just another adventure story, the studio tried to pass it off as a spy melodrama since that was the best market. The story first appeared in serial form in *The Saturday Evening Post*. The director was able to get the United States Navy to provide him with one of its very few submarine for use in the film.

A Farewell to Arms (1932)

Produced by Edward Blatt and Benjamin Glazer, Paramount Pictures (United States). Directed by Frank Borzage and written by Benjamin Glazer, Oliver H.P.

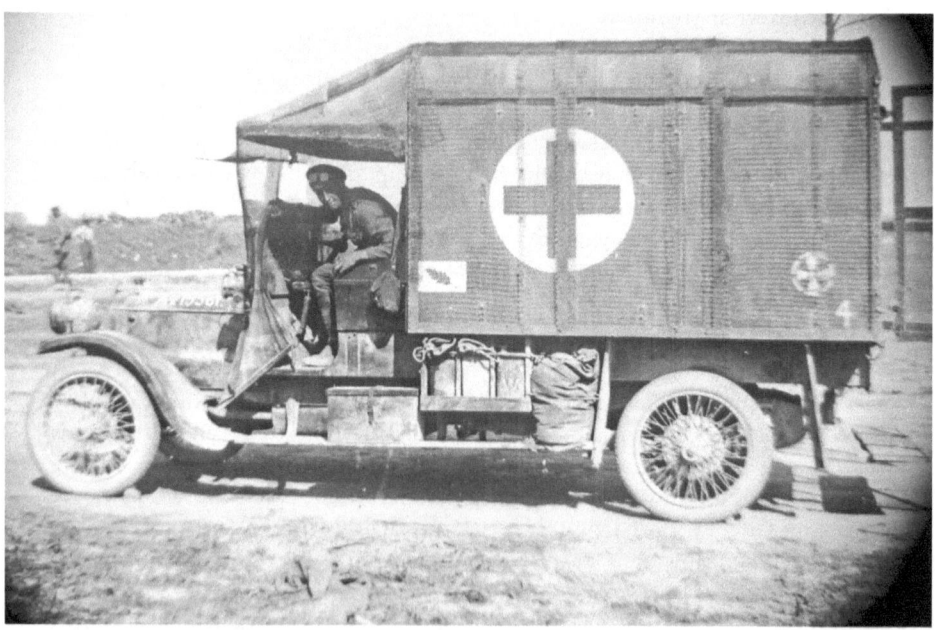

A U.S. Army ambulance of the type featured in *A Farewell to Arms* (courtesy Center for the Study of the Korean War, Independence, Missouri).

Garrett, based on the novel by Ernest Hemingway. The cinematographer was Charles Lang. The 90-minute black and white film starred Gary Cooper, Helen Hayes, Adolphe Menjou, Mary Phillips, Jack La Rue, Blanche Friderici, Alice Adair, Herman Bing, Agostino Borgato, Robert Cauterio, Peggy Cunningham, Mary Forbes, Gilbert Emery, and Henry Armetta.

Story: This screen version of Ernest Hemingway's novel is about romance and desertion in Italy during World War I. A wounded American officer, Lieutenant Henry (Gary Cooper), falls in love with an English Red Cross nurse, Catherine Barkley (Helen Hayes), and agrees to desert and join her in Switzerland. The stars try desperately to suggest that spiritual love can transcend its earthly counterpart and that it somehow rises above national loyalty. In this film, like so many of the period, the female role is identified primarily for their gender, as sexual objects or at best love interests, and discounting the horror, danger, and discomfort of the situation that they put up with just to serve. The war scenes are excellent and even moving but they are not matched by the same sort of sensitivity when it comes to the predictable romance.

Military Correlation: Spotty

Comment: Ruth Chatterton, Claudette Colbert and Eleanor Boardman were considered for the film before Paramount decided on stage actress Helen Hayes. Some of the early scenes were shot with Boardman and had to be reshot. Oscars were won by Charles Lang for cinematography and Harold C. Lewis for sound recording. It was the first of Hemingway's novels to be filmed. The Hemingway story was basically pirated in the movie *Force of Arms* (1951). This Hemingway movie was remade in 1957.

This being the last vestige of the Victorian age, the various women's corps were carefully chaperoned and men were not free to roam around as they often did in these movies.

Blooper: Helen Hayes'

Helen Hayes and Gary Cooper starred in *A Farewell to Arms* (courtesy Center for the Study of the Korean War, Independence, Missouri).

character of Catherine is described as being "very tall" while Hayes was only five feet in height.

A Farewell to Arms (1957)

Produced by David O. Selznick and 20th Century-Fox (United States). Directed by Charles Vidor and written by Ben Hecht, based on a novel by Ernest Hemingway. Cinematography by Piero Portalupi and Oswald Morris. It stars Rock Hudson, Jennifer Jones, Vittorio De Sica, Alberto Sordi, Mercedes McCambridge, Elaine Stritch, Oskar Homolka, Jose Nieto, Kurt Kasznar, Franco Interlenghi, Leopoldo Trieste, and Victor Francen.

Story: This remake has the same basic story as the 1932 version, as English nurse Catherine Barkley (Jennifer Jones) falls in love with a wounded American ambulance driver, Lieutenant Henry (Rock Hudson), in Italy during World War I. They plan to desert their posts and move to Switzerland where love can triumph. Long on scenes of stolen love and short on the importance of the war or the morality of their planned desertion, it is not as good a film as the earlier effort.

Military Correlation: Spotty

Comment: Despite the change in attitudes toward women, the producers did little to alter the image that Hemingway, and the film, projected of women as objects rather than significant participants in the war effort. Jennifer Jones was producer Selznick's wife. This was a somewhat bloated version of the early film. The first intent was to provide theater managers with both a happy and sad ending but when Hemingway learned of it they decided to make the managers request the version they wanted. John Huston the original director resigned and Vidor substituted There was considerable infighting during the filming of the movie and Hemingway, asked to help out, refused the $100,000 offer and suggested that Selznick should change it into nickels and "shove them" until he filled himself.[16] The technical quality and the many advances in technique and styles should have made this a much better film than the earlier version, but that is not the case.

Blooper: The film contains several continuity errors; for example, the number of sugar cubes on the table keeps changing in number, as does the amount of wine in Catherine's glass.

The Fifth Commandment (1932)
see *Broken Lullaby* (1932)

The Fighting 69th (1940)

Produced by Louis F. Edelman and Hal B. Wallis for Warner Brothers (United States). Directed by William Keighley and written by Norman Reilly Raine and Fred Niblo, Jr. Cinematography by Tony Gaudio. This 90-minute black and white film starred James Cagney, Pat O'Brien, George Brent, Jeffrey Lynn, Alan Hale,

Frank McHugh, Dick Foran, William Lundigan, Guinn "Big Boy" Williams, Henry O'Neil, John Litel, Sammy Cohan, Harvey Stephens, William Hopper, Frank Wilcox, Trevor Bardette, Herbert Anderson, John Arledge, Jack Boyle, Jr., Richard Clayton, Frank Coghlan, Jr., Joseph Crehan, Eddie Dew, Ralph Dunn, Edgar Edwards, Frank Faylen, James Flavin, Jerry Fletcher, Arno Frey, Edmund Glover, Chuck Hamilton, John Harron, J. Anthony Hughes, Layne Ireland, Donald Kerr, George Kilgen, Jacques Lory, Wilfred Lucas, Frank Mayo, and Dennis Morgan.

Story: This movie was based on the exploits of a World War I regiment consisting mostly of New York Irish. Jerry Plunkett (James Cagney) plays a loud-mouthed braggart who looks out for himself while he alienates most of the officers and his own comrades. The chaplain, Father Duffy (Pat O'Brienn), has a great deal of unfounded faith that the young man is basically good and tries to make him see his larger responsibility to himself, the regiment, and the country. Eventually Plunkett performs a selfish and cowardly act that eventually costs the lives of many of his fellow soldiers. A final act of cowardice leads to terrible consequences but Plunkett sees in them a chance to redeem himself and does so.

Military Correlation: Helpful

Comment: Hollywood loved the "bad boy does good" theme and this is a better-than-average example with two highly respected actors. The funeral scene in which the poem "Rouge Bouquet" by Joyce Kilmer is read is based on a true event. This film is basically a remake of *Angles with Dirty Faces* (1938) in khaki.

Bloopers: In one scene an "unconscious" German who was about to be carried off suddenly stands up as if the day's work was over.

The Flags of Mothers (1918) see *The Service Stars* (1918)

Flight Commander (1930) see *The Dawn Patrol* (1930)

Flyboys (2006)

Production by Dean Devin, Electric Entertainment, Flyboys Films, Ingenius Film Partners (United States). Directed by Tony Bill and written by Phil Sears and Blake Evans. Cinematograph by Henry Braham. This 140-minute film starred James Franco, Jean Reno, Jennifer Decker, Scott Hazell, Mac McDonald, Todd Boyce, Karen Ford, Ruth Bradley, Abdul Salis, Tim Pigott Smith, Philip Winchester, Jean-Philippe Ecoffey, Gail Downey, David Ellison, Jean Evans, Augustin Legrand, and Tyler Labine.

Story: For their own personal reasons, several young men enlist in the French Air Force, joining the 124 Air Squadron, the Lafayette Escadrille with five French officers and 38 American flyers. Blaine Rawlings (James Franco) is faced with foreclosure of the family farm. Eugene Skinner (Abdul Salis), a African-American boxer, was accepted in France and wants to repay them with his service. Eddie Beagle (David Ellison), a thief, is escaping the law. Porter, a pastor, seeks a mission.

Jamie, upset with American neutrality, wants to go to war. On the first mission Jamie is killed. Rawlings is spared from death by a kind German, and Beagle (whose crimes are exposed) is forgiven. The crew of Americans is slowly whittled down by the constant fighting. Rawlings finds some peace in his affection for Lucienne (Jennifer Decker), who is leery about his dangerous life. After an air battle in which the evil German Black Falcon is killed, Jensen, Skinner, Beagle and Rawlings survive under the watchful eye of Captain Thenault and Cassidy the resident ace. Rawlings is never able to locate Lucienne again. The film ends with a short account of what happened to the men portrayed in the movie.

Military Correlation: Good

Comment. The film is not much in terms of plot or performance, but worth watching for the air scenes (all very well staged) and the love interest which is believable. It is an old story worn thin and acted out by less than energetic actors.

Bloopers: The film is riddled with factual errors, most of which could easily have been avoided. In one scene we see a column of German tanks when the Germans had very few tanks and even then did not put them into service until March 1918. What tanks they had were ones captured from the French and British. The shots of French pilots being trained in British Sopwith Struters is ridiculous.

Follow the Girl (1917)

Produced and distributed by Universal Film Manufacturing Corporation (United States). Directed by Louis William Chaudet. Written by Fred Myton. This five-reel, silent, black and white film starred Ruth Stonehouse, Jack Dill, Roy Stewart, Mattie Witting, Claire Du Brey, Alfred Allen and Harry Dunkinson.

Story: This is one of the very few wartime espionage films that is set in the American west. Hilda Swanson (Ruth Stonehouse), a Swedish immigrant who works as a maid in the home of a wealthy family, discovers and unwittingly becomes involved in a plot by reactionaries to overthrow the American government. While she is not an American citizen, she acts to stop the plot before it gets going.

Military Correlation: Poor

Comment: Only marginally a war film, it is nevertheless illustrative of the manner in which Hollywood brought the war into just about every type of film. It also rather unusually addresses the issue of the loyalty of the many persons who today would be identified as hyphenated Americans or undocumented aliens. The question of loyalty was the subplot of many movies and, in many cases, the character being portrayed turn out to be disloyal.

For France (1917)

Produced by Vitagraph Company of America: A Blue Ribbon Feature (United States). Directed by Wesley Ruggles. It was written by Will Courtney and Cyrus Townsend Brady. Photography by Jules Cronjager. This five-reel silent black and white film, with English intertitles, starred Edward Earle, Betty Howe, Arthur Donaldson, Mary Maurice, Frank Anderson, and Erich von Stroheim.

Story: An American West Point cadet, in France studying flying, joins the French army as a pilot when war breaks out. His fiancée Marthe Landeau and her father turn to the family farm on the Marne for safety. When flying a scouting mission over the Landeau farm, Gerald spots some Germans attacking Marthe. He swoops down and is able to save Marthe and her father. They take refuge awaiting the arrival of the British cavalry. In the morning the three are attacked by the Germans. Gerald, with Marthe's help and a British machine gun, fights them off. Badly wounded, he and the Landeaus are saved by the arrival of French troops. Gerald is sent to a Red Cross Hospital where he is nursed to health by Marthe.

Military Correlation: Helpful

Comment: Some catalogues report that Henry Cronjager was the cameraman on this film. The battle scenes were shot with the aid of 400 American soldiers provided by the Army for the making of the film.

For King and Country (1964) see *King and Country* (1964)

For Liberty (1917) / aka ***The Patriot***

Produced by William Fox of Fox Film Corporation (United States). Directed by Bertram Bracken and written by Bennett Cohen. Photography by Charles Kaufman. This five-reel silent black and white film, with English intertitles, starred Gladys Brockwell, Charles Clary, Bertram Grassby, Willard Louis, Colin Chase, Clara Graham, Norbet A. Myles, William Ryno and George Routh.

Story: Marcia Glendon (Gladys Brockwell), an expatriate in Berlin, is courted by the American spy Frank Graham (Charles Clary) and the German General Von Lentz (Bertram Grassby). Marcia believes she can help her country by taking advantage of the general's affection for her. Graham misunderstands and thinks she is a traitor to the cause. Eventually Graham is caught and Marcia agrees to purchase his freedom by offering herself to the German general. Once freed, Frank is able to transport some secret plans across the German border to the American lines. Returning in command of an American regiment, he manages to save Marcia's life and her endangered honor.

Military Correlation: Poor

Comment: One of the many spy-melodramas designed for what was later called the B film system, okay but hardly out of the ordinary. Weak lighting, shadowed corners, fixed camera and intimate close-ups provided the atmosphere of skullduggery. Inexpensive to produce and profitable at the box office, they were turned out by the dozens.

For Me and My Gal (1942) / aka **The Big Time**

Produced by Arthur Freed for Metro-Goldwyn-Mayer (United States). Directed by Busby Berkeley and written by Howard Emmett Rogers, Richard Sherman, Fred F. Finklehoffe and Sid Silvers. Cinematography by William H. Daniels. Music by Roger Edens. This 104-minute black and white film starred Judy Garland, Gene Kelly, George Murphy, Martha Eggerth, Ben Blue, Stephen McNally, Richard Quine, Lucille Norman, and Keenan Wynn.

Story: Vaudevillians Jo Hayden (Judy Garland) and Harry Palmer (Gene Kelly), about to reach the height of their careers, prepare to perform their act the Palace Theatre on Broadway. Harry unexpectedly gets a draft notice and, hoping to create a short delay, he smashes his hand in a steamer trunk. The same day Jo learns that her brother Danny (Richard Quine), who had been studying to be a doctor, has been killed on the battlefields of France. When she realized what Harry has done, she dumps him and the act. Harry tries to enlist but his hand is permanently damaged and he cannot. He goes to France with the YMCA shows to entertain the troops. When he and his friends find themselves too close to the front, Harry heroically warns an ambulance unit heading into artillery fire. Although wounded, he destroys an enemy machine gun emplacement waiting to ambushing the convoy. He is commended for his bravery. After the war at a victory performance at the Palace Theatre, Jo sees Harry watching her from the audience and goes to him. They agree to forgive and reunite on stage singing "For Me and My Gal."

Military Correlation: Helpful

Comment: There are many excellent numbers in the film and they seem to fit around an interesting and well told story, matched by an unusual romance. It was inspired by a true story about vaudeville actors Harry Palmer and Jo Hayden. The musical numbers are performed as if acted out on a vaudeville stage. While very entertaining and in some ways a light movie; there is far more to it than at first appears. This was Gene Kelly's screen debut. George Murphy, who was originally to play Harry Palmer, was switched to the role of Jimmy Metcalf, a backup man who befriends Jo. At an early screening the audience felt Jo should end up with Jimmy and so Louis B. Mayer reshot part of it to give Kelly's character more of a conscience and to reduce Murphy's role in the film. Garland did not like director Busby Berkeley and often sided with Kelly against him. (She and Kelly later made *The Pirate* [1948] and *Summer Stock* [1950] together.) The film received Academy Award nominations for best score and musical direction. Kelly received a Best Actor award from the National Board of Review.

The songs that made the movie so popular included "For Me and My Gal," "Oh, You Beautiful Doll," "When You Wore a Tulip and I wore a Big Red Rose," "Ballin the Jack," and "After You're Gone." The songs "Spell of the Waltz" and "Three Cheers for the Yanks" did not make it in.

Blooper: In one scene a Southern Pacific Railway cab-forward steam locomotive pulls a passenger train; such engines were used only to pull freight trains.

Forever England (1934) see Brown on Resolution (1934)

For the Freedom of the World (1917)

Produced by Ira M. Lowry, S&M Film Company, Goldwyn Distributing Company (United States). Directed by Romaine Fielding and written by Edwin Bowser Hesser. Cinematography by Fred Chaston and William S. Cooper. This 80-minute silent black and white film starred E.K. Lincoln, Barbara Castleton, Romaine Fielding, Neil Moran, Jane Adler, Walter Weems and Emily Lubin.

Story: Wealthy American Gordon Harvey (E.K. Lincoln) joins the American Legion of the Canadian Army prior to America's entry into the war. He meets and marries Betty Milburn (Barbara Castleton). She cannot stand to see him leave so they disguise her as a Red Cross nurse and she follows him overseas. Ralph Perry (Romaine Fielding), who was once rejected by Betty, wants to get even and turns them in to the authorities believing they will be shot for disobeying military orders. Fearing the firing squad, Gordon shoots his wife and then volunteers for a suicide mission. At the last minute he is saved by the repentant Perry and awarded the Victoria Cross for his role in the mission. Betty, who was only wounded, recovers enough to be reunited with her husband and all is well.

Military Correlation: Helpful

Comment: This is a film in which realism is totally ignored for the sake of the plot and incredible events are the order of the day. As it is, the movie moves slowly and without much interest. In this film you see the same gender images being suggested, in this case the role of the Red Cross nurse which is only a means to disguise and not as a significant service in its own right.

For Valour (1928)

Produced by G.B. Samuelson, Samuelson-Victoria Film Productions (United Kingdom). Directed and written by G. B. Samuelson. This six-reel silent black and white film, with English intertitles, starred Dallas Cairns, Mary Rorke, Roy Travers, Marjorie Stallor, Millicent Wolf, Leonard Keysor, and George Findlater.

Story: A blind grandmother (Mary Rorke) recounts the story of how her husband (Dallas Cairns) was awarded the Victoria Cross, Great Britain's highest honor.

Military Correlation: Unknown

Comment: This was an attempt to capitalize on memories of the war, but it was poorly received and a commercial failure.

Forbidden Ground (2013) / aka Battle Ground

Produced by 24/7films, Armzfx, Scarlet Fire Films (Australia). Directed by John Earl and Adrian Powers. Written by Johan Earl and Powers. This 95-minute color film starred Johan Earl, Tim Pocock, Martin Copping, Denai Gracie, Sarah Mawbey, Barry Quin, Damian Sommerlad, Oliver Trajkovski, Igor Breakenback, Byron J. Brochmann, Alex Jewson, Steve Maxwell, Craig Walker and James Shepherd.

Story: Soldiers (Johan Earl, Tim Pocock, Martin Copping) find themselves in no-man's-land after an attack on the German lines has isolated them. Seeking to escape to their own lines, the three men, one of whom is wounded, cross the muddy wasteland as the Germans begin to follow. During the horrible ordeal the men become brothers. They make it back to their lines as an attack is just starting. The film does a good job of identifying the distinction between heroism and reality. While not preachy the director does not hold back from reflecting the grievances of military politics and the loss of innocence.

Military Correlation: Good

Comment: The original version ended after the prison scene but test audiences did not like it and a homecoming scene was added. The director later suggested that he preferred the first version. The visual effects, especially some of the explosions, are not well done. The opening sequence, a charge against the enemy, took two weeks to film. The film was shot in twenty-one days.

Bloopers: Some minor goofs like the wearing of modern wrist watches in the final scene as the soldier puts flowers on the grave.

Forty Thousand Horsemen (1940) / aka *Thunder Over the Desert*

Produced by Charles Chauvel for Famous Feature Films, Universal Pictures (Australia), Monophonicgram Pictures (United States). Directed by Charles Chauvel and written by E.V. Timms and Charles and Elsa Chauvel. Cinematography by George Heath, Frank Hurley, and John Hayer. This film (100 minutes in Australia, 89 in the U.S.) starred Grant Taylor, Betty Bryant, Pat Twohill, Chips Rafferty, Eric Reiman, Joe Valli, Kenneth Brampton, Albert C. Winn, Harvey Adams, Norman Maxwell, Harry Abdy, Pat Penny, Charles Zoli, Claude Turton, Theo Lianos, Roy Mannix. Edna Emmett, Vera Kandy, Iris Kennedy, Joy Hart and Michael Pate.

Story: In 1916 the Germans in Jerusalem under the command of Von Schiller (Eric Reiman) arrest French wine merchant Paul Rouget (Harry Abdy) for spying and hang him. His daughter Juliet (Betty Bryant) dresses as a man, goes into hiding, and spies on the Germans. Three young Australian of the Lighthorse, Red (Grant Taylor), Larry (Pat Twohill) and Jim (Chips Rafferty), are there fighting the Turks in a series of battles that include the march to Ogratina. The Lighthorse was a unit of mounted infantry recruited for this operation. Red is separated from the others and his life is saved by Juliet, who he thinks is an Arab boy. At the battle of Gaza, Kim and Larry are badly wounded and Red is captured. The British forces are defeated. Red is sent to do slave labor and discovers that the village is wired with explosives. Juliet rescues him and they spend the night together in the hut. Jim gets back to his unit in time to take part in the charge of the Lighthorse at the Battle of Beersheba. Von Schiller is spotted and caught before he can set off the explosives. The Turks and the Germans are defeated and Red, wounded, is reunited with Juliet.

Military Correlation: Excellent

Comment: The director Charles Chauvel was the nephew of General Sir Harry Chauvel who commanded the Australian Lighthorse during the Sinai and Palestine campaigns Charles' objective was to make the Australians look good. The writers are a little loose with some of the facts but do a good job of setting the stage to understand the theater's military significance. The combat scenes were shot using the First Lighthorse (machine-gun) regiment on loan. The censors had trouble with the overnight scene with Red and Juliet (feeling it did not matter at this point if Juliet was either a girl or a boy) and what looked like cruelty to some of the horses in the charge; the company was cleared of any mistreatment of animals and the film was finally released. The Australian people have a much greater interest in World War I than do Americans and the film was very popular there.

Forward March (1930) see *Doughboys* (1930)

Four Horsemen of the Apocalypse (1921)

Produced by Rex Ingram for Metro Pictures (United States). Directed by Rex Ingram and written by June Mathis, and based on the Spanish novel of the same name by Vicente Blasco Ibanez. Cinematography by John F. Seitz. Music by Louis F. Gotschalk. This 132-minute silent black and white film with English intertitles starred Bridgetta Clark, Rudolph Valentino, Virginia Warwick, Alan Hale, Mable Van Buren, Stuart Holmes, John St. Polis, Alice Terry, Mark Fenton, Derek Ghent, Nigel de Brulier, Pomery Cannon, Bowditch M. Turner, Wallace Beery, Jean Hersholt, and Edward Connelly.

Story: A rich Argentina leader, Madariaga (Pomery Cannon), has two daughters; one marred a Frenchman and the other a German. Madariaga prefers the Frenchman, which causes jealousy with the German and his three sons. He is particularly taken by his grandson Julio (Rudolph Valentino), with whom he drinks nightly at the clubs. When the old man dies, the family splits up, some of them going back to Germany and some to France. In Paris, Julio becomes an artist and has an affair with an unhappily married woman, Marguerite Laurier (Alice Terry). When war breaks out, Marguerite becomes a nurse in London and Etienne (John St. Polis) goes into battle where he is wounded. Ashamed of his wasted life, Julio enlists. When the Germans overrun the family estate, among those who occupy it is Marcelo's German nephew who tries to protect him. It does not work and Marcelo is sentenced to be executed for interfering when a German assaulted a woman. He is saved by the arrival of the French in the counterattack known as the Miracle of the Marne. Julio is recognized for bravery before he and one of his German cousins are killed. Back in Paris Marguerite gives thought to abandoning the blinded Etienne but Julio's ghost directs her to remain with him as they all try to recover from the effects of the war. In this film, perhaps more than in any other of his films, Ingram gave way the fact that he was essentially a painter and used light to create breathtaking effects.[17]

Military Correlation: Good

Comment: The image of the four horsemen (Book of Revelations, Chapter Six, 1–8) riding across the screen becomes a compelling reminder of man's inhumanity for even at this date the nation was still full of maimed men and fatherless children. It was the largest grossing film of 1921, even beating out Chaplin's *The Kid*. The film brought Valentino, who had been a taxi dancer in New York, to the front even though he was the lowest paid actor on the set. Alice Terry, who played Julio's lover, was a former Follies Girl and married the director the same year the film came out. During the love scenes Valentino and Terry spoke French to impress the lip readers. Generally not commented on, but nevertheless highly significant, was screenwriter Mathis' depiction of German officers coming down the stairs in drag.[18] The tango scene, which for some is the best remembered part of the movie, was parodied by Gene Wilder in *The World's Greatest Lover* (1977).

Four Horsemen was remade in 1961 starring Glenn Ford and Ingrid Thule and directed by Vincente Minnelli; the storyline was updated to the "more popular" World War II though the message was basically the same. Some film critics often suggest that the 1921 version was the first "real anti-war" film. Jean Hersholt played an uncredited part as the bearded son.

The film was placed on the National Film Registry in 1995 because it was "culturally, historically or aesthetically significant."

Four Sons (1928)

Produced and distributed by Fox Film Corporation (United States). Directed by John Ford and written by Philip Klein and I.A.R. Wylie. This 100-minute silent black and white film starred Margaret Mann, James Hall, Charles Morton, Ralph Bushman, Frank Reicher, Ferdinand Schumann-Heink, Jack Pennick, Earle Foxe, June Collyer, and George Meeker.

Story: A powerful saga of the widow Mother Bernie (Margaret Mann) who has four productive sons. When war breaks out, three go into the army to fight for Germany, while one goes to America to take a job. Living there happily married, he nevertheless feels the need to join the army when America enters the war. Once he is in the service, he must deal with the challenges of altered loyalty. The story is so simple and straightforward in the telling that very few title cards were used.

Military Correlation: Helpful

Comment: This movie was long considered lost; when found, it showed that John Ford was just as powerful a director without sound as he was with it. This very popular film, with its blistering attack on the horrors of war, set a new attendance record at the Roxy Theatre in New York. The initial scenes of the Germans fighting the Russians are outstanding as are the many highly emotive episodes. Seen in the film are the sets of the small European village from the film *Sunrise* (1927). Director Archie Mayo remade this movie in 1940 as a warning of coming disaster, changing the location and nations involved to make it more appropriate.

Bloopers: Like so many Fox movies made at this time, no effort was made to keep the dresses and cars within the period being portrayed (1919).

From Flower Girl to Red Cross Nurse (1915)

Produced and distributed by Zenith Film Company (United Kingdom). Directed by Leedham Bantock and written by Karina Mile. This silent black and white film, with English intertitles, starred Karina Mile.

Story: A young girl named Nelly (Karina Mile) is saved from a suicide attempt and becomes a dancer and then a Red Cross nurse in wartime France.

Military Correlation: None

Comment: There is a significant gap between what the producer and director must have had in mind, and what was actually produced. We know little of the film's content but are aware that the image of the nurse is, once again, an escape, not a goal. There is no mention of the fantastic responsibilities these women took on during the war. Many a movie patron came away from these early films with some serious misconceptions of the role of women.

Gallipoli (1981)

Produced by Robert Stigwood and Patricia Lovell for Associated Village Roadshow (Australia) and R & R Films, Paramount Pictures (United States). Directed by Peter Weir and written by Weir and David Williamson, based on a story by Weir. Cinematography by Russell Boyd. Music by Brian May. This 111-minute Eastmancolor film starred Mel Gibson, Mark Lee, Bill Kerr, Charles Lathalu, Yunipingu, Heath Harris, Gerda Nicolson, Robert Grubb, David Argue, Brian Anderson, Reg Evans, Rau Graham, Jack Giddy, Dane Peterson, and Tim McKenzie.

Story: The movie relates the events that took place during the disastrous World War I battle at Gallipoli in 1915. In this effort, British and Australian troops are trying to capture Istanbul. Incredible mistakes made by higher command lead to massive casualties among the Allied troops. Two young Australian men form a friendship that is tested by the circumstances. They are just about as nice a bunch as you will meet. In the background is a portrayal of the military and political mishandling suffered by these men who are called to fight a war in places they do not know and for reasons they do not understand. It ends with the futile attack at the Battle of the Nek on August 7, 1915. The mismanaged attack of ANZAC troops is unforgettable.

Military Correlation: Excellent

Comment: The depiction of life in Australia at the time is highly faithful and the story of the young runners is well developed. The motivation for participation in the war are well reviewed: ultra-nationalism, anti–German propaganda. The attraction of the uniform and a sense of adventure (as well as, for many, the need to get away quickly). The theme, the loss of innocence and the coming of age, though old and worn, is well cultivated. It came at a time when Australia was in need of its own identity fix, and stressed such things as the significance of mates and the distrust of authority. It also deals with the national willingness to support England in this struggle, as against the situation of Frank's (Mel Gibson) Irish uncle who does not believe in it. The many reasons for being involved show up in the characters; ultra-nationalism, anti–German propaganda, the lure of adventure, pride and to some extent ego. This very successful film won several Australian Film Institute awards including best film, director, actor, supporting actor, screenplay and cinematography. At the time it was the most expensive film ever made in Australia.

A poster for *Gallipoli*, Peter Weir's 1981 film (courtesy Center for the Study of the Korean War, Independence, Missouri).

Bloopers: The British are seriously bashed on several occasions in the film. The character who appears to be the real villain, General Frederic Hughes, gets off easily. The gesture of the benevolent General Gardiner (who supposedly called off the attack) did not happen; the attack actually simply failed and petered out.[19] And, despite the depiction suggesting otherwise, the British were not drinking tea on the beach as the attack took place. There were several old antagonisms being displayed in this bit of footage.

The Geezer of Berlin (1918)

Produced by Universal Film Manufacturing Company (United States). Directed by Arthur Hotaling and written by Tom Bret and Frank Howard Clark. Cinematography by Park Ries. This 20-minute silent black and white film, with

English intertitles, starred Roy Hansford, Jack Steward, Marvin Loback, Walter Bytell, R.O. Pennell, Earl Lynn, Hughie Mack, Bartine Burrett, Monty Banks, Bert Roach, and Raymond Hatton.

Story: A broad parody of Germany under the control of the Kaiser. It is very much of the same variety as *Shoulder Arms* (1918) and *Yankee Doodle in Berlin* (1919).

Military Correlation: None

Comment: Raymond Hatton was in numerous films and did not stop working until his death. His last film appearance was as an old man collecting bottles along the highway in *In Cold Blood* (1967).

The German Spy Peril (1914)

Produced and distributed by the Barker Motion Picture Company (United Kingdom). It was directed by Bert Haldane and written by Rowland Talbot. This silent black and white silent film, with English intertitles, starred J. Hastings Batson.

Story: A propaganda film seeking to muster patriotic support for the war. The plot is loosely based on the Guy Fawkes 1605 plot to blow up Parliament. The hero, disheartened when ill health prevents him from enlisting in the army, overhears a group of German spies planning on blowing up the Houses of Parliament. Determined to stop them, he counter-bombs the tunnels they have constructed. As Big Ben counts off the seconds, the explosion brings the plot to an end.

Military Correlation: Helpful

Comment: One review of the film called it "a most exciting and thoroughly topical subject." This was one of the first "spy films" to name the country of origin of the evildoers. While the plot is a little thin, it is fun viewing. Guy Fawkes is not mentioned. This was somewhat unusual for a spy drama as it went beyond the formula dialogue and had a somewhat innovative storyline. Few directors were as capable of creating the suspense and tension powerful enough to carry the weak plot.

The Girl Who Stayed at Home (1919)

Produced and distributed by D.W. Griffith Productions (United States). Directed by D.W. Griffith and written by Griffith and Stanner E.V. Taylor. This 60-minute silent black and white film, with English intertitles, starred Carol Dempster, Adolph Lestina, Francis Parks. Richard Barthelmess, Robert Harron, Syn De Conde, George Fawcett, Kate Bruce, Edward Peil, Sr., Clarine Seymour, Tully Marshall, David Butler, Joseph Scott, H.H. Crowder and General March as himself.

Story: Brothers Ralph (Richard Barthelmess) and James (Robert Harron) face the coming of the war. Ralph the good brother enlists and goes to France to fight. There he falls in love with Atoline France (Carol Dempster). James, the lazy brother with little interest in his responsibilities, stays home where, in time, he is

redeemed by the love of a cabaret singer with the unbelievable name of Cutie Beautiful (Clarine Seymour).
Military Correlation: Poor
Comment: The movie makes some reference to General H.H. Crowder, the main force behind the Selective Service Act of 1917. One of Griffith's least impressive films, it is a highly predictable "last-minute-that-restored-the-fighting-spirit" film.

Good-Bye Bill (1918) see *Good Bye Bill* (1918)

Good Bye Bill (1918) / aka *Good-Bye Bill; Gosh Darn the Kaiser*

Produced and distributed by Famous Players–Lasky Corporation and John Emerson and Anita Loos Productions (United States). Directed by John Emerson and written by Anita Loos and John, based on the story "Gosh Darn the Kaiser." Cinematography by Jacques Monteran. This silent black and white comedy-war drama starred Shirley Mason, Ernest Truex, Joseph Allan, Sr., Henry Koser, Joseph Burke, and Carl de Planta.
Story: I could not find a synopsis.
Military Correlation: Unknown
Comment: The author Anita Loos, who was married to John Emeson, also wrote the screenplay for *Gentlemen Prefer Blondes*.

Gosh Darn the Kaiser (1918) see *Good Bye Bill* (1918)

The Grand Illusion (1937)

Produced by Albert Pinkovitch and Frank Rollmer, World Picture Corporation (United States). The film was directed by Jean Renoir and written by Renoir and Charles Spaak.[20] Cinematography by Charles (Christian) Matras. Music by Joseph Kosha. This 111-minute anti-war film starred Jean Gabin, Dita Parlo, Pierre Fresnay, Erich von Stroheim, Jullian Carette, Georges Peclet, Werner Florian, Jean Daste, Sylvain Itkine, Gaston Modot, and Marcel Dalio.
Story: Set in 1916 before American involvement in the war, the story is based in a prisoner of war camp and deals with the disillusionment of captors (the Germans) and prisoners (British and French). Into this camp comes Captain de Boeldieu (Pierre Fresnay), who has been shot down by the German von Rauffestein (Erich von Stroheim). He becomes friendly not only with the other prisoners but Rauffestein as well. Eventually it is necessary for the German to kill his friend. Two prisoners, Marelhal (Jean Gabin) and Rosenthal (Marcel Dalio) recede into the background and we are left with the ultimate question: Can humanity start again? This is not a prisoner of war film nor is it jingoistic, but rather a melodra-

matic effort to deal with the changing order in Europe and the fact that in the long run the world is being taken over by the commoner.

Military Correlation: Excellent

Comment: This was the first foreign film to be nominated by the Academy for Best Picture but it lost. Director Jean Renoir, son of the painter Auguste Renoir, was a French Air Force pilot during the war and had his own agenda for the film. He received an Oscar for Lifetime Achievement in 1975. When Goebbels came to power in Germany, he proclaimed this film to be a Cinematic Public Enemy. Renoir had a lot of influence on later films, and in at least two cases they have scenes "stolen" from *Grand Illusion*. One had to do with a finely detailed copy of the building of the escape tunnel, including the dropping of dirt from pants legs as they walked about the compound in *The Great Escape* (1963); also the singing of "La Marseillaise" to anger the Germans in *Casablanca* (1942). *Grand Illusion* of the very few war movies in which there are no battle scenes but the impact of the war is everpresent. Erich von Stroheim, though born in Austria, did not speak German well enough and had an awful time learning his lines. A close look will also suggest that much of the sexual symbolism found in, say, von Stroheim's military apartment scenes was taken in detail from Griffith's *Intolerance*.

Bloopers: When Boeldieu died, Rauffestein moves to close his eyes with his hand, but as he does, Boeldieu blinks.

The Gray Nun of Belgium (1915)

Produced by L. Frank Baum and Nat G. Deuerich, Alliance Program, Oz Film Manufacturing, Dramatic Feature Films (United States). Directed by Francis Powers, it was written by Baum. The silent black and white film starred Betty Pierce, Cathleen Countiss, and David Proctor.

Story: Mother Superior (Betty Pierce) helps wounded Allied soldiers escape.

Military Correlation: Unknown

Comment: The distributor, rather arbitrarily it appears, made the decision that the picture was basically without merit and refused to release it. The exhibitor copy, made as a sales tool for theaters, is the only copy known to exist.

The Great Love (1918)

Produced by D.W. Griffith, Famous Players–Lasky Corporation, Artcraft Pictures, Paramount (United States). Directed by D.W. Griffith and written by Stanner E.V. Taylor. Photography, G.W. Bitzer. This seven-reel silent black and white film, with English intertitles, starred Lillian Gish, Robert Harron, Henry B. Walthall, Gloria Hope, Maxfield Standey, George Fawcett, Rosemary Theby, and George Siegmann.

Story: James Young (Robert Harron), an American, enlists in the Canadian Army early in the war and is sent to London. There he meets and falls in love with Susanna Broadplains (Lillian Gish), the lovely daughter of Reverend Joseph Broadplains (George Fawcett). In the meantime Sir Robert Brighton (Henry B. Walthall) makes love to a local village girl, Jessie Lovewell. When reassigned, he leaves her and returns to London where he meets with groups of communists and pacifists. Jessie is brokenhearted and pregnant. Brighton agrees to help the Germans and drives through London in a car with flashing lights to direct zeppelins in order for them to bomb an important munitions plant. James catches up with him and smashes the light. He then sets up a light signal of his own and leads the Germans astray. Brighton shoots himself. James and Susanna, who has been spending time as a nurse in France, are wed.

Military Correlation: Helpful

Comment: Lillian Gish, as always beautiful, manages to give great support to the film. It is not a powerful part for her, relying on looks rather than performance. The public liked the zeppelins as they always appeared mysterious and formidable, but the action scenes involving them are unbelievable. Film of British nobility, shot by the director when in London, was to be used in *Hearts of the World* (1918) but he used them in this film instead.

The Great War (2004)

Produced by Galafilm Productions, Canadian Production Company (Canada). Directed and written by Brian McKenna. This color film available in both English and French stars Justin Trudeau, Michael Rudder, Maxime Cournoyer, Arthur Holden, Pat Kiely, Justin Walsh, Noel Burton, Sasche Cole, Francis X. McCarthy, Jean-Francios Blanchard, Susan Almgren, John Dee Delorimier, Glen Bowser, Paul van Dyck, Niel Napier, and Paul Stewart.

Story: A cross between a feature film and a documentary, this is a story about Canada's involvement in the Great War. The war experience is described by 125 descendants of persons who participated at one level or another. It was filmed at Saint Bruno military range near Montreal where a World War I battlefield was recreated. It is acted out by a mix of professional actors and amateurs from both sides of the war.

Military Correlation: Good

Comment: The McKenna brothers also worked with historical re-enactors on movies about the War of 1812 and World War II. The primary criticism was that those involved appeared too emotional to tell the story.

The Greatest Power (1917) / aka *Her Greatest Power*

Produced and distributed by Rolfe Photoplays, Metro Pictures Corporation (United States). Directed by Edwin Carewe and Edward LeSaint and written by Albert S. Le Vino and Louis Wolheim. Cinematography by Arthur Martineili. This 130-minute silent black and white film, with English intertitles, starred Ethel Barrymore, William B. Davidson, Henry Northrup, Redfield Clarke, Rudolph de Cordova, W.M. Armstrong, Frederick Truesdell, and Frank Currier.

Story: With backing from Randolph Monroe (Frank Currier), chemist John Conrad (William B. Davidson), assisted by Monroe's lovely daughter Miriam (Ethel Barrymore), invents a high explosive. John and Miriam fall in love. Conrad thinks that the sale of his weapon to every nation will prevent future wars because it is so deadly that no one will use it. His humanitarian concerns are not shared by, Miriam, who believes he should preserve it for the defense of his own country. It is only when he nearly loses the invention to Albert Bernard (Harry S. Northrup), a clever German spy, that he decides she is right.

Military Correlation: Spotty

Comment: Prior to the war, the film companies were careful how they identified the bad guys though the characters are terribly stereotyped, suggesting a nationality. When, however the United States entered the war, this theme became a standard one and the bad guys were quickly identified.

Promotion of films, and this is an excellent example, either show America unleashing its unlimited military power or dropped down the intensity to show the support of the American people. In this case Ethel Barrymore is shown grappling with a large round of artillery as she loads it into the breach of a cannon.

The Greatest Thing in Life (1918) / aka *The Cradle of Souls*

Produced by D. W. Griffith with Famous Players–Lasky/Artcraft Company and Paramount Pictures (United States). Directed and written by Captain Victor Marier (pseudonym for D.W. Griffith, Lillian Gish and Stanner E.V. Taylor). Cinematography by G.W. Bitzer and Henrik Sarton This 70-minute silent black and white film, with English intertitles, starred Robert Harron, Lillian Gish, Peaches Jackson, Elmo Lincoln, Zasu Pitts, Kate Bruce, Adolphe Lestina, and David Butler.

Story: In England, Jeannette Peret (Lillian Gish) meets the young and somewhat arrogant Edward (Robert Harron). On a trip to France with her father (secretly paid for by her admirer, Edward), Jeannette meets and marries a stodgy but wealthy grocer named le Bebe (David Butler). When war breaks out, both le Bebe and Edward find themselves on the field of battle where Edward learns a good deal about humanity. During the war, le Bebe is killed. When Edward returns to England a much changed man, he and Jeannette get together. In the film there is a rather touching scene when Edward comes across a dying black man calling for his mother. Edward holds him in his arms, and even kisses him, until the man dies.

Military Correlation: Good

Comment: D.W. Griffith, having been recognized for his earlier work, was invited by the United Kingdom to film on the actual battlegrounds of World War I. When the director got there he shot nearly 86,000 feet of film primarily near the Marne River in Chateau-Thierry, France. In time this film would be the basis for three films, *Hearts of the World*, *The Great Love*, and *The Greatest Thing in Life*. Some of the footage, it is rumored, was purchased from Franz Kleinschmidt.[21]

This film, like others, shows his astonishing ability to crystallize the awful, massive destruction of war into shots of simple symbolism or metaphor. Despite the grimness of the often authentic war scene in his film *Hearts of the World*, its most moving shot is a brace of swans swimming away from the ripples of their pond caused by the falling of debris from a bomb explosion.

The film was groundbreaking in a variety of ways but perhaps the most "daring" was that it included the kiss between a white officer and a black soldier, both male. The "black" man was Elmo Lincoln in blackface. While it was a significant acknowledgment that African-American soldiers were fighting in France, it was also a heavy reminder that they were not working in Hollywood. It was also considered to be the first, and best, example of the portrait photographic style of Henrik Sartov.

The use of the battlefield footage, plus the Griffith touch, provided viewers with a much more realistic perception of the war than many other films. It is hard to determine just how deliberate this was but the Harron-Lincoln kiss provided some insights into racial relations at the time. Zasu Pitts was hired for the film and several shots were taken with her in them. However, it was decided that she looked too much like Lillian Gish and so she was fired and all those short retaken. There are no known complete prints of this film. Recently it was announced that a complete print was located in the Raymond Rohauer Collection at the Cohen Media Group but this turned out not to be true.

The Guns of Loos (1928)

Produced and distributed by Stoll Picture Production Company and New Era (United Kingdom). It was directed by Sinclair Hill and written by Reginald Fogwell and Leslie Howard Gordon. Cinematography by D.P. Cooper, Desmond Dickinson, and Sidney Eaton. The 84-minute silent black and white film, with English intertitles, starred Henry Victor, Madeleine Carroll, Bobby Howes, Hermione Baddeley, Donald Macardle, Adeline Hayden Coffin, Jeanne le Vaye, Philip Hewland, Frank Goldsmith, William Freshman, David Laidlaw, Tom Coventry, and Wally Patch.

Story: A tough soldier, John Grimlaw (Henry Victor), is blinded while saving some of his comrades during the war. He and his friend Clive (Donald Macardle) try to win the love of Diana (Madeleine Carroll), whom they left behind. When Victor returns home to take over the family's industrial business, he must fight off a strike effort and win the love of a lady's daughter.

Military Correlation: None

Comment: The movie carefully puts in juxtaposition the war and its problems with the mystery of the home front and the differing views each presents. And yet it is another example of the romantic triangle that appears rather consistently in these dramas of the First World War. It is not clear if this is just a way to include more men and fewer women, or if there was some assumed glamour to be found in that particular situation. One thing is for sure: That is a no-win situation.

The one thing that seems to be consistent is that the woman involved is too fickle to make up her mind and allows the winds of fate to determine her future. This was the film debut of Madeleine Carroll, who was selected for the role over 150 other contenders and went on to enjoy a long career.

Half Shot at Sunrise (1930)

Produced and distributed by RKO Radio (United States). It was directed by Paul Sloan and written by James Ashmore Creelman. This 78-minute film stars the musical comedy team of Bert Wheeler and Robert Woolsey, John Rutherford, and Dorothy Lee and the Tiller Sunshine Girls dance team.

Story. Two doughboys, AWOL in Paris, spend most of their time ducking the military police. In an entanglement with French politicians and ladies, the twosome are entrusted with secret orders. They are caught and about to be shot when it is discovered that the secret messages being smuggled out was nothing but love letters between the French Colonel Marshall and the flirtatious Olga (Dorothy Lee). Considered slapstick, this movie nevertheless has some significant scenes, one of which depicts Woolsey risking death to rescue the injured Wheeler from No Man's Land. It contains several musical numbers that became very popular including "Whistling the Blues Away."

Military Correlation: None

Comment: This movie is fun and worth watching if only for the early appearance of the Tiller Girls. They were the first dance team to include a routine that included linked arms and high kicks. It was later adopted by the Rockettes.

Ham and Eggs (1927) / aka *Ham and Eggs at the Front*

Produced and distributed by Vitaphone Productions, Warner Brothers (United States). Directed by Roy Del Ruth and written by Robert Dillon, James Starr and Darryl F. Zanuck. This 60-minute silent black and white comedy starred Tom Wilson, Heinie Conklin, Myrna Loy, William Irving, Noah Young, Louise Fazenda, Tom Kennedy, and Cameo the Dog.

Story: African-Americans doughboys Ham (Tom Wilson) and Eggs (Heinie Conklin) go AWOL in a small French village. Both fall in love with the beautiful Fifi (Myrna Loy), who leads them on. When they discover she is a spy reporting to the Germans, it stirs their loyalty. They eventually redeem themselves, and set things right with the Army, by going behind the lines and capturing a German general. The comedy is primarily slapstick.

Military Correlation: Poor

Comment: This is an awful film and by today's standards totally unacceptable. The two soldiers were played by white actors in blackface, and their activities were so stereotyped as to be ridiculous. Zanuck later went on to produce the anti-racist film *Pinky* (1949).

It does have one redeeming quality and that is that while the vast majority of

African-Americans who served in the military did so in construction or service jobs, there were black troops (such as the Harlem Hell Fighters) who fought bravely and effectively throughout the war.[22] This is one of the very few movies that even recognized the appearance of African-Americans in the war.

Ham and Eggs at the Front (1927)
see *Ham and Eggs* (1927)

The Hands of the Hun (1918)
see *The Claws of the Hun* (1918)

Havoc (1925)

Produced and distributed by Fox Film Corporation (United States). Directed by Rowland V. Lee and written by Edmund Goulding and Henry Wall, based on a play by Wall. Cinematography by G.O. Post. This nine-reel silent black and white film starred Madge Bellamy, George O'Brien, Walter McGrail, Eulalie Jensen, Margaret Livingston, Leslie Fenton, David Butler, Harvey Clark, Wade Boteler, Edythe Chapman, E.H. Calvert, and Bertram Grassby.

Story: Englishmen Dick Chappel (George O'Brien) and Roddy Dunton (Walter McGrail) are both in love with the beautiful but fickle Violet Deering (Margaret Livingston), who loves them both. When war breaks out, both men join up. Chappel proposes to Violet prior to leaving for the front. Once he is gone, she decides she loves Dunton instead and insists that he tell his friend. He does not; when he has the chance, he leaves Chappel behind at the trench line when the Germans attack. Chappel survives but is blinded. Dunton is so ashamed that he takes his own life. Back in London, Tessie (Madge Bellamy), Dunton's sister, nurses Chappel back to health and he regains his sight. At this point, having lost Dunton, Violet decided she loves Chappel. Chappel, however, dumps her and marries Tessie.

Military Correlation: Helpful

Comment: This plot was used over and over in American- and British-made silent films. The point, when there is a point, is that patriotism always wins out.

Heart of Humanity (1918) /
aka *Hearts of Humanity; The Dawn of Reckoning*

Produced by Carl Laemmle and Jewel Productions, Universal Film Manufacturing Company (United States). Directed by Allen Holubar and written by Ogla Linek Scholl and Holubar. Cinematography by Fred LeRoy Granville. This 110-minute silent black and white film starred Dorothy Phillips, William Stowell, Pat O'Malley, Gloria Joy, George Hackathorne, Walt Whitman, Erich von Stroheim, Lloyd Hughes, William Welsh, Joseph Girard, and Robert Anderson.

Story: Nanette (Dorothy Phillips) lives in a small Canadian village where she is in love with John (William Stowell), the oldest of five brothers. When war breaks out, all the boys go to war, as does Nanette (via the Red Cross). In Belgium she is accosted by Lieutenant Von Eberhard (Erich von Stroheim) but she is saved by John. Many critics claim that this was a rip-off of *Hearts of the World* (1918): Not only was the plot the same but so were many of the individual scenes. Star Dorothy Phillips copies almost word for word, gesture for gesture, Lillian Gish's lines as she descended into madness. The overbearing power of war scenes suggests that Erich von Stroheim may well have had more to do with it than at first suggested, for they are well beyond what might be anticipated from Holubar.

Military Correlation: Good

Comment: Erich von Stroheim, a brilliant director and actor, was billed as "The man we most love to hate" and he earned the reputation with such scenes as ripping the buttons from a woman's blouse with his teeth, or throwing a baby out the window. He was very good at being very bad. Dorothy Phillips did a poor job impersonating Lillian Gish.

Heart of the World (1918) see *Hearts of the World* (1918)

Hearts of Humanity (1918) see *Heart of Humanity* (1918)

Hearts of the World (1918) / aka *Love's Struggle*

Produced and distributed by D.W. Griffith Productions, Famous Players–Lasky Corporation (United States). Directed and written by D.W. Griffith. Cinematography by Billy Bitzer, Alfred Machin and Hendrik Sartov. Music by Carli Elinor. This 117-minute silent black and white film, with English intertitles, starred Lillian Gish, Dorothy Gish, Erich von Stroheim, Noël Coward, Adolph Lestina, Robert Harron, Jack Cosgrave, Kate Bruce, Ben Alexander, Marion Emmons, Robert Anderson, George Fawcett, George Siegmann, Fay Holderness, Josephine Crowell, and L Lowry.

Story: A sentimental propagandistic film produced primarily to encourage the United States' entry into the war. The romance between the children of American neighbors (Lillian Gish and Robert Harron) living peacefully in a French village is a plea for the unity of the nations. When the village is invaded by the Germans, the young people band together to cause difficulties. The revolt was costly but the two survived long enough to be saved by French troops. In many respects its most noteworthy accomplishment was its advances in lighting and pictorial composition which were the most sophisticated to date and the close-up shots of Lillian Gish that were stunningly beautiful.

Military Correlation: Good

Comment: This film was financed by the British War Office to make the point of the Allied involvement. It went out of its way to display the viciousness of the German soldier. In the credits, Griffith listed himself as the writer Gaston de Tolignac. The harshness of the film was personified by the actions of actor Erich von Stroheim. Sisters Lillian and Dorothy Gish appeared together in several films. Billy Bitzer the original cameraman was not allowed in France since he was of German ancestry and so Griffith used an Army camera crew. Griffith purchased film of the German chief of staff from an Austrian-American officer named Kleinschmit who was arrested in the United States for espionage. After completion of the film, Griffith suggested that he wanted to get back to making films about "the sun and the wind on the corn."

This virtually a remake of *The Birth of the Nation* which the director transposed into World War I. It has the same rhythms of separation and reunions, and the same sensational scenes in which he has a brigade of French volunteers substitute for the Ku Klux Klan. And, once more, their leader arrives just in time to save Lillian Gish from being raped by George Siegmann.

The cast included a 19-year-old Noël Coward in a small part pushing a wheelbarrow. The movie ran an unprecedented six weeks (twice a day) at the Davidson Theatre with prices from 25¢ to $1.50 This film was the longest-running and most prestigious film produced and released during the period of the United States participation in the war. While considered one of the best American war films, it is less than pure American since it was financed by the British War Office and filmed in France.[23]

Hedd Wyn (1992)

Produced by Shan Davis, Pendefig Tyo Cefn Sianel 4 Cymru (Wales) Modern Art Entertainment (United States). Directed by Paul Turner and written by Alan Llwyd, based on his play. Cinematography by Ray Orthon. Music by John E.R. Hardy. This 123-minutes color film stars Huw Garmon, Catrin Fychen, Ceri Cunnington, Lilo Silyn, Grey Evans, Gwen Ellis, Emma Kelly, Sioned Jones Williams, Llyr Joshua, Angharad Roberts, Emlyn Gomer, Guto Roberts, Manon Prysor, and Gruffudd Aled.

Story: A highly sensitive young farmer, Ellis Humphrey Evans, born in Gwynedd and living in North Wales, competes for the Chair of the National Eisteddfod, the prize given for poetry. He is totally against the war and refuses to enlist but soon finds that he must in order to relieve his younger brother from conscription. Regretfully he leaves his young sweetheart, ill with consumption, and joins the 15th Royal Welch Fusiliers who are being sent to fight in support of English troops. Under the pen name Hedd Wyn, meaning "blessed peace" and inspired by the rays of the sun penetrating the mist in the valley of Meironydd, he writes "Yr Arwr" ("The Hero") and addresses the conditions, the violence, the fear, and the desire for peace. After he has submitted his poem, and in the course of the senseless slaughter, he is killed at the Battle of Passcheudaele (Third Battle of Ypres). More than 31,000 died that day.[24] The poem wins the award as he has promised his sweetheart. In the final scene the chair, swathed in black, is brought to the Evans farmhouse where his parents receive it with dignity.

Military Correlation: Helpful

Comment: A reviewer called *Hedd Wyn* a "beautifully acted, directed, and photographed film worthy of its Oscar nomination." This delightful and highly romanticized film suggested the idea of a "poets war" in which sensibility was the gauge of its success; the remembering was more important than the war. This film, released in both English and Welsh, is based on the true story of poet Ellis Evans and was the only Welsh-language film nominated for an Academy Award. Besides being an impressive denunciation of war, the film is also a well planned attack on the British domination of Wales. It was well received, especially in Wales where it reflected the nation's pride in its contribution to the war. The chair awarded is to this day known as the National Eisteddfod Chair in Black.

Hell Below (1933) / *aka* **Pigboat; Conflict**

Produced and distributed by Metro Goldwyn-Mayer (United States). Directed by Jack Conway and written by Laird Doyle, John Lee Mahin, and Raymond L. Schrock, based on Commander Edward Ellsberg's novel *Pigboats*. Cinematography by Harold Rosson. This 101-minute black and white film starred Robert Montgomery, Walter Huston, Robert Young, Madge Evans, Eugene Pallette, Edwin Styles, David Newell, Charles Irwin, Sterling Holloway, and Jimmy Durante.

Story: When the commander of U.S. AL-14 is wounded on its last cruise, Lieutenant Thomas Knowlton (Robert Montgomery) hopes to be promoted but Lieutenant Commander T.J. Toler (Walter Huston) shows up and takes over. Toler's daughter, whom Knowlton meets at a party, becomes the love interest. After disobeying orders not to fight some German ships, he is court-martialed and leaves the Navy in disgrace. Toler is given a hazardous mission, loading the AL-14 with explosives to ram a fortification at a narrow point in the channel. During the mission he sacrifices his life for the good of the service.

Military Correlation: Helpful

Comment: While the acting is good, the atmosphere of the submarine is the most interesting thing about the movie. It was very up-to-date in the presentation of the technical apparatus shown. Submarines were undergoing tremendous growth in the inter-war period. The destroyer shown sinking was the decommissioned World War I destroyer USS *Moody*, with adjustments to its hull. MGM bought the Moody for $35,000. The film was re-released in 1937 with some dialogue eliminated in order to meet the standards of the Production Code.

Bloopers: The clothes and hair styles of the movie are pure 1933, not 1918.

Hell Bent on Glory (1958) see *Lafayette Escadrille* (1958)

Hell on Earth (1931) / aka *No Man's Land*

Produced and distributed by Resco-Filmproduktion (Germany), Aeolian (United States). Directed by Victor Trivas and George Shdanoff (uncredited). Written by Leonhard Frank, Shdanoff (uncredited) and Victor Trivas (uncredited). Cinematography by George Stilanudis and Alexander von Lagorio. This 93-minute black and white film stars Ernst Busch, Vladimir Sokoloff, Renee Stobrawa, Elisabeth Lennartz, Hugh Douglas, Louis Douglas, Zoe Frank, George Peclet and Rose-Mai.

Story: A dugout is made out of a basement in no man's land at the height of the war. Two soldiers are stranded there avoiding capture. After a while they find a wounded man who is trapped inside. He has no uniform but they soon discover they are from different sides. When they make an attempt to leave, they are fired on by the armies of both sides. As time passes, more soldiers join them and soon they find they have an Englishman, a Frenchman, a Russian Jew, a German and a vaudevillian (nationally not given and his profession unimportant). They argue among themselves about the merits of the war, eventually agreeing on its irrationally, and marching out together with the commentary "Marching forward, Defying their common enemy, War."

Military Correlation: Helpful

Comment: Filmed in German with English, French, German and Yiddish dialogue, it reeks of its anti-war message and offers little as either entertainment or instruction. Dark and depressing, it is a pieced-together story of comradeship and international unity. It provides little but frustration since nothing is cleared up and no questions solved.

Hell's Angels (1930)

Produced and distributed by Caddo Corporation, United Artists (United States). Directed by Howard Hughes, Marshall Neilan (uncredited), Luther Reed (uncredited) and James Whate (uncredited) and written by Harry Behn and Howard Estabrook. Cinematography by Tony Gaudio and Harry Perry. This 129-minute black and white (with one Technicolor scene) film starred Ben Lyon, James Hall, Fred Clark, Roy Wilson, Douglas Gilmore, Jane Winton, Evelyn Hall, William B. Davidson, Wyndham Standing, Lena Malena, Marian Marsh, Carl Von Hartman, Jean Harlow, John Darrow, and Lucien Prival.

Story: Three Oxford friends—English brothers Monte (Ben Lyon) and Roy (James Hall) and a German—are called to war by their countries. Their lives are complicated by the love of the same woman (Jean Harlow) who turns out to be less than they expected. A tough, by-the-book commanding officer makes life uncomfortable for Monte and Roy. The boys take on a desperate mission primarily to prove Monte is not the coward that he is believed to be, and for Roy to forget his love troubles. When the brothers are captured, there is a risk that the Allied attack will be thwarted. Ray kills Monte to prevent him from talking, and then is himself executed. The film features a good number of exciting dogfight sequences between the Royal Flying Corps and Germany, but the ground action leaves much to be desired.

Military Correlation: Good

Comment: During filming, 137 different pilots were required, and several were killed in accidents. Greta Nissen, who was originally to play the female lead, was pushed out when director Howard Hughes decided to make *Hell's Angels* a talkie and she, they discovered, had a heavy Norwegian accent. Perhaps the film is most notable for introducing her replacement Jean Harlow to the screen. Harlow was the one who made famous the line "Excuse me while I slip into something more comfortable." The film won the Academy Award for cinematography. It was reissued in 1946 in a 96-minute version.

Wyndham Standing was noted for his exceptional performance as the captain who, fed up with the antics of Ben Lyon and James Hall, sends them on a dangerous mission.

Her Boy (1918) / aka *Conscription*

Jean Harlow on the stylized poster for *Hell's Angels* (courtesy Center for the Study of the Korean War, Independence, Missouri).

Produced and distributed by Metro Film Corporation (United States). Directed by George Irving. Written by Albert S. Le Vito and W. Carrey Wonderly. Cinematography by Harry Davis. This 90-minute, silent, black and white film, with English intertitles, starred Effie Shannon, Niles Welch, Pauline Curley, James T. Galloway, Pat O'Malley, William Bechtel, Charles Sutton, Charles Riegel, Violet Axzelle, George Demarest, James Robert Chandler, Ferike Boros, Anthony Byrd, S. McAlpin, J.C. Bates, and Edmund Wright.

Story: A nice but determined widow (Effie Shannon) is against the war. She is able to prevent her boy (Niles Walsh) from enlisting even though he is upset and prefers to do his duty. Then he is caught up in the conscription. To prevent him from going, his mother illegally alters his birth certificate showing that he is too young to be drafted. In doing so, she has unwittingly listed him as born ten months prior to his father's death. This makes the young man both a slacker *and* a bastard in the eyes of the town. Finally realizing what she has done she has a totally unexplained change of heart and confesses to the village that she lied. All is forgiven and the mother, now filled with patriotic fever, stands proud as her son marches off to France.

Military Correlation: Poor

Comment: This was one of a half-dozen slacker movies that focused on the "better late than never" redemption of patriotism. The film was not much; they could easily have told the story in half the time. The director appears to know the story so well that he does not feel the need to explain it to the audience; there are too many long pauses without explanation, and little to no explanation by way of intertitles. However, it does deal directly with an issue that was generally ignored: The reluctant participant in the conscription system (introduced by President Wilson) posed a considerable problem.

Her Greatest Power (1917) see *The Greatest Power* (1917)

The Hero of Submarine D-2 (1916) / aka *Colton, U.S. N.*

Produced and distributed by Vitagraph Company of America and U-L-S-E Distributors (United States). Directed by Paul Scardon and written by Cyrus Townsend Brady and Joseph Ewing Brady. This 90-minute silent black and white film, with English intertitles, starred Charles Richman, James Morrison, Anders Randolf, Charles Wellesley, Thomas Mills, L. Rogers Lytton, Eleanor Woodruff, and Zena Keefe.

Story: The story of a Naval Academy official, submarine commander Colton (Charles Richman) discovers a Ruanian (meaning German) plot to destroy the United States fleet at harbor. Colton sails to the rescue only to discover that his submarine is too large to sail into the mine-infested waters of the harbor. Donning diving gear, he orders his men to shoot him out the torpedo tube. He then swims into the harbor, defuses all the mines and saves the fleet.

Military Correlation: Helpful

Comment: Submarine movies have always been popular. The nature of the submarine limits the extent of the action and the consolidated situation expands the opportunity for emotional interaction. The hero of this film is fighting the emotions of the crew as well as the imaginary Ruanian navy. In this case the plot is so ridiculous that it makes the rest of the film, which is somewhat interesting, hard to watch.

Heroes of the Marne (1938)

Produced and distributed by Andre Hugon (United States). Directed by Andre Hugon. Written by Paul Achard (from his novel), Hugon and Georges Fagot. Cinematography by Marc Bujard. Music by Jacques Ibert. This 93-minute monophonic black and white film starred Georges Paulais, Germaine Dermoz, Jacqueline Porel, Albert Bassermann, Camile Bert, Georges Peclet, Endouard Delmont, Pierre-Louise, Richard Lancret, Raimu, Bernard Lancret, Denis d'Ines, Jean Toulout, Fransined, Andre Nox, Catherine Fonteney, Lise Florelly, Paul Cambo, Jean Buquet, and Paul Marthes.

Story: Bernard LeFrancois (Raimu), a prosperous farmer on the River Marne, has a neighbor who is very poor and out of his class. The rich man strongly objects to his daughter's romance with the man's son, but despite the objection the two continue to see each other. When World War I breaks out, the son enlists and becomes a pilot. The unmarried daughter, is now pregnant, returns home to live with her father. When the Germans invade she becomes a spy to help the French. LeFrancois finally joins up as a soldier.

Military Correlation: Spotty

Comment: Something has to be said about the incredibly slow pacing of the movie and, if there is a point to this story, it was missed by critics at the time, and it seems no clearer today. The atmosphere is well established but the love interest is not very moving. The equality story was done so many times that if *that* is the message, it was unnecessary. The unwed mother has little to no bearing on the film.

The Heroine of Mons (1914)

Produced and distributed by Clarendon British Film Productions, Gaumont British (United Kingdom). Directed by Wilfred Noy. This silent black and white film, with English intertitles, starred Dorothy Bellew, Leslie Howard, and Bert Wayne.

Story: A beautiful young girl in Belgium (Dorothy Bellew) become friends with Captain Arnaud (Leslie Howard) who lives in the home of her banker family. When Germans invade her small town and occupy the town bank, she sees an opportunity to take action. She escapes in a stolen motor car and drives to the British lines. There she tells her story and then brings troops who are able to capture all the Germans and save Captain Arnaud in the nick of time.

Military Correlation: Helpful

Comment: This is a film in which a woman plays a key role, in this case a legitimate heroine. This was the first film for Leslie Howard, who had been released from the British army as a result of shell shock and steered toward acting as a means of recovery. Howard, born is Hungary, quickly becomes known as "the perfect Englishman." The film does not do a good job of depicting the First Battle of Mons (August 24–28, 1914), the first British encounter with the German army. The

Prahran Chronicle (January 23, 1915) called the movie it as "exciting from start to finish," but the dialogue appeared somewhat too witty for the situation.

Hotel Imperial (1927) / aka *I Love a Soldier*

Produced by Erich Pommer and Famous Lasky Productions (United States). Directed by Mauritz Stiller and written by Lajos Biro and Jules Furthman, based on a play by Biro. Cinematography by William Mellon. This 85-minute film starred Pola Negri, James Hall, George Siegmann, Michael Vivitch, and Otto Fries.

Story: Lieutenant Paul Almasy (James Hall), an Austrian officer caught behind Russian lines, takes refuge in a small hotel. A chambermaid (Pola Negri) allows him to pose at the hotel butler. Soon they fall in love. Russian General Juschkiewitsch (George Siegmann) makes the hotel his headquarters and immediately takes an interest in the lovely chambermaid. Almasy is also involved in trying to locate a spy, Tabakowitsch (Michael Vavitch), who has been sending important information to the Russian. In a series of conflicting and generally confusing scenes, Almasy shoots the spy, thwarts the Russian general, saves the Austrian army, and wins the chambermaid.

Military Correlation: Good

Comment: The movie was considered by many who participated, cursed as several of those involved, died shortly after the filming. Stiller made only a handful of films in America and this was certainly his best. The movie was confusing and the plot too twisty.

Hotel Imperial (1939)

Produced and distributed by Paramount Pictures (United States). Directed by Robert Florey and written by Lajos Biro and Gilbert Gabriel, based on Biro's play. Cinematography by William Mellon. This 67-minute black and white movie starred Ray Milland, Isa Miranda, Gene Lockhart, Henry Victor, Albert Dekker, and Reginald Owen.

Story: In a small hotel behind the Russian lines, a young Austrian officer, Almasy, seeks refuge. There he finds comfort and help from the chambermaid. Almasy is trying to identify the spy who is passing essential information to the enemies of his country. With the help of the chambermaid he is able to catch the Russian general as the spy and save the day.

Military Correlation: Spotty

Comment: This movie was remade yet again as *Five Graves to Cairo* (1943) with the action moved up to World War II. Ray Milland was badly injured during the making of this film when his horse failed to make a jump and he was thrown off. Milland, who had been a member of the British Household Cavalry insisted on doing his own riding in the film.

The Hun Within (1918) / aka The Enemy Within; F-4

Produced and distributed by F-4 Picture Corporation, Famous Lasky Corporation (United States). Directed by D.W. Griffith and Chester Withey (as Chet Withey) and written by Griffith and Stanner E.V. Tanner. Cinematography by David Abel. This silent black and white 50-minute movie stars Dorothy Gish, George Fawcett, Charles K. Gerrard, Lillian Clark, Douglas MacLean, Herbert Sutch, Max Davidson, Robert Anderson, Erich von Stroheim, Kate Bruce, and Adolph Lestina.

Story: Beth (Dorothy Gish) lives with her dying father (Adolph Lestina). Before he dies Lestina entrusts his daughter to his friend Henry Winger (Douglas Fawcett). While the German-born Winger is basically loyal to America, his son Karl (Charles K. Gerrard), who has been studying in Germany, tosses his hat in with the Fatherland. Frank Douglas (Douglas MacLean), an old school friend of Beth's, has joined the United States Secret Service. When Karl returns to America he becomes involved in a plot to blow up an American ship that is transporting soldiers to France. Beth overhears Karl talking about these plans. To keep her quiet, Karl locks her in the basement the Germans are using as a headquarters. Frank rescues Beth and the two of them head for the ship. Karl's bomb is discovered and thrown overboard just in time.

Military Correlation: Helpful

Comment: In this film Dorothy Gish gives up her usual comedy roles and plays the melodramatic daughter of the confused German. Made with Griffith style, though really directed by his longtime assistant Chester Withey, it was well received as were the performances of Gish and the "awful German" who was nearly a standard in such movies, Erich von Stroheim. The divided family is employed in a good many of these early war films, providing domestic tension to match the tension of the battlefield.

The use of Hun in the title is significant to understanding the story. It refers to that evil that is not only living among us, but is within us. It was a part of the campaign to identify the enemy.

Huns and Hyphens (1918)

Produced and distributed by the Vitagraph Company (United States). Directed and written by Larry Semon. Music by Kevin Mac Leodtars. This 20-minute silent black and white film, with English intertitles, starred Larry Semon, Madge Kirby, Stan Laurel, Mae Laurel, William McCall, Frank Alexander, William Hauber and Pete Gordon.

Story: Larry Semon is a wealthy man courting a rich young lady named Vera Bright (Madge Kirby). The young lady, who lives with her stepfather, has invented a gas mask that the government wants to mass produce. Semon is not what he appears for he is in fact a somewhat clumsy, dullish man working in a restaurant where most of the staff and nearly all the customers are sympathetic to the Kaiser. They plan to get Vera to the restaurant where they can steal her gas mask. When she sees Semon she realizes that he is not what he had said he was. He redeems himself when he rescues Vera and her stepfather from the spies and saves the plans.

Military Correlation: Helpful

Comment: This pro-war film is made up of a series of bad clichés, gags and situation comedy as the hero was far more interested in making the viewers laugh than in sending a message. The man who plays the German who gets the egg down his pants is none other than Stan Laurel in one of his first film roles. This is not a great comedy and has little to say about the Great War.

Huns of the North Sea (1914)

Produced by John M. Payne (aka John Castle), P & M Films and Feature Supply Company (United Kingdom). It was directed and written by Sidney Morgan. This two-reel silent black and white film, with English intertitles, starred Harry Lorraine, Norman Royce, Eva Norman, and Nora Wolfe.

Story: There is very little available on this movie with the only plot synopsis coming from the British Film Institute catalogue. It has to do with a German spy (Harry Lorraine) whose English-born wife (Nora Wolfe) prevents him from laying down a mine field from his fishing shack in order to harass the British navy.

Military Correlation: Unknown

Comment: The available reviews suggest that the movie was greatly underplayed and draggy. The critics suggest that the director may have known the story so well that he does not feel the need to explain it to the audience; there are too many long pauses without explanation, and little to no explanation by way of intertitles.

The use of the term Huns, applied to mean all Germans whether in the military or not, was a part of the campaign to identify the enemy. Even before the United States entered the war, the movies as well as the press used the term to provide a ready-made enemy. In World War II the Nazis were the European enemy, not the German people, but in the Great War no such distinction was made. The characteristic of the Hun, seen often and exaggerated on movie posters, was one of piggish evil.

Hunting the U-Boat (1918)

Produced and distributed by Bud Fisher Film Company, Celebrated Players (United States). Directed by Harry Conway "Bud" Fisher, Raoul Barre and Charles Bowers, it was written by Fisher, based on the Mutt and Jeff comic series. Animation was by Fisher and Edgar Norach. The short (seven minutes) silent black and white film starred Augustus J. Mutt and Edgar Horace Jeff.

Story: The Kaiser's military is again exposed to the stupid duo's antics.

Military Correlation: None

Comment: These Mutt and Jeff films are not really war films as much as they are anti–Kaiser films. The comedians—animated or actual—make the war personal for they are not really anti–German as much as they are anti-authority (identified as the Kaiser). Neither of the characters has much intelligence but the cartoonist is highly imaginative and clever in his plots.

I Didn't Raise My Boy to Be a Soldier (1915) see *I'm Glad My Boy Grew Up to Be a Soldier* (1915)

I Love a Soldier (1927) see *Hotel Imperial* (1927)

If England Were Invaded (1909) see *The Invaders* (1909)

I'll Say So (1918)

Produced and distributed by Fox Victory Pictures, Fox Film Corporation (United States). Directed by Raoul Walsh and written by Ralph Spence. This silent black and white film, with English intertitles, starred George Walsh, Regina Quinn, William Bailey, James Black, and Ed Keeley.

Story: New Yorker Bill Durham (George Walsh) tries to enlist but is turned down because of flat feet. He is devastated by this failure and by the fact that people who do not understand assume he is a slacker. He meets and starts a fight with a pacifist who is advocating on the streets. In the incident he meets the beautiful Barbara (Regina Quinn) and they soon fall in love. Her guardian turns out to be a German spy who is planning to go to the border to cause trouble between the United States and Mexico. Walsh follows the German sympathizer and he and Barbara thwart him. The guardian manages to whisk Barbara off to New York where he plans for her to marry a fellow spy. At the last minute Walsh turns up at the church and substitutes himself for the bridegroom, thus saving Barbara.

Military Correlation: Poor

Comment: This film came out after the Armistice and was not popular as spies were no longer seen as a threat. In fact the appearance of the spy in these later movies brought on hissing and ill-mannered remarks rather than fear and loathing as hoped. The minor players seemed to have more conviction than the major ones, and the long unexplained moments left the viewer wondering if they were missing something. There are too many long pauses without explanation, and little to no explanation by way of intertitles. In this case the spy story became the sad story.

I'm Glad My Boy Grew Up to Be a Soldier (1915) / aka *I Didn't Raise My Boy to Be a Soldier*

Produced and distributed by Selig Polyscope Company, V-L-S-E (United States). Directed by Frank Beal and written by Alfred Bryant and Gilson Willets.

This 90-minute silent black and white film, with English intertitles, starred Guy Oliver, Frank Beal, Eugenie Besserer, Anna Luther, Harry Mestayer, and Harry De Vere.

Story: James Warrington (Harry De Vere) feels the call of patriotism and leaves his wife and child to enlist in the army. When his friend Arthur Archer (Guy Oliver) returns from the war after losing his arm, he tells James' wife that her husband has died a hero. Seventeen years later, in a different war, her son also goes off to fight and falls in love with a Red Cross nurse (Anna Luther) who in time has to return to tell the mother that her son is dead. Inconsolable, Mrs. Warrington has a vision in which she sees a battleship being transformed into a threshing machine, and takes comfort from the mystical experience.

Military Correlation: Helpful

Comment: The film does not tell us why the mystical experience was so profound and it seems out of place with the rest of the movie. This film was produced after the war had started in Europe and before the United States got involved. The nation was going through a debate about preparedness and this did not seem to address the issue. The film was basic propaganda promoting something but it is not exactly clear how that was supposed to work.

In the Hands of the Enemy (1915)

Produced by Edwin Thanhauser, Mutual Films and Thanhauser Film Corporation (United States). Directed by Theo Frenkle (unconfirmed). The musical score was by Ben Model. This 28-minute silent, black and white film, with English intertitles, starred J. Morris Foster and Inda Palmer.

Story: During the war Constance (Inda Palmer), a countess, and her young son Albert (J. Morris Foster) agree to take on disguises and attempt to deliver secret messages through enemy lines. The mission is critical to the Allies' success. Now the movie expands to include some well produced battle scenes of both artillery and cavalry action as well as strong performances by its stars. The firing squad depiction at the end is well done; the combining of distant shots with quick intimate close-ups creates a sense of drama unrecorded in words.

Military Correlation: Good

Comment: This film is considered remarkable because of the artistry and techniques involved, the film's use of close shots for expressiveness and intimacy. Some of these techniques become standard in years to come. The subject is very melodramatic but the director avoided the usual hokum. The simple plot adds to the complication of emotions it produces. It's considered one of the best movies of 1915.

In the Name of the Prince of Peace (1914)

Produced and distributed by Dryeda Art Film Corporation, Prince of Peace Corporation, World Films (United States). Directed and written by J. Searle Dawley. Cinematography by Irwin Willet. This four-reel, silent, black and white film, with English intertitles, starred Robert Broderick, Laura Sawyer, George Stillwell, and Arthur Evers.

Story: Following a battle in which many members of their unit are killed, a group of French artillerymen take refuge in a church. Among them is Baron von Krapt, whom none suspect is a German spy. Also at the church is a beautiful young nun who was the sweetheart of von Krapt's son Waldo. The nun accidently betrays the baron and he is captured and ordered executed. The nun, feeling guilty, tries to stop the execution and in the process she is shot and killed. The message is loud and clear: In war, not only the guilty but also the innocent are punished.

Military Correlation: Helpful

Comment: The men of the United States Army 22nd Field Artillery appear in several scenes and are credited.

The Inn (1982) see *Austeria* (1982)

The Invaders (1909) / aka *If England Were Invaded*

Produced by the Clarendon Company (United Kingdom). It was directed by Perry Stow and inspired by the William La Quex book *The Invasion of 1915*. This is a ten-minute, silent, black and white film with English intertitles.

Story: When a young girl's home is commandeered by the enemy because of its strategic location, she takes matters in her own hands. She sends a message by pigeon to call for the territorial troops to save her from a group of spies who, of all things, were posing as a group of Jewish tailors.

Military Correlation: Poor

Comment: In this somewhat strange film the enemy appears to reflect the growing fear that many held that the outbreak of war would cause an influx of immigrants from the European community. It may have been in response to the passing of the Alien Act in the United Kingdom in 1905 which greatly limited immigration. As was common in these early films, the national origin of the spies is not identified. A later version of this story, *The Raid of 1915* (1913), was never released.

The Invasion of Britain (1918) / aka *Victory and Peace*

Produced and distributed by National War Aims Commission (United Kingdom). Directed by Herbert Brenon and written by novelist Hall Caine. The 130-minute silent black and white film, with English intertitles, starred Ellen Terry, Matheson Lang, Marie Lohe, and James Carew.

Story: This is primarily a propaganda film capitalizing on Britain's great fear of being invaded. Though not invaded since 1066, the island maintained a healthy paranoia about it.

Military Correlation: Poor

Comment: The movie is harsh and overdone. Since it came out after the Armistice, the National War Aims Commission decided not to release it and it was never available for general distribution. About 1000 feet of it is still available but while listed in some British film catalogues no copies appear to be available. Remnants of reviews suggest that the film was not all that good.

Island of Adventure (1919)
see *Light of Victory* (1919)

It's a Long Way to Tipperary (1914)

Produced by Ernest Higgins, British and Colonial Kinematograph Company (United Kingdom). Directed by Maurice Elvey and written by Eliot Stannard. This short silent black and white film, with English intertitles, stars Elisabeth Risdon, James Russell, A.V. Bramble, M. Gary Murray, Ernest A. Cox, and A.C. Ogan.

Story: In this highly melodramatic story, Irish Nationalist Mike (A.V. Bramble) gives up his life at the Western front to save that of his rival Paddy (James Russell), a Ulster volunteer. This act of heroics and political acceptance is all for the love of Molly Malone (Elisabeth Risdon).

Military Correlation: Helpful

Comment: The title is based on a music hall favorite written by Jack Judge that became closely associated with the British troops in World War I. Tipperary is a small Irish village that during the war somehow became a symbol for home. On entering this small town, there is a sign that says "You've Come a Long Way." A song with a hint of sadness to it, it is often used to suggest a somber situation. The cast of *The Mary Tyler Moore Show* sang it as they ended the last episode. The popular song gave rise to an increasingly popular response "What's the Wrong Way to Tickle Mary?"

J'accuse! (1919)

Produced and distributed by Chaples Pathe, United Artists (United States). Directed by Abel Gance and Blaise Cendrars and written by Gance. Cinematography by Marc Bujard, Leonce-Henri Buell and Maurice Foster. This 166-minute silent black and white film, with French and English titles, starred Romuald Joube, Maxime Desjardins, Severin-Mars, Angele Guys, Maryse Dauvray, Elizabeth Nissan, and Blaise Cendrars.

Story: Lovely young Maria Lazare (Maxime Desjardins) is in love with poet Jean Diaz (Romuald Joube) while unhappily married to an older man, Francois. War breaks out and both men end up on the front line. Edith is captured by the German forces and suffers violation at their hands. In the story, the horror of war both on an individual and collective basis is contrasted by a series of nearly comical looks at life in Paris at this time. In time the two men meet, become friends, and share their love for Edith. However when they return home Edith (who now has a half–German daughter) does not tell of the rape, and the two men fight again. Finally they decide to take vengeance on the enemy and return to the front where one is killed and the other goes mad.

Military Correlation: Good

Comment: Considered by many to be one of the most technically advanced film of the era is also one of the first of the more specific pacifist film. It was billed as "a human cry against the bellicose din of armies." Gance's assistant director Blaise Cendrars lost an arm during the war.

Portions of the film were shot during the battle of St. Mihiel. Soldiers featured in those scenes were, within a week, back at the front and nearly 80 percent of them were killed.

Bloopers: Blaise Cendrars is seen standing in the back of a field of supposedly dead soldiers.

J'accuse! (1938) / aka *That They May Live*

Produced by Abel Gance, Forrester-Parent (France). Directed by Abel Gance and written by Gance and Steve Passeur. Cinematography by Robert Hubeert. This 125-minute black and white film starred Victor Francen, Line Noro, Jean-Max, Jean Louis Barrault, Renee Devillers, Marie Lou, Romuald Joube, Paul Amiot, Andre Nox, Georges Saillard, George Rollins, and Marcel Delaitre.

Story: Research scientist Jean Diaz (Victor Francen), a World War I veteran, is so horrified by the war that he discards all other activities and dedicates his life to bringing an end to all wars. When he discovers that the military is exploiting his work, he summons up the spirits of the millions who died on the field of battle during the Great War, to bring the world to its senses. Director Gance has an almost prophetic view of the power and destruction of modern weapons, and makes a significant and emotional statement.

Military Correlation: Helpful

Comment: This is Abel Gance's remake of the silent film he made in 1919. He was so upset at the thought of another world war that he reaffirmed his concern by telling the story in a different fashion, calling this time on the mystic powers of the remembered dead. Again there was reluctance in the United States to distribute the film but finally it came out, classified it as a horror film. Many critics say it is the French response to *The Birth of a Nation*.

Joan of Plattsburg (1918)

Produced and distributed by Goldwyn Production Company, Goldwyn Distribution Corporation (United States). Directed by William Humphrey and George Loane Tucker, it was written by Tucker and Porter Emerson Browne and based on his play. This 60-minute silent black and white film, with English intertitles, starred

Mabel Normand, Robert Elliott, Joseph W. Smiley, Edward Elkas, John Webb Dillon, Willard Dashiell, Edith McAlpin and Isabel Vernon.

Story: Reeking of teenage sexuality, a young orphan girl becomes the darling of a group of Army trainees in Plattsburg, New York. She has visions of being a heroine like Joan of Arc with whom she identifies, and dreams of a great adventure. One night while in the orphanage she hears voices in the basement. When she goes to listen, she discovers they are not saints waiting to call her to great things, but a group of German spies plotting to do damage to the military. Taking matters in her own hands she enlists the aid of some of the Plattsburg boys at camp and they are able to thwart the plan and save the day. She ends up praised as a heroine, a modern-day Joan of Plattsburg.

Military Correlation: Poor

Comment: The film is a disaster. Normand was a well-known and highly popular comedienne who made this film to help the war effort. But she simply could not pull it off as a serious actress, particularly with such a stupid plot and outlandish dialogue. The film does not even manage to maintain the evil image of the Hun that had become such a part of the war movie presentation. Critics went to great lengths to point out that neither Normand nor Joan was anything like Joan of Arc.

The Jockstrap Raiders (2011)

Produced and distributed by Mark Wilson (United States). Directed by Mark Wilson, Written by Wilson with animation by Wilson and Jason Thielen. Music by Gordy Haab. This 19-minute color short features the voices of Anthony DiMonte, Fred Tatasciore and Devin Uzan.

Story: This animated short film takes place in Leeds, England, where a group of underdog misfits make an attempt to enter the military but are denied because they have various abnormalities. Their ills range from being drunks to having flat feet or tumors. When there is the sudden danger that Great Britain will be invaded by Germans who are building a bridge by which to attack, "the Leeds Raiders" must stop them. They manage to gather together to overcome their many differences and defeat the enemy for crown and country.

Military Correlation: None

Comment: This animated film, produced by a UCLA student, was inspired by the film *Kelly's Heroes* and took four years to produce. The animation is good and the voices, while obviously done with good spirit, could have been more consistent. It won the Student Academy Award.

Johnny Got His Gun (1971)

Produced and distributed by Bruce Campbell World Entertainment Company (United States). Directed and written by Dalton Trumbo. Cinematography by Jules Brenner. This 106-minute, color–black and white stars Timothy Bottoms, Kathy Fields, Marsha Hunt, Jason Robards, Jr., Donald Sutherland, and Diane Varsi.

Story: In 1918 American soldier Joe Bonham (Timothy Bottoms) lies in bed with both arms and legs amputated as well as having lost his hearing and sight when his face was blown off. Eventually the nurse-caretaker discovers that, while the young soldier appears to be in a coma, he is alert. The military-medical authorities, fearful of the message it might be sending, does not allow anyone to see him, and denies him the mercy killing he is able to suggest he wants. In the prolonged nightmare which is his life, we hear the voice of the young man articulating his thoughts, and making some effort to understand what is going on and to communicate. We hear the young war victim's thoughts during his treatment. Neither his face or missing limbs are ever shown in the films.

Military Correlation: Excellent

Comment: This powerful anti-war film's message is delivered primarily by silence. A *Time Out* critic defined it as "often sentimental, sometimes brilliant, as well as a horrifying and intriguing film" (February 9, 2006). Trumbo published the book in 1938. This film looks at the female lead as a significant person—in this case a careful, caring, and professional nurse—rather than simply the necessary member in a love triangle. The combining of distance shots with quick intimate close-ups provides a sense of drama unrecorded in words.

The movie won the Grand Prize at the Cannes Film Festival in 1971. In 1988 the Metallica, a heavy metal band, wrote the song "One" based on the book and showing a movie clip. The movie was remade in 2008.

Johnny Got His Gun (2008)

Produced and distributed by Greenwood Hill Productions, Tres Hermano Productions (United States). Directed by Rowan Joseph, it was written by Bradley Rand Smith and Dalton Trumbo. This 75-minute color film starred Matty Ferraro (voice), Rowan Joseph (voice), Meredith Kendall, Ben McKenzie, and Shane Partlow.

Story: Hit by an artillery shell on the last day of the Great War, 20-year-old soldier Joe Bonham (Ben McKenzie) wakes to discover that he has lost all his limbs and his eyes, ears, nose, and mouth. Regaining consciousness and aware that his brain is fully functional, he finally discovers a means to communicate with his nurse. Tapping his head in Morse Code he manages to plead first to be taken out and put on display as an example of the evils of war, and then for a mercy killing. The military unsympathetically denies both requests. Most critics found it to be well done, "basically the book on film with few Hollywood interruptions."

Military Correlation: Good

Comment: A "live on stage," film version of the 1982 Broadway play, starred Benjamin McKenzie. McKenzie earned critical acclaim for his performance as Joe. In 2010 a DVD of the McKenzie version was made available free to every high school library in the United States as an indictment against war. It included discussions guides for students, a 15-minutes short on the making of the film, and a brief history of the novel.

Joining the Tanks (1918)

Produced and distributed by American Pathe, B.F. Production Company, Celebrated Players, Fox Company (United States). Directed by Harry Conway "Bud" Fisher, Raoul Barre and Charles Bowers, it was written by Fisher based on the Mutt and Jeff comic series. Animation by Dick Huemer. The seven-minute silent black and white film starred Augustus J. Mutt and Edgar Horace Jeff.

Story: The film focuses on the antics of the "two mismatched tinhorns" Augustus J. Mutt, an incurable gambler, and his dimwitted friend Edgar Horace Jeff (always called Jeff) who join the Army and fight the Kaiser.

Military Correlation: None

Comment: The producers developed a system where the dialogue was carried on the bottom of the screen rather than on intertitles and the films were billed as "talking."

Journey's End (1930)

Produced and distributed by Gainsborough Films, Woolf Freedom Film Service (United Kingdom), Tiffany Productions (United States). Directed by James Whale and written by Gareth Gundrey and Joseph Moncure March, based on the play by R.C. Sherriff. Cinematography by Benjamin H. Kline. This 150-minute black and white film starred Colin Clive, Ian MacLaren, David Manners, Anthony Bushell, Billy Bevan, Robert Adair, Tom Whiteley, Jack Pitcairn, Warner Klingler, Leslie Sketchley, and Gil Perkins.

Story: Second Lieutenant Raleigh (David Manners) joins up with old school friend Captain Stanhope (Colin Clive) in the trenches in France. Raleigh, who had been the schoolmaster at the school where Raleigh had attended, is having a lot of trouble keeping his nerves in check as the war goes on. He is drinking more and seems close to a breakdown. He is very afraid that Raleigh will tell his sister, who Raleigh plans to marry after the war, that he is in such trouble. But he does not, and he and his friend Lieutenant Osborne work to keep the captain out of danger. Raleigh and Osborne are called upon to undertake an especially dangerous mission. Osborne is killed and Raleigh badly wounded. Raleigh is later killed and Captain Stanhope is left trying to deal with these losses and his own diminishing capabilities.

Military Correlation: Excellent

Comment: Well produced and highly sensitive, this production was considered by many to be the British version of *What Price Glory*; it had the added advantage of sound, but it was not nearly *that* good a movie. The production, much of which took place in a sort of mess hall carved out of one end of the trenches, took full advantage of the lights and shadows to emphasize the psychological tensions that were being dealt with. It was the first of a good many Anglo-American productions. The German version *Die Audere seitz* was banned by the German government in 1933 because of its harsh portrayal of the German people. James Whale, who was asked to direct the film, had been the director of the stage play and Colin

Clive had played the lead on Broadway. Clive went on to play the title role in the original version of *Frankenstein*. *Journey's End* was David Manners' film debut. The movie was remade as *Aces High* (1976).

Joyeux Noel (2005) see *Merry Christmas* (2005)

The Kaiser, the Beast of Berlin (1918) / aka *Beast of Berlin*

Produced by Rupert Julian for Renowned Pictures[25] (United States). It was directed by Rupert Julian and written by Julian and Elliott Clawson. Cinematography by Edward Kull. This 70-minute silent, black and white film, with English intertitles, starred Rupert Julian, Elmo Lincoln, Nigel De Brulier, Lon Chaney, Harry von Meter, Harry Carter, Joseph W. Girard, Alfred Allen, C.E. Anderson, W.H. Bainbridge, Henry A. Barrows, F. Beauregard, Walter Belasco, Betty Carpenter, Edward Clark, Ruth Clifford, Wallace Coburn, F. Corcoran, Orlo Eastman, Mark Fenton, Robert Gordon, Winter Hall, Wadsworth Harris, Georgie Hupp, Ruby Lafayette, Frankie Lee, Jack MacDonald, General Hans von Beseler, Zoe Rae, Allan Sears, Jay Smith, Pedro Sose, and Gretchen Lederer.

Story: In the town of Louvain, Belgium, blacksmith Marcus (Elmo Lincoln) lives with his grandmother (Ruby Lafayette), his son Jean (Georgie Hupp), and his daughter Gabrielle (Ruth Clifford). Far away in Berlin lives Kaiser William II of Germany (Rupert Julian). When the Kaiser is in a foul mood, Captain von Wohlbold (Allan Sears) is driven to anger and he strikes the Kaiser. In an effort to atone for his actions and the disgrace he faces, he kills himself. Shortly afterwards the Kaiser announces his intention to invade Belgium. In Belgium, Marcus tries to dispel the fears of his community by telling them there is a treaty of neutrality signed with the Germans that will protect them. But of course it does not, and troops march into Louvain. When a German soldier seizes Gabriel, March kills the soldier and throws the body into a building. The passenger ship *Lusitania* is sunk and the captain responsible is given a special medal. But the man himself is heartbroken over his actions and he goes mad. As a result of the sinking, the president of the United States orders troops to Germany. When the Kaiser recognizes what is happening, he is frightened and ends the war. Somehow the Kaiser becomes a prisoner of the Belgians.

Military Correlation: Spotty

Comment: A highly anti–German film, this was designed to show the greed of the German leadership, the height of the mistrust among his own people as well as among the members of the armed forces, and to provide a highly fantastic prediction about how the war will end. Billed as an "expose of the Kaiser's intimate life," it really does not deliver."[26] In fact, it tells us very little about the ruler of Germany. The degree of incredibility runs high and the context is somewhat shaky. It was considered a great commercial success; it is claimed that more than 14,000 patrons saw the film during the first week in Omaha, Nebraska. The film is on the AFI's lost film list and is identified as one of the Ten Most Wanted films. Rupert Julian was so well received for his portrayal of the Kaiser that he repeated it in several films. In their advertising for the film, theatres boasted that "all pro–Germans will be admitted free." In 1919 a short parody came out called *The Geezer of Berlin*. There are no known prints of this film available.

The Kaiser's Finish (1918)

Produced by Warner Brothers, States Rights Production Company (United States) It was directed by Jack Harvey and written by Harvey and Cliff P. Saum. Cinematography by Rial Schellinger. This eight-reel, silent, black and white film, with English intertitles, starred Earl Schenck, Claire Whitney, Percy Standing, Louis Dean, John Sunderland, Fred Hearn, Charles Parr, Philip Van Loan, Billie Wagner, and Victor De Linsky.

Story: The Kaiser (Louis Dean) is planning to start a war and believes that he will eventually own the Unites States. He sends his bastard son (Earl Schenck) to live in America; he is adopted by the family of Robert Busch (Percy Standing). The young man grows up thinking he is a Busch; he is astounded to learn he is the son of the Kaiser. He realizes that he has no ties to Germany and has come to love his adopted home and determines to come to its aid. Returning to Germany, he signs up with the American Secret Service. Taking advantage of the fact that he looks like the Kaiser, he is able to gain entry to the most secret places and manages to blow up both the Kaiser and the German Military Staff. The movie ends after he delivers a long lecture on the evils of Germany.

Military Correlation: None

Comment: This movie came out just before the end of the war. It would have been laughed at during any other period. It was so irrationally strained that it put constant pressure on credibility. That and the fact that it was not well acted nor produced made it one of the poorer WWI movies. It was not well received by even the most patient movie buffs. Warner Brothers' first distribution film, it was not a commercial success.

The Kaiser's Last Sequel (1919)
see *Yankee Doodle in Berlin* (1919)

The Kaiser's New Dentist (1918)

Produced and distributed by Celebrated Players, Fox Pathe, B.F. Production Company (United States). Directed by Harry Conway "Bud" Fisher, Raoul Barre and Charles Bowers, it was written by Fisher, based on the Mutt and Jeff comic series. Animation by Dick Huemer. The 7-minute silent, black and white film starred Augustus J. Mutt and Edgar Horace Jeff.

Story: The Mutt and Jeff shorts were shown prior to a feature film.
Military Correlation: None

The Kaiser's Shadow (1918)

Produced by Thomas H. Ince, Thomas H. Ince Corporation, Famous Players–Lasky, Paramount Pictures (United States). Directed by Roy William Neill (as R. William Neill) and written by Octavus Roy Cohen and J.U. Glesy based on a series of magazine articles ("The Triple Cross") by Cohen. Photography by John Stumar. The 50-minute silent black and white film, with English intertitles, starred Dorothy Dalton, Thurston Hall, Edward Cecil, Leota Lorraine, Otto Hoffman, and Charles K. French.

Story: Clement Boyd (Edward Cecil) invents a new rifle that he believes will end the war immediately. But on his wedding day to Dorothy Robinson (Dorothy Dalton), he is kidnapped by a German spy named Paula Harris and whisked off to the home of master spy William Kremlin (Charles K. French). Their plan is to steal the invention and to execute him. Another spy, Hugo Wagner (Thurston Hall), appearing to be equally bad, takes Dorothy to witness Charles' interrogation. Things are looking pretty bad. Boyd is about to be injected with bacteria when the true colors of the Secret Service team of Paula Harris and Hugo Wagner are shown. The master spy tries to escape and is chased by Hugo but his gun jams and it is up to Paula to shoot him. When all is said and done, the invention is safe.

Military Correlation: Poor

Comment: Another "Secret Service saves the day" film that came out just as the war was ending and as interest was diminishing. Ince made dozens of these fast and furious films relying on the power of the war and the worn-out dialogue, and most were commercial if not artistic success. This one was poorly and quickly done.

The Kaiser's Spies (1914)

Produced by J. B. Davidson, Kinematograph Trading Company (United States). Directed by Charles Raymond and written by Harry Blythe and Raymond. It is believed to be based on a pulp fiction work by William Le Queux, *Spies of the Kaiser*. The silent black and white film starred Philip Kay and Lewis Carlton.

Story: All that is known is the brief description left over from a sales effort: "An entomologist runs a spy ring made up of bus drivers working in the Eppin Forest."

Military Correlation: Unknown

Comment: This presumably lost film gives every indication of being a formula picture that takes advantage of the natural darkness of the silent black and white films to provide an atmosphere for secret activities and betrayal.

The Kid Who Couldn't Miss (1983) / aka Billy Bishop Goes to War

Produced by Adam Symansky, National Film Board (Canada), Public Broadcasting System (United States). Directed by Paul Cowan and written by John Gray, Eric Peterson and based on the musical *Billy Bishop Goes to War* by Gray. Cinematography by Paul Cowan. Music by Ben Low. This 79-minute black and white film starred William Hutt, Eric Peterson, Walter Borden, Cecil Knight, H.H. Asquith, Albert Bell, W.A. Bishop, Robert Borden, John Gray, and George Guynemer.

Story: Presented as a semi-documentary, this is an attempt to challenge the claims of Billy Bishop, World War I ace and Canadian national hero, the man the world believed had shot down the infamous Red Baron. The movie posits that the raid for which he was awarded the Victoria Cross did not happen. According to Bishop, on June 2, 1917, he made a solo raid on a German airfield for which he was awarded the Victoria Cross. In the film, his mechanic claims that the bullet holes in Bishop's plane were in such a tight cluster that they must have been fired from a fixed position on a non-moving plane and could not have been done as Bishop claimed.

Military Correlation: Poor

Comment: The evidence provided comes across much like that provided by "Ancient Aliens" documentaries where a string of maybes support some form of conclusions. This attack on a national hero followed the production of a musical *Billy Bishop Goes to War* and reflected the growing belief among historians that Bishop was not responsible for the downing of the Red Baron as claimed.[27] The Standing Committee on Social Affairs, Science and Technology (Canada) discounted the film as totally unfair. And they are right in that nothing in the film proves anything one way or the other. The movie, patched together from archival film, interviews, and staged situations, leaves a great deal to be desired. Michael Dorosh summed up the general response in 2013: "The NFB treatment of Canada's military history has been an international embarrassment, particularly due to the necessary intervention of other levels of government who have stepped in and had to reel in film-makers with an unabashed zeal for fabricating adverse stories about Canada's Service personnel." It is hard to understand why it was seen as important to make this movie or, if you were going to challenge the ace, why pick the far lesser accomplishment for which he is known. The story was told again, this time from the perspective of his granddaughter Diana, in the 2013 TV special *A Hero to Me: The Billy Bishop Story—World War I Canadian Ace*.

Kiddies in the Ruins (1918)

Produced by George Pearson, Jury Films, Welsh-Pearson Company (United States). Directed by George Pearson and written by Paul Gsell, Pearson and Francisque Poulbot and based on Poulbot's play *Les Grosses dans les Ruins*. Cinematography by M. Rollins. This three-reel, silent, black and white film, with English intertitles, stars Emmy Lynn, Hugh E. Wright, Georges Colin, Simone Prevost, Georges Merouze, and Berthe Jalabert.

Story: In the ruins of a war-torn French city, a group of orphans who live in the rubble come to the aid of Private Tommy (Hugh E. Wright). While the plot is very thin, the depiction of the conditions under which the children live were remarkable and opened a lot of eyes just as the war was ending and thoughts were turning to rebuilding. A very human picture.

Military Correlation: None

Comment: Put out just a few days after the Armistice was signed, this movie fit in well with the beginning of a changing mood about the "enemy." The nations of the world had to come together now to assure that peace could be established and the destruction of the war be reversed. The plight of the children was an issue that all nations needed to face.

King and Country (1964) / aka *For King and Country*

Production by Norman Priggen and Richard B. Goodwin (United Kingdom). It was directed by Joseph Losey and written by Evan Jones, J.L. Hodson, A. E. Housman, based on the play *Hamp* by John Wilson. Cinematography by David Cook. This 86-minute black and white film starred Dirk Bogarde, Tom Courtenay, Leo McKern, Barry Foster, Peter Copley, James Villiers, Vivian Matalon, Jeremy Spenser, Barry Justice, Keith Buckley, James Hunter, Jonah Seymour, Larry Taylor, Richard Arthure, Raymond Brody, Terry Palmer, Dan Cornwall, Brian Tipping, and David Cook.

Story: Amidst the horrors of World War I, an army private (Tom Courtney)—after spending three years at the front, being the only survivor of a unit, and shell shocked—leaves his post and starts to walk back to England. When stopped, he is accused of desertion and put on trial. Captain Hargraves (Dick Bogarde), assigned the job of defending him, has little interest. Hargraves is very arrogant concerning this simple-minded boy who he believes is a deserter and should be punished. But in time he begins to learn that there is more to the story and begins to side with his client. But he is aware that the military requires that an example be made of the man and does not interfere with the order of execution when it is given. When the execution is carried out, the gunshots fail to kill the young private and Captain Hargraves is forced to shoot him with his revolver.

Military Correlation: Good

Comment: It takes place primarily in a dark trench holding area and is acted very much like it was a stage play. Most reviewers described it as a non-stop emotional experience in which they watched the human spirit being crushed and innocence lost due to the mechanical cruelties of war. There is nothing in the film to provide a saving grace for the military attitude being expressed at the time or for those driven insane by the turmoil of battle. The treatment and mistreatment of shell-shocked soldiers is a subject often hovering in the background of World War I movies but it is rarely openly addressed as it is in this film. While the message is an important one, the momentum of the movie slows to a crawl and, unfortunately the ending, while meant to be dramatic, is something of a fizzle.

King of Hearts (1966)

Produced by Philippe de Broca, Les Production Artistes Associe (France), United Artists (United States). Directed by Philippe de Broca and written by Daniel Boulanger and Maurice Bessy. Cinematography by Pierre Lhomme. This 102-minute movie stars Alan Bates, Jacques Baultin, Daniel Boulanger, Pierre Brasseur, Jean-Claude Brialy, Genevieve Bujold, Pier Paolo Capponi, Adolfo Celi, Francoise Christophe, Madeleine Clervanne, Marc Dudicourt, Julien Guiomar, Palau, Micheline Presle and Michel Serrault.

Story: A Scot private, ornithologist Charles Plumpick (Alan Bates), is mistaken by the army for an explosives expert. When word comes from the French Resistance that the Germans have planted a bomb at a weapons cache in a nearby town, he is sent by the outlandish British Colonel Alexander MacBibernbrook (Adolfo Celi) to defuse it. Bewildered, he travels to the French town of Mariville but discovers that the Germans are not all gone. The village people have all disappeared but when the Germans see Plumpick, they chase him. Seeking a place to hide, he comes upon the village insane asylum. The inmates there greet him with great joy and, having decided he is the King of Hearts, they conduct an elaborate inauguration. Believing that he must help them escape before the bomb goes off, Plumpick makes an effort to lead them out of the village, but they will not take him seriously and frolic about in a variety of costumes they have acquired. When he tries to leave he is kidnapped by friends of the beautiful Coquelicot (Genevieve Bujold), who has fallen in love with him. While tied up, he watches in the distance while the Germans and British fight it out over the empty village. It's hard to tell which of those involved are really the insane ones. The final scene shows a nude Plumpick carrying a birdcage and walking up to the asylum door demanding that he be admitted.

Military Correlation: Helpful

Comment: *King of Hearts* was marketed as a comedy and in most respects it comes off that way but there is a very interesting underlying message concerning both the insanity of war and the acceptance of life by the insane. The ending was predictable but that does not diminish its impact. Audiences laughed but it was not the hearty laughter of the light-hearted. The film is well staged, particularly the soft love of the insane Coquelicot and the happy inmates singing and dancing in the streets.

Bloopers: One must wonder: When Plumpick suddenly decides to climb to the top of the blockhouse, where does the ladder suddenly come from.

Kultur (1918)

Produced by William Fox, Victory Pictures, Fox Film Corporation (United States). Directed by Edward J. LeSaint and written by Fred Myton and J. Grubb

Alexander. Cimematography by Friend F. Baker. This six-reel, silent, black and white film with English intertitles starred Gladys Brockwell, Georgia Woodthorpe, William Scott, Willard Louis, Charles Clary, Nigel de Brulier, William Burress, and Al Fremont.

Story: Countess Griselda von Arenburg (Gladys Brockwell) is the mistress of the old Emperor Franz Josef (Alfred Fremont). His son, the Archduke Ferdinand (Charles Clary), hates the woman and makes every effort to get rid of her. She rebels and makes the first move: She convinces Danilo (Nigel de Brulier), one of her fanatical admirers, to assassinate the Archduke. She knows she can avoid implication in the crime through the intervention of Baron von Zeller (Willard Louis), who is also in love with her and willing to do anything. He has figured out that since Danilo is a Serb, and given the ethnic hatred that exists, he and the Serbian people will be held accountable. In the meantime, secret agent Rene de Bornay (William Scott) arrives from France to investigate. The countess, redirecting her affection, falls in love with him almost at once. When war is declared he is suddenly in danger and she manages to save him from being taken prisoner. While he is escaping, the countess is shot for protecting him.

Military Correlation: Poor

Comment: A highly fictionalized melodrama where historical facts are used as tools much like an alternative history. It is well scripted and certainly provides an interesting twist on world history, but there is not much meat on the bone. The unusual plot provides some opportunities for clever film work that does not materialize.

Lafayette Escadrille (1958) / aka **Hell Bent on Glory**

Produced and distributed by Warner Brothers (United States). Directed by William A. Wellman and written by Albert Sidney Fleishmann and Wellman. Cinematography by William H. Clothier. Music by Leonard Rosenman. This black and white film starred Tab Hunter, Etchika Choureau, Will Hutchins, Paul Fix, Jody McCrea, Clint Eastwood, Brett Halsey, Raymond Bailey, William Wellman, Jr., Denny Devine, Ralph Guldahl, Sam Boghosian, Veola Vonn, Robert Hoover, Tom Laughlin, Henry Nakamura, and David Janssen.

Story: Spoiled kid Thad Walker (Tab Hunter) gets in trouble at home in Boston and escapes to France where he hopes he can join the French Foreign Legion. Once overseas he and some friends join up with the Lafayette Escadrille. His friends include "Dude" Sinclair (David Janssen), Dave Pugtman (Will Hutchins), Tom Hitchcock (Jody McCrea) and Bill Wellman (William Wellman, Jr.). While in training, Walker falls in love with prostitute Renee Beauieu (Etchika Choureau). She loves him and decides to reforms in order to help him. Walker, who was repeatedly hit by his father when he was young, does not do well with authority. A French officer strikes Walker, and Walker knocks him down. He runs to avoid capture and goes into hiding at the brothel of the Madam (Veola Vonn). He begins working there hoping to raise enough money for he and Renee to go to

South America. But when he sees his companions he realizes that he belongs in the army. When the United States enters the war he pleads with the military command to let him join the American Air Service. They incredibly agree and he soon becomes an ace and then is free to return to France with his companions to marry Renee.

Military Correlation: Spotty

Comment: Wellman had served with the American Ambulance Service and then with the Lafayette Escadrille where he had three kills and won the Croix de Guerre with two palms. The companions were all based on men he had known in the squadron. But this film did not turn out the way that he had wanted. The budget was too small for the task, and actor Tab Hunter was out of place. The air scenes were cut to a minimum. James Garner had a walk-on part as Lufberry. The original ending had Walker killed but there was so much criticism that the end was rewritten, making it even weaker. The acting was flat, the plot mediocre, the dialogue silly and the romance irrelevant. As it was, the Lafayette Escadrille veterans disassociated themselves from the movie saying it was Pollyanna and reflected poorly on their service.

The Land That Time Forgot (1975)

Produced by John Dark and Samuel Z. Arkoff, Amicus Productions, American International Pictures (United States). Directed by Kevin Connor and Allan James. It was written by James Cawthorn and Michael Moorcock and based on a 1924 novel of the same name by Edgar Rice Burroughs. Cinematography by Alan Hume, Charles Staffel, Derick Browne, Mike Frift and George Robertson. Music by Douglas Gamley. This 90-minute Technicolor film starred Doug McClure, John McEnery, Susan Penhaligon, Kieth Barron, Anthony Ainley, Declan Mulholland, Godfrey James, Byron Story, Roy Holder, Ben Howard, Brian Hall, Andrew McCullouch, Colin Farrell, Grahame Mallard, Bobby Parr, Ron Pember, Andrew Lodge, Stanley McGreagh, Peter Sproule and Steven James.

Story: Survivors from a World War I merchant ship sunk by a U-boat are taken aboard a German submarine. After some time, Bowen Tyler (Doug McClure) and Captain Bradley (Keith Barron) take over the sub. Finally they discover and land on an island called Caprona. They realize that the island reflects several levels of evolution that are going on at the same time. This means that there are not only several species of prehistoric animals (dinosaurs and the like) but also types of human characters. With the aid of the lovely Lisa Clayton (Susan Penhaligon), the crew fights a variety of battles with animals and ancestors and survives.

Military Correlation: Poor

Comment: Hardly a remarkable film and only peripherally a World War I film but the directors make quite a point of the war. It is made even more difficult to believe by the poor use of model submarines and animals portrayed by puppets worked by strings rather than stop motion.

Landing a Spy (1918)

Produced and distributed by American Pathe, B. F. Production Company (United States). Directed by Harry Conway "Bud" Fisher, Raoul Barre and Charles Bowers, it was written by Fisher based on the Mutt and Jeff comic series. Animation by Dick Huemer. The seven-minute silent black and white film starred Augustus J. Mutt and Edgar Horace Jeff.

Story: Edgar Horace Jeff (always called Jeff) and his friend Mutt join the Army to fight the Kaiser, this time dealing with spies.

Military Correlation: None

Comment: This was one of more than 300 such films made by Fisher's company between 1913 and 1926 and one of ten that focuses on World War I.

The Last Volunteer (1914)

Produced and distributed by Pathe Freres Electric Film Company (France). Directed by Oscar Apfel. This 74-minute silent black and white film, with English intertitles, starred Robert Broderick, Paul Panzer, Eleanor Woodruff, Edward Hoyt, A.H. Barstar, Mary Gray, Doc Crane, and Irving Cummings.

Story: Katrina (Eleanor Woodruff), the young daughter of a European innkeeper, doubles as an anarchist. Despite her fierce anti-royalist feelings she falls in love with a German prince, Ludwig of Saxe-Thunberg (Irving Cummings) who arrives at her inn traveling incognito. She discovers two spies planning an attack and with the aid of her brother Roalf (Doc Crane) kills one of them. It turns out he was the Austrian ambassador (Paul Panzer). Even though she confesses her crime to Marshall Von Trump (Robert Broderick), the politician is determined to execute Roalf in order to appease the angry Austrians. She is able to convince the Marshall not to execute her brother but the Austrians, as anticipated, declare war over the incident. When war breaks out she discovers the prince's true identify, and must decide where she will place her loyalty. In the end she chooses to cast her lot with her heart, the prince and his country. As the enemy advances toward her town, she becomes a hero by signaling the advance of oncoming troops. In the final battle she gives her life to save that of her lover, the prince.

Military Correlation: Helpful

Comment: This was filmed early enough in the period of the war that an English-speaking company was able to produce something that showed the German people, and its military, in such a favorable light. But even this early tolerance could not make up for the incredible nature of the plot and the stagnant moments that permeate the film. It was not well-received.

Lawrence of Arabia (1962)

Produced by Sam Spiegel and Horizon Pictures, Columbia Pictures (United Kingdom). Directed by David Lean and written by Michael Wilson and Robert Bolt,

A playbill for *Lawrence of Arabia* (courtesy Center for the Study of the Korean War, Independence, Missouri).

based on T.E. Lawrence's *The Seven Pillars of Wisdom*. Cinematography by Freddie A. Young. Music by Maurice Jarre. This 222-minute Super Panavision film starred Peter O'Toole, Claude Rains, Jack Hawkins, Arthur Kennedy, Anthony Quinn, Omar Sharif, I.S. Johar, Gamil Ratib, Alex Guinness, Jose Ferrer, Michel Ray, John Dimech, Zia Mohyeddin, Harry Fowler, Anthony Quayle, Donald Wolfit, Peter Burton, Hugh Miller, Ferando Sancho, Stuart Saunders, Jack Gwillim, Kenneth Fortescue, Jack Hedley, Henry Oscar, John Ruddock, Norman Rossington, and Howard Marion-Crawford.

Story: The movie is based on the real-life experience of British soldier T. E. Lawrence (Peter O'Toole) who served in Cairo in 1916. It covers the follies of colonialism and the hypocrisies of war in stark relief with few punches pulled. Lawrence is a spy sent to gather information on Prince Faisel (Alec Guinness), leader of the Allied Arabs. The plan established by the French and the British was designed to turn the Arabs against the Turks at Aquaba in return for their freedom after the war. During the course of the film we realize that the dream of Arabian unity dissolves following the fall of Damascus, the taking of the port city of Aquaba, the no-prisoner massacre at Tafas and the capture, torture, and rape of Lawrence at Daraa. The film displayed not only the military and political problems of the time, but the conflicts of powerful and often dishonorable men. Lawrence himself was tormented by the change that occurred in him after his own act of killing and the massacre of Turkish soldiers, as well as the growing question of his loyalty that he acknowledges is divided between his mother country and the adopted one. The politics of empire are laid bare in all their dishonesty.

Albert Finney was a contender to play Lawrence. Montgomery Clift wanted the part but they finally went with O'Toole whose "eyes had an astonishing poetry in them" (producer Sam Spiegel). The part of Prince Faisel was originally offered to Laurence Olivier but he was not available. Michael Wilson was the original screenwriter but he and the director fought over dialogue and he resigned; Robert Bolt took his place. The role of the reporter was given to Arthur Kennedy after Edmond O'Brian suffered a heart attack after doing some on-camera work. The director, cinematographer and film won Academy Awards. One critic described it as "just a huge thundering camel opera." The film was banned in most Arabic countries and has never been shown in Turkey. It was placed on the National Film Registry in 1991.

Bloopers: While a wonderful film and masterfully done, it needs to be criticized for its outlandish misrepresentation of the historical situation. For anyone interested in the historical events, the timeline in the film is way off. Heavy with historical characters, it is deeply fictionalized, making any attempt to justify it with known historical events impossible. Notice the foam rubber that O'Toole used to soften his camel saddle; it can be seen in several shots.

Legion of the Condemned (1928)

Produced by Jesse L. Lasky, E. Lloyd Shelton, William A. Wellman and Adolph Zukor, Paramount–Famous Lasky (United States). Directed by William A. Wellman and written by John Monk Saunders, Jean de Limur and George Marion, Jr.

Cinematography by Henry W. Gerrard. This 80-minute silent black and white film starred Fay Wray, Gary Cooper, Barry Norton, Lane Chandler, Francis McDonald, George Voya, Freeman Wood, Albert Conti, Charlotte Bird, E.H. Calvert, Joe Darensbourg, Satchel McVea, and Toto Guette.

Story: Four young men from a variety of walks of life, all running away from something or someone, are in the service of the French air squadron Lafayette Escadrille. While on a mission to deliver a spy, the hero Gale Price (Gary Cooper) remembers past events in his life as a flyer. Among these is the fact that he found his sweetheart Christina Charteris (Fay Wray) in the arms of a German officer. He believed she was really a German spy and just plying him for information. He then realizes that his passenger, who he has picked up to deliver on a secret mission, is in fact Christine who, it turns out, is a French agent being sent on a dangerous mission. Before she can explain it all to him, they land and are caught by the Germans and sentenced to die. The execution is halted when the members of the Lafayette Escadrille bomb the area, and then help all involved to escape unharmed.

Military Correlation: Good

Comment: Produced as a follow-up to *Wings*, this film contained much of *Wings'* flying combat footage and some that was not seen in *Wings*. But *Legion* is not as good a movie as *Wings*. Gary Cooper is showing some of the promise of later films but still spends a lot of time in this movie deadpan as if he does not know what is going on. Fay, who went on to become known as a "scream queen" because of her success in horror films, is much better (and far better-looking). *Legion* is considered a lost film. There is a 1928 Grosset-Dunlap book with Gary Cooper and Fay Wray on the cover that looks like a promotional piece and has a lot of information about the film.

The film is a good example of the extended plot, which in so many of these films entailed the presence of a spy. As if the war itself was not enough, or the romance generated not all that satisfying, it was felt necessary to throw in an element of betrayal, or at least suspected betrayal. This subplot was so well defined that it became a formula production around which films were constructed. The spy element was usually poorly explained and simplistic. If they represented the abilities of the real spies, the nation was in no danger.

Lest We Forget (1918) / aka *N'oublion Jamais*

Produced by Giuseppe de Cippico (Italy) and Rita Jolivet Film Corporation, Screen Classics (United States). Directed and written by Leonce Perret. This eight-reel silent black and white film, with English intertitles, starred Rita Jolivet, Hamilton Revelle, L. Rogers Lytton, Kate Blancke, Cliff Saum, Emil Roe, Henry Smith, Gaby Perrier, Texas Cooper, H.P. St. Leger, Ernest Maupain, Edward Gerstle, Dolores Cassinelli, and Georges Flateau.

Story: This semi-documentary–style film focused on the U-boat sinking of the ocean liner *Lusitania* in 1915 and it does it well. But not willing to leave it at that, the director has the heroine Rita Herolt (Rita Jolivet) be captured by the Germans and sentenced to be executed by firing squad ("No blindfold if you please"). Escaping from that situation, she goes in search of her fiancé Harry Winslow (Hamilton Revelle), who has also survived the sinking and been captured. She manages to help him escape but in the process somehow makes him suspicious that she has developed pro–German sympathies. Deeply hurt and determined to prove otherwise, she corrects this image in a dramatic episode where she strangles a Prussian baron with a bed sheet. Pretty thin.

Military Correlation: Helpful

Comment: Rita Jolivet was actually someone who did survive the sinking of the ocean liner *Lusitania*. The film was produced by her husband in an effort for her to tell her story. The portrayal of the sinking is one of the best pieces of special effects in these early films. The unnecessary sinking, the many deaths, the innocence of those aboard is all fit around the emphasis on the brutality (even inhumanity) of the Germans. The rest of the story is meaningless, totally unhistorical, and irrational. They weakened the amazing story by the addition of vast amounts of fiction.

Letters of the Great War (2004)

Produced and distributed California State University. Directed and written by Charles R. Ortiz. This 20-minute color film stars Bill Billions, Lain Hanna, and Jeremy Thorsen

Story: A short film, told in documentary form, it is basically the reading of letters from a World War I American soldier.

Military Correlation: Helpful

Lieutenant Pimple and the Stolen Submarine (1914)

Produced by Folly Films, Phoenix (United Kingdom) It was directed by Fred Evans and written by Fred and Joe Evans. This 14-minute silent, black and white film, with English intertitles, starred the comedy team of Joe Evans and Fred Evans.

Story: One in a series of Pimple movies, this depicts Lieutenant Pimple (Fred Evans) posing as a diver in order to rescue men from a sunken submarine. The only thing funny about it is the blatantly, unashamedly fake special effects. It was billed as an American sailor daydreaming his way through a series of submarine adventures but it is primarily slapstick. It could have taken place anywhere.

Military Correlation: None

Comment: There were more than 100 of these Pimple comedies that parodied what was happening at the time, in this case the growing rivalry in the naval expansion between Germany and Great Britain. Much of the film is reminiscent of the later work produced by Monty Python and they made just about the same amount of sense.

The Life and Death of Colonel Blimp (1943) / aka Colonel Blimp

Produced by Michael Powell and Emeric Pressburger, Richard Vervon, Archer, United Artists, Independent Film Production (United Kingdom). Directed and written by Michael Powell and Emeric Pressburger, based (at least the title) on the same-name comic strip by David Lee. Photography by Georges Perinal. Music by Allan Gray. This 163-minute Technicolor film starred Roger Livesey, Deborah Kerr, Anton Walbrook, Roland Culver, James McKechnie, David Hutcheson, Ursula Jeans, John Laurie, Harry Welchmen, Reginald Tate, A.E. Matthews, Carl Jaffe, Dennis Arundell, James Knight, Spencer Trevor, Neville Mapp, Vincent Holeman, and Valentine Dyall.

Story: Major General Clive Wynne-Candy (Roger Livesey), a lovable, blustery, rotund British officer, is captured in a training exercise and held in a Turkish bath. While there he remembers his forty years of adventures in a series of epochs that deal with the Boer War and World War I and Two. The old soldier has survived three awful wars and three aggressive women, all played by Deborah Kerr.

Military Correlation: Good

Comment: Comic and romantic, this movie was not well received by either the British government or the English people. It was re-released in 1983 to a much better reception. It is an interesting chronology of the character of warfare in the twentieth century. Powell wanted Laurence Olivier to play the lead but Olivier was on active service with the Navy and Winston Churchill would not allow him to be released to make the film because he did not want a well-known actor to play the part of a blustering, probably incompetent British officer. The director's decision to go with Deborah Kerr came only after his first choice turned up on the set pregnant. The movie was disapproved of by the British Government on the grounds that it made fun of the British Army. It inspired the book *The Shame and Disgrace of Colonel Blimp* by E.W. and M. M. Robson, who saw it as a mockery.

While the title came from a comic strip, the idea emerged from a discussion while filming *Wings*, in which it was said, "You don't know what it is like to be old." This film does not tell us what it is like, but provides some potential illustrations. The credits for the major characters were sewn into a tapestry like pictures on a scroll (they were done by the Royal Council on Needlework). At the end of the film it scrolls down a tapestry on which is written in Latin "Sic transit Gloria Candy" that translates into "Thus Passeth Away the Glory of Candy." The film suggests that the term "concentration camp" first appeared in South Africa during the Boer War (1899–1902).

Film critic Roger Ebert wrote that this movie transformed "a blustering pigheaded caricature into one of the more lovable of all movie characters." Sociologist E.W. Robson, a member of the Sidneyan Society, called it a "highly elaborate, flash, flabby and costly film, the most disgraceful production that has ever emanated from a British film studio." Michael Powell called it a 100 percent British film "but it's photographed by a Frenchman, it's written by a Hungarian, the musical score is by a German Jew, the director was English, the man who did the costumes was a Czech; in other words, it was the kind of film that I've always worked on with a mixed crew of every nationality, no frontiers of any kind."[28]

Bloopers: In the colonel's account of imprisonment by the Boers, he says he was held for seven months in one scene and seven weeks in another.

The Light of Victory (1919) / aka *The Renegade; The Island of Adventure*

Produced and distributed by Blirdbird Photoplay, Universal Film Manufacturing Company (United States). It was directed by William Wolbert and written by George C. Hull and Waldemar Young. Cinematography by Harry B. Harris. This 53-minute silent black and white film, with English intertitles, starred Andrew Robson, Fred Kelsey, Norval MacGregor, Beatrice Dominquez, George Nichols, Betty Compson, Monroe Salisbury, Bob Emmons, and Fred L. Wilson.

Story: An alcoholic young American naval officer (Monroe Salisbury) has been court martial for losing a code book containing vital documents. In the process of his drunken decline he also loses the love of his fiancée. The navy apparently feels he should take his own life, and when he does not do so, they exile him to a distant island called Tafofu. While there he meets a native girl and they stay together until even she cannot take him any more. A second girl helps him get control over his drinking and he begin to regain some of his self-dignity. In the meantime, his original girlfriend decides she really does love him, drink or not, and tries to follow him. She is a passenger on a ship heading to his island when it is hit by a German submarine and sunk. She manages to get to Tafofu where she discovers her lover has become a changed man. He aids in the sinking of a German U-boat but in his heroic exploits he is eventually killed by the Germans.

Military Correlation: Poor

Comment: This is an example of the movie trade at its sloppiest. It's a formula production where the formula simply does not work. There is no justification for the behavior of the characters, no credibility in the actions taken or the events that happen, and little if any interest in the characters themselves. Surrounded by the characters we met, it is no wonder that the naval officer turned to drink.

The Lighthorsemen (1987)

Produced by Jon Bladier, Australian Film Company, FGH Film (Victoria, Australia). Directed by Simon Wincer and written by Ian Jones. Cinematography by Dean Semler. Music by Mario Millo. This 131-minute color film starred Di O'Connor, Anthony Andrews, John Walton, Gary Sweet, Jon Blake, Bill Kerr, John Larking, Peter Phelps, Nick Waters, John Haywood, Shane Briant, Ralph Cotterill, Grant Piro, Tony Bonner, Seage Larzareff, and Tim McKenzie.

Story: Palestine, 1917: The British advance is stopped by the Turks; the attack on Gaza has failed. Facing the Turks along a line from Gazal to Beersheba is a regiment of Australian Mounted infantry, the Lighthorse. Dave Mitchell (Peter Phelps), an excellent shot, is reluctant to fire at the enemy. He finally proves himself during an air attack where he was wounded by a strafing plane. He goes to the hospital where he meets nurse Anne (Sigrid Thorton) and they quickly fall in love. When he returns to the front line he and the rest of the unit are faced with the challenge of breaking the Turkish line.

Military Correlation: Excellent

Comment: Probably the best cavalry charge ever recorded on film: long, harsh, emotional—and foolhardy. The horses play a significant role in this film and a good portion of the movie shows not only the care and feeling of the animals, but the relationship they establish with the men. There was a fair share of "Pommy bashing" and more than enough clichés. Segments of the film appear in the *Young Indiana Jones Chronicles*. Joan Blake was injured in an auto accident on the last day of filming.

Lilac Time (1928) / aka *Love Never Dies*

Produced by George Fitzmaurice and John McCormick, Vitaphone, First National Pictures (United States). Directed by George Fitzmaurice and Frank Lloyd (uncredited) and written by Carey Wilson, Jane Cowl, George Marion, Jr., Jane Murfin, Willis Goldbeck, and Adela Rogers St. Johns, based on the novel *Lilac Time* by Guy Fowler. Cinematography by Sidney Hickox. Music by Nathanel Shilkret and Cecil Copping. This 80-minute silent (with sound effects) black and white film starred Colleen Moore, Gary Cooper, Burr McIntosh, George Cooper, Cleve Moore, Kathryn McGuire, Eugenie Besserer, Jack Stoney, Emile Chautard, Dick Grace, Edward Dillion, Stuart Knox, Harlan Hilton, Richard Jarvis, Arthur Lake, Eddie Clayton, Dan Dowling, Philo McCullough, J. Gunnis Davis, Paul Hurst, Nelson McDowell, Harold Lockwood, and Jack Ponder.

Story: An English airfield is located in France's lilac fields next to a large farm owned by the Widow Berthelot (Eugenie Besserer). Her daughter Jeannine (Colleen Moore) is very interested in all the young men she sees at the airfield and in time they adopt her as a little sister and mascot. Captain Philip Blythe (Gary Cooper) at first hates her when she walks on the airfield where he is trying to land, but he falls in love with her when he sees her walking in the field of lilacs. When the pilots are all called away on a dangerous mission, Blythe promises her that he will return. He is wounded and crashes in the village. Philip and Jeannine are finally reunited and she nurses him back to health.

Military Correlation: Poor

Comment: The film was adapted from a play by the same name, which was also based on the novel by Guy Fowler. The play ran 176 performances on Broadway. Colleen Moore, who was the director's wife, provided a varied dramatic-romantic performance. Dice Grace, the head stunt pilot, had just finished filming *Wings* (1927) where we had been injured in a minor crash. Colleen Moore's brother played the role of Cleve and her cousin Eugenie Besserer was Madame Berthelot.

The Little American (1917)

Produced by Cecil B. DeMille, Mary Pickford Films, Jesse Lasky Studio (United States). Directed by Cecil B. DeMille and Joseph Levering (both uncredited), it was written by Jeanie Macpherson and DeMille (uncredited).[29] Cinematography by Alvin Wyckoff. This 80-minute silent black and white film, with English intertitles, starred Mary Pickford, Jack Holt, Raymond Hatton, Hobart Bosworth, Walter Long, James Neill, Ben Alexander, Guy Oliver, Edythe Chapman, Lillian Leighton, DeWitt Jennings, Bernard Niemeyer, Charles Macdonald, Wallace Beery, Olive Corbett, Lucile Dorrington, Clarence Geldart, Carl Gerard, Robert Gordon, Gordon Griffith, Norman Kerry, Ramon Novarro, Sam Robinson, Marian Swayne, Sam Wood, and Mrs. Allan Walker.

Story: On a ship of Americans heading to France is a young woman who agreed to help the French against the Germans. When she arrives she finds that the aunt that she had expected to live with has died, and that her lover has switched sides and is fighting for the Germans. Karl (Jack Holt) is not only drunk and evil but nearly rapes Angelia (Mary Pickford) when they first come together. He comes to his senses when another officer humiliates Angelia by making her pull off his muddy boot, and Karl defends her. Then Angelia is caught red-handed transmitting highly secret information about Germany to the Allies. Captured and found guilty, she is facing a firing squad when she escapes just in time. The French forces bombard the area. She also somehow gets Karl to America. One film historian describes it this way: "Although we have seen Germans torpedoing the ship of a neutral country, and killing the American women and children passengers on board, the raping of French civilians, and shooting old men, mothers and young children, and although we have even seen Karl beat her, betray her and nearly rape her, she still loves him and manages to bring him home and, we presume, marries him in the shadow of Lady Liberty."[30]

Military Correlation: Helpful

Comment: This is without question a propaganda film played out as a love story with a intertitles foretelling the many disasters; for example, "The shadow of coming events" is displayed in front of a throne-like chair with a royal person sitting in it and a German double eagle behind the chair. The next title suggests, "We shall not let a mere scrap of paper interfere with the vigorous advancement of prussianism."[31] There is a definite tone of *The Four Horsemen of the Apocalypse* in the film and the display of the German evilness is totally exaggerated. The sinking of the *Veritania* (read *Lusitania*) was remarkably filmed and was so realistic it caused injury to several extras.[32] Mary Pickford, it was discovered, could hardly swim.

Some scenes appear a little extreme even today. The German officer who opens his beer bottle by breaking off the neck is explained by the intertitles "Hunnish Efficiency." The fact that in the film none of the Germans have names, only ranks, was deliberately insulting.

The film received almost universal acceptance with the one significant exception being a criticism from Major Funkouser, a Chicago movie critic who wrote, "I cannot pass this picture because it would offend the Germans who live here and who did not start the war."[33] This is hard to understand considering the circumstances; it did not encounter this sort of criticism anywhere else. As a part of the promotion of this film, Pickford donated a fully equipped ambulance to the Red Cross for use overseas, then offered a second, and dedicated herself to maintaining the cost of their involvement. Her title "America's Sweetheart" was first used by the manager of the Grauman Theater in San Francisco in 1914 but Leslie Midkiff De Bauche provides evidence that it was not used consistently until the release of *The Little American* in 1917.[34] Mary Pickford who was absolutely beautiful on screen and who was always the star, was somewhat difficult to work with and sometimes referred to "Attila of Sunnybrook Farm." Wallace Beery made his debut in this film.

The Little Comrade (1917)
see *On Dangerous Ground* (1917)

Little Miss Hoover (1918)

Produced and distributed by Famous Players–Lasky Corporation, Paramount Pictures (United States) . Directed by John S. Robertson and written by Adrian Gil-Spear, based on the book *The Golden Bird* by Maria Thompson Davies. Cinematography by William Marshall. This 87-minute silent, black and white film, with English intertitles, starred Marguerite Clark, Alfred Hickman, Eugene O'Brien, Forrest Robinson, Hal Reid, Frances Kaye, J.M. Mason, John Tansey, Dorothy Walters, and John J. Williams.

Story: A rural romance with surprising characters and a heroine who is so naive that she does not know the rooster has a role in producing eggs. The rural simplicity is way overdone (shades of Ma and Pa Kettle in the 1940s) but the point is well made. It is focused on the highly significant role of the American farmer who was responsible for the production of food for the soldiers at the front and the starving Europeans.

Military Correlation: Helpful

Comment: Marginally a war film, this is a wonderful example of the "support the war front from at home" that was pushed by presidential hopeful Herbert Hoover (hence the title). The film reminds one of *Mrs. Wiggs of the Cabbage Patch* (1934). While little about her is known today, star Marguerite Clark was nearly as popular as Mary Pickford. In 1920 the Quigley Poll voted her the top female box office actress of the year.

The Little Patriot (1917)

Produced and distributed by Diando Pathe Films (United States). Directed by William Bertram and written by Lela E. Rogers and John W. Grey. Cinematography by William Norris. This 50-minute, silent, black and white film, with English intertitles, stars Marie "Baby" Osborne, Herbert Standing, Marian Warner, Jack Connolly, Frank Lanning, Florence Sottong, and Madge Evans.

Story: At the outbreak of war, Mary (Madge Evans) is inspired by stories of the French heroine Joan of Arc and determined to do what she can for the war effort. She organizes her young friends into a sort of a semi-military association designed to fight for freedom. In time they go to the aid of an old inventor (Herbert Standing) who believes that his new invention, an aerial torpedo that will change the nature of warfare, has been stolen by a gang of local German spies. The children manage to identify the spies, save the old man, and keep the invention out of the hands of the enemy. In the process it is discovered that the old man is really Mary's long-lost grandfather. The film ends with the family reunited.

Military Correlation: Spotty

Comment: The success of this film started a whole series of children's films of the *Emil and the Detectives* variety. While the ability of children to defeat the local bad guys is hard to believe, there seems to have been no difficulty in believing that every town in America possessed its own German spy ring intent on destroying us all.

Little Patriots (1917) see *The Volunteer* (1917)

The Littlest Scout (1919)

Film: Produced by J. Stuart Blackton Productions, Country Life Series, Independent Sales Corporation (United States). It was directed and written by Paula Blackton (aka Paula Dean). This silent, black and white film, with English intertitles, starred Paula Blackton, Charles Stuart Blackton, Violet Blackton, and William Bittne.

Story: Charles Stuart Wyngate, who is three, and her older sister Violet, who thinks she is a boy named Bill, want to be involved in the war and work with the Red Cross. They meet Harold at the playground, there is a fight and Charles hits Harold. Harold's father is a pacifist. Later, wearing scout uniforms, the children are kidnapped while playing near the waterfront. The Boy Scouts come to the rescue and the spies are captured. A German submarine is found and destroyed by gunboats.

Military Correlation: Poor

Comment: This totally unbelievable tale was scheduled to be released at the opening of Boy Scout Week but was delayed. Paula Blackton aka Paula Hilburn and Paula Dean was J. Stuart Blackton's wife and Charles Stuart Blackton and Violet Blackton were their children. The Roosevelt Boy Scout troops from Oyster Bay, New York, play the scouts in the film.

The Littlest Volunteer (1917) see *The Volunteer* (1917)

The Lone Wolf (1919) see *The False Face* (1919)

Lost at the Front (1927)

Produced by Frank Griffin, John McCormick Productions, First National Pictures (United States). Directed by Del Lord and written by Hampton Del Ruth, Frank Griffin, Clarence Hennecke and Ralph Spence. Photography by James Van Trees. This six-reel black and white movie starred George Sidney, Charles Murray, Natalie Kingston, John Kolb, Max Asher, Brooks Benedict, Ed Brady, Harry Lipman, Nita Martan, and Nina Romano.

Story: Despite their rivalry over Olga (Natalie Kingston), a beautiful local girl, Patrick (Charles Murray) and German bartender Adolph (Max Asher) are good friends. When Adolph is called back to Germany as an army reservist, he takes with him a wireless set that Patrick believes will hurt the Allied war effort. In order to stop the transfer, Patrick, too old for the American army, enlists in the Russian army. He meets up with Adolph on the border where they are stationed. At this point Patrick takes his friend prisoner. Then, to avoid the wrath of both armies, they disguise themselves as women. In that role they are conscripted into the infamous Russian Legion of Death. Just before going back into battle, the Armistice is signed and both men return to New York where they discover that Olga has married someone else in their absence.

Military Correlation: Poor

Comment. This film lacks whatever it is that makes a movie coherent. While sometimes a serious director, Del Lord was also the director of many of the Three Stooges shorts. This film was clever and well produced but lacked any content.

The Lost Battalion (2001)

Produced by David Craig, David Gerber, Avi Levy, Tom Reeve, Romain Schroeder and Michael Weisbarth, A & E Home Television Networks (United States). Directed by Russell Mulcahy and written by James Carabatson. Cinematography by Jonathan Freeman. Music by Richard Marvin. This 100-minute made-for-television film starred Ricky Schroder, Michael Brandon, Jamie Harris, Jay Rodan, Adam James, Daniel Caltagirone, Michael Goldstrom, Andre Vippolis, Rhys Miles Thomas, Arthur Kremer, Adam Kotz, Justin Scot, Anthony Azizi, George Calil, Wolf Kahler, Joachim Paul Assbock, Philip McKee, and Michael Brandon.

Story: In the closing days of the Great War, the United States 77th Infantry Division's 308th battalion, about 550 men, was surrounded by the Germans and cut off from supplies and communication near the Argonne Forest. Their leader, Major Charles W. Whittlesey (Rick Schroeder) had attacked that morning according to plan, while the French and British on both sides had failed to advance. At first the American artillery kept the Germans at bay but soon the shells were hitting the American lines. Despite dwindling supplies and constant bombardment and attacks by the assaulting German forces, they held on. One of the captured soldiers tried to explain to his German captors what they were up against: "a bunch of Mick, Dago, Polack, and Jew-boy gangsters from New York City. They will never surrender." The Americans refused to surrender and the attacks continued day after day. Finally an American pilot spotted the battalion from the air and called in a plea for help despite the fact he was badly wounded. After six more days of fighting, Allied reinforcements arrived and the men of the lost battalion were finally saved—but not before Whittlesey lets his commanders know how they have been mistreated.

Military Correlation: Excellent

Comment: A typical David and Goliath military story, it rises above many other films as a result of the accurate way it depicts an actual incident and the excellent manner in which the cinematography is handled. The pacing of the film makes the unit's wait for help understandable and the tensions within the ranks, as well as the dangers imposed by the enemy, are carefully matched. Many critics suggest that director Russell Mulcahy was trying to mimic Kubrick's style but it seems to stand on its own. It was nominated for three Emmy Awards, and won the Motion Picture Sound Editors Award.

Bloopers. While the historical accuracy is fairly high, there are some silly mistakes like the inclusion of Zippo lighters, a post–World War I invention. Some of the military dialogue is too modern to be accurate. When the troops turn up their boots, we see rubber soles, a much later development.

The Lost Patrol (1929)

Produced by Harry Bruce Woolfe, British Instructional Pictures (United Kingdom), Fox Film Corporation (United States). Directed by Summers. It was written by Walter Summers and Philip MacDonald, based on MacDonald's novel *Patrol*. This British-made silent black and white film stars Cyril McLaglen, Sam Wilkinson, Terence Collier, Arthur B. Woods, Hamilton Keern, Fred Dyer, Charles Emerald, Andrew McMaster, James Watts, John Valentine, and Frank Barker.

Story: A tense "hunt and seek" drama about twelve British cavalryman who are lost following a failed attack in the Mesopotamian desert during World War I. The film becomes the highly elongated story of how they were being followed and cut down by a determined unit of Arab sharpshooters. When his commander is killed, a soldier (Cyril McLaglen) takes over and tries to save some of the ragged survivors. The film features a series of flashbacks that identify each of the beleaguered soldiers and tell their part of the story.

Military Correlation: Good

Comment: Cyril McLaglen was the brother of Victor McLaglen who starred in the same role in the 1934 production of *The Lost Patrol*. The flashbacks routine is very much the same as used in the *Legion of the Condemned* though it is not as well done. Many of the flashback, in fact, seem totally out of place and generally unrelated to the progress of the film. The desert is well presented and there is a sense of both the heat and the distance, but the oasis looks more like a giant sandbox with kiddy pool.

The Lost Patrol (1934) / aka *Patrol*

Produced by Merian C. Cooper, John Ford Productions, RKO Radio Pictures (United States). It was directed by John Ford and written by Dudley Nichols and Garrett Fort, based on the novel *Patrol* by Philip MacDonald.[35] Music by Max Steiner. Cinematography by Harold Wenstrom. This 72-minute black and white film starred Victor McLaglen, Boris Karloff, Wallace Ford, Reginald Denny, J.M. Kerrigan, Sammy Stein, Alan Hale, Douglas Walton, Brandon Hurst, Paul Hanson, Howard Wilson, Neville Clark, and Billy Bevan.

Story: Twelve British cavalryman are lost in the Mesopotamian desert during World War I. Tracked and fired upon by a group of determined Arab soldiers, they are involved in a torturous journey across the massive desert where they must fight the heat, the thirst, and the loneliness as well as dealing with each other's emotions. They find brief salvation in an oasis before Arab sharpshooters begin cutting down their numbers. When the commander is killed, a reluctant sergeant takes over the small unit. By drawing straws, one of their number is selected to go for help but he is soon cut down. When the group has been reduced to three they are spotted by a pilot who is shot when he sets his plane down. The plane is set on fire and, as hoped the smoke signals others to come to their aid. Prior to the well-timed arrival of help, the remaining survivors, almost insane under the circumstances, are killed by Arabs. Only the sergeant is alive when help arrives. Somehow it seems pointless.

Military Correlation: Good

Comment: The conditions when making the film in Yuma, Arizona, were very harsh, the heat sometimes rising to more than 120 degrees. This led to delays causes by sickness among the crew. This is a remake of the 1929 silent film. Some critics feel that this is this movie that gave director John Ford an international reputation. Star Victor McLeglen was a member of the Irish Fusiliers in Mesopotamia during the World War I period covered by this movie. He is the brother of Cyril McLeglen, who played the sergeant in the 1929 version. The technical aspects of the film are much better than the earlier version but not enough to justify the remake.

The Love Light (1921)

Produced by Mary Pickford for the Mary Pickford Company (United States). It was directed and written by Frances Marion. Cinematography by Henry Cronjager and Charles Rosher This 89-minute, silent, black and white film starred Mary Pickford, Evelyn Dumo, Raymond Bloomer, Fred Thomson, Albert Prisco, George Regas, Eddie Phillips, and Jean de Briac.

Story: In Italy, Angela (Mary Pickford) lives in a lighthouse where she keeps the flame alive as long as her brothers (Jean de Briac and Eddie Phillips) are off fighting in the war. When she learns of the death of her older brother, she takes refuge in the arms of a man named Joseph (Fred Thomson) who identifies himself as an American; he has washed ashore apparently from a shipwreck. Soon the loving Joseph turns out to be a German spy who sends nightly messages to German ships. One of his messages had led to an attack on the ship that was bringing her younger brother home. With determination and loyalty Angela gives up her lover, turning him over to the angry villagers. During this time she fights for the protection of her newborn child and suffers through a shipwreck during a storm. In the end she seeks safety, lured on by love's light.

Military Correlation: Helpful

Comment: Mary Pickford was one of the original members of the United Artists group and co-founder of the American Motion Picture Academy of America. This was a different role for her. She had been "America's Sweetheart" for several years but about the time of this picture the nature of her beauty and allure changed, and in her movie roles she went from the sexy lady who had to win her man, to the alluring beauty that men must win. One contemporary critic identified this film as "a virtually stunning if somewhat overblown melodrama." The film had just about everything you could want from a movie: war, betrayal, love (both honest and unrequited), blindness, death, theft, disaster, and insanity.

Nat G. Devenish, an uncredited assistant director, was nearly killed in the scene that shows the destruction of a ship. The scene was shot off the coast of Monterey. Actor Fred Thompson died shortly after the completion of the film from tetanus complications.

Love Never Dies (1925) see *Lilac Time* (1925)

Love's Struggle (1918) see *Heart of the World* (1918)

Lucille Love: The Girl of Mystery (1914)

Produced and distributed by Thomas H. Ince Corp., Universal Gold, Universal Film Manufacturing Company (United States). It was directed by Francis Ford and written by Grace Cunard and Ford. This 300-minute serial was composed of 15 episodes. A silent black and white film, with English intertitles, it starred Grace Cunard, Francis Ford, Harry Schumm, Ernest Shields, Edgar Keller, Eddie Boland, Wilbur Higby, Burton Law, Jean Hathaway, William White, Harry L. Rattenberry, Lionel Bradshaw, Louise Glaum, and John Ford.

Story Heroine Lucille Love (Grace Cunard) and her sidekick Hugo Loubeque (Francis Ford) share adventures designed to rival the success of Pearl White's short films. Basically it is a western but part of the story deals with World War I.

Military Correlation: None

Comment: Several of the scenes come from the 1914 silent film serial *The Girl of Mystery*. It was never a serious contender for Pearl White–level success.

Eight episodes (2, 3, 6, 8, 10, 12, 13 and 14) of *Lucille Love* survive and can be found at the Library of Congress. In 1920 an effort was made to use the film already shot and produce a feature-length film called *The Woman of Mystery*.

Lucky Star (1929)

Produced by William Fox, Fox Film Corporation. Directed by Frank Borzage and written by John Hunter Booth, Sonya Levien, Tristram Tupper, and M.H. Caldwell, based on the short story "Three Episodes in the Life of Timothy Osborn" by Tristan Tupper. Cinematography by Charles Lyons and William Cooper Smith. Music by Christopher Caliendo. This 90-minute mixed sound and silent, black and white film starred Janet Gaynor, Charles Farrell, Paul Fix, Hedwigs Reicher, Gloria Grey, Billy O'Brien, Jack Pennick, Delmar Watson, Guinn "Big Boy" Williams, and Hector Sarno.

Story: A poor farm girl (Janet Gaynor) living a simple life meets Tim (Charles Farrell) just before he is called into service. He is wounded while in Europe and loses the use of his legs. While the two are powerfully attracted to one another, Tim believes that his physical handicap means he should not declare his love for her. He tells any who will listen that she should be allowed to make a life of her own. The plot thickens when Tim's former sergeant (Guinn "Big Boy" Williams), a bully, meets Janet and takes a liking to her. Now Tim must fight for his girl.

Military Correlation: Poor

Comment: This was considered by some early reviewers to be one of "Hollywood's greatest romances." This is a tag line that was often used by the promoters but this time it received some support from critics who believed the romantic scenes were beautifully done. This film had been considered lost but a 35mm copy was located and restored by the Netherlands Film Museum. The talking parts of the film are still lost.

Mademoiselle from Armentieres (1926)

Produced and distributed by Gaumont British Picture Company (United Kingdom). Directed by Maurice Elvey and written by Elvey and Victor Saville. Cinematography by William Shenton. This 55-minute silent, black and white film starred Estelle Brody, John Stuart, Alf Goodard, Boris Ranevsky, Clifford Heatherley, Humberston Wright, Marie Ault, and John F. Hamilton.

Story: The unnamed mademoiselle works with her aunt in a restaurant in Armentieres. There she meets Johnny (John Stuart), a British soldier who falls in love with her. She is somewhat interested. A local liaison with the military authorities asks her if she can investigate a man named Branz, who they suspect might be a German spy. She turns on the charm, attention and quickly collects evidence that he is a spy. But Johnny saw the two of them together and came to the conclusion that she is not true to him. Before she can tell him the truth, he is sent off to the front line. Once in battle he is wounded and left in the trenches when his comrades retreat. The mademoiselle, knowing she must make things right, goes in search of him. She finds him in a trench but then they are captured by the Germans. They are released when the British move forward and they return to England to be married.

Military Correlation: Helpful

Comment: This was the most profitable film made in England up until this time. The British Film Institute has about two thirds of the film. The title is based on the song "Mademoiselle from Armentieres," usually known in America as "Hinky Dinky Parlez Vous." It was probably written by Harry Wincott but others have claimed credit.

Mamba (1930)

Produced by Rudolph Flothow, Tiffany Pictures (United States). Directed by Albert Rogell and written by Ferdinand Schumann-Heink, John Reinhardt, Tom Miranda and Winifred Dunn. Cinematography by Charles P. Boyle. This 78-minute Technicolor film stars Jean Hersholt, Eleanor Boardman, Ralph Forbes, Josef Swickard, Claude Fleming, Wilhelm von Brincken, Will Stanton, Hazel Jones, Arthur Stone, Torben Meyer, Andres de Segurola, Edward Martindel, and Noble Johnson.

Story: An evil man with a lot of money, August Bolte (Jean Hersholt) lives in German South Africa where he is hated by just about everyone. He forces a debtor to give him his beautiful daughter Helen (Eleanor Boardman) in marriage, then goes to Europe and brings his reluctant bride home by ship. While in passage she meets a young and charming German officer, Karl von Reiden (Ralph Forbes), and they fall in love. Acknowledging that she is married, they remain platonic. When Bolte becomes enraged with his wife and is about to beat her, Karl steps in. When war breaks out, Bolte is conscripted; he tries to buy his way out but cannot, so decides to incite the local natives to revolution. In the fighting that follows, Bolte is shot. Karl rescues Helen from an onslaught of natives and they are wed.

Military Correlation: Helpful

Comment: Billed as the "first drama in natural color," the film is not really anti-anything but it was banned in Germany because it made German officers look weak. The plot line is old and the love affair simplistic but it made a good story. Of interest is the fact that it leads into part of the war—German South Africa—which is rarely considered. Most producers believed, or thought that audiences believed, that the war was fought only in Europe. Bolte comes across as a really evil man.

The movie was produced by Tiffany Films, a company that soon went out of business. Prints of their films were used to set the fire for the burning of Atlanta in *Gone with the Wind*. There are no complete copies of the film available.

The Man I Killed (1932) see *Broken Lullaby* (1932)

Mare Nostrum (1926) / aka ***Our Sea***

Produced by John Birkel, Metro-Goldwyn-Mayer (United States). Directed by Rex Ingram and written by Willis Goldbeck and Vincente Blasco Ibanez, from Ibanez's book. Cinematography by John F. Seitz. Music by William Axt and David Mendoza. This 102-minute silent black and white film starred Alice Terry, Antonio Moreno, Apollon (Louis Uni), Alex Nova, Hughie Mack, Mickey Brantford, Rosita Ramirez, Frederic Mariotti, Paquerette, Fernand Mailly, Andrews Englemann, Mademoiselle Kithnog, and Kada-Abd-el-Kader.

Story: Almost a seagoing *Mata Hari*, this far-fetched story is about a boy who loves the sea, Ulysses Ferragot (Kada-Abd-el-Kader as a child and Antonio Moreno as an adult). Despite his wife's objections he buys the merchant ship *Mare Nostrum* and enters the pre-war shipping business. At her insistence he soon plans to sell the business but then the war breaks out and he realizes what great profits can be made. On one of his trips to Europe he meets Freya (Alice Terry) who among other things is an Austrian spy. She talks Ulysses (a neutral Spaniard) into delivering her to a submarine at sea and providing the sub with fuel. She convinces him that the submarine crew does not fire on passenger ships. Later he learns that his son Esteben has been killed when the neutral ship upon which he was traveling was sunk by the same submarine that he had helped. The captain of the *Mare Nostrum* decides to take revenge and in the end, though his ship is sunk and he loses his life, he manages to sink the German U-boat with all its crew.

Military Correlation: Spotty

Comment: This is a heartfelt but painfully slow adaptation of Ibanez's novel. The author wrote with an overall tone of disillusionment and defeatism that seemed to echo America's general feeling of vague discontent that prevailed in the nation following the end of the war. The special effects, while primitive, are very good but the general feeling of exhaustion with war and its betrayal is not present in the movie. During the filming, director Ingram and his wife Alice Terry adopted the young native actor who was in the film, Kada-Abd-el-Kader. A 1948 version was made in Spanish.

Marianne (1929)

Produced and distributed by Marion Davies, Cosmopolitan Productions, Metro-Goldwyn-Mayer (United States). Directed by Robert Z. Leonard and written by Laurence Stallings, Gladys Unger, Dale van Every and Joseph Farmham. Cinematography by Oliver T. Marsh. Music by William Axt and Charles Maxwell. This 111-minute black and white film starred Marion Davies, Cliff Edwards, George Baxter, Benny Rubin, Robert Edeson, Oscar Apfel, Fred Solm, Lawrence Gray, Scott Kolk, Emile Chautard, and Mack Sean.

Story: Marianne (Marion Davies), a lovely French farm girl, stays at home on the farm as her lover Andre (George Baxter) goes off to war. Soon the Americans move in near her farm and after much effort to avoid these crude young men, she meets and falls in love with Stagg (Lawrence Gray). Then her French lover returns—but during the war he has lost his sight. Concerned with her own future, she convinces herself that he is in love with the nurse who has been treating him. She now leaves him and joins up with her Yank and moves to 42nd Street.

Military Correlation: Poor

Comment: *Marianne* is light and airy and without many saving graces. The acting, it was reported at the time, appeared stilted and claustrophobic. It had been originally produced as a silent film but was turned in to a musical with Marion Davies and Cliff "Ukulele Ike" Edwards[36] breaking out in song. The film has a dark feel to it. Like some of Laurence Stallings' other films it raised the question how Stallings, like many of those who participated in the war and now wrote about it, could not bring himself to admit the war itself might well have been meaningless, unnecessary, and finally disastrous.

Marianne is one of the very few films which allows the heroine to make what many would consider a selfish decision. In most war films, for World War I at least, the lady in question usually gives up what she wants and regardless of the circumstances is loyal to her wounded man, beaten and disabled as he might be.

The Martyrdom of Nurse Cavell (1916)

Produced and distributed by Famous Feature Company (Australia). It was directed by Jack Gavin and Charles Post Mason and written by Agnes Gavin. This 44-minute silent, black and white film, with English intertitles, starred Robert Floyd, Jack Gavin, James Martin, Vera Pearce, George Portus, Harrington Reynolds, Roland Stavely, Charles Villiers, and Perry Walshe.

Story: This movie pretty much follows the facts that were known at the time of its production: British nurse Edith Cavell (Vera Pearce) who served as the head of a Belgian hospital, took matters into her own hands after the Germans invaded her town. She decided to spy for the Allies and to provide aid and comfort to Allied prisoners of war trying to escape across neutral lines. After some time, during which she was very successful, she was betrayed and captured by the Germans. Determined to make an example out of her, she was sentenced to be executed. Despite a wide and loud international uproar she was shot by a firing squad and became an instant martyr and for the English a symbol of Germany's lack of humanity.

Military Correlation: Good

Comment: This was a highly popular film and, some believed, the best of the many films dealing with the execution of nurse Cavell. No complete copies are known to exist. The director Jack Gavin sued W.J. Lincoln, producer of another Cavell film, for making basically the same film. Several films have been made about this event including *The Woman the Germans Shot* (1918), *Dawn* (1928), and *Nurse Edith Cavell* (1939).

Little was done in this film, or in any of the others, to explain why the Germans, usually so in touch with public opinion, would allow this to occur.

Mata Hari (1931)

Produced by George Fitzmaurice and Irving Thalberg for Metro-Goldwyn-Mayer (United States). Directed by George Fitzmaurice and written by Benjamin Glazer, Leo Birinsky, Doris Anderson, and Gilbert Emery. Cinematography by William Daniels. Music by William Axt (uncredited). This 89-minute black and white film stars Greta Garbo, Ramon Novarro, Lionel Barrymore, Lewis Stone, C. Henry Gordon, Karen Morley, Alec B. Francis, Blanche Friderici, Edmund Breese, Helen Jerome Eddy and Frank Reicher.

Story: An agent who has been captured is promised freedom if he exposes the agent he is hiding. Dubois (C. Henry Gordon), the head of the French intelligence, believes the spy is Mata Hari (Greta Garbo), a popular exotic dancer with friends in high places. But the prisoner chooses death instead. Arriving from Russia with important papers, Lieutenant Alexis Rosanoff (Ramon Novarro) convinces his superior (Lionel Barrymore) to take him to see the famous Mata Hari. He instantly falls in love with her and, turning on the charm, he manages to persuade her to let him spend the night with her. She wants to know what is in the secret papers he is carrying. While General Shubin, Rosanoff's superior, has been warned about her, he had himself given her information in exchange for favors. During an evening encounter, Mata Hari steals the papers, copies them, and returns them. When the general catches on, she kills him and goes into hiding. Rosanoff's plane crashes and he is injured and she goes after her love. She is arrested, found guilty and sentenced to death. To protect his feelings, she pretends to be in a sanatorium for her health. When Rosanoff is brought to see her, all of the staff members maintain the pretense and he believe they will be together. She is then led off to the firing squad.

Military Correlation: Spotty

Comment: This was Garbo's most successful film, a smash hit (especially in Europe). It was largely responsible for the popularity of both the actress and the Mata Hari myth. When reissued in May 1939 the far stricter moral codes were in effect and it was highly censored, including the famous seduction scene of Lieutenant Rosanoff. The movie tagline got right to the point: "Men worshipped her like a goddess, only to be betrayed by a kiss!"

This unexplained connection between the exotic dancer and the spy started early and was well developed through the Mata Hari films up to and including James Bond. Exotic and seductive seem to go together like Tom and Jerry, allowing the ladies with fewer morals to appear as dancers rather than the prostitutes they were.

Male lead Novarro had to wear lifts in his boots to make him as tall as Garbo.

Mata Hari (1985)

Produced by Yoram Globus, Menahem Golan and Roni Ya'achov, Golan-Globus, Cannon City Distributors (Netherlands). Directed by Curtis Harrington and written by Joel Ziskin. Cinematography by David Gurfinkel. This 108-minute Eastmancolor film starred Sylvia Kristel, Christopher Cazenove, Oliver Tobias, Gaye Brown, Gottfried John, William Fox, Michael Anthony, Vernon Dobtcheff, Anthony Newlands, Brian Badcoe, Tutte Lemkow, Taylor Ryan, Victor Langley, Nicholas Selby, Malcolm Terris, Carios Sutton, Neil Robinson, Agnes David, Odon Gyalog, Ferenc Nemethy, Csaba Jakab, Erzsi Cserhalmi, Matyas Usztics, Laszio Baranyi, Gabor Reviczky, Gabor Nagy, Georg Maday, Marta Bako, Virmos Izsof, Laszlo Nemeth, Magda Darvas, Janos Bata, and Karoly Vogt.

Story: The exotic dancer (Sylvia Kristel) is portrayed as an innocent woman forced to work for the German government during the war, but who at the same time provided secret documents for France; in both cases her motives were based on the desire to save lives. The French, on the other hand, see her capture and execution as a morale booster. It is based on a love triangle between Mata Hari and the French Georges Ladoux (Oliver Tobias) and the German Karl von Bayerling (Christopher Cazenove) who are personal friends but who have ended up on opposite sides in the war. They are all being worked by the amoral Fräulein Doktor (Gaye Brown), a psychologist and leading German intelligence officer. Mata Hari's best intentions are thwarted by

Greta Garbo starred as the infamous spy in *Mata Hari* (courtesy Center for the Study of the Korean War, Independence, Missouri).

an assassination plot using a concealed bomb that lead her to be caught in a compromising situation. Despite Ladoux's efforts she is tried and executed. The two men are reconciled after the war.

Military Correlation: Poor

Comment: Though this movie was advertised as a true story, it was far from the truth; it is in fact ridiculous. All that seems to be real is that there was a dancer by the name of Lady MacLeod who adopted the name Mata Hari, which means the eye of the day, during her more successful years around 1906. She did dance a strip tease number and, after her popularity died, lived on "gifts" from admirers. Apparently she rather naively became involved with the French and German intelligence networks during the war and she was executed on October 17, 1917, as a spy. She had been a spy for all of two weeks. The rest is pure fantasy.

There is a scene in which a man watches through the keyhole of her room as Mata Hari masturbates. Star Sylvia Kristel claimed the director forced her, and included so much unnecessary sex that she considered the film to be little more than soft porn.

Men Without Women (1930)

Produced and distributed by Fox Film Corporation (United States). It was directed by John Ford and written by Ford and James Kevin McGuiness. Cinematography by Joseph H. August. This 77-minute black and white film starred Kenneth MacKenna, Frank Albertson, J. Farrell MacDonald, Charles K. Gerrard, Warren Hymer, Paul Page, Pat Somerset, and Stuart Erwin.

Story: Chief torpedo man Burks (Kenneth MacKenna) aboard the U.S. Submarine 513 in the China Sea, is actually Quartermaine the infamous former commander of the British Ship *Royal Scot* that was sunk by Germans with a field marshal on aboard. He tells his sweetheart who, it turns out, is an enemy agent. When the submarine collides with a ship and begins to sink, Burke has to take charge as Ensign Price is unable to command. Burke must keep the sailors alive long enough for them to be rescued by destroyers that have been alerted. At the time of its production the film received high praise both for the technological advances but also for the capable presentation by the actors involved. In his *New York Times* review (February 1930) Mordaun Hall wrote, "Absorbing pictorial study in which subtle comedy relief came to the rescue of incisive dramatic moments."

Military Correlation: Helpful

Comment: The film was probably suggested by the growing interest in submarines, particularly how one escapes from them if they begin to sink.[37] Historically this film is of great interest as it was one of the early transitions between silent and sound. The film actually has only limited sound as well as title cards. A few scenes have both. The only sound version of this film is held by the Museum of Modern Art. "Star of the future" John Wayne, plays a very minor role as the on-shore radio man; you hear his voice before you see him.

Merry Christmas (2005) / aka *Joyeux Noel*

Produced and distributed by Nord-Quest Production, Senator Film Produkton (France). Directed and written by Christian Carion. Cinematography by Walter van den Ende. Music by Philippe Rombi. This 116-minute color film, with English, French, German, and Rumanian titles, stars Diane Kruger, Benno Furmann, Guillaume Canet, Gary Lewis, Dany Boon, Daniel Bruhl, Alex Ferns, Steven Robertson, Frank Witter, Bernard Le Coq, Ian Richardson, Thomas Schmauser, Lucas Belvaux, and the singing voices of Natalie Desspy and Roland Villazor.

Story: The film is very loosely based on a World War I episode when the German Horstmayer (Daniel Bruhl), a Jew from the 93rd Infantry; a Frenchman named Audebert (Guillaume Canet) from the 26th Infantry; and the Scottish Lieutenant Gordon (Alex Ferns) of the Fusiliers, put down their guns, fraternized with the enemy, and celebrated Christmas Eve together. That December 1914 several sections shut down and did not fire, proclaiming an unofficial truce for a day at least. This incident is remembered because of the problems it causes the authorities. The story focuses on a Scottish priest, a German tenor, a Dutch soprano (the German's lover, a young woman who was visiting the front to entertain the troops) and a French lieutenant who allow the music of the season to take over and create a bond between them. Together they sang traditional songs and played football (soccer). The film also follows the punishment each of those officers faced as the military authorities decided that such humane behavior at a time of war was unacceptable.

Military Correlation: None

Comment: The spirit of the Christmas story is over-told and in this case most likely not totally accurate. The acting was considered poor and the justification for this behavior is left more to the mystical for some sort of explanation than it is to the human. The football game displayed did not happen but is rather based on a game played on Christmas Eve 1914 between the Saxton Infantry and the 2nd Battalion of the Royal Welch Fusiliers. Reported by critics as feeling "squishy and vague as a handsome greeting card calling for peace on earth" and as having a cast of "equal opportunity peace makers," it was not well received. The story had been around a long time and told in several short stories so it was only a matter of time before someone decided to make a movie. The primary problem seems to be the lack of any real story other than the event itself, and the added material is often not contextual. Most certainly it was not started by an opera singer marching forth with a lighted Christmas Tree. The 2011 opera *Silent Night* was based on the movie script.[38] It was the last film of Ian Richardson who died soon after this performance.

Might and the Man (1917)

Produced and distributed by Triangle Distribution Company (United States). It was directed by Edward Dillon and written by F.M. Pierson. This five-reel silent black and white film, with English intertitles, starred Elmo Lincoln, Carmel Myers, Lillian Langson, and Clyde Hopkins.

Story: An adventure story where the only consistency seems to come from the number of really bad guys who are trying to rape, kill, and/or kidnap our heroine (Carmel Myers). Strongman Elma Lincoln is able to fight them off with a miraculous single blow or a fantastic swift kick.

Military Correlation: Poor

Comment: The plot and action is so silly and the characters so unattractive, it is hard to believe it was intended to be serious, but if identified as a comedy it did fairly well. Carmel is beautiful and plays it straight. Elmo Lincoln was the first actor to play Tarzan. He was first noticed by D.W. Griffith because of his large and powerful body and was assigned the role of White Armed Joe in *The Birth of a Nation*.

Miss Jackie of the Army (1917)

Produced and distributed by American Film Company, Mutual Film Company (United States). Directed by Lloyd Ingraham and written by Beatrice Van, and William Parker. This five-reel silent, black and white film, with English intertitles, starred Lee Shumway, Loise Guire, John Steppings, Marguerita Fischer, Hal Clements, and Jack Mower.

Story: Mackie (Marguerita Fischer) is a cute little army brat with little to do other than harass her father Colonel Kerwood (Hal Clements) and hang around the base upsetting the troops. She has a boyfriend of sorts, Lieutenant Adair (Jack Mower), who shows how desperate the army much have been for men at the time. She decides, primarily out of boredom and without any hint of rational thought, that her boyfriend must be an enemy spy. She conducts her own investigation into the matter and discovers it is not her boyfriend who is the spy, but rather a local group of Germans planning to blow up a train full of military officials. She and her lieutenant, with the help of the army, thwart the Germans.

Military Correlation: None

Comment: A light comedy with limited entertainment value, this is the sequel to *Miss Jackie of the Navy* (1916) which has even less to do with the military and was just as shallow. One critic explained it this way: "Audiences are impressed with child actors even if not too pleased with children in movies." Nevertheless, the teenager with budding sex appeal apparently was a good sell.

Mons (1926)

Produced by H. Bruce Woolfe, British Instructional Film, New Era Films (United Kingdom). Directed and written by Walter Summers. Photography by Horace Wheddon, Jack Parker, and Stanley Rodwell. This 60-minute silent, black and white movie is primarily a documentary but is listed here because the director staged the story by focusing on individuals who were often played by uncredited actors.

Story: The story follows the British "Contemptibles"[39] and recounts the retreat from Belgium to Paris during the early months of the war. It is directed at the attack itself and at the eventual retreat at the Battle of Mons. Director Summers captures some of the impact of the "duration of defeat" and the slow disillusionment of thousands upon thousands of men who were slowly learning the cost of the war and the possibility of losing it. The director restages several incidents of individual bravery, particularly among the officers from Scotland.

Military Correlation: Good

Comment: *Mons* was made with the official sanction of the British Army Council and made available at the Imperial War Museum so that much of the footage has been copied in war dramas of the '40s and '50s. The movie inspired the British poet Teresa Hooley to write the much loved poem "A War Movie" in 1927. While the movie received high honors for its presentation of the battle, it was criticized for the overacting of some of the performers, many of whom had little or no experience. No complete copy of the film exists; only reels one and three are available, but some 80 percent of these have been restored.

Motherland (1927)

Produced by G.B. Samuelson and Reciprocity Films (United Kingdom). Directed by G.B. Samuelson. Cinematography by A.A. Tunwell. Music by W.L. Trytel. This 104-minute silent black and white film starred Alec Alexander, Rex Davis, Eva Moore, James Knight, Dorinea Shirley, Peggy Carlisle, Lena Halliday, and A. Harding Steerman.

Story: A lonely soldier (Rex Davis) poses as a dead captain in order to bring comfort to a blind woman and a girl poses as a dead Jew to comfort a family.

Military Correlation: Unknown

Comment: *Motherland* was seen as a quickie designed to copy the success of a series of war films released by British Instructional Films but the reception was highly negative. There is no screenable film available and the information we have about the film comes from posters.

Mrs. Slacker (1918)

Produced and distributed by Gold Rooster Plays, Astra Film, Pathe Exchange (United States). Directed by Hobart Henley and written by Agnes Christine Johnston. Cinematography by Albert Richard. This five-reel silent black and white film, with English intertitles, starred Creighton Hale, Gladys Hulet, Paul Clere, and Walter Hiens.

Story: The wealthy wimp Robert Gibbs (Creighton Hale) is too cowardly to enlist when the war breaks out. Seeking a deferment, he hastily marries his laundress Susie Simpkins (Gladys Hulet). When she later learns why he has married her, she rebels and gives him the air, saying she does not want to be Mrs. Slacker. This does not make a difference to her wimp husband, so she sets out on her own to contribute to the war effort. She soon discovers a German plot to sabotage a munitions factory, and manages to thwart their plans.

Military Correlation: Poor

Comment: Because of the times, the movie went over fairly well, but in more normal times Mrs. Slacker would have been declared unstable and locked up.

My Boy Jack (2007)

Produced by Ecosse Films, Grandada International (United Kingdom). Directed by Brian Kirk and written by David Haig, based on a 1997 play by the same name. Cinematography by David Odd. This 95-minute film starred Daniel Radcliffe, Kim Cattrall, Carey Mulliagan, Julian Wadham, Martin McCann, Richard Dormer, David Haig, Peter Gowen, Brian de Salvo, Simon Coury, and Ciaran Noland.

Story: When World War I broke out, Rudyard Kipling's son—underage, frail, and suffering from poor eyesight—was not what the military wanted. But the famous and adventurous father (David Haig) was determined that he get in the war. In response to his considerable influence, the military located a position for the young man with the Irish Guards. John was just turning eighteen when he went to France as a platoon leader. At the Battle of Loos he was badly wounded—most of his face blown away—and soon died of his wounds. He was not identified nor his grave marked. On hearing that he was missing, Caroline "Carry" Kipling demanded that they use the same influence they possessed to locate him. What they discovered was composed of far less glory than it was of gore and they finally have to deal with his death.

Military Correlation: Helpful

Comment: The best evidence is that John "Jack" Kipling died of wounds suffered at the Battle of Loos. At one time it was suggested that his grave had been found but it turned out not to be the case. Following their efforts to locate their son, Rudyard became deeply involved in the War Graves Commission and later wrote a poem in memory of his boy.

The Kipling story was tragic in itself and is also a tragic illustration of the influence Victorian-minded fathers had on the willingness of young men and boys to go to war. Many of the war films use the parent's (father's) pressure to either explain or justify the enlistment of a young son apparently seeking their father's approval. "I am a man" was such a sad theme played out.

Bloopers: There are some contextual problems. Also cars shown in the film are much later than the period in which the film is set. The British troops are wearing steel helmets that were not invented or distributed prior to late 1916.

My Country (1917)
see *War and the Women* (1917)

My Four Years in Germany (1917)

Produced by Mark M. Dintenfass and Jack L. Warner, My Four Years in Germany, Inc., and Warner Brothers (United States). It was directed by William Nigh and written by James W. Gerard and Charles Logue. Cinematography by Rial Schellinger. This 123-minute, silent, black and white film, with English intertitles, stars Halbert Brown, Anne Dearing (as Ann Dearing), Willard Dashiell, Louis Dean, Earl Schenck, George Ridell, Frank Stone, Karl Dane, Percy Standing, Fred Hearn, William Bittner and Arthur C. Duvel.

Story: The film is a dramatization of the life of the American ambassador to Germany, James Gerard (Halbert Brown), basically as he outlined it in his book. It tells of his pre-war life working with the Germans, a life filled with German intrigue and cruelties. and includes several witnesses to German atrocities, many of which were greatly exaggerated in reenactment. The assignment to deal with Germany at the diplomatic level was a hard one indeed and at the end it was basically a no-win situation. The German-American clash was not determined there, nor could it have been prevented there. James Gerard's competence is another question and one that is not well addressed.

Military Correlation: Helpful

Comment: This film, produced for less than $50,000, grossed more than $1.5 million and was the first Warner Brothers success. It made good use of newsreel footage. The moviemakers obviously were willing to leave artistic value behind in order to make their point. With director Nigh's aristocratic tendencies the film often sacrifices artistic presentation and historical accuracy for propaganda presentations.

The Mystery Girl (1938)

Produced and distributed by Famous Player-Lasky Corporation (United States). Directed by William C. DeMille. Written by Marion Fairfax and George Barr McCutcheon, based on the novel *Green Fancy* by McCutcheon. This silent, black and white film, with English intertitles, starred Ethel Clayton, Harry Woodward, Clarence Burton, Charles West, Winter Hall, Mayme Kelso, and J. Parks Jones.

Story: Prince Sebastian of Lurania (Winter Hall) has to go into hiding when his country is invaded by the Germans. His niece the Countess Therese (Ethel Clayton), is an ambulance driver with the French army serving at the front. She hears from her uncle who asks her to meet him in a small village and to bring the crown jewels that have been entrusted to her care. She decides to follow his directions, unaware that a pretender to the Luranian throne and a jewel thief have conspired to steal the jewels and capture the countess.

Military Correlation: Poor

Comment: This was primarily a vehicle for the very pretty and highly popular Ethel Clayton. One columnist complained, "Why will Paramount cast that fine actress Ethel Clayton in wild melodramas? She suffered through the same kind of plots at World." The film is entertaining but the critics are right, for this film is way below Clayton's talents. The film appears to be lost but the novel is still available.

No Man's Land (1931) see *Hell on Earth* (1931)

Nurse Cavell (1916) see *Edith Cavell* (1916)

Nurse Edith Cavell (1939)

Produced by Merrill G. White and Herbert Wilcox, Imperadio Pictures, Ltd. (United Kingdom), RKO (United States). Directed by Herbert Wilcox and written by Michael Hogan, from the story *Dawn* by Reginald Berkeley. Cinematography by Joseph H. August. Music by Anthony Collins. This 105-minute, black and white film starred Anne Neagle, Edna May Oliver, George Sanders, May Robson, Zasu Pitts, H.B. Warner, Sophie Stewart, Mary Howard, Robert Coote, Martin Kosleck, Jimmy Butler, Rex Downing, and Lionel Royce.

Story: English nurse Edith Cavell (Anne Neagle) had risen in her profession to become the head of a small private hospital in Brussels. In England when war breaks out, she returns to her post. When the Germans occupied the country she remains at the hospital and aids the wounded from both sides. In time she recognizes the need to help the Allied cause and with the support of another woman from town, an aristocrat, she organizes an underground system to help French, British and Belgian soldiers escape to a neutral country. She is very successful but eventually someone betrays her and she is caught and charged with treason.[40] Despite a wide range of international protests she is ordered executed and shot by a German firing squad. The closing scenes, moving quickly through her capture, the execution by the "dastardly Deutschlanders" and the memorial at Westminster, are all done with a drama and a dignity that gives credit to the whole story. Her final comment "Patriotism is not enough" was used as a tag line.

Military Correlation: Good

Comment: There was an earlier (silent) version of this story, *Edith Cavell* (1916), produced in Australia. At the time it caused considered turmoil in England because of the violence of the war scenes. This film opened in the United States in 1939 just a few days before war broke out in Europe. Cavell's strong beliefs, symbolized by the parting statement attributed to her, "Patriotism is not enough," were immortalized by a statue at London's Charing Cross Road. George Sanders greatly expanded his reputation by his portrayal of the stiff aristocrat. Producer-director Herbert Wilcox also made a movie about Nurse Cavell called *Dawn* (1928).

The Officer's Ward (2001)

Produced by Laurent and Michele Petin, Art House and International Drama (France). Directed and written by Francois Dupeyron, based on a novel by Marc

Dugain. Cinematography by Tetsuo Nagata. This 135-minute color film stars Andre Dussollier, Eric Caravaca, Sabine Azema, Denis Podalydes, Gregori Derangere, Isabelle Renauld, Geraldine Paihas, Jean-Michael Portal, Guy Trejan, Xavier de Guillebon, Catherine Arditi, Paul Le Person, Circe Lethem, Elise Tielrooy, Agatha Dronne, Renaud Lebas, and Alain Rimoux.

Story: A sensitive young lieutenant, Adrian (Eric Caravaca), enjoys an afternoon of lovemaking with Clemence (Geraldine Paihas) before heading overseas. He leaves for the front accidentally carrying with him one of her earrings. Once in combat he is horribly wounded and spends the rest of the war in the Val-de-Grace hospital for those with disfigured faces. We do not see him, just the reaction of doctors and nurses. Since he no longer has a tongue he cannot talk so all we hear from him are his thoughts (via voiceover). When he receives a Dear John letter from Clemence, he tries to decide what he wants to make of the event. Does he want to consider it a nostalgic love to be remembered for all time, or an awful act of betrayal to be avenged? During his consideration he makes a prescient play on words, "No clemency in wartime." Most of the film takes place in the Officer's Ward where mirrors have been removed and in which men act out their own spiritual war. "Why aren't we dead?" they ask each other as their thoughts range from subject to subject. Once the hero arrives at the hospital, the film is really not going anywhere, but it rather reinforces the awesomeness of the situation.

Military Correlation: Excellent

Comment: An anti-war movie in which there are no war scenes. The impact is in the silence. *The Guardian* reported that the movie was "superbly furnished, passionately acted, and exquisitely photographed and lit." It was first shown at the Cannes Festival in 2003. While a horrible film to watch (it is awesomely reminiscent of *Johnny Got His Gun*), there are some soft and beautiful parts to it including a platonic love with one of the nurses. This aspect of the story was aptly told in *Johnny Got His Gun* but there is a different atmosphere here, a sense perhaps of muted hope. The desperation in the consideration of what happened is there but not the most lasting question of what will become of me.

Bloopers: As the lieutenant is passing through a French village on his way to the front, there is a British 18-pound artillery piece in the background. At this point in the war Britain was not involved in the war and the only artillery used by the French was the 75mm.

Oh! What a Lovely War (1969)

Produced by Richard Attenborough and Brian Duffy, Accord Productions, Paramount Pictures (United States). Directed by Richard Attenborough and written by Charles Chilton, Joan Littlewood, and Len Deighton (uncredited), based on the stage musical *Oh What a Lovely War* by Chilton. (It was first presented as a radio play, "The Long Long Train."[41]) Cinematography by Gary Turpin. This 144-minute film starred Wendy Allnut, Colin Farrell, Malcolm McFee, John Rae,

Corin Redgrave, Maurice Roeves, Paul Shelley, Kim Smith, Mary Wimbush, Jane Seymour, and Nanette Newman.

Story: This film was based on the 1917 stage musical *Oh What a Lovely War* by J.P. Long and Maurice Scott in which a family member goes off to fight. Much of the action revolves around World War I, based on a series of popular songs of the time. The movie mimics the political and military authorities who were involved in the outbreak of war and follows the American Smith family through the war. With the American arrival the British general begins to sing "Over There" with the words changed to "We won't come back—we'll be buried over there." It is not unnoticed that as the war comes to an end, Jack (Paul Shelley) realizes that they are back where they stood having accomplished nothing, and dies lying down on the grass with his dead friend as their bodies turn into memorial stones. It ends with an aerial view of thousands of soldiers' graves as the voices of the dead men sound off with "We'll Never Tell Them" as a parody to the Jerome Kern song, "They Didn't Believe Me."

Military Correlation: Helpful

Comments: Len Deighton, who wrote and produced the film, decided that, in order to shame others who claimed credit for things they did not do, he would not list himself on the credits. It was a move he later said was "stupid and infantile." The climatic helicopter shot of the thousands of graves is considered by many film critics to be one of the most memorable moments ever filmed. The director explained that 16,000 white crosses had to be hammered into individually dug holes. Jane Seymour debuted in this film.

O.H.M.S. (1913)

Produced and distributed by the Barker Motion Photography (United Kingdom). Directed by Alexander Butler and written by Rowland Talbot. This 1,450-foot silent black and white film starred Harry Scaddan, Blanche Forsythe, Fred Paul, and Doreen O'Connor.

Story: Made in the pre-war period, *O.H.M.S.* depicts the tensions and suspicions between Germany and the United Kingdom at this time. The beginning of the film is missing but it is assumed that a German spy (Fred Paul) is blackmailing a woman (Blanche Forsythe). Showing great courage she is finally able to confront the situation and kill the German spy by shooting him as he is about to run his sword through her husband.

Military Correlation: Helpful

Comment: In the main it is not unusual for a woman to be attached to a spy team, but in this case the female is the strongest role. It was heralded by Sybil *in Dr. Brian Pellie and the Secret Dispatch* (1912).The plots of most of these films were simple with studio screenwriters producing different dialogue but generally the same story. While these pre-war movies did not identify the nationality of the spy involved, this one certainly had a very German-sounding name, Colonel Von Harlan. The film won the Gold Medal at the National Kinematographic Exhibit.

On Dangerous Ground (1917) / aka The Little Comrade

Produced by William A. Brady, Peerless Productions, World Film Corporation (United States). Directed by Robert G. Thornby and written by Frances Marion and Burton E. Stevenson, based on the novel *The Littlest Comrade* by Burton E. Stevenson. Cinematography by Lucien N. Andriot. This five-reel silent black and white film, with English intertitles, starred Carlyle Blackwell, Gail Kane, William Bailey, Stanhope Wheatcroft, Frank Leigh, John Burkell, and Florence Ashbrook.

Story: A visiting American (Carlyle Blackwell) is in his hotel room when a strange woman (Gail Kane) comes in, hugs him, and calls him her husband. A spy, she has some important papers that must be delivered to the French and needs his help. The astonished American willingly helps her for the sake of the nation and then just as easily falls in love with her, and she with him. Together they face danger as they engage in equal amounts of intrigue and romance.

Military Correlation: None

Comment: In some places it is hard to determine if it is a comedy as advertised or something more is being slipped in. Even when making a comedy, it is easy to use the natural atmosphere of the silent black and white films to provide the setting of evildoing and backyard betrayal. No effort is made to explain what is happening.

On the Jump (1918)

Produced by Hal Roach, Rolin Films, Pathe Exchange (United States). It was directed by Alf Goulding. This silent black and white film stars Harold Lloyd, "Snub" Pollard, Bebe Daniels, James Blyler, Jane Blyton, Florence Brewster, Sammy Brooks, Harry Burns, Lige Conley, Billy Fay, Genevieve Cunningham, William Gillespie, Helen Gilmore, and Max Hamburger.

Story: This comic film takes place at Squirrel Inn where Harold Lloyd the bellboy must deal with the house detective. Not much to it.

Military Correlation: Poor

Comment: These films in which Harold Lloyd did most of his own stunts were popular though not *as* popular as Chaplin's films.

On the Russian Frontier (1915)

Produced by Arthur Finn and Charles Westen (United States). Directed by Charles Westen. This four-reel silent black and white film, with English intertitles, stars Charles Westen and Gordon Begg.

Story: In a village on the Russian-German border at the outbreak of World War I, a Russian soldier falls deeply in love with a lovely German peasant girl. The girl's loyalties are in question but when she discovers that her father is a German spy she decides to side with Russia and her Russian lover. The two lovers are then involved in a series of overworked situations dealing with stolen war plans.

Military Correlation: Helpful

Comment: Perhaps the best part of the movie is that it features some remarkable newsreel footage of the early days on the Russian front. As an added value it reminded theater audiences that the war was not limited to the Western Front.

One Man Mutiny (1955)
see *The Court Martial of Billy Mitchell* (1955)

Only One Night (1936) see *Cafe Moscow* (1936)

Our Four Days in Germany (1918)

Produced and distributed by American Pathe, B.F. Production Company (United States). Directed by Harry Conway "Bud" Fisher, Raoul Barre and Charles Bowers. Written by Fisher, based on the Mutt and Jeff comic series. Animation by Dick Huemer. The seven-minute silent black and white film starred Augustus J. Mutt and Edgar Horace Jeff.

Story: The film focus on the antics of the "two mismatched tinhorns," the gambler Augustus J. Mutt and his friend Jeff.

Military Correlation: None

Comment: This appears to be a mockery of the U.S. ambassador's book and film *My Four Years in Germany* (1917).

Our Sea (1926) see *Mare Nostrum* (1926)

The Outrage (1915)

Produced and distributed by Hepworth Production Company, Thompson (United Kingdom). Directed by Cecil M. Hepworth and written by Albert Chevalier. This silent, three-reel, black and white film, with English intertitles, starred Henry Ainley, Alma Taylor, Lionelle Howard, John McAndrews, Violet Hopson, and Marnie Murray.

Story: A Prussian lieutenant (Lionelle Howard) rapes a girl (Alma Taylor) in 1870 and is later killed by his illegitimate son in 1914.

Military Correlation: Unknown

Comment: Violet Hopson, known for her roles as a villain, was one of the few women to own a production studio and mostly starred in her own films.

Over the Top (1918)

Produced and distributed by Vitagraph Company of America, Greater V-L-S-E (United States). Directed by Wilfrid North and written by Robert Gordon Anderson and Arthur Guy Empey, based on Empey's book by the same name. Cinematography by Tom Mallory. This nine-reel silent, black and white film, with English intertitles, starred Arthur Guy Empey, Lois Meredith, James Morrison, Mary Maurice, Betty Blythe, Nellie Anderson, William H. Stucky, William Calhoun, Arthur Donaldson, and Julia Swayne Gordon.

Story: A German U-boat commander is in charge of a submarine that for some unexplained reason transports kidnapped American women to his headquarters in Belgium. He is chased by a British secret service man who is the sweetheart of one of the women.

Military Correlation: Poor

Comment: Little is known of the film but the book is still available and provides some clues. A significant number of early films were based on books or plays.

Passchendaele (2008)

Produced by Paul Gross, Niv Fichman and Frank Siracusa, Bell Broadcast News Media Fund, Damberger Film and Cattle Company, Whizbang Film Industry (United States). Directed and written by Paul Gross based on a book by Michael Dunn. Cinematography by Greg Middleton. This 114-minute film stars Paul Gross, Caroline Dhavernas, Gil Bellows, Jesse Frechette, Rainer Kahl, Brian Dooley, Meredith Bailey, Jim Mezon, Michael Greyeyes, James Kot, Landon Liboiron, Hugh Probyn, and Joe Dinicol.

Story: A hopelessly garbled story of a young soldier (Paul Gross), wounded in France, who meets nurse Sarah (Caroline Dhavernas) in the hospital. She is drummed out of the hospital because her father, a German, went back to his country to fight. David Mann (Joe Dinicol), Sarah's brother, manages to enlist despite numerous strikes against him. Sarah, David, and Dunn all meet at a forward aid station. The movie then follows the 10th Battalion, 1st Canadian Division through the battle of Passchendaele (Second Ypres).

Military Correlation: Good

Comment: The movie is based on the experiences of Michael Dunn of the 10th Battalion, a unit made up primarily of Albertans, Saskatchewan and Manitobans. The film was shot in 45 days. The cast includes many soldiers who had recently returned from Afghanistan. The movie was not well received and was a financial failure. A viewer can't tell if the moviemakers think that war was something dreadful and to be avoided, or a somewhat romantic episode for all to experience. Windy Ida of the *Times of London* reported, "It is hard to overstate how unimaginably dreadful *Passchendaele* is." Paul Gross, who wrote, directed, produced and starred in the film, received the National Arts Council Award. The book was reasonably successful.

The Patent Leather Kid (1927)

Produced by Alfred Santell, First National Pictures (United States). Directed by Alfred Santell and written by Gerald C. Duffy and Winifred Dunn, from a story by Rupert Hughes. Cinematography by Arthur Edeson, Ralph Hammeras and Alvin Knechtel. Music by Cecil Copping. This 150-minute silent black and white film starred Richard Barthelmess, Molly O'Day, Lawford Davison, Matthew Betz, Raymond Turner, Hank Mann, Walter James, Lucien Prival, Nigel de Brulier, Fred O'Beck, Clifford Salam, Henry Murdock, Charles Sullivan, John Kolb, and Al Alleborn.

Story: A young unpatriotic boxer is having trouble balancing his sport and his girlfriend Curley. Things get worse when he goes into the army, becomes a hero, cleans up his attitude—and is badly injured. He is so covered with mud that Curley, now a nurse working at the front, hardly recognizes him. The doctor believes he is beyond help and is going to leave him unattended; when she realizes who it is, she talks them into helping. He lives but is badly crippled. Having lost much of his cockiness, he is eventually reunited with his love.

This movie featured a favorite Hollywood theme, cocky young man finds humility and maybe even the love of a good woman while on the field of battle. The fact that it often leaves the soldier sightless or without a limb in generally not considered.

Military Correlation: Helpful

Comment; The movie, despite its author's highly publicized intention, did not become one of the greatest war stories ever portrayed. The *New York Times* questioned if the film devoted too much time to the agony of the military operations.

Paths of Glory (1957)

Produced by Stanley Kubrick, Kirk Douglas and James B. Harris, Bryna Production Company, United Artists (United States). It was directed by Stanley Kubrick and written by Kubrick, Calder Willingham and Jim Thompson, based on Humphrey Cobbs' scathing antiwar novel of the same name. Cinematography by George Kruse. This 88-minute black and white film starred Kirk Douglas, Adolphe Menjou, Ralph Meeker, George Macready, Wayne Morris, Richard Anderson, Joe Turkel, Christane Kubrick, Jerry Hausner, Peter Capell, Emile Meyer, Bert Freed, Kem Dibbs, Timothy Carey, John Stein, Harold Benedict, and Fred Bell.

Story: This film tells of injustice within the French army as they try to fight off German forces in 1916. It comes to a head when some of the French soldiers refuse to fight under the existing conditions and the jingoistic generals decide to make an issue out of it. The enlisted pawns are the cannon fodder as two commanders consider the taking of "The Anthill" from the Germans and General Mireau refused to let the attack proceed because of the danger to his men. Everyone is aware that millions of men are dying over gains that can be measured in meters. His attitude changes when there is consideration that a success on the field might well lead to a promotion. When men refuse to fight, the general insists on the execution of 100 of them. He is eventually talked down to three men who will be drawn by lot. The three are Joseph Turkel, Ralph Meeker and Timothy Carey. The commander (Kirk Douglas) makes an effort to defend them but the fix is in and they are executed.

Military Correlation: Excellent

Comment: *Paths of Glory* is highlighted by long dallying shots moving through the claustrophobic trenches as officers watch through in safely. Initially it was banned from American military bases and remained unseen in France for a long time (their military considered it slanderous). The plot was based in part on a mutiny that took place among French troops who refused to attack against impossible odds. The execution of men for desertion (or what was often called mutiny) was far more common than reported. Nearly every army during the war faced this problem one time or another.

The book on which it was based was well received and considered a masterpiece of anti-war writing.

Bloopers. There are several uniform problems as illustrated by the fact that all the guards of the firing squad have 710 regiment numbers while the Sergeant has 701 on his.

Patriot (1917) see *For Liberty* (1917)

Patriot and the Spy (1915) / aka *The Spy and the Patriot*

Produced and distributed by Mutual Film, Edwin Thanhauser Film Company (United States). Directed by Jack Harvey. Cinematography by Carl Louis Gregory. This four-reel, silent, black and white melodrama, with English intertitles, starred James Cruze, Marguerite Snow, Alphonse Ethier, Hal Clarendon, Samuel N. Niblack, Frank L. Gereghty, and Albert L. Reitz.

Story: Pietro (James Cruze) and his wife Blanchette (Marguerite Snow) live in a small unidentified nation in Europe. When war breaks out, Pietro cannot serve because of an injury. He is made to feel bad by townsman Johannes (Alphonse Ethier) who, despite his pretensions, is really an enemy spy. In a mixed-up belief he is helping his country, Pietro becomes involved in a plot to blow up a bridge, but at the last minute discovers the duplicity. When confronted, Johannes escapes and stops in the village to rape Blanchette. Pietro finds him and in the fight that follows he is exonerated from any blame. The spies are all caught and Pietro is no longer considered a coward.

Military Correlation: Poor

Comment: There seemed to be no end to the ways in which Hollywood could take advantage of the spy formula to produce these quick and fairly inexpensive productions.

Patriotism (1918)

Produced and distributed by Paralta Plays (United States). Directed by Raymond B. West and written by Jane Holly and R.B. Kidd. This silent, black and white film, with English intertitles, starred Bessie Barriscale, Charles Gunn, Herschel Mayall, Arthur Allardt, Joseph J. Dowling, Mary Jane Irving, Ida Lewis, and Clifford Alexander.

Story: Robin Cameron (Bessie Barriscale), a nurse in a hospital in Scotland, works with Dr. Hyde (Arthur Allardt). A rich merchant decides to provide safety razors to all the troops. In the meantime Robin's uncle Sir John Cameron (Joseph J. Dowling) comes to town looking for spies. Add to this mix the arrival of Charles Hamilton (Charles Gunn) who has been saved from a shipwreck. He is accused of sending messages with secret information to submarines passing offshore. Robin is able to find the real spies and saves Charles, leaving him free to join the American forces in France.

Military Correlation: Poor

Comment: The owners of the newly developed Gillette Safety Razor Company made itself famous by providing free razors to troops going overseas. That seems to have impressed the director. This film, considered a spy melodrama, is hardly more than an adventure film. Whatever spying was involved was somehow lost in the stupidity of the plot and the silly dialogue.

The Peril of the Fleet (1909)

Produced by S. Wormaid, London Cinematograph Company and Electric Theatres (United Kingdom). It was directed by S. Wormaid. This 550-foot silent, black and white film came with English intertitles.

Story: Spies, easily identified by their long hair and beards, are aided by a woman as they seek to destroy the Royal fleet at Southampton via a system of sea mines (originally planted to *protect* the fleet from attack). After having survived being thrown off a cliff by the spies, a detective manages to save the fleet with only moments to spare. As the film ends we see the HMS *Drake* steaming by to assure us that all is well.

Military Correlation: Good

Comment: The movie can claim to be the first British spy film and took advantage of the Royal Navy gathering at Spithead in 1909 as a part of a conference to discuss imperial policy. Therefore, it is one of the first films to actually use footage of the Royal Navy; catching the battleships *Drake, Agamemnon* and *Irresistible* at sea. The film is very typical of the invasion literature of the period and focuses on the threats imposed by the expanding German navy. It was "intensely sensational" according to many reviewers, but it was also hampered by cardboard sets and limited dialogue. The country of origin of the spies is not identified, and only later identified in such films as *The German Spy Peril, Huns of the North Sea* and *The Kaiser's Spies* (all 1914). The film was distributed in Germany as well as

Great Britain. The only copy is at the National Film and Television Archives and ironically has German intertitles.

Pigboat (1933) see *Hell Below* (1933)

Pimple's Dream of Victory (1915)

Produced and distributed by the British firm Folly Films, Phoenix (United Kingdom). It was directed by Fred Evans and written by Fred and Joe Evans. This 964-foot film was silent, black and white, with English intertitles, and starred the comedy team of Joe Evans and Fred Evans.

Story: One in a series of Pimple movie comedies, this depicts an American sailor daydreaming his way through a series of submarine adventures.

Military Correlation: None

Poppies of Flanders (1927)

Produced and distributed by British International Pictures, Wardour Films (United Kingdom). It was directed by Arthur Maude and written by Herman C. McNeile and Violet E. Powell, based on McNeile's novel *The Hopeless Case*. Cinematography by George Pocknail. This nine-reel, silent, black and white film, with English intertitles, starred Jameson Thomas, Eve Gray, Malcolm Tod, Gibb McLaughlin, Henry Vibart, Daisy Campbell, Tubby Phillips, and Cameron Carr.

Story: The reformed son (Jameson Thomas) of an wealthy earl (Henry Vibart) pretends to have a relapse when he learns that his sweetheart (Eve Gray) has fallen in love with another man. He finds the courage to give his life in order to save that of his love's new affection.

Military Correlation: Helpful

Comment: The movie makes reference to "the poppies that grow between the rows" of crosses at Flanders field, and to the well-known poem, but the connection pretty much ends there. Of all the battlefield cemeteries in Europe, Flanders seems to have become the symbol of the rows of thousands of white crosses that mark the wanton killing. The film was adapted from a short story by Herman McNeile, based on his own World War I experiences. He served as an engineer in the British army. Because officers were not allowed to publish articles, he wrote under the name "Sapper."

Pot Luck in the Army (1918)

Produced and distributed by American Pathe, Bud Fisher Production Company (United States). Directed by Harry Conway "Bud" Fisher, Raoul Barre and Charles Bowers, it was written by Fisher, Al Smith, George Breisacher and based on the Mutt and Jeff comic series. Animation by Dick Huemer. The seven-minute silent black and white film starred Augustus J. Mutt and Edgar Horace Jeff.

Story: This film was based on the first daily comic strip "Mutt and Jeff." It focuses on the antics of the "two mismatched tinhorns" who bring chaos to the Army and fight the Kaiser by making fun of him.

Military Correlation: None

Comment: This was one of more than 300 films made by "Bud" Fisher's company between 1913 and 1926 and one of ten that in some way reflected on World War I.

President Wilson (1944) see *Wilson* (1944)

Private Peaceful (2012)

Produced by Jack Bowers, Fluidity Films (United Kingdom). It was directed by Pat O'Connor. Screenplay by Simon Reade, based on a book by the same name by Michael Morpurgo. Cinematography by Jerzy Zielinski. Music by Rachel Portman. This 100-minute color film starred Jack O'Connell, George McKay, Richard Griffiths, Alexandra Roach, Maxine Peake, Frances de la Tour, Izzy Meikle Small, John Lynch, Anthony Flanagan, Hero Fiennes-Tiffin, Gregg Lowe, Paul Ready, David Yelland, Eline Powell, Paul Chequer, James Laurenson, and Rita Davis.

Story: Tommo (George McKay) and Charlie Peaceful (Jack O'Connell) are brothers from a poor English family in Devon. They live a simple life as members of feudal families. During their school years they both fall in love with the beautiful and vivacious Molly (Alexandra Roach) and the three of them share a playful childhood together. Tommo soon learns that Molly is seeing Charles on the side and it becomes apparent that she has become pregnant by him. Heartbroken and feeling badly betrayed by them, he joins the army. Charles, feeling that he is responsible, follows him in, leaving the unhappy Molly and her child behind. The brothers endure the horrors of battle, gas attacks, artillery fire, and bombardment but in the end cannot escape from summary military justice. The two brothers' relationship has changed but Charles nevertheless looks out for Tommo. When he finds his brother wounded in an trench, he refuses orders to attack. Court martialed, he is found guilty of desertion and executed. After the war Tommo returns home and reunites with Molly, and they decide to raise the child together.

Military Correlation: Good

Comment: The movie was not well received and many believed that it didn't have the charm of the book from which it was taken. The story was better than many but not well presented. The practice of basing films on popular books sometimes went astray when the producers took the plots in a different direction, thus ruining the context as the author had first seen it. The plot was well used and the settings not well selected for the message of courage and cowardice it was trying to convey. There were also gaps of logic.

Private Peat (1918)

Produced and distributed by Famous Players–Lasky Corporation of America, Paramount Artcraft Special (United States). Directed by Edward Jose and written by Charles E. Whittaker, based on a book of the same name by Harold R. Peat. This 50-minute silent, black and white film, with English intertitles, starred Harold Peat (as himself), Miriam Fouche, William Sorelle, and Edwin Grant.

Story: Alone in the world with the sole exception of his girlfriend Mary (Miriam Fouche), Harold Peat (as himself) tries to enlist in the Army but is rejected on the grounds that his chest size is too small. Determined, he and his friend Bill (Edwin Grant) make up a story about Harold losing his mother, father and sister to the Germans, and ask special permission to join; it is granted. After training together the two friends go to France. Peat is wounded while on a mission to locate more ammunition. He is nevertheless able to help stop the German advance. Named a hero and sent home, he meets Mary in Europe and they marry and sail home together.

Military Correlation: Helpful

Comment: The author of the source book (a *New York Times* bestselling author for two years) was a Canadian citizen who served in France with the 3rd Battalion of the First Canadian Contingency. In the movie, however, he plays a red-blooded American. The movie has a heavy reliance on newsreel films to serve for the combat scenes and expected that the beauty of Miriam Fouche to carry the love scenes. After the war, Peat became the owner of a speakers bureau and worked with rich and famous people all over the world.

The Profiteer (1919)

Produced and distributed by Arrow Film Corporation (United States). Directed by John K. Holbrook. Written by Jack Sherrill, Alma Hanlon, and Robin H. Townley. This six-reel silent black and white film, with English intertitles, starred Jack Sherrill, Alma Hanlon, Robin H. Townley, Charles Bowell, F.W. Stewart, Dorothy Kingdon, E.L. Howard, Max Ruhbeck, and Louise Hotaling.

Story: Tom Merritt (Jack Sherrill) is the assistant director at a major industrial plant. When he tries to enlist, the army turns him down on the grounds that he's needed on the home front. On the side he is working on an invention that will help raise sunken ships. His employer, Henry Fair, sees the potential of great profit and tries to secure control of the new invention. Vera, Henry's sister, is in love with Tom and is trying to get him to break up with his girlfriend. The movie then takes us through a variety of episodes: an attempt to put Tom and his girlfriend in a compromising situation, an effort on the part of Fair to sell the invention to a group of Germans who had not really given up and who plan to reestablish the old German nation state, Tom's sweetheart being kidnapped by Henry's driver, a mutiny put down by Marines, and the arrival of the American fleet back home.

Military Correlation: Spotty

Comment: During the war, the "bad guys" were those who tried to make a profit off the necessities of the war. It was a constant problem both at the domestic level—the control and jacking up of prices over small home items—and at the industrial level. This was the final film for Alma Hanlon who had a brilliant but very short career.

The Prussian Cur (1918)

Produced and distributed by Fox Films (United States) Directed and written by Raoul Walsh (as R.A. Walsh). Cinematography by Roy F. Overbaugh. This 70-minute, silent, black and white film, with English intertitles, starred Miriam Cooper, Sidney Mason, H. von der Goltz, Leonora Stewart, James Marcus, Pat O'Malley, John E. Franklin, Walter McEwen, Charles Reynolds, William Harrison, Pat Hartigan, Ralph Faulkner, Walter Lawrence, James Hathaway, and William Black.

Military Correlation: Poor

Comment: Raoul Walsh claimed it was "his rottenest picture" and Miriam Cooper said that it was the worst movie she ever made. They blamed the executives at Fox Corporation for forcing them into the production of a vastly exaggerated depiction of the Germans. It's best known for its inclusion of the crucified soldier (propaganda had it that a Canadian soldier was crucified with a bayonet on a barn door while fighting on the Western Front). There was no proof or witnesses but the story appears again in World War II when the Germans used it against the British. In many scenes Raoul Walsh pushes modern technology into the background and takes on the Kaiser in hand-to-hand fighting, with the Kaiser living in an alley surrounded by figures that look like women—victims, we can only suppose, of German atrocities. With today's eyes the extent of propaganda and the violent nature of all the Germans involved seems harsh, but the film was well accepted and the propaganda swallowed.

Actor H. Von der Goltz, who played the German heavy, was in reality a spy working for the Germans. He had been caught by British Intelligence spying for the enemy and turned.[42] In return for his help in identifying and locating other spies working in England, the British gave him safe passage to the United States where he went to work for the film industry. Miriam Cooper was Walsh's wife. The film used a great deal of newsreel footage which, in itself, was sometimes staged. The film is considered to be lost and many critics think that is probably just as well.

The Queen's African Rifles (1953)
see *Royal African Rifles* (1953)

The Red Baron (1971)
see *Von Richthofen and Brown* (1971)

The Red Baron (2008)

Produced by Dan Magg, Thomas Reisser, Roland Pellegraino, Warner Brothers, Monteray Media (United States). Directed and written by Nikolai Mullerschon. Cinematography by Klause Merkel. Music by Stefan Hansen and Dirk Reichardt. This 123-minute film starred Thomas Koutik, Tomas Ibi, Albert Franc, Matthais Schweighofer, Maxim Miehmet, Hanno Koffler, Til Schweiger, Richard Krajco, Joseph Fiennes, Steffen Schroeder, Lukas Prikazsky, Lena Headey, Ondrej Volejnik, and Jiri Wohanka.

Story: Manfred von Richthofen (Matthais Schweighofer) of the Imperial German Air Service, known historically as the Red Baron, flew over the lines of the Western front where he was a perfect gentleman, telling his men not to kill pilots if it could be avoided. He runs into and shoots down Royal Canadian Flying Club pilot Roy Brown (Joseph Fiennes) and lands beside his plane to make sure he is okay. With the help of Kate Otersdorf (Lena Headey) they nurse him back to health. Soon Brown escapes from the POW camp and meets the German ace on the ground where they share a drink and exchange crude comments about Kate. The German ace is offered a ground job which he refuses because he will not leave his men behind. This angers Kate, who is the object of his affection. An Allied air raid interrupts the love scene between the two and he flies off to save his squadron. As fate would have it, he is shot down by the very same British pilot, Roy Brown.

Military Correlation: Helpful

Comment: A poorly acted, singularly sloppy, but lively adventure story that among other things plays havoc with the truth. Brown was never shot down by von Richthofen, nor was he ever a prisoner of war. As far as we can tell there was no Kate in his life or the baron's. The injection of the nurse at this point was to reflect the long tradition of providing a love object. The portrayal of the Red Baron is totally out of character with what is known about him, for he was neither aristocratic nor a gentleman. The film is lacking in engaging characters and the plot so disjointed that one anxiously awaits another air battle. The coverage of the war, while providing some excellent air shots, suggests an attitude about it that would not represent those who fought it.

Bloopers: The film has many bloopers such as the fact that the Royal Canadian Flying Club did not exist.

Red Salute (1917) see *Arms and the Girl* (1917)

Remember Belgium (1915)

Produced and distributed by Burlingham Standard Corporation, Walturdaw Distribution (United Kingdom). Directed by Ethyle Batley. This two-reel silent, black and white film, with English intertitles, starred Dorothy Batley, Ernest G. Batley, Martin Valmour and James Russell.

Story: No copies of the film exist. I could not locate any reviews.

Military Correlation: Unknown

Comments: This was primarily a family affair: Dorothy Batley was the daughter of producer-director Ethyle Batley and actor Ernest G. Batley. Ethyle died shortly after the film was released.

The Renegade (1914) see *The Light of Victory* (1919)

The Return of the Soldier (1982)

Produced by J. Gordon Arnold and Barry R. Cooper Productions, Brent Walker Pictures, Skreba Films (United Kingdom). Directed by Alan Bridges and written by Hugh Whitemore and Rebecca West, based on West's novel. Cinematography by Stephen Goldblatt. Music by Richard Rodney Bennett. This Technicolor film starred Julie Christie, Glenda Jackson, Ann-Margret, Alan Bates, Ian Holm, Frank Finlay, Jeremy Kemp, Hilary Mason, John Sharp, Elizabeth Edmonds, Valerie Whittington, Patsy Byrne, Amanda Grinling, Edward de Souza, Vickery Turner, Sheila Keith, Shirley Caine, Emily Irvin, William Booker, Valerie Aitken, Nicholas Frankau, Robin Langsford, Stephen Finlay, and Michael Cochrane.

Story: Kitty Baldry (Julie Christie), a stuck-up society queen, has a rather narrow view of life and its values. All of this is challenged when her husband Captain Chris Baldry (Alan Bates) returns from the war shell shocked and suffering from amnesia. He does not know who she is but instead remembers, and wants a reunion with, Margaret Grey (Glenda Jackson), his working class lover from the distant past. Gilbert Anderson (Ian Holm) is hired to unscramble the man's feelings for his past love and for his all-too-caring cousin Jenny (Ann Margret). Ultimately all come to realize that he is unstable and unreachable, lost in the past. Throughout the story Kitty remains the selfish and shallow beauty who never seems to understand or, really, to care.

Military Correlation: Good

Comments: This complex psychological melodrama contains many violent images and situations. It did justice to the book from which it was taken. It's a very powerful film if for no other reason than it acknowledges the generally ignored plight of those suffering from mental breakdown. The war that this film shows is far from the romantic versions found in many of the early "devil may care" movies. It was the first film in the United Kingdom to be rated with the new PG certification that was designed to give audiences a better idea of what they would be seeing. Glenda Jackson, who played Margaret, would leave acting and go into politics, finally serving as a member of the British House of Parliament.

La Revanche (1916) / aka *Vengeance*

Produced by W. J. Lincoln (Australia). Directed by W.J. Lincoln and G.H. Barnes. Written by Lincoln and Fred Kehoe. The 4,000-foot silent black and white film, with English intertitles, starred Arthur Styan, Agnes Keogh Stewart Garner, W.J. Lincoln, and a host of Australian servicemen who had returned from the war and were used as extras.

Story: Friends of the executed nurse Edith Cavell, led by Captain Devreaux (Stewart Garner), seek revenge against those who caused the betrayal and ultimate death of the heroine during World War I. In the complicated outpouring of the plot, the spy who betrayed Cavell is shot by the Belgians, and a German who was involved in her execution is shot by a woman he was trying to assault. The film is quite graphic and shows the flogging of a Belgian man, and the Kaiser awarding the Iron Cross to an officer who murdered an innocent woman. In the background is depicted the German capture of Wavre, Belgium.

Military Correlation: Spotty

Comment: This was seen as a sequel to *Edith Cavell* (1916). Director W.J. Lincoln used many of the cast and crew as well as some of the footage from the earlier movie. It was one of many films inspired by the execution of Nurse Cavell. It was the totally unnecessary harshness of the sentence that bothered most persons. It is somehow sad, however, that what is remembered of this fine lady are the circumstances of her death and not a celebration of her remarkable life. Lincoln played the role of the Kaiser. The film is considered lost.

Reveille (1924)

Produced by George Pearson and Robert Cullen, Walch Pearson (United Kingdom). Directed and written by George Pearson. Cinematography by Basil Emmott and Percival Strong. The 93-minute, silent, black and white film, with English intertitles, starred Betty Balfour, Stewart Rome, Ralph Forbes, Sidney Fairbrother, Frank Stanmore, Henrietta Watson, Guy Phillips, Walter Tennyson, Charles Ashton, Donald Searle, Buena Bent, and Simeon Stuart.

Story: This is a rather diffused and ill-crafted story of how the war affects a wide variety of persons with different backgrounds; it's designed to show the courage displayed by all involved. A seamstress (Betty Balfour) stops a poor ex-soldier from becoming a left-wing agitator. The author-director did not want a describable script. He wrote to his crew in January 1924, "There is no story, as such. I hate the well-made Story with its Exposition, Denouncement, Crisis, etc., as materials for my elusive Screen. I confess I cannot write one."[43] The best that can be said is that it follows several British soldiers through and after World War I. The one print that has been located was stolen from the British Film Institute National Archives and so *Reveille* is now listed as one of the "Most Wanted" lost films.

Military Correlation: Good

Comment: The "participant-story" style was used in several films when the director pulled together individual accounts of personal experience to create a tapestry-like overview of the war. Like a collection of essays, the process suffered from a lack of performance standards and often sent mixed messages.

The Road Back (1937)

Produced by Edmund Grainger and Universal Pictures (United States). Directed by James Whale and written by Charles Kenyon, R.C. Sherriff, based on Erich Maria Remarque's novel of the same name. Cinematography by John J. Mescall and George Robinson. Music by Dimitri Tiomkin. The 97-minute film starred John King, Richard Cromwell, Slim Summerville, Maurice Murphy, Andy Devine, Larry Blake, John Emery, Henry Hunter, Noah Beery, Jr., Gene Gericke, Barbara Read, Spring Byington, Frank Reicher, Marilyn Harris, Jean Rouverol, Etienne Girardot, Charles Halton, Laura Hope Crews, Louise Fazenda, Robert Warwick, Samuel S. Hinds, Arthur Hohl, William B. Davidson, Lionel Atwill, Al Shean, Clara Blandick, Reginald Barlow, Edwin Maxwell, E. E. Clive, Edward Van Sloan, Francis Ford, Margaret Seddon, Greta Meyer and Dwight Frye.

Story. The plot is built around the despair and disillusionment of men returning to civilian life in Germany after the end of World War I. It was supposed to be a sequel to *All Quiet on the Western Front* but it did not accomplish that, primarily because of outside influence. Even with cutbacks it combined a strong anti-war message about the horrors of World War I, and at the same time warned against the lingering dangers of the rising Nazi regime.

Military Correlation: Good

Comment: Universal was threatened with a boycott of all their films by the German government unless the anti–Nazi sentiment in the film was deleted, and the owners of the company caved in. They also called for the addition of some comedy scenes with Slim Summerville and Andy Devine, scenes which director James Whale considered to be totally unsuitable; Whale left Universal shortly after that. The battle scenes, shot with a special traveling crane, were magnificent. The original version made a strong preparedness statement but it was withdrawn and seen by only a few. It is too bad that those who chose to restore the film have restored the cut version.

Germany was one of the few nations that took such actions against film companies, forever sensitive to how they looked to the public. Film companies, in business for commercial purposes, were often willing to go along with them.

The Road to Glory (1936) / aka *Wooden Crosses*

Produced by Darryl F. Zanuck, 20th Century-Fox (United States). Directed by Howard Hawks and written by Joel Sayre and William Faulkner. Cinematography by Gregg Toland. The 103-minutes black and white film starred Fredric March, Warner Baxter, Lionel Barrymore, Gregory Ratoff, June Lang, Victor Kilian, Paul Stanton, John Qualen, Julius Tannen, Theodore Von Eltz, Paul Fix, Leonid Kinskey, Jacques Lory, Jacques Vanaire, Edythe Raymore, George Warrington, and John Bleifer.

Story: This melodramatic anti-war film follows the adventures of Lieutenant Denet (Fredric March), Captain La Roche (Warner Baxter) and Monique LaCoste

(June Lang). La Roche is in charge of the 5th Company, 2nd Battalion, 39th Regiment of French troops who, as each new set of replacement arrives, gives them a phony speech about honor and courage and duty. No one believes it. One set of replacements includes Lieutenant Denet and a private who La Roche recognizes as being his father. When Denet meets the lovely Monique La Coste, who he does not know is La Roche's mistress, they fall in love. Back on the battlefield they are sent on a mission to install phone lines and there both La Roche and his father are killed. Denet wins the girl but soon finds himself involved in the destruction of minds and bodies and he now must give the same insane speech to all the new replacement.

Military Correlation: Excellent

Comment: The movie somewhat disgracefully used large amounts of film from the French film *Wooden Crosses* (1932) never released in English. The "father's a spy" and triangle love affairs was a well-worn plot, but in the hands of Howard Hawks it came out as a fairly good film. It certainly exposed the insanity of men willingly going into battle spurred on by the phony words of their officers.

Bloopers: There is no explanation why Lionel Barrymore was chosen for this part as he was so old-looking that no enlistment officer would have allowed him to join, nor would any officer have sent him on a mission.

The Road to Honor (1917) see *The Dark Road* (1917)

Roses of Picardy (1927)

Produced by Maurice Elvey, M.A. Wetherell, Victor Saville, Cricklewood Studios, Gaumont British Picture Corporation (United Kingdom). Directed by Maurice Elvey and written by Gareth Gundrey, Fred V. Merrick, and Jack Harris, based on the books *The Spanish Farm* and *Sixty Four Ninety Four* by R.H. Mottram. This 124-minute silent, black and white film, with English intertitles, starred Lillian Hall-Davis, John Stuart, Jameson Thomas, Marie Ault, A. Bromley Davenport, Clifford Heatherley, and Humberton Wright.

Story: A British officer, Lieutenant Skene (John Stuart), returns to Belgium after the war and meets with Madame Vanderlynden (Lillian Hall-Davis) who had comforted him when he nearly lost his mind following an all-night attack. She is now caring for the blind son of a local baron (A. Bromley Davenport). A young, wealthy and aristocratic French officer, Lieutenant George D'Archeville (Jameson Thomas), is in love with her. She cannot decide between them and must let the war determine the outcome.

Military Correlation: Poor

Comment: This film seems to have lost something in the adaptation for R.H. Mottram's books were far better than the movie. The title comes from the popular song of the same name. The lyric was, if nothing else, symbolic of the war and appeared in dozens of films. The movie leaves a lot to be desired as many of the characters seem to believe a long stare is a sufficient replacement for action. The plot, though nearly worn out by this time, is further weakened by the lack of any real belief in the girl's indecision. She apparently is unaware of the reality that "no decision is a decision."

The line between entertainment, literary creation, propaganda and information is so blurred at times that it is easily crossed over when that was not the intention. In this case the underlying agenda seems to push too hard against the simple entertainment suggested.

The Royal African Rifles (1953) / aka *The Queen's African Rifles; Storm Over Africa*

Produced by Richard V. Heermance, Louis Hayward Production Company, Allied Artists Pictures (United States). Directed by Lesley Selander, written by Daniel B. Ullman. Cinematography by Ellis W. Carter. Music by Paul Dunlap. This 75-minute Cinecolor film starred Louis Hayward, Veronica Hurst, Michael Pate, Bruce Lester, Steven Geray, Angela Greene, Barry Bernard, Robert Osterloh, John Warburton, Patrick Aherne, Don Blackman, Louis Polliman Brown, Naaman Brown, James Craven, and Roy Glenn.

Story: As war breaks out all over the world, a consignment of valuable Vickers machine-guns is stolen from the Royal Navy ship HMS *Marlin,*. The ship had been docked at Bombasa Harbor, Africa, and it was believed that is where they went missing.. One of the ship's officers, Lieutenant Denham (Louis Hayward), goes undercover posing as a hunter working in British East Africa. His assignment is to get the guns back before they can be delivered to the Germans. The central theme, however, is the playing out of an effort to avoid disturbing the balance of power in Africa. Lieutenant Denham's efforts finally lead him to a German officer named Cunningham (Michael Pate) who, incidentally is the father of Jennifer (Veronica Hurst), the love of Denham's life.

Military Correlation: Spotty

Comment: The whole movie was filmed in the Arboretum and Botanic Gardens in Los Angeles Country, California, and was the first and only production of Hayward's Associated Film Artists, Inc. It's a good adventure film in which the war plays a minor role. It's also one of the few movies that took the war out of Europe. As far as Hollywood was concerned, the war was fought in France and Belgium, ignoring the fact that it was in all ways a world war, involving more than a hundred nations.

Bloopers: There were no Royal African Rifles in World War I.

Runaway Daughter (1917) see *Arms and the Girl* (1917)

Saving the Colours (1914)

Produced by Arthur Finn and Charles Weston, Regent Films, Motion Picture Sales Company (United Kingdom), Coismofotofilm Corporation (United States). Directed by Charles Weston, it was written by Rowland Moore and Jane Gail. The silent black and white film, with English intertitles, starred Rowland Moore and Jane Gail.

Story: This is the much repeated story of the cowardly son (Rowland Moore) of a wealthy squire who finally enlists in the army and finds that he is more of a man than he thought. Responding to the conditions and the patriotism of his companions, he rises to the occasion. Though badly wounded, our hero is involved in an act of selfless courage during which he is able to save the English flag that had fallen during the Battle of the Mons. He makes his father proud.

Military Correlation: Spotty

Comments: There is something said about democracy in this, and other films like it. The man of questionable character is almost always a wealthy aristocrat's pampered son forced to face his responsibilities. But when faced with the equality of the battlefield he, as the theme goes, finds himself and becomes capable of performing heroic acts. But there is also something being said about the presentation of war, for in this case it comes across as the natural duty for any "normal" man, and the war itself pressures our hero to perform as a man.

Seas Beneath (1931)

Produced by Fox Film Company (United States). It was directed by John Ford and written by Dudley Nichols, William Collier, Sr., Curt Furburg, and James Parker, Jr. Cinematography by Joseph H. August. Music by Peter Brunelli. This 69-minute black and white film starred George O'Brien, Marion Lessing, Mona Maris, Walter C. Kelly, Warren Hymer, Steve Pendleton, Walter McGrail, Larry Kent, Henry Victor, Philip Ahlm, Al Bennett, Earl Wayland Bowman, Bill Brande, Leonard Davidson, Joseph Depew, Francis Ford, Hans Ferber, Robert Fort, and John Loder.

Story: In the last days of World War I an American mystery ship sailed for the coast of Spain pulling a submarine. Their mission was to locate and sink a U–boat that had been effective in attacking Allied shipping. Posing as a harmless three-mast schooner, the ship is in fact a formidable vessel carrying a gun capable of sinking the U–boat. Stopping in the Canary Island to refuel, the crew members interact with locals and become involved with German sympathizers who give away their assignment. The hero Bob Kingsley (George O'Brien) learns that his own sweetheart Anna Maria von Stubven (Marion Lessing) is really an enemy spy and that she has a brother and a lover on the very German submarine they are seeking.

Military Correlation: Poor

Comment: If this is supposed to be serious, then there is far too much comic relief. It was highly criticized at the time for the poor acting and unbelievable circumstances. The submarine identified as U172 is the USS *166* the *Argonaut,* at the time the largest submarine in the world. The three-mast schooner used in the film also appeared in *The Sea Wolf* (1930). The Navy made available several vessels from the fleet to make the movie that is little more than a reworking of *Men Without Women* (1930). Jona Loder was paid an extra $1000 for her part because it called for her to have especially short hair.

Blooper: The German U-boat 172 was not launched until July 1941.

Secret Agent (1936)

Produced by Michael Balcon and Ivor Montagu, Gainsborough (United Kingdom). Directed by Alfred Hitchcock and written by Charles Bennett, Jesse Laskey, Jr., Campbell Dixon, Alma Reville and Ian Hay, from a story by W. Somerset Maugham. Cinematography by Bernard Knowles. This 86-minute film stars John Gielgud, Peter Lorre, Madeleine Carroll, Robert Young, Percy Marmont, Florence Kahn, Charles Carson, Lilli Palmer, Rene Ray, Andreas Malandrinos and (uncredited) Michael Redgrave and Michael Rennie.

Story: British officer Edgar Brodie (John Gielgud) is a famous author who faked his death in order to go underground. He is being sent by R (Charles Carson), the head of British Intelligence, to Switzerland. A female agent (Madeleine Carroll) goes along posing as his wife. They also work with a British agent (Peter Lorre) who is known as "The Hairless Mexican" and "The General." Brodie, posing as Ashenden, is to prevent the German agent from leaving with the information he has managed to collect. In the end the German is killed and the two English agents have grown ambivalent about the war and their involvement in it. This seems to be happening because the mission violates their consciences and, most likely, interferes with their romance. The tension needed for the success of the movie is maintained but it does not have the same sort of sensitivity when it comes to the romance that, at best, seems blundering.

Military Correlation: Helpful

Comment: Perhaps the best thing about this movie was that it provided the uncredited film debuts for Michael Redgrave and Michael Rennie, who would go on to become fine actors. John Gielgud, who was busy filming the movie during the day, was also performing in *Romeo and Juliet* on the stage in the evening. The movie was voted the fifth best British film of 1936.

The Secret Game (1917)

Produced and distributed by Jesse L. Lasky Feature Play Company, Paramount Pictures (United States). Directed by William C. DeMille and written by Marton Fairfax. The 67-minute silent black and white film, with English intertitles, starred Sessue Hayakawa and Jack Holt, and Florence Vidor.

Story: A German secret agent named Schmidt (Charles Ogle) is passing himself off as Dr. Ebell Smith. On the West Coast, Jack Holt works with his beautiful assistant Kitty Little (Florence Vidor) who is loyal to Germany and her brother who is in the army. Enemy spies have been gaining access to American scientific secrets through a quartermaster officer named Northfield. Nara-Nara (Sessue Hayakawa), a special agent working with the government of Japan (a country aligned with the Allies in World War I), is trying to determine who the leak is. The immediate problem is that a troop transport is in danger of being sunk if the spies can get the information out. The evil Dr. Smith takes Northfield's secretary captive and puts Kitty in her place. Nara-Nara saves his love and the United States transport at the expense of his own life.

Military Correlation: Poor

Comment: A contemporary critic called this a "static but watchable story." The director employed a series of well-composed shots but the camera was motionless, giving it a sensation of stillness. Charles Ogle stood out as a villain beyond all villains. At this time the casting of Sessue Hayakawa as a hero was both daring and unusual. This was the height of the Yellow Peril scare generated in part by William Randolph Hearst, so public sentiment toward Orientals was not high. Even in the film the lovely Kitty Little shies away from the casual touch of the Japanese hero and later romantic scenes show some of the "Japanese lustfulness" that was a part of the stereotype. This was a recurring theme of those early melodramas as the peril of the yellow man who schemes to marry a white girl comes to light. The implausibility of such a union is taken for granted and the fact that the villain is even thinking about it is all the proof needed to show that he is indeed a villain at heart.

The Secret of the Submarine (1915)

Produced and distributed by American Film Manufacturing Company, Manuel Films (United States). Directed by George L. Sargent and written by war correspondent Richard Berry. This silent, black and white film, with English intertitles, ran for 15 episodes (24 minutes each and starred Juanita Henson, Tom Chatterton, Hylda Hollis, George Clancy, William Tedmarsh, Harry Edmondson, George Webb, Hugh Bennett, Perry Banks, Joseph Beaudry, Leona Hutton, and George Gebhardt.

Story: This serial was based on the United States Navy underwater service. It depicted the experiences of Lieutenant Jarvis Hope (Tom Chatterton) as he works to prevent the enemy (suggested as being from Russia or Japan) from gaining information about or control of the titular submarine.

Military Correlation: Spotty

Comment: Submarines are an odd kind of background for a war film. The sets themselves are claustrophobic and there is limited space for the characters to act out their roles. This was especially true in silent films. The conflict must come either from an external source, that is an enemy the crew cannot see, or it is an internal conflict acted out between the personalities of the characters. The rest of the time the men (and until recently it was always men) are sitting around looking at the various screens or listening to the sound of beeps. Written by Richard Berry, a war correspondent, this serial was an effort to urge America to make preparations for the war Berry knew was coming. The series began just 15 days after the *Lusitania* was sunk. All of the episodes in this series are presumed to have been lost.

The serial was a popular format that began early and ran well into the 1950s. It allowed multiple use of sets and the cost-effective repeating of scenes under different circumstances. They were usually shown in theaters before the feature films.

Sergeant York (1941)

Film: Produced by Howard Hawks, Jesse L. Lasky and Hal B. Wallis for Warner Brothers (United States). It was directed by Howard Hawks and written by Harry Chandlee, Aben Finkel, John Huston, Howard Koch, Tom Skeyhill, and Sam Cowan (uncredited). Cinematography by Sol Polito. Music by Max Steiner. This 134-minute black and white film stars Gary Cooper, Walter Brennan, Joan Leslie, George Tobias, Margaret Wycherly, Ward Bond, Noah Beery, Jr., June Lockhart, Dickie Moore, Clem Bevens, Howard Da Silva, Charles Trowbridge, Harvey Stephens, David Bruce, Carl Esmond, Joe Sawyer, Pat Flaherty, Robert Porterfield, Erville Alderson, Murray Alper, James Anderson, Arthur Aylesworth and Stanley Ridges.

Story: Tennessean Alvin C. York (Gary Cooper), an enlisted man in France, is torn between religious pacifism learned from his mother (Margaret Wycherly) and his sense of patriotic duty. He becomes the most famous hero of the war after he captures 132 German soldiers during the Meuse-Argonne offensive in October 1918. For this action he wins the Congressional Medal of Honor. A significant part of the movie takes place in his Tennessee hometown where he lives with his deeply religious parents . After he meets Gracie William (Joan Leslie) and, incidentally is struck by lightning, he adopts his parents' religious attitude and does odd jobs to make a living. He is drafted despite his pleas as a conscientious objector because his religion had no official standing. During training, it is discovered that York is a terrific marksman.

Determined not to kill anyone, he is sent home to think it over. There he has an experience where the wind blows open a Bible to the passage that instructs all to "render therefore unto Caesar the things which are Caesar's and unto God those things that are God's." He takes this as a sign and returns to the army willing to fight for his Caesar. In France he is tagged by an officer to join with Sergeant Earley (Joe Sawyer) in attacking a German position, but they are soon trapped and must go on the defensive. Marksman York kills so many Germans that the enemy finally surrenders. After the war he turns down all offers presented and return to his home in Tennessee.

Military Correlation: Good

Comment: In 2008 this film was selected for preservation in the National Film Registry as being "culturally, historically, or aesthetically significant." The battle scenes in the movie have the distinct feeling of having been staged and as such has the tendency to reduce York's heroic action to just one more of Hollywood's war films. This is one of the films that suffers from Hollywood's attempts to combine studio set footage and natural footage. When they are combined, if the sets are not superbly done, the juxtaposition with the natural settings make the sets look even more unrealistic.

York refused many offers to make a movie about his life and adventures. He finally gave in when the studio agreed to pay for the creation of an interdenominational bible school. He also insisted that Gary Cooper play him. Cooper won the Academy Award for Best Actor. Editor William Holmes received an award, and the film got nine other nominations: Best Director, Writing, Supporting Actress, Supporting Actor, Cinematography, Music, and Sound. It helped the film's success that it came along about the time of the attack on Pearl Harbor. It was a huge success both as a commercial venture and as a boost to national pride. As one military man said, the film sent men directly from the theater to the enlistment offices. The American Film Institute ranked the film 57th in its 100 most inspirational American movies, and rated York #35 among American heroes in cinema.

The line between agenda and entertainment was too easily crossed in this film as the message (the necessary defense of one's nation even in the face of God's concern) suffered from the need to make the movie entertaining. Ward Bond, who appeared in the film, was an epileptic and was rejected from service during World War II.

Bloopers: While American troops were assigned the M 1917 rifle, the movie has York using an M1903 Springfield.

The Service Star (1918) / aka *The Flag of Mothers*

Production by Samuel Goldwyn (United States). Directed by Charles Miller and written by Charles Logue. Cinematography by Louis Dunmyre and Ned Van Bureen. This 60-minute silent black and white film, with English intertitles, starred Clarence Oliver, Maude Turner Gordon, Mable Ballin, Victory Bateman, Tammany Young, William Bechtel, Jules Cowles, Zula Ellsworth, John Hemmingway, Phineas Billings, Isaac Wentworth, Madge Kennedy, and David Schuyler.

Story: Marilyn March (Madge Kennedy), a homely young woman, displays a service star in her window because she wants to be a part of the war effort. When she takes a job in Washington, her co-workers do not believe that the flag stands for anyone so Marilyn makes up a story about her secret marriage to John Whitney Marshall (Clarence Oliver), a well-known air ace. When the girls challenge this, Marshall's mother (Maude Turner Gordon) verifies the story, not because she believes it but because she knows her son is not an ace but a chemist working on a secret project for the government, and any publicity might endanger him. The two women keep the secret, allowing themselves to be involved in a vast number of difficult situations.

Military Correlation: None

Comment: In World War I as in World War II, small flags were available for display with a star for each person the house had in the armed services. Some homes had as many as six stars. Gold stars were displayed for a man killed. This film is considered lost.

The Seventy-Five Mile Gun (1918) see *The Seventy Mile Gun* (1918)

The Seventy Mile Gun (1918) / aka *The Seventy-Five Mile Gun*

Produced by Raoul Barre and Charles Bowers, American Pathe, B.F. Production Company (United States). Directed by Harry Conway "Bud" Fisher, Raoul Barre and Charles Bowers, it was written by Fisher, based on the Mutt and Jeff comic series. Animation by Dick Huemer. The seven-minute silent black and white film starred Augustus J. Mutt and Edgar Horace Jeff.

Story: The film focus on the antics of the "two mismatched tinhorns" Augustus J. Mutt, an incurable gambler, and his dimwitted friend Jeff, who join the Army and fight the Kaiser by making fun of him. The situation, in this case the artillery, was only a stage for the conduct of these anti-authoritarian characters.

Military Correlation: None

Comment: This was one of more than 300 such films made by Fisher's company between 1913 and 1926 and one of ten that in some way involved on World War I.

She Goes to War (1929)

Produced by Edward Halpaerin, Inspirational Pictures, United Artists (United States). Directed by Henry King and written by Fred de Gresac, Rupert Hughes, John Monk Saunders and Howard Estabrook. Cinematography by John P. Fulton and Tony Gaudio. Music by Modest Altscholer. The 87-minute, black and white, limited sound movie starred Eleanor Boardman, John Holland, Edmund Burns, Alma Rubens, Al St. John, Glen Walters, Margaret Seddon, Yola d'Avril, Evelyn Hall, Agostino Borgato, Dina Smirnova, Yvonne Starke, Eddy Chandler, Gretchen Hartman, Tiny Jones, H.M. Zier, Ann Warrington, and Eulalie Jensen.

Story: A bored and totally naive socialite, Joan Morans (Eleanor Boardman), follows her drunken boyfriend into the war. When her boyfriend proves to be a coward, and unable to fight, she goes to the line to take his place. In a swift and basically unexplained combat scene, she saves them all. The battle scenes are good and the close-up shots of men inside a burning tank are exceptional. But the story is so far-fetched as to be unbelievable even in this well-presented film. While Boardman does a good job and makes it almost believable, Alma Rubens (playing a minor character) stole the show. Unfortunately this was her last film as she succumbed to drugs shortly after its release.

Military Correlation: Helpful

Comment: The only surviving copy of this movie is a 50-minute cut-down with no intertitles, making it very hard to follow. Nevertheless the "blistering" action scenes are even more shattering than those seen in *All Quiet on the Western Front*.

Shoulder Arms (1918)

Produced and distributed by Charlie Chaplin Productions, First National (United States). Directed and written by Charlie Chaplin. The 46-minute black and white film stars Charlie Chaplin, Edna Purviance, Syd Chaplin, Jack Wilson, Tom Wilson, Henry Bergman, Albert Austin, J. Parks Jones and Loyal Underwood.

Story: A doughboy (Charlie Chaplin), stuck in boot camp in the Awkward Squad, spends too much of his time with dreams of glory. In one scene he receives some Limburger cheese, throws it behind the enemy lines, and then captures thirteen Germans. "I surrounded them," he explained, He then agreed to move through enemy lines disguised as a tree, and goes from there to help a French lady, win the love of a beautiful Belgian girl, and captures the Kaiser. All of this happens in his dreams.

Military Correlation: None

Comments: Charlie Chaplin received some complaints about being the first to produce a comedy about the war. (Actually the first was Captain Harry Conway "Bud" Fisher, creator of the Mutt and Jeff cartoons.) *Shoulder Arms* opened on Armistice Day in Chicago and was hailed by the *Chicago Tribune* as "a great picture with a great man on a great day." Charlie's brother Sydney plays a dual role in the film. True Boardman, Marion Feducha and Frankee Lee played Charles' sons in an early domestic scene that was cut, as were scenes of Peggy Preuose and Nina Trask as draft board clerks, Alf Reeves as a sergeant and Albert Austin as a doctor. The movie had an incredibly long life, reissued in 1922, 1927, 1943, 1959, 1963, 1971, and 1986. Chaplin, Douglas Fairbanks and Mary Pickford were all involved in bond drives. Chaplain was supportive of the war, a somewhat unexpected view considering his left-leaning attitudes about many contemporary issues.

Blooper: In such a film it is hard to tell what was intended and what was not but in one scene when Chaplin is hiding in a tube, a German tries to pull him out and in doing so pulls off his shoes. Then when Chaplin comes out, he is still wearing his shoes.

Shout at the Devil (1976)

Produced and distributed by Tonau Production Services (United States). Directed by Peter R. Hunt and written by Stanley Price and Alastair Reid, from a book by Will Smith. This 150-minute Technicolor film starred Lee Marvin, Roger

Moore, Barbara Parkins, Ian Holm, Reinhard Kolldehoff, Gernot Endermann, Karl Michael Vogler, Horst Janson, Gerald Paquis, Jean Kent, Heather Wright, George Coulouris, Maurice Denham, Murray Melvin, and Renu Setna.

Story: A drunken ivory poacher in pre–WWI German Africa, Captain O'Flynn (Lee Marvin) is aided by British aristocrat Sebastian Oldsmith (Roger Moore) in his illegal trade. This puts them at odds with the German provincial commissioner Herman Fletcher (Reinhold Kolldehoff). When Sebastian gets sick, Flynn's daughter Rose (Barbara Parkins) nurses him back to health. They fall in love and get married. When war breaks out they join together against their common enemy and decide to destroy a German battle-cruiser being repaired in an inlet not far from Zanzibar.

Military Correlation: Good

Comment: Not a bad movie but with all the modern techniques it could have been better. Roger Moore plays his usual emotionless role while Lee Marvin steals what there is of the show. The location is isolated and beautiful. During the filming Marvin and Moore got into a fistfight and most were very surprised when Moore came out ahead. Moore was forty-seven at the time.

Bloopers: There were several minor mistakes, as in the case of the crocodile that appears with four fingers and a thumb and the fact that the Portuguese choir singing at the wedding are singing in Maltese.

The Showdown (1917) / *aka* **Back to the Primitive**

Produced by Blue Bird Photoplays, Universal Studios (United States). Directed by Lynn E. Reynolds, and written by Waldemar Young and Reynolds. Cinematography by Clyde R. Cook. This five-reel silent black and white film, with English intertitles, starred Myrtle Gonzales, George Hernandez, Arthur Hoyt, Jean Hersholt, and George Chesebro.

Story: A group of wealthy passengers is aboard an ocean liner that is sunk by a German submarine. Left to survive as best they can, they make their way toward a deserted isle and wash up on the shore where they are totally unequipped to survive. After the anticipated tensions between the alpha dogs and a series of disasters, the commoner Bob Curtis (George Chesebro) takes charge and shows the others how to live off the land. In doing so he soon wins the love of Lydia Benson (Myrtle Gonzales) and the respect of the other shipwrecked passengers.

Military Correlation: None

Comments: While Lynn E. Reynolds directed a lot of films, primarily westerns, he never rose far above the technical abilities of the job, leaving the actors to pretty much direct themselves. He was known among movie critics as a "traffic cop" director. In this case it did not work out very well. In a fit of anger after arguing with his wife at a party, Reynolds shot himself in the head.

The Sky Hawk (1929)

Produced and distributed by Fox Film Corporation (United States). Directed by John G. Blystone, it was written by Llewellyn Hughes and Campbell Gullan. Cinematography by Conrad Wells. Music by Alfred Dalby and Jack Virgil. This 67-minute black and white film starred Helen Chandler, John Garrick, Gilbert Emery, Lennox Pawle, Lumsden Hare, Billy Bevan, Daphne Pollard, Joyce Compton, Jimmy Aubrey, Hans Fuerberg, Mary Gordon, David Manners, Ellinor Vanderveer, and Percy Challenger.

Story: Jack Bardell (John Garrick) disgraces himself and his father Lord Bardell (Lennox Pawle) when his plane mysteriously crashes on his way to fight the Germans. Both the military and his friends suspect he was a coward and may have been trying to avoid combat. Actually he has stopped to see his girlfriend Joan (Helen Chandler) and was not running away as he is suspected of doing. He eventually gets to regain his reputation when the Germans stage a huge zeppelin raid on London: By daring and heroic action he prevents them from completing their mission.

Military Correlation: Helpful

Comment: The movie is poorly done and the two leads are adequate at best. The air action is the best part of the movie and zeppelins are always attractive (and scary) to audiences. But the highly predictable story is so thin it does not carry the movie. For the time, the air battles that were filmed primarily with miniatures were remarkably well done.

The Slacker (1917)

Produced and distributed by Metro Film Corporation (United States). Directed by Christy Cabanne (as William Christy Cabanne) and written by Cabanne. This seven-reel silent black and white film, with English intertitles, starred Emily Stevens, Leo Delaney, Walter Miller, Eugene Borden, Daniel Jarrett, Millicent Fisher, Sue Balfour, Baby "Ivy" Ward, Charles Fang, Belle Bruce, Dorothy Haydel, W.E. Lawrence, Mathilde Brundage, Evelyn Converse, and Gilbert P. Hamilton.

Story: Two men, both in love with Margaret Christy (Emily Stevens), find themselves facing the draft. John Hardy (Leo Delaney) and his friend Robert Wallace (Walter Miller) both seek ways to avoid service if they can. Wallace urges Margaret, who works at the recruiting station, to marry him because he has learned that single men will be taken first. At a party for Wallace's brother (Eugene Borden), who has volunteered and is about to leave for the front, Margaret learns why Wallace was pushing for marriage. She calls him a slacker and breaks from him Later, suffering the effects of the insult, he sees a man take an American flag from a little girl. Without explanation he attacks the man. This apparently causes a change of heart and we see him at the end of the film wearing his uniform and marching happily off to France as his wife rejoices in his actions.

Military Correlation: Poor

Comment: This was one of many films designed to encourage men to respond to the draft lottery as it was called. Despite what appeared to be American enthusiasm for the war, and the large number of enlistments, Americans generally did not like the draft—it seemed sort of un–American. Nevertheless it was the law and the government went to a lot of effort convincing young men to obey it. It was considered a pretty good film in addition to its propaganda value. Some cast listing suggest that Ben Lyon played the juvenile lead but that is not confirmed by the film or other sources.

The Slacker's Heart (1917)

Produced and distributed by the American Emerald Motion Picture Company (United States). It was directed and written by Frederick J. Ireland. Cinematography by John J. Pasztor. This 90-minute silent black and white film, with English intertitles, starred Edward Arnold, Lillian De Turck, Bernadine Zuber, Tony West, Chester Woods, Phea Catto Laughlin, T.H. Westfall, Marion Skinner, Gustave Kleeman, Oscar G. Briggs, and Hilda Holberg.

Story: American pacifist Frank Allen (Edward Arnold) is determined not to fight, but finally decides to support the war effort after a vessel carrying his family is torpedoed and sunk by a German U-boat. His friend turns out to be a German spy who is working to get Mexico to come into the war supporting Germany. Allen, who has now become a staunch supporter of the Allied cause, decides that loyalty to country trumps loyalty to a friend, and exposes his German friend and brings a halt to the plans he had underway. The new hero unites with his girlfriend Phyllis (Lillian De Turck). Critics generally accepted it as a good and entertaining movie but one that did not quite live up to the potential of the fine actors that were involved.

Military Correlation: Spotty

Comment: There is a sub-theme running in many of these war production films that has to do with justification for involvement. It is in the national interest to support the war once involved but there were not a lot of reasons for Americans to *be* involved. Vast numbers of Americans had German roots and were not happy to turn against them. One obvious reason was to identify the individual harm that had been done to Americans—friends lost on the *Lusitania* or some such thing, to justify their involvement. Another tie-in here may well be the stir caused by the exposure of the Zimmerman telegram that caused a great deal of concern about our neighbors to the south.[44] In the case of this film, the jingoism of the hero is hard to explain even under the circumstances provided.

Somewhere in France (1915)

Produced and distributed by Thomas H. Ince, Kay-Bee Productions, New York Motion Picture Corporation, Triangle Films (United States). Directed by

Charles Giblyn and written by J.G. Hawks, based on the 1915 novel by Richard Hardin Davis. Cinematography by Dal Clawson. This 50-minute, silent, black and white film starred Louise Glaum, Howard C. Hickman, Joseph Dowling, Fanny Midgley, George Fisher, William Fairbanks, and Jerome Storm.

Story: An evil German woman, Marie Chaumontel (Louise Glaum), serves as a German spy, using her charms to seduce French officers and steal their secrets. Once she has what she wants, she leaves them. She becomes the mistress of French Captain Henry Ravignac (Jerome Storm), steals his papers and delivers them to the Germans. When the loss is discovered, he is charged with treason and found guilty. Unable to live with the shame he takes his own life. His brother Charles (Howard C. Hickman) vows revenge. He poses as a spy and works with Chaumontel until he has gathered enough information to have her arrested. In doing so he closes down the spy ring and clears his brother's reputation.

Military Correlation: Helpful

Comment: Another run-of-the-mill spy drama where the lady in question is first the betrayer and then the betrayed. The drama was the output of the studio formula system of overlapping plots and dialogue to get the most out of their contract stars. If we were assume these films told the true story, we would be left with the idea that American men went into battle with courage and determination and a patriotic if fatalistic attitude, while the women became seductive spies or sexual vamps plying their trade in the guise of nurses or entertainers.

Sonny (1922)

Produced by Henry King, Inspiration Pictures, Associated First Nation Distributors (United States). Directed by Henry King and written by King, Frances Marion, George V. Hobart, and Raymond Hubbell. Cinematography by Henry Cronjager. This 70-minute silent, black and white film, with English intertitles, stars Richard Barthelmess, Margaret Seddon, Pauline Garon, Lucy Fox, Herbert Grimwood, Patterson Dial, Fred Nicholls, James Tarbell, Margaret Elizabeth Falconer, and Virginia Magee.

Story: Sonny Crosby and Joe Marden (both played by Richard Barthelmess) join the army to fight in France. Sonny belongs to a well-to-do family, Joe is down on his luck and manages a pool hall. On the night before they leave, Sonny almost marries his sweetheart Madge Craig (Lucy Fox) and Joe, with no one else around, spends the evening with his faithful dog. When the two men meet on the battlefield in France they note their uncanny resemblance to each other and become good friends. When Sonny is wounded and knows he is about to die, he asks Joe to impersonate him when he returns home. Joe, who feels that he has nothing to lose, agrees and they switch dog tags and identities. After the armistice is signed, Joe heads home where he pretends to be the badly shell-shocked Sonny. With the help of a friend, Alicia (Patterson Dial), he gets away with it for some time. The plot thickens when Joe is attracted to Sonny's younger sister Florence (Pauline Garon). Not knowing what to do, he decides to do nothing. On the other hand he has no interest in Madge, with whom Sonny had had a fling, and who expects some attention. Madge's father (Herbert Grimwood), a social climber, finds out about the impersonation and threatens to blackmail Joe. Joe decides to do what is right and goes to Sonny's mother and tells her the whole story. She, of course, already knew what was going on, and was only playing along for his sake. All ends well because now he can join up with Florence.

Military Correlation: Spotty

Comment: The film was well received and Richard Barthelmess was applauded for his performance(s). The plot twist was not all that unexpected but it did not seem to detract from the film's popularity. The lookalike double identify was a highly popular theme in silent films and can be found in a good many of the war films.

The Spreading Evil (1918)

Produced and distributed by James K. Keane Feature Photo Play Production (United States). Directed and written by James Keane. This silent, seven-reel, black and white film with English intertitles starred Leo Pierson, Irene Wyllie, Carolyn Wagner, Joseph Clancy, William Hackett, Josephus Daniels, James Keane, Quex Bellamy, George B. Williams, and Howard Davies.

Story: A German submarine torpedoes a boat on which a German scientist was traveling to New York with a cure for syphilis. While posing as an adventure film, this is a very clever anti–venereal disease film put out to warn the soldier heading to Europe about the dangers of immoral conduct with foreign women. It does not say it, but the film clearly suggests that only European women had syphilis. Since the word "syphilis" was not publishable in many cities, it was referred to as "the blood disease." A tagline that appeared with some of the versions was "You wouldn't share your toothbrush, why share your woman." This film is presumed to have been lost.

Military Correlation: Good

Comment: Thousands upon thousands of American servicemen had to be treated for venereal diseases throughout the war, and this kept them off the battlefield. The effort to "keep American boys clean" was complicated by the fact that both the British and French military provided "clean houses" for their men and took a much more realistic attitude toward control of the disease. America's "just say no" campaign did not work. Not only were the authorities worried about the disease being contracted, but also about the veterans bringing it home to their loved ones.

The Spy (1917)

Produced and distributed by Fox Film Corporation, A William Fox Special (United States). Directed by Richard Stanton and written by George Bronson Howard. Cinematography by Dev Jennings. This silent, black and white film, with

English intertitles, starred Dustin Farnum, Winifred Kingston, William Burress, Charles Clary, William Lowry, May Abby and Howard Gaye.

Story: Anticipating that America will soon be involved in the war, the government sends an agent into Germany to learn the names and locations of German spies operating in the United States. The agent manages to infiltrate the German intelligence network and makes an effort to steal the list and escape with the list.

Comment: Another Hollywood story about seeking out German spies, whom everyone seemed to believe abounded in America.

The Spy and the Patriot (1915) see *Patriot and the Spy* (1915)

The Spy in Black (1939) / aka *U–Boat 29*

Produced by Alexander Korda and Irving Asher, London Film Productions (United Kingdom) and Columbia Pictures (United States). Directed by Michael Powell. Written by Robert Pertwee and Emeric Pressburger, on a novel by J. Storer Clouston. Cinematography by Bernard Browne. Music by Miklos Rozsa. This 82-minute black and white film starred Conrad Veidt, Valerie Hobson, Sebastian Shaw, Agnes Lauchlan, Athole Stewart, Helen Haye, June Duprez, Cyril Raymond, Mary Morris, George Summers, Hay Petrie, Grant Sutherland, Robert Rendel, Kenneth Warrington, Marius Goring, Bernard Miles, Graham Stark and Skelton Knaggs.

Story: German submarine commander Ernest Hardt (Conrad Veidt) is ordered to attack the British fleet at Scapa Flow. He goes ashore at the Orkney Islands to meet his contact who, it turns out, is masquerading at a schoolmistress (Valerie Hobson) The captain is in for more than he anticipated. The lovely spy is in fact a double agent for the British. Warned of the danger he was imposing on his own people, Hardt escapes and sinks his own submarine rather than cause the country any unnecessary harm. The Hun in this case is clearly presented, often with sophisticated black humor, as the bad guy.

Military Correlation: Poor

Comment: This World War I spy thriller was made as a "quota quickie" and released in order to fulfill the contract demand that the company produce a certain amount of British films. It went on to be named one of the ten best films of the year by the National Board of Review. The steamer *St. Magnus*, seen in the background of several shots, is the patron saint of Orkney. It's one of the few films to show any part of the war from the German point of view. The opening credits include a word of appreciation to "Kiel Base of the German Grand Fleet."

Bloopers: There are some weak spots as, for example, the rear projection of landscape for the kidnapping scene allows the edges to be seen. The dials and the officer's commands on the German submarine are in feet, not meters.

Stars of Glory (1919) see *Unknown Love* (1919)

Storm Over Africa (1955) see *The Royal African Rifles* (1955)

Submarine (1928)

Produced and distributed by Harry Cohn, Columbia Pictures (United States). Directed by Frank Capra and Irvin Willat (uncredited). Written by Dorothy Howell and Norman Springer. Cinematography by Joseph Walker. Music by David Brockman. This 93-minute black and white film with monophonic sound (for music and sound effects) starred Jack Holt, Dorothy Revier, Ralph Graves, Clarence Burton, Arthur Rankin, and Joe Bordeaux.

Story: Despite their long-standing friendship, two sailors have a major clash when they both fall in love with the same dance hall girl (Dorothy Revier). When Reagan (Jack Holt) wins her hand and marries her; his friend Bob Mason (Ralph Graves) is heartbroken. Bessie is not cut out for marriage and begins an affair with Mason, splitting the friends entirely. However, when Reagan is trapped underwater in a submarine, Mason is sent to rescue him. After the rescue Bessie confesses her infidelity but assures Reagan of Mason's loyalty and the friends reunite.

Military Correlation: Helpful

Comment: Submarine films were always popular and had many of the qualities of a stage play with which the audience was more familiar. It presented the story in a confined and controlled space, using dialogue to explain what was happening, with the everpresent tension of emotions waiting to surface. The sexual obsessions and witty reactions seem out of place with the rest of the film. It is hard to know if this use of the romantic triangle was simply a device to use fewer women in the films or if someone in Hollywood thought it was particularly romantic, maybe even tragic.

This was Capra's first effort at an A film. He was so pleased with the success of the film that he put its male heroes in two more talkies, *Flight* (1929) and *Dirigible* (1931). In the background of the rescue scene one can see the USS *Langley*, America's first aircraft carrier. The soundtrack that is available for this film is not the original track and is not well-coordinated.

Submarine D-1 (1937)

Produced and distributed by First National Films, Warner Brothers (United States). Directed by Lloyd Bacon. Written by Warren Duff, Frank "Spig" Wead, and Lawrence Kimble. Cinematography by Arthur Edeson. Music by Leo F. Forbstein. This 100-minute, black and white film stars Pat O'Brien, George Brent, Wayne Morris, Doris Weston, Veda Ann Borg, Dennie Moore, Henry O'Neill, Regis Toomey, and Frank McHugh.

Story: This movie involves the McCann Rescue Chamber, a piece of equipment used to save the men of a sinking submarine. Two sailors are in love with the same girl. The rivalry and the typical love triangle between "Butch" Rogers (Pat O'Brien), "Sock" McGill (Wayne Morris) and Ann Sawyer (Doris Weston) forms the crux of this story.
Military Correlation: Good
Comment: This film appears to have been designed to show off the newest ships, the strength of the submarine service and recruit sailors. Two actors who played minor parts, Ronald Reagan and Broderick Crawford, both ended up on the cutting room floor. Lieutenant Commander Frank Wead was an early naval aviator who turned to writing after an accident deprived him of the use of his legs.
Bloopers: During the film the sailors continue to wear their hats when inside, violating the rule that cover was worn inside only when on watch. This mistake is made in several movies.

Submarine Patrol (1938)

Produced by Ralph Dietrich, Gene Markey, and Darryl F. Zanuck, 20th Century-Fox (United States). Directed by John Ford. Written by William Faulkner, Sheridan Gibney, Rian James, Kathryn Scola, Darrell Ware, Gene Markey. Cinematography by Arthur C. Miller. Music by Arthur Lange and Charles Maywell (uncredited). This 95-minute black and white film starred Richard Greene, Nancy Kelly, Preston Foster, George Bancroft, Slim Summerville, John Carradine, Joan Valerie, Henry Armetta, Dick Hogan, Warren Hymer, Elisha Cook, Jr., Douglas Fowley, J. Farrell MacDonald, George E. Stone, Jack Pennick, Charles Trowbridge, Moroni Olsen, Ward Bond, Robert Lowery, Harry Strang, Lon Chaney, Jr., Max "Slapsie Maxie" Rosenbloom, Victor Varconi, Russ Clark, Charles Tannon, Ernie Alexander, Murray Alper, Dorothy Christy, Ray Cooke, Alan Davis, Duke Green, Fred Malatesta, Frank Moran, Ferdinand Schumann-Heink, Dick Wessel, and Manuel Paris.
Story: A wealthy playboy, Perry Townsend III (Richard Greene), joins the navy believing his father's influence will get him a high command, honor, and fame. Instead he is assigned as the engineer in the smallest boat in the splinter fleet under Lieutenant Drake (Preston Foster), who has been demoted on a charge of neglect and given a crew of undesirables. Much of the time Townsend directs his efforts to chasing Susan Leads (Nancy Kelly) whose disapproving father is the captain of a munitions boat. Her previous companion was the sour-looking McAllison (John Carradine), who simply cannot compete with the charm of the engineer. Drake shapes up the crew, helps Townsend find himself while, and in charge of a worn-out antique sub-chaser, he takes on a German U-boat during World War I. Through these exploits he regains his honor, the girl, and the fame he was seeking.
Military Correlation: Helpful
Comment: Some critics report that this was John Ford's favorite film, a claim

that seems hard to believe when considering some of his far more famous films. This was Nancy Kelly's first adult role.

A Submarine Pirate (1915) / aka *Submarine Story*

Produced and distributed by Keystone Film Company (United States). Directed by Charles Avery and Syd Chaplin and written by Mack Sennett. This 24-minute silent, black and white comedy, with English intertitles, starred Syd Chaplin, Phyllis Allen, Glen Cavender and featured an uncredited appearance by Harold Lloyd.

Story: A trouble-making waiter (Syd Chaplin) at a fancy restaurant overhears an inventor (Glen Cavender) and a friend talking about a submarine they are going to use to rob a passenger ship that is carrying gold. The waiter decides to thwart the plot. He buys an admiral's uniform and cons his way onto the submarine, then comes up with a plan to take the money for himself.

Military Correlation: None

Comment: Producer Mack Sennett brought his slapstick comedy from vaudeville with him and then was equally as successful making the transition from silent to talkies. This typical Sennett movie has no reasonable plot but is only a situation in which Syd Chaplin can perform his skits. Glen Cavender was one of the original Keystone Kops.

Submarine Story (1915)
see *The Submarine Pirate* (1915)

Suspense (1930)

Produced by Walter Summers, British International Pictures, Wardour Films (United Kingdom). Directed by Walter Summers and written by Summers and Patrick MacGil. Cinematography by Theodor Sparkuhl and Hal Young. This 75-minute black and white film starred Mickey Brantford, Cyril McLaglen, Jack Raine, Hay Petrie, Fred Groves, Percy Parsons, Syd Crossley, and Hamilton Keene.

Story: A platoon of new men is sent in to take over an area on the line that they consider quiet. Private Pettigrew's (Mickey Brantford) first clue that something is wrong is the tense and exhausted faces of the men they are relieving. The platoon is a mixed bag of British commoners who react differently, but who as a group represent the unity of the force. In the still of the night, they can hear Germans underneath them digging tunnels to blow up the British trenches. Night after night they listen, unable to do anything about it. An officer (Hamilton Keene), when told about it, does not seem to care.

Military Correlation: Good

Comment: Tunneling was an important and acceptable part of World War I warfare (see 2010s *Beneath Hill 60*). This highly psychological film mirrors the tensions of such warfare. The battle effects created by Cliff Richardson at Elstree Studio are very good. The character of Private Bill Baldrick of Blackadder steals the show. While this is a very early film and much of the acting is somewhat theatrical, it goes over well.

Tell England (1931) / aka *The Battle of Gallipoli*

Produced by H. Bruce Woolfe, British Instructional Films, Wardour Films (United Kingdom). Directed by Anthony Asquith and Geoffrey Barkas. Written by A P. Herbert and Asquith, based on a novel by Ernest Raymond. Cinematography by Jack Parker, Stanley Rodwell and James E. Rogers. Music by Hubert Bath. This 80-minute film stars Fay Compton, Tony Bruce, Carl Harbord, Dennis Hoey, C.M. Hallard, Gerald Rawlinson, Frederick Lloyd, Sam Wilkinson, Wally Patch, and Hubert Harben.

Story; Two young men, Edgar Doe (Carl Harbord) and Rupert Ray (Tony Bruce), one rich and one poor, are chums and friendly competitors. They both join the army that has been conscripted to fight at the front at Gallipoli. Caught in a stalemate in Europe, the Allied leaders search for a way to break out. Pushed on by Winston Churchill[45] to strike at the "soft underbelly of Europe," the campaign against the Turks was a fiasco, poorly planned and badly executed. When the young men get there, the glory they expected becomes hell on earth and they encounter not only great danger but great disillusionment about the war. The war there is even more devastating than it was in the trenches. The film ends with the death of one of the men.

Military Correlation: Good

Comment: Both of this movie's directors had memories of Gallipoli as did Fay Compton's brother Compton Mackenzie. The fact that Anthony Asquith's father Herbert Asquith was prime minister at the time of the Gallipoli landings drew considerable press attention. Some critics suggested that the movie's intended purpose was to clear the British of responsibility for the failures at Gallipoli but there is little evidence that this is the case. If that *was* the intention, it did not work. Co-director Geoffrey Barkas also fought at Gallipoli. The movie was originally designed to be a silent film but was delayed so long they were able to produce it in sound.

That They Might Live (1938)
see *J'accuse!* (1938)

13 Men and a Gun (1938)

Produced by Mario Zampi, Pisorno Cinematografica, Two Cities, British Independent Films (United Kingdom). Directed by Mario Zampi and written by Kathleen Connors, Basil Dillion, and Giovanni Gorzano. Cinematography by

Mario Albertelli. Music by Ronald Binge. This 64-minute black and white film starred Arthur Wontner, Donald Gray, Scott Harold, Bernard Miles, Andre Morell, John Kevan, Clifford Evans, Howard Marion Crawford, Allen Jeayes, Gibb McLaughlin, and Wally Patch.

Story: Set along the Austrian-Russian border during World War I, this highly intense drama involves artillery that is maintained in strict secrecy, and its thirteen-man crew led by a captain (Arthur Wontner). When the Russians locate the artillery and destroy it, the authorities believe that a member of the gun crew must have betrayed them. When the identity of the traitor remains a mystery; the Austrian commander (Allen Jeayes), acting under intense pressure from above, decides to execute the entire crew. Before the sentence is carried out, the traitor is identified and the lives of the other crew members are spared.

Military Correlation: Good

Comment: An interesting film set in a fascinating location. The themes alternate between duty, loyal comradeship, and the lasting effects of official stupidity. Numerous cases came out of the war where the official response to individual failure was to punish a group. This story, we are told, was based on a real event. In 1942, Zampi founded Two Cities Films. This is the English version of *Tredici unmin e un cannone*.

Three Comrades (1938)

Produced and distributed by Metro-Goldwyn-Mayer (United States). It was directed by Frank Borzage and written by F. Scott Fitzgerald and Edward A. Paramore, from a book by Erich Maria Remarque. The 95-minute black and white film, with English intertitles, starred Margaret Sullavan, Robert Taylor, Robert Young, Franchot Tone, Guy Kibbee, Lionel Atwill, Henry Hull, Charley Grapwin, and Monty Woolley.

Story: This somewhat melodramatic postwar love story involves three disillusioned soldiers, Erich Lohkand (Robert Taylor), Otto Koster (Franchot Tone) and Gottfried Lenz (Robert Young), returning to Germany. Their mutual friendship is strengthened, but complicated, by the fact they all share a love for the same woman, Patricia Hollmann (Margaret Sullavan) who, though she finally marries one of them, is dying from tuberculosis.

Military Correlation: Helpful

Comment: This movie was carefully tailored so as not to too heavily indict the leading party in Germany. The Nazi party was just coming to power and very sensitive about such things as the treatment of the Jews and the burning of books. The movie still conveys the haunting sense of hopelessness and waste of war, as these brave but obviously neurotic men become upset with the growth of Fascism in Germany, and with the lack of opportunities for them upon their return the nation. It is among other things a hauntingly beautiful love story but one without much hope. This is one of the few films that credits F. Scott Fitzgerald as a writer.

Three Faces East (1926)

Produced and distributed by Cecil B. DeMille, Cinema Corporation of America, Producers Distributing Corporation (United States). Directed by Rupert Julian and written by Monte M. Katterjohn and Anthony Paul Kelly. Cinematography by J. Peverell Marley. Music by Hugo Riesenfeld. The film stars Jetta Goudal, Clive Brook, Henry B. Walthall, Edythe Chapman, Clarence Burton, Rupert Julian and Ed Brady.

Story; Frances Hawtree (Jetta Goudal) is in reality British secret agent Z-1. At the moment she is posing as British Army nurse Fraulein Marks and working to secure some secret files. She must first deal with master spy Valdar (Clive Brook), who is serving as the butler in the home of a British diplomat. We are not sure if he is a German spy or a British spy.

Military Correlation: Helpful

Comment: The film was reformatted in 1930 as a talkie and then again in 1940 as *British Intelligence*. The film gave director Rupert Julian yet another chance to play the role of the Kaiser, which he had done in several films, and seemed to enjoy.

Three Faces East (1930)

Produced by Darryl F. Zanuck, Warner Brothers (United States). Directed by Roy Del Ruth and written by Arthur Caesar and Oliver H.P. Garrett, from a play by Anthony Paul Kelly. Cinematography by Bernard McGill. Music by Paul Lamkoff. This black and white film stars Constance Bennett, Erich von Stroheim, Anthony Bushell, William Courtenay, Crauford Kent, Charlotte Walker, William Holden, Ullrich Haupt, Paul Panzer, and Wilhelm von Brincken.

Story; British Army nurse Frances Hawtree (Constance Bennett) is in reality British secret agent Z-1. Posing as Fraulein Marks, she is working to aid her co-agent Schiller Blecher smuggle some important secrets from the home of Winston Chamberlain (William Holden). Using the three word code "three faces east," she contacts Valdar (Erich von Stroheim) who is, as all can see, very German and a serious risk. Working the double agent idea to the hilt, the movie fades out with the audience still not sure if Valdar is an English agent or a German one.

Military Correlation: Helpful

Comment: Even the best of reviews pointed out that this film creaked as only a stage play adapted for talkie could. The characters move about with the exaggerated histrionics of a much earlier period. Erich von Stroheim is, as is often the case, the best performer especially when playing his leering (going through the ladies' suitcase of underwear) self. There is so little action it could have been filmed on a single sound stage. Each actor seems to give a good performance, they just don't seem to always be in the same movie. Constance Bennett is the exception but while she is attractive in this role, you see little of the acting ability that comes in later films.

Bloopers: In this film Captain Arthur wonders if Frances was her brother's boyfriend, apparently forgetting that the brother was gay.

Thunder Over the Desert (1940) see *Forty Thousand Horsemen* (1940)

Till I Come Back to You (1918)

Produced by Jesse L. Lasky, Famous Players Artcraft (United States). Directed by Cecil B. DeMille and written by Jeanie Macpherson, Clarence Gildart, Frank Butterworth. Cinematography by Alvin Wyckoft. This silent, black and white film, with English intertitles, starred Bryant Washburn, C. Renfield, Florence Vidor, Gustav von Seyffertitz, Winter Hall, George Stone, Julia Faye, Lillian Leighton, Mae Giraci and William Irving.

Story: A young Belgian girl, Yvonne (Florence Vidor), is married to a German, Karl von Krutz (Gustav von Seyffertitz), who confesses to her after their marriage that he is a spy. He soon leaves for Germany to join the armed forces. When the United States enters the war, Jefferson Strong (Bryant Washburn) becomes a spy for America and he is ordered to take on Krutz's identify so he can go behind the lines and blow up a liquid fire base. Yvonne is now in charge of 65 war orphans who will be killed in the explosion if this happens. Strong can't do it and cuts the fuse. He is tried for his actions but King Albert of Belgium unexpectedly frees him. Von Krutz conveniently dies and opens the way for Strong and Yvonne to get together.

Military Correlation: Helpful

Comment: It is never explained just why the spy, if he is working in America to bring about its defeat, had to go to Germany to join the army. In later years DeMille admitted that he did not consider it one of his better works.

To Hell with the Kaiser (1918)

Produced and distributed by Screen Classics (United States). Directed by George Irving. Written by June Mathis. This silent, black and white film, with English intertitles, starred Lawrence Grant, Mary McAvoy, Betty Howe, and Olive Tell.

Story: The Kaiser, afraid he will be assassinated, decides to hire a lookalike actor to take his place on some occasions. The actor uses the opportunity to cause all sorts of mischief. The crown prince thinks little of the rape of girls from the nunnery or the mistreatment of the nuns. One of the prince's conquests is the daughter of an American inventor; the inventor protests what has happened and is killed. The girl, seeking revenge, uses a newly invented wireless machine to contact a squadron of planes to bomb the village where the Kaiser and the crown prince are located. The Kaiser is captured and put into a POW camp.

Military Correlation: None

Comment: This movie harshly depicting the German leaders. It is often considered to be in the same league as the highly popular *Shoulder Arms*. It came out after the war was over and was sold to a less interested public as "It was great before. It is even greater now." This film is considered lost.

To the Rescue (1918)

Produced by Raoul Barre and Charles Bowers, American Pathe, B.F. Production Company (United States). Directed by Harry Conway "Bud" Fisher, Raoul Barre and Charles Bowers, it was written by Fisher, based on the Mutt and Jeff comic series. Animation by Dick Huemer. The silent black and white film starred Augustus J. Mutt and Edgar Horace Jeff.

Story: The film focus on the antics of the comic characters Mutt and Jeff, who become involved in a haphazard rescue attempt.

Military Correlation: None

Comment: This was one of more than 300 such films made by Fisher's company between 1913 and 1926 and one of ten that focuses on World War I.

Tommy Atkins (1915)

Produced and distributed by Barker Production Corporation, I.C.C. (United Kingdom). Directed by Bert Haldane. Written by Ben Landeck, Rowland Talbot, and Arthur Shirley, based on a play by the same name. This five-reel silent, black and white film, with English intertitles, stars Blanche Forsythe, Jack Tessier, Roy Travers, Maud Yates and Barbara Rutland.

Story: A German-born captain (Roy Travers) kills his wife and frames his fiancée.

Military Correlation: Unknown

Comment: Tommy Atkins is the nickname long associated with the common British soldiers. A 1928 film of the same name, with primarily the same cast, and basically the same plot, is set in the Sudan.

Treason (1917)

Produced and distributed by Universal Film Manufacturing Company (United States). Directed by Allen Holubar and written by Robert Lee Weigert. Cinematography by Roy H. Klaffki. This five-reel, silent, black and white film, with English intertitles, starred Allen Holubar, Lois Wilson, Dorothy Davenport, Burton Law, Joseph W. Girard, George Pearce, Edward Hearn, and L.M. Wells.

Story: "Somewhere in Europe," in a land called Statiria, the men of the army wears French-looking uniforms. Our Hero Baariot (Allen Holubar) and his rival Danick Rysson (Edward Hearn) are in the service. Baariot has the cushy job as telegraph operator on the line. They are also rivals for the hand of Flora Nature

(Lois Wilson). Baariot's position is overrun and he is wounded. While he's in the hospital, Flora starts going out with Rysson. Baariot, angry over the whole affair, gives away some secrets to a spy from an unnamed nation. When his true loyalty takes over, he chases the spy, retrieves his secrets and wins back the hand of Flora Nature.

Military Correlation: Poor

Comment: Pretty low-key and slow-moving, half spy and half war drama. There is very little that is fresh and quite a bit that is old-hat. The action is stilted and the dialogue, what there is of it, is dull.

The Trench (1999)

Produced by Mairi Bett, Bray Films, Art Council of England (United Kingdom), Bonaparte Films (France). Directed and written by William Boyd. Cinematography by Tony Pierce-Roberts. Music by Evelyn Glennie and Greg Malcangi. This 98-minute film stars Paul Nicholls, Daniel Craig, Julian Rhind-Tutt, Danny Dyer, James D'Arcy, Tam Williams, Anthony Strachan, Michael Moreland, Adrian Lukis, Clarian McMenamin, Cillian Murphy, John Higgins, Ben Whishaw, Tim Murphy, Charles Cartmell, Tom Mullion, Jenny Pickering, Tom Silburn, Dahren Davey, Jamie Newell, Stan Charity, Chris Bridgeman, Luke Duckett, Guy Barrett, and Danny Nutt.

Story: In 1916 on the eve of the catastrophic Battle of the Somme, a group of young English soldiers wait for the order to go into battle. The movie is there with them as they deal with the waiting. The plot deals with the terrible boredom, the awesome fear, the moments of extended panic, their profound restlessness and total confusion. They are led by the jingoistic Sergeant Winter (Daniel Craig) and a scholarly lieutenant (Julian Rhind-Tutt). It's a character study as soldier after soldier remembers his past in an effort to avoid contemplating his fate.

Military Correlation: Helpful

Comment: This movie provides an unusual perspective on the bloodiest day in the history of the British Empire. It owes something to R.C. Sheriff's *Journey' End* (1930) but by itself is ultimately heartbreaking. The director had the whole cast spend a night in a recreated trench where they could get a feel for it. There are, it appears, too many characters for the length of the film, so much so that it all seems rushed even though the movie itself appears to move very slowly. This was Ben Whishaw's first film.

U–Boat 29 (1939) see *The Spy in Black* (1939)

U-9 Weddigen (1927)

Produced and distributed by Johannisthaler Filmanstalten (Germany). Directed by Heinz Paul and written by Willy Rath. The silent, black and white movie stars Gerd Briese, Ernest Hofmann, Fred Solm, Hella Moja, Mathirde Sussin, Fritz Alberti, Hans Mierendorff, Carl de Vogt, Hanne Brinkmann, and Willy Mendan.

Story: A generally true story based on the exploits of the German submarine *U-9* under the command of Captain Weddigen (Carl de Vogt), who managed to sink three British cruisers, the *Aboukir*, *Hogue* and *Cressy*, with the loss of more than 1,400 men, in just under an hour. The sinkings occurred on the evening of December 22, 1914. The boat and its crew were hailed as heroes by the German high command. Captain Weddigen and most of his crew were later killed in action.

Military Correlation: Good

Comment: This is a fairly straightforward film effectively presented with little exaggeration or distortion. Kapitanleutnant Otto Weddigen had been forced to dive deep to sit out a storm and when he rose he discovered three British armored cruisers of the Cressy Class, sailing abreast at about ten knots. He managed to destroy all three. It's one of the few movies that looks at the sea war, and one of the very few that lets the Germans come out ahead. *The Sound of Music* (1965) also featured a U-boat captain, Von Trapp, from this same period though it was not about his World War I service. He ranked sixth in the number of sinkings among submarine captains, and was the only one of that group to survive.

Ultimatum (1938)

Produced by Herman Millakowsky and Robert Wiene, Films Ultimatum, Forrester Parant (France), Milo Films (United States). Directed by Robert Wiene and Robert Siodmak. Written by Edwal Bertram, Pierre Allary, Alexandre Arnoux and Leo Lania, based on Bertram's novel *Days Before the Storm*. Cinematography by Robert Lefebvre, Jacques Mercanton, and Theodore J. Pahle. Music by Adolphe Borchard. This 83-minute (French), and 73-minute (United States) film starred Dita Parlo, Erich von Stroheim, Abel Jacaquin, Bernard Lancret, Georges Rollin, Marcel Andre, Raymond Aimos, Lila Kedrova, Pierre Nay, Rene Alle, Nino Constantini, Lucien Pascal, Andre Nox, Georges Vitray, Jacques Henley, Georges Paulais, Frederic Mariotti, Frederic O'Brady, Louis Vonelly, Edith Gallia, Michele Lahaye, and Marcel Peres.

Story: Set in July 1914 against the assassination of Archduke Franz Ferdinand and the opening days of the First World War, *Ultimatum* focuses on the strained relationship between a Serbian-born officer and his Austrian-born wife as they become involved in espionage between their two countries. Messing up the situation is the presence of a fellow Austrian with an eye for the wife.

Military Correlation: Spotty

Comment: This was not a very good film. The only really interesting role is played by the forever Prussian Erich von Stroheim. Robert Wiene was a famous German film director who had been forced to flee from Germany when the Nazis came to power. This was his final film as he died while filming and was replaced by Robert Siodmak. The fact that the cast included Dita Parlo and von Stroheim led many to compare it with Renoir's *The Grand Illusion* (1937). The "ultimatum" of the title is a reference to the Austrian demands issued to Serbia which, it is generally held, led to war.

The Unbeliever (1918)

Produced and distributed by Perfection Production, Edison Company (United States). Directed by Alan Crossland, it was adapted from a novelette (*The Three Things*) by Mary Raymond Shipman Andrews. This 80-minute silent black and white film, with English intertitles, starred Marguerite Courtot, Raymond McKee, Erich von Stroheim, Kate Lester, Frank DeVernon, Mortimer Martine, Blanche Davenport, Harold Hollacher, Darwin Karr, Earl Schenck, Gertrude Norman, Lew Hart, Thomas Holcomb, J. F. Rorke, and Moss Gill.

Story: This film depicts the trauma of young Philip Landiscutt (Raymond McKee) who has three identifiable failings: he is an atheist, he hates all Germans, and he considers himself superior to all other persons. For unidentifiable reasons Phil enlists in the Marines and through a series of nearly improbable coincidences, lucky wounds and unbelievable luck, he comes to accept religion and believe in God, fall in love with a poor working class Belgian girl, Virginia Hartbrok (Marguerite Courtot), come to love democracy and even appreciate some Germans.

Military Correlation: Good

Comment: A well-made and entertaining movie with the characters playing in such a way as to speak louder than their gestures or actions. It was made with the help of Marine extras from the 78th, 79th, 80th, and 96th company. The idea was to engage real Marines and work them into the narrative in such a way as to link real officers and men of the 3rd Battalion of the 6th Regiment of the United States Marines with the movie Marines. The movie was sanctioned by the attaches of the allied governments. J.C.E. Guggenheim of the local Marine station said that as a result of *The Unbeliever's* run at the Rialto Theatre, they had secured at least one hundred recruits.[46] Erich von Stroheim, who plays his usual role as the man you love to hate, is unaccountably billed as Karl von Stroheim. In the film he even attacks his own men, destroying a young soldier's musical instrument and yelling, "You are here to fight not to fiddle." The Edison Company made only one more film after this and then closed its doors in March of 1918.

Under the German Yoke (1915)

Produced and distributed by Clarendon Production, Pathe Executive (United States), Pathe Freres (France). Directed by Wilfred Noy. This silent, black and white film, with English intertitles, starred Dorothy Bellew, George Keene, and Elizabeth Grayson.

Story. A major's daughter shoots a Prussian captain. Her old nurse brings back the British army to save the major from execution.

Military Correlation: Unknown

Comment: This appears to be one of the quickies designed to meet a quota set by contract with distributors.

Unknown Love (1919) / aka *Stars of Glory*

Produced by Léonce Perrett, Perrett Productions, Pathe Exchange (United States), Pathe Freres (France). Directed and written by Leonce Perrett. This 60-minute black and white film, with English intertitles, starred Dolores Cassinelli, E.K. Lincoln, Bradley Barker, Robert Elliott, and Warren Cook.

Story: The young pen pal (Dolores Cassinelli) of a wounded soldier (E.K. Lincoln) decides to go to Europe to see him. Unbeknownst to her, he has sent her the picture of his friend rather than his own. She talks a naval friend into taking her on board his ship to France, but the ship is sunk by German submarines, and her naval friend killed. She finally manages to get to France and locates her wounded friend who, his face covered with bandages, is unrecognizable. In the next few months, however, she falls in love with the person, not the face, and they marry and live happily together after the War.

Military Correlation: Poor

Comment: *Unknown Love* was generally well received by the public but most critics seemed to agree that the movie was "corny and unrealistic." "Corny" probably; "unrealistic" most certainly. Léonce Perret was involved in more than 400 films as actor, director, or producer and was the innovator of numerous camera shots. He came to the U.S. in 1917; most of the movies he directed were produced by the French company Pathe of France. The French outsourced the films because they were cheaper to produce in the United States, and being silent, the language made no difference.

The Unpardonable Sin (1919)

Produced by Harry Garson, Blanche Sweet Productions of World Pictures (United States). It was directed by Marshall Neilan and Alfred E. Green and written by Kathryn Stuart, based on the book of the same name by Rupert Hughes. Music by Frederick V. Bowers. This 90-minute silent, black and white film, with English intertitles, starred Blanche Sweet, Edwin Stevens, Mary Alden, Matt Moore, Wesley Barry, Wallace Beery, Bull Montana, Bobby Connelly, Dick Curtis and John De Lacy.

Military Correlation: Poor

Comment: The title was enough to attract attention. The film was banned by the Kansas Board of Review became of its vivid scene depicting rape. Several things were wrong with the film, among them the injection of some totally inappropriate comedy scenes. In general it was rejected by the American people, who wanted no more reminders of the awful events.

Vengeance (1916) see *La Revanche* (1916)

A Very Long Engagement (2004)

Produced and distributed by Warner Brothers, Tapioca Films (United States). Directed by Jean-Pierre Jeunet and written by Sabastien Japrisot and Jean-Pierre Jeunet. This 133-minute color film stars Audrey Tautou, Gaspard Ulliel, Jodie Foster, Dominque Pinon, Clovis Cornillac, Andre Dussollier, Ticky Holgado, Dominque Bettenfield, Marion Cotillard, Denis Lavant, and Alvert Dupontel.

Story: Five young soldiers give themselves minor injuries in an effort to avoid being sent to the front line. When the authorities discover what they have done, it is decided that they have to be punished immediately. They are forcefully taken up to the front and pushed into the attack, and within a few minutes all of them are dead. No records were kept of the event nor were the families informed of what happened. One of the young men had a fiancée, Mathilde (Audrey Tautou), who decides to find out what happened and goes to France. She discovers what the horrors of war does to men, especially those in command, and what ghastly treatment is meted out to soldiers who seek to escape from the onslaught. During all this time Mathilde is fighting her own battle with polio. She learns a great deal about the heart and soul of the human spirit.

Military Correlation: Spotty

Comment: Several World War I movies address this issue of the execution of men for a variety of crimes. The willingness of a man to flee when faced with enemy fire depends on many things, often other than courage. There were such cases, without a doubt, but the films tended to make more of them than was known at the time. It would be twenty years before most of the information about unit executions was known.

Victory (1928)

Produced and distributed by Gaumont British Picture Corporation, Woolf and Freedman Film Service (United Kingdom). Directed by M.A. Wetherell and written by Boyd Cable. Cinematography by Freddie Young and Joe Rosenthal. This silent, black and white film, with English intertitles, starred Moore Marriott, Walter Byron, Julie Suedo, Marie Ault, Griffith Humphreys, Douglas Herald, Marjorie Gaffney, and Victor Maxim Moorkins.

Story: Fleeing the German advance, many refugees go into England. One of these is the very rich Marie Dulac (Julie Suedo), who was helped in her escape by Seth Lee (Moore Marriott), a British pilot. Assigned to take a Canadian officer, Major King (Walter Byron), on a dangerous mission of sabotage behind the enemy lines, Lee and his passenger are shot down and hide in a cottage near to where Marie had lived. Much to their surprise, they discover that Marie is there and it looks very much like she is consorting with the enemy. Marie, however, is really involved in counterespionage efforts without the Germans knowing it. All this allows the major to complete his effort. Marie and the major, now lovers, escape.

Military Correlation: Helpful

Comment: Considered a specialist in military melodramas, Boyd Cable was the author of *Between the Lines* that provided a look at life in the trenches. When he paired with M.A.Wetherell, who had done *The Somme* (1916), they came up with a pretty good film. The plot is old and tired but the actors brought some new life in to it, and were able to keep the tensions high.

Victory and Peace (1918)
see *The Invasion of Britain* (1918)

The Volunteer (1917) /
aka The Littlest Volunteer; Little Patriots

Produced and distributed by World Film (United States). Directed by Harley Knoles and written by Julia Burnham. This 50-minute silent black and white film, with English intertitles, starred Madge Evans, Henry Hull, Muriel Ostriche, Victor Kennard, Jack Drumier, Kate Lester, Charles W. Charles, William A. Brady, Kitty Gordon, Ethel Clayton, June Elvidge, Evelyn Greely, Carlyle Blackwell, Harley Knoles, and Montagu Love.

Story: When her father and mother go off to serve in the war, child star Madge Evans (playing herself) is sent to live with her grandparents, Timothy (Jack Drumier) and Tabitha (Kate Lester) Mandenhall. They are Quakers and very stern disciplinarians. Her uncle Jonathan (Henry Hull) wants to enlist and does so when he comes of age. He is disowned by his father. When Madge's film comes to town, she begs to see it but they will not let her. Timothy secretly attends the showing and is so won over by it that he has a change of heart, embraces Madge, forgives his son and reunites with her mother, whom he cast out earlier for marrying against his will. He urges them all to come home safely.

Military Correlation: None

Comment: One of the more interesting "conversion" films, *The Volunteer* made good use of the Quaker angle to show that even the traditionally peaceful are aware that you sometimes have to fight. *Sergeant York* (1941) makes this same appeal. The film includes scenes from the World Film Corporation at Fort Lee, New Jersey, and cameo appearances by the director general William A. Brady as well as Harley Knoles. Stars William A. Brady, Kitty Gordon, Ethel Clayton, June Elvidge, Evelyn Greeley, Carlyle Blackwell and Montagu Love make cameo appearances themselves. It is Hollywood's version of the deus ex machina where all things are corrected in a single incident.

Von Richthofen and Brown (1971) /
aka The Red Baron

Produced by Gene Corman, Corman Company, United Artists (United States). Directed by Roger Corman and written by John William Corrington and

Joyce Hooper Corrington. Cinematography by Michael Reed. This 97-minute color film stars John Phillip Law, Don Stroud, Barry Primus, Corin Redgrave, Karen Ericson, Hurd Hatfield, Stephen McHattie, Robert La Tourneaux, Peter Masterson, Clint Kimbrough, Tom Adams, Ferdy Mayne, David Weston, John Flanagan, and Brian Foley.

Story: The storyline is based loosely on the life of the German ace, the Red Baron, who must deal with the flying attacks of his enemies but also the insults of other German officers jealous of his success. He is, in this film, dedicated to the code despite his desire to win. His counterpoint was the Canadian flyer Arthur Roy Brown who in this film is depicted as cynical and ruthless. Eventually the Red Baron, already weakened by a head wound, is shot down by Brown. The Baron is the "faithful enemy."

Military Correlation: Poor

Comment: The movie, filmed in Ireland, was shut down for some time when an air crash caused the government to cancel all flights. The film seems more interested in exposing the class struggles that existed in both armies during this time than it is in suggesting any real importance to the war itself. Also emphasized is von Richthofen's personal fight between the harsh brutality of war and the code of ethics that he was brought up with. After all this, the final scene is anti-climactic.

The movie reports to be a true story but there are a lot of historians who see it differently, with the best current information suggesting the Red Baron was brought down by a rifleman on the ground. The air scenes are quite factual with vintage planes but the crashes were done by a hobby club of teenagers at Andrews Air Force Base using models. One of the pilots in the film was Richard Bach, the author of *Jonathan Livingston Seagull* (1973).

Blooper: The interruption gear, that allowed machine-guns to fire through the propellers, caused a much slower rate of fire than was shown in the movie.

The W Plan (1930)

Production by Victor Saville, British International Pictures, Elstree Studio (United Kingdom), RKO Radio Pictures (United States). Directed by Saville and written by Victor Saville, Miles Malleson and Frank Launder. Cinematography by Rene Guissart and Freddie Young. This 87-minute black and white film starred C.M. Hallard, Frederick Lloyd, B. Gregory, Mary Jerrold, Clifford Heatherlay, Austin Trevor, Norah Howard, Cameron Carr, Milton Rosmer, Charles Paton, Wilhem Konig, Brian Aherne, Madeleine Carroll, Gibb McLaughlin, Gordon Harker, George Merritt.

Story: High-ranking British officer Duncan Grant (Brian Aherne) learns from a dying German officer (George Merritt) about a secret W plan. When Grant talks with his superior about it, they decide to send him (he speaks German) to find out what it is. He is dropped by plane near the area where they believe it is being undertaken. There he meets old sweetheart Rose Hartmann (Madeleine Carroll). While they are dining, a German officer becomes suspicious of Grant and he runs away.

The plane that was supposed to pick him up has been destroyed in a dog fight and so Grant is finally taken prisoner. Instead of shooting him, the Germans decide to use him as forced labor and he is sent to the very area he had come to investigate. With other British POWs he discovers that the Germans are burrowing below the British lines and plan to conduct a surprise attack. Grant is able to organize the other prisoners and they blow up a significant part of the underground works. Grant is rescued and we are left with the impression he is on his way to see Rose.

Military Correlation: Helpful

Comment: The Elstres Studios were well-known for producing "quickies" but *The W Plan* is a rather remarkable film in terms of both plot and acting. It is one of the several films that acknowledges the role of both English and German sappers during the war.

War and the Women (1917) / aka *My Country*

Produced by Edwin Thanhauser, Thanhauser Film Corporation (United States). Directed by Ernest C. Warde and written by Phillip Lonergan. This silent, black and white film, with English intertitles, starred Florence La Badie, Ernest C. Warde, Tom Brooke, Wayne Arey, Grace Henderson, Arthur Bauer, and Ralph Faulkner.

Story: Ruth (Florence La Badie) is loyal to the United States but because her stepfather Braun (Tom Brooke) is a German spy, she is somewhat naturally rebuffed by most of the community. Aviator Barker (Wayne Arey) falls in love and marries her. When the nation is attacked by an unidentified country, Barker goes off to fight in the war. Somehow the enemy manages to gain control of Ruth's house, which is in a strategic location. She is able to set off some bombs that she had brilliantly stashed in her basement and then get away with Barker who has appeared in his plane. The house explodes and kills the enemy leaders and, apparently as a result, the invasion fails.

Military Correlation: Poor

Comment: An inconsequential film with few redeeming graces. The dialogue is standard and of the type heard in war films since they first began. There is nothing in the script that would allow for the film to make any sort of a point and the film's idea of preparedness, if that is the point, is so stupid as to be meaningless.

War Brides (1916)

Produced and distributed by Herbert Brenon Film Corporation, Selznick Distribution Company (United States). Directed by Herbert Brenon and written by Brenon and Marion Craig Wentworth, based on her one-act play. This silent, black and white film, with English intertitles, stars Alla Nazimova, Richard Barthelmess, Charles Bryant, Alex Shannon, William Bailey, Nila Mac, Gertrude Berkeley, Robert Whitworth, Ned Burton, Theodora Warfield, Charles Challies, and Charles Hutchinson.

Story: A young man, Franz (Charles Bryant), recently married to Joan (Alla Nazimova), is sent off to war from his European village. Word comes back that he has been killed along with his brothers. Joan, who is pregnant, considers suicide but decides she must take responsibility for their child. The government starts a program to get young women to marry a departing soldier so as to raise up a new generation of fighting men. When word is received that the king will be passing through the village, she organizes the women, all dressed in black, to protest his plan. When she comes face to face with the king (Alex Shannon), soldiers threaten to shoot her if she does not back off. Instead she kills herself in front of him as an act of protest and so demonstrates the message that women will not create another generation to be killed in another war.

Military Correlation: Poor

Comment: A sad idea sadly presented. Alla Nazimova, a stage actress, had avoided the films but when she was offered this part, based on a one-act play by Marion Craig Wentworth, she took it. Reviewers suggested that this stage actress overplayed the part. Charles Bryant, her co-star, was also her longtime lover and there was little spontaneous emotion between them. America entered the war just one month after its release and this heavily anti-war movie did not have a lot of success. The studio pulled it back, changed the name of the country in question to Germany and re-released it. It then made money. The film was later spoofed in a movie called *War Prides* (1917).

The War Bride's Secret (1916)

Produced and distributed by Fox Film Company (United States). Directed by Kenean Buel and written by Mary Murillo. Cinematography by Frank Kugler. This silent, black and white film, with English intertitles, stars Billy Lynbook, Glen White, Walter Law, Virginia Pearson, Henry Hallam, Oliver Corbett, Stuart Sage, and Robert Vivino.

Story: Scottish lass Jean MacDougal (Virginia Pearson) and her lover Colin Douglas (Glen White) are secretly married before he goes off to the front line. When word comes back that he has been killed, Jean, pregnant with his child, wants a father for her baby and marries Robin Gray (Walter Law), an old farmer who has long loved her from a distance. When Colin returns from the war, wounded but very much alive, there is some confusion but the old farmer, aware that the young family should be together, gives up his wife to the one she loves.

Military Correlation: None

Comment: Even by 1916 this plot had worn pretty thin and the acting did not do much to save it. A surprising number of war films are based on the false reporting of a soldier's death. While a good plot line, it nevertheless identified a problem generally unaddressed: The very nature of war, the massive confusion with millions of men involved, and the poor accounting efforts employed, meant that many families were falsely informed, or in some cases never informed. Since so many units were made up of men from the same area, news of a death was often passed along by a soldier who served with the dead man. And this information was often wrong.

War Horse (2011)

Produced by Frank Marshall, Revel Guest, Steven Spielberg and Kathleen Kennedy, DreamWorks Pictures, Touchstone Pictures, Reliance Entertainment, Walt Disney Studios (United States). It was directed by Steven Spielberg and written by Lee Hall and Richard Curtis, based on a children's book by Michael Morpurgo and a stage play by Nick Stafford. Cinematography by Janusz Kaminski. Music by John Williams. This 90-minute color film starred Jeremy Irvine, Emily Watson, Peter Mullan, Niels Arestrup, David Thewlis, Tom Hiddleston, Benedict Cumberbatch, Celine Buckens, Toby Kebbell, Patrick Kennedy, Leonard Carow, David Kross, Matt Milne, Robert Emms, Eddie Marsan, Nicholas Bro, Rainer Bock, Hinnerk Schonemann, Geoff Bell, Liam Cunningham, Gerald McSorley, Tom Pitts, Pip Torrens, Philippe Nahon, Julian Wadham, David Dencik, Edward Bennett, Johnny Harris, Tam Dean Burn, and Maximillian Brucker.

Story: The story begins with the friendship of a teenage boy, Albert Marriott (Jeremy Irvine), and his horse Joey. The horse, when put to the plow, manages to help save the family farm in Devon much to the dismay of Albert's mother Rose (Emily Watson) and father Ted (Peter Mullen). When the horse is taken off to war, the film follows the horse and the lives of persons the animal meets and the variety of situations in which it finds itself—with British cavalry officer Captain James Nicholls (Tom Hiddleston), with teams pulling German artillery, and with two men who desert with the plan of riding to Italy. The men are caught and executed but it allows for the horse to have a brief stay with a French farmer and his granddaughter, Emile (Celine Buckens). But they soon lose him. When the war is over, horses are sold either for stock or as meat to feed the starving French. It is decided that only officers' horses will be shipped home. Joey is saved when Emile's grandfather buys him and the boy and his horse are reunited.

Military Correlation: Excellent

Comment: This film did a great deal to convey the situation of World War I to a generation that had no comprehension of what it was like. While some of the scenes appear almost idealist, others (especially the scenes with the horses dying of exhaustion while pulling impossible loads of artillery) are overwhelming. There is a strange cleanliness about it, however, with the filming too clear and the individuals too distinct. Perhaps that was intended.

During the filming, fourteen different horses played Joey, eight as an adult and four as a colt and foal. For one scene more than two hundred horses were used. An animatronics horse is used in just a few scenes as when Joey's skin is torn by barbed wire. The film employed actors from more than a dozen nations and nearly 6,000 extras including the granddaughter of Captain Budgett, one of the World War I veterans who had inspired Michael Morpurgo to write the original book. Perhaps the most impressive thing about the movie was the sight of the men on horses "meeting the absolute destruction of those tools of mass slaughter" as the British troops moved into a nest of machine-guns. It was the end of the old ways of warfare.

The film was well received and profitable but there was some criticism, primarily the disjointed feeling one got as the transitions between adventures were often ragged. There were no accidents to the animals while filming though there was one charge that a horse had died and it had been covered up; that proved not to be true. The London opening was attended by Prince William and his wife Catherine. The *New York Observer* said, "*War Horse* is a don't miss Spielberg classic that reaches true perfection. It's as good as movies can get, and one of the greatest triumphs of this or any other year." The film received Oscar nominated for Best Picture, Best Art Director, Best Cinematography, Best Original Score, Best Sound Editing and Mixing and won none.

War Is Hell (1915)

Produced and distributed by Burlington Standard, Walturdaw (United Kingdom). Directed by Ethyle Batley. The silent, black and white film, with English intertitles, starred Martin Valmour, Nancy Bevington, Dorothy Batley, Schach Johnson, and James Russell.

Story: A Belgian boy, ordered to shoot his father by a German major, shoots the major instead."

Military Correlation: Unknown

Comment: An amazing number of books and movies use this title, based, it is assumed, on General Sherman's comment.

War Nurse (1930)

Produced and distributed by Metro-Goldwyn-Mayer (United States). Directed by Edgar Selwyn and written by Becky Gardiner and Joe Farnham. This 81-minute black and white film stars Robert Montgomery, Anita Page, June Walker, Robert Ames, Zasu Pitts, Marie Prevost, Helen Jerome Eddy, Hedda Hopper, Edward J. Nugent, Martha Sleeper and Michael Vavitci.

Story: American women responded to the war by volunteering for service as nurses and aids. Some sought to do their duty while some were just anxious to go to France where the men were. One pretty young lady, Joy (Anita Page), goes with highly romantic notions but finds instead desperation and suffering. The women are faced with dangers and discomforts they did not expect, and were around men who were in need and desperately looking for female companionship. Joy is attracted to young Robin (Robert Ames) while the no-nonsense Barbara (June Walker) fights off the advances of Wally (Robert Montgomery). Both the romances turn out different than they expected. The war does not provide the sort of life either of the women had anticipated. The movie gives the impression that the nurses spent as much time in the beds of the patients as beside them.

Military Correlation: Spotty

Comment: The script was based on the anonymous memoirs of an American woman who served with the French Army as a nurse. The lady in question had several sexual encounters that made many wonder if the book was too hot for Hollywood. But the screenplay managed to keep the intent of the book and yet soften it enough for film. The women seemed determined to be involved in one ill-conceived relationship after another and in the end find themselves, or at least their ideals, betrayed. In the end, both of the major characters die.

There are a lot of female stereotypes in the film with women shown afraid of spiders and mice and squeamish around blood. If we were to believe what was shown, we would think that American men went to war with courage and fatalism, while the women went as seductive spies or sexual vamps. Loretta Young had a small bit but it was cut before released. It leaves a lot to be desired.

The Water Diviner (2015)

Produced by Troy Lum, Andrew Mason, and Keith Rodger of Fear of God Films, Hopscotch Features (Australia). Directed by Russell Crowe. Written by Andrew Anastasios and Andrew Knight. Cimematography by Andrew Lesnie. This color film stars Russell Crowe, Olga Kurylenko, Jai Courtney, Jacqueline McKenzie, Cem Yilmaz, Yilmaz Erdogan, Daniel Wyllie, Ryan Corr, and James Fraser.

Story: In 1919, Australian farmer Connor (Russell Crowe) travels to the site of the battle of Gallipoli to find the bones of his three missing sons. In 1915 ANZAC troops attacked Gallipoli in their effort to take Constantinople and open a sea route to Russia but the Turks fought a terrific defense and more than 10,000 Allied troops were killed.

Military Correlation: Unknown

Comment: This movie will be Australian Russell Crowe's first movie as a director.

Waterloo Bridge (1931)

Produced by Carl Laemmie, Universal Studios (United States). Directed by James Whale. Written by Benn Levy and Tom Reed, based on a play by Robert Sherwood. Cinematography by Arthur Edeson. Music by Val Burton. This 81-minute film starred Mae Clarke, Douglass Montgomery, Doris Lloyd, Frederick Kerr, Enid Bennett, Bette Davis, and Ethel Griffies.

Story: Myra Deauville (Mae Clarke), an unemployed American singer, has taken to the London streets to make a living. She meets her clients, most of them soldiers on their way to battle, at Waterloo Bridge. One evening she meets Canadian soldier Roy Cronin (Douglass Montgomery), who takes a shine to her and offers to help. When he takes her to his mother's home she decides to break free of him, feeling she is not good enough for him. She returns to the streets but he follows her and asks her to marry him. She says no, but he turns on the pressure as he is about to leave for France. She finally agrees that she will marry him when he returns. As his train pulls out of the station, an air raid begins and Myra is killed.

Military Correlation: Spotty

Comment: A generally good film. The Cockney characters are somewhat forced and some parts of the story seem contrived to give the film length. Billy Wilkerson of *The Hollywood Reporter* said, "It is grown-up entertainment, not sophisticated, but mature..." It really tells us very little about World War I. This is an excellent example of the effect of sound on films. It can be safely said that a significant sub-genre of the silent film was the love story. But with the coming of sound they sought new dimensions in which the love story could be played out. In the silent film the story was deliberately non-realistic, using elements of fantasy and mysticism that were to be far less common in the more realistic sound era. Studios made the mistake of thinking that since they were now real because they talked, that they had to be realistic in all other respects. This had the effect, for a while, of eliminating many of the qualities of poetry and lyricism from most films.

After the Production Code came into effect, the picture could not be rereleased. Metro-Goldwyn-Mayer bought the film rights and remade it in 1940 with the situation updated to World War II. *Gaby* (1956) is also basically the same film.

A couple of actors were in both the 1931 and 1940 versions. Rita Carlyle played the Old Woman on the Bridge in both movies: In the first she drops a basket of potatoes and cabbage and in the second a basket of flowers. Ethel Griffies played the landlady in both films, Mrs. Hobley in the first and Mrs. Clark in the second.

We Are French (1916) see *Bugler of Algiers* (1916)

What Price Glory? (1926)

Produced by William Fox and Fox Film Corporation (United States). Directed by Raoul Walsh. Written by James O'Donohoe and Malcolm Stuart Boylan, based on a book by Maxwell Anderson and a play by Laurence Stallings and Anderson. Cinematography by Barney McGill, John Smith and John Marta. Music by Erno Rapee. This 116-silent, black and white film with synchronized sound effects, starred William V. Mong, Elena Jurado, Jack Fay, Edmund Lowe, Victor McLaglen, Dolores del Rio, Leslie Fenton, Phyllis Haver, Barry Norton, and August Tollair.

Story: Two oldtime Marine sergeants, having served together in China and the Philippines, are sent to France when war breaks out. Flagg (Victor McLaglen) is promoted to Captain and his sidekick Quirt (Edmund Lowe) is assigned to him. Their rivalry expands when they meet the flirt Charmaine (Dolores del Rio). This begins a series of episodes that combine comedy, witty one-liners, war-torn battlefields, and the possibility of a shotgun wedding.

Military Correlation: Spotty

Comment: The special effects were outstanding, though costly. It was the first film to acknowledge special effects as a credit. Actor Jack Fay died at the age of 25 as the result of injuries suffered in one of the staged explosions. The fireworks also damaged houses nearby. Rough and gritty, the stage version was nearly banned because many believed it mocked military authority. In the heat of filming the actors actually swore at each other and a bevy of lip readers complained. To add to the movie's unique appeal the female members of the cast were introduced not with shots of their faces, but with the image of their seated behinds.

The movie produced in 1926 includes a question mark at the end of the title, but the 1952 version does not. Movie buffs and sometimes historians like Darian Cobb suggest that in the first case it was a question, while in the second the producers knew what the cost was.

What Price Glory (1952)

Produced and distributed by 20th Century–Fox (United States). It was directed by John Ford and written by Phoebe Ephron. This 116-minute Technicolor film starred James Cagney, Corinne Calvet, Dan Dailey, William Demarest, Craig Hill, Marisa Pavan, Max Showalter, James Gleason, Wally Vernon, Henri Letondal, and Robert Wagner.

Story: This comedy-drama is a remake of Raoul Walsh's silent classic. Two American Marine sergeants (James Cagney and Dan Dailey) in France are determined to battle each other as well as the Germans at the front and the women in the villages. The relationship between the two heats up when Flagg gets promoted to captain and Quirt is assigned as his NCO. The competition is further complicated when they both fall for Charmaine (Corinne Calvet) who urges them on. The rivalry follows the Marines through much of the fighting in France and through many romantic episodes with the two stars busy yelling at each other.

Military Correlation: Spotty

Comment: Apparently James Cagney agreed to star in the remake of this 1926 classic when they told him that some musical numbers were added to the Anderson-Stallings play. When he found out there were none for him, he decided to go ahead anyway. The powerful anti-war message of the original film is lost somewhere in this portrayal of the cowardly, drunken Captain Flagg and the good-natured Quirt brawling over the very sexy Charmaine. While interesting and well acted, the remake lacks the impact of the original. It does uncover something that few films had taken on, and that is the effect of shell shock on the morale of the other troops.

Bloopers: Captain Flagg commands Company M. In the Marines during World Wars, companies were numbered.

Where Were You the Night I Shot Down Baron von Richthofen? (1970) see *Darling Lili* (1970)

Wilson (1944) / aka ***President Wilson***

Produced by 20th Century-Fox and Darryl F. Zanuck. Directed by Henry King. Written by Lamar Trotti. Cinematography by Leon Shamroy. This 154-minute Technicolor movie starred Alexander Knox, Charles Coburn, Geraldine Fitzgerald, Ruth Nelson, Cedric Hardwicke, Vincent Price, William Eythe, Mary Anderson, Ruth Ford, Sidney Blackmer, Madeleine Forbes, Thomas Mitchell, Eddie Foy, Jr., and Charles Harton.

Story: The life of President Woodrow Wilson (Alexander Knox) from the time he was president of Princeton University to his death. It deals with the major issues he faced including the death of his first wife, the fight for peace, the outbreak of World War I, the failed efforts at the League of Nations, and his own lingering illness.

Military Correlation: Helpful

Comment: *Wilson* was highly acclaimed, winning the Academy Award for Best Director and several others. But all in all it was a long picture about a basically boring man. It was the most expensive movie produced up to that time, surpassing *Gone with the Wind*, and yet was a commercial flop. It was the only film to received ten Academy Award nominations and ten awards and still be a commercial failure. The use of newsreels from World War I were well done but placed in such a manner that they seemed out of context.

This was producer Darryl F. Zanuck's first film after returning from North Africa in World War II and he was very proud of it. When it was such a box-office failure, he asked people to never speak to him of it again. Alexander Knox, who played the president, was a Canadian.

Bloopers: On the train in 1919 as Wilson travels the country promoting the League of Nations, cars outside the window are from the 1940s. When he is in his office, the map on the wall shows nations that did not exist until after the war. In one shot you can see the Washington Monument which had not been built when he took office in 1913. In one scene it is mentioned that he won all of New Jersey's 22 counties. New Jersey only has 21 counties.

Wings (1927)

Produced and distributed by Paramount, Famous Lasky Corporation (United States). Directed by William Wellman and Harry d'Arrass (uncredited). Written by John Monk Saunders and Hope Loring. Cinematography by Harry Perry. Music by J.S. Aamechik. This 144-minute, silent, black and white movie, with English, Spanish, and French intertitles, starred Clara Bow, Charles "Buddy" Rogers, Richard Arlen, Gunboat Smith, Richard Rucker, Jobyna Ralston, El Brendel, and Gary Cooper.

Story: Two men who have been friends for a long time ("Buddy" Rogers and Richard Arlen) fall for the same girl. They join the Army Air Corps during World War I and maintain the friendship despite the difficulties. In the background a

An American Friends Ambulance of the type driven by Clara Bow in *Wings* (courtesy Center for the Study of the Korean War, Independence, Missouri).

social hierarchy is established as Armstrong and Sylvia (the love object) belong to the upper class while Powell and Clara (Bow) are from the middle class. Powell mistakenly believes that his friend has been killed and in a rage goes off and shoots down a German plane that Armstrong had commandeered. Powell returns to America to a parade of honor but with the awesome task of explaining it all to Armstrong's aged parents. He comes to realize that he was not in love with Sylvia but rather with the effervescent short-haired skimpy-skirted neighbor who loves cars.

Military Correlation: Excellent

Comment: The plot is thin and predictable but the action is so good that most ignore the lack of substance. Other than a short romantic phase at the opening of the movie and an occasions effort at dialogue, the movie consists of dogfights. While some contemporary reviewers felt that the movie had not made it clear if it was a serious war drama or a romantic comedy, most agree that director William Wellman captured the feeling and realism of aerial combat. Many of the battle scenes have become standard for air-war movies: a plane spinning to earth trailing a cloud of smoke, and a bridge from which soldiers are jumping to avoid being cut down by fire from the plane.

Many believed that *Wings* provided an authentic view of the war because the story was authored directed by veterans who had taken part in the war. Even though the narrative of the film was by far its weakest point, many believed it inspired admiration for the brave deeds of those involved and a real sadness for the loss of lives. Ultimately, however, the airplane activity overrode everything else, driving the rather thin love story into the background.

It was the first and only silent film to win an Academy Award and is generally remembered as a classic. Jobyna Ralston and Richard Arlen met on the set and were married during the filming; the marriage lasted to 1946. Gregory Weinkauf, in a revisit to the movie, reported it was "nice, not thrilling, but nice" (*New Times*, April 25, 2004). Paramount and General Electric had worked together to create a special sound effect for planes and machine-guns, taking sounds that had been used in other pictures to supplement their effect.

Brock Garland, film historian, suggests that George Lucas modeled his *Star Wars* dogfights after those in *Wings*.

Wings (1977)

Produced by Barry Thomas as a BBC-TV production (United Kingdom). Directed by Jim Goddard, Gareth Davies, Donald McWhinnie and Desmond Davis, it was written by Barry Thomas, Julian Bond, and Arden Winch. Music by Alexander Faris. This TV series starred Tim Woodward, Michael Cochrane, Nicholas Jones, John Hallan, David Troughton, Anne Kristen, Reg Lye and Sarah Porter.

Story: Alan Farmer (Tim Woodward), a blacksmith turned fighter pilot, and his mentor Captain Triggers (Michael Cochrane) are in the service together. Triggers begins dating Farmer's girlfriend when it is believed he was shot down over France. In twenty-five 50-minute episodes the series drags the viewer through repeated romances, dramatic revelations of problems with old weapons, considerable comment about class distinction and concerns, as well as some rare fighting scenes that seem staged.

Military Correlation: Good

Comments: The producers were very careful to be accurate with historical details and they allow the men and equipment to reflect the passage of time. What they cannot seem to do is to get the characters to assume any of the attitudes or even expressions of the early war. Some World War I planes that were still airworthy were used but most of the flying shots were made with 1/6th scale radio-controlled models.

Winnie the Bear (2004)
see *A Bear Named Winnie* (2004)

The Woman the Germans Shot (1918) / aka *The Cavell Case*

Produced and distributed by Frank J. Carroll Productions, Joseph L. Plunkett (United States). Directed by John G. Adolfi. Written by Anthony Paul Kelly. This

60-minute silent, black and white film with English intertitles starred Julie Arthur, Creighton Hale, Thomas Brooks, George LeGuere, William Tooker, Jack W. Johnston, Paul Panzer, Joyce Fair, Martin Faust, Fred Kalgren, Sara Alexander, Amy Dennis, George Majeroni, and George Dupree.

Story: Famed stage star Julie Arthur has her film debut as the Englishwoman Edith Cavell, who was shot by the Germans for espionage. As the matron of a major Belgian hospital when war broke out, she not only nursed the soldiers of both sides, but aided hundreds of Allied soldiers to escape across the border to a neutral country. After a while she was betrayed and the Germans decided to make an example of her. She was sentenced to death and, despite international protests, she was executed by firing squad.

Military Correlation: Good

Comment: The movie was billed as the "the true story of Edith Cavell, a British nurse who served with the underground in Belgium during the First World War." Her actions and contributions were really not all that significant for many women would offer like service. But hers were exaggerated by the fact that she was executed. The film is interesting and does not waver too far from the facts that are known, but does present the case in moral tones of black and white. The case was highly significant to the British, and several movies and stage plays were made about the event.

When the British decided to make this case the basis of a huge propaganda campaign, they made Nurse Cavell the most prominent female British casualty of the war. They also used the story well into the years of World War II.

Womanhood, the Glory of the Nation (1917) / aka *Battle Cry of War*

Produced by J. Stuart Blackton, Albert Smith and Vitagraph Company of America (United States). Directed by J. Stuart Blackton and William P.S. Earl. Written by Helmer Bergman, Blackton, and Cyrus Townsend Brady. Cinematography by Clark R. Nickerson. The seven-reel silent, black and white film, with English intertitles, starred Alice Joyce, Harry T. Morey, Naomi Childers, Joseph Kilgour, Walter McGrail, Mary Maurice, James Morrison, Templar Saxe, Bobby Connelly, Edward Elkas, Bernard Siegel, and Peggy Hyland.

Story: In this highly propagandized film for the preparedness movement, the United States is invaded by the mythical country of Ruthania and they take over New York. Mary Ward (Alice Joyce), returning from Europe, learns that her sweetheart is an officer in the invading army and she must acknowledge her loyalty. The scenes are full of fake battleships blowing up and fiery love scenes but in the main it shows how America can fight back against the invader because, having been forewarned, it was prepared: hiding bombs and weapons and organizing the people.

Military Correlation: Poor

Comment: This was designed to be a sequel to *The Battle Cry of Peace*. It is said that Presidents Theodore Roosevelt and Woodrow Wilson both were behind the film and that numerous national organization like the Daughters of the Americana Revolution were determined that every American see this film.

Wooden Crosses (1932)

Produced and distributed by Pathe-Natan (France). Directed by Raymond Bernard. Based on a novel by Roland Dorgeles. Cinematography by Julie Kruger and Rene Ribault. This 113-minute black and white film starred Pierre Blanchar, Charles Vanel, Gabriel Gabrio, Henry Blair, Raymond Aimos, Paul Azais, Raymond Cordy, Marchel Delaitre, Jean Galland, Pierre Labry, Rene Montis, Jean-Francois Martial, and Marc Valbel.

Story: The movie follows the men of a French regiment into battle. The new arrival thinks he is too late for the war but soon finds that he is fighting to stay alive. The main character carries a picture of his girl and gets letters from her, thus providing some insight. The bits of background information we get from the other characters seem irrelevant and simply add to the despondency of the situation.

Military Correlation: Good

Comment: A depressing film as we see little but war for nearly two hours in a film that is essentially designed to bombard the audience with the "randomness and pointlessness of warfare." The majestic filming, especially the use of long-distance and crane shots, is indeed powerful. Filmed in French, it was finally released in English and received only moderate attention. Perhaps it was too long after the fact.

Wooden Crosses (1936) see *The Road to Glory* (1936)

Yankee Doodle Dandy (1942)

Produced by Hal B. Wallis, Jack Warner, William Cagney, and Warner Brothers. Directed by Michael Curtiz and written by Robert Buckner and Edmund Joseph. Cinematography by James Wong Howe. This 126-minute black and white musical comedy stars James Cagney, Joan Leslie, Walter Huston, Frances Langford, Richard Whorf, Jeanne Cagney, George Barbier, Irene Manning, George Tobias, S.Z. Sakall, Walter Catlett, Douglas Croft, Eddie Foy, Jr., Minor Watson, and Rosemary DeCamp.

Story: The film biography of George M. Cohan the song and dance man (and composer of "It's A Grand Old Flag" is told in a series of overlapping flashbacks that range from his birth on July 4 (it was really the 3rd). A typical Hollywood biography, it takes many liberties with fact in order to make its jingoistic points. Nostalgic and unashamedly patriotic, it was a perfect film for the early war years, and was very popular. Cohan wrote some of the period's best music. It is a fun story with great music and James Cagney, who was too old for World War I, is at his best.

Fred Astaire was first offered the role but turned it down. Cohan himself suggested Cagney.

Military Correlation: Helpful

Comment: In many respects Cagney was a far better star in this film than in any of his more famous roles. It is played out in innocence and childish playfulness but also with elegant sincerity. Orson Welles commented, "There was never a moment in which he was not true." Director Michael Curtiz reportedly wept as Cagney's Cohan reacted to the death of his father.

The film was placed on the National Film Registry in 1993.

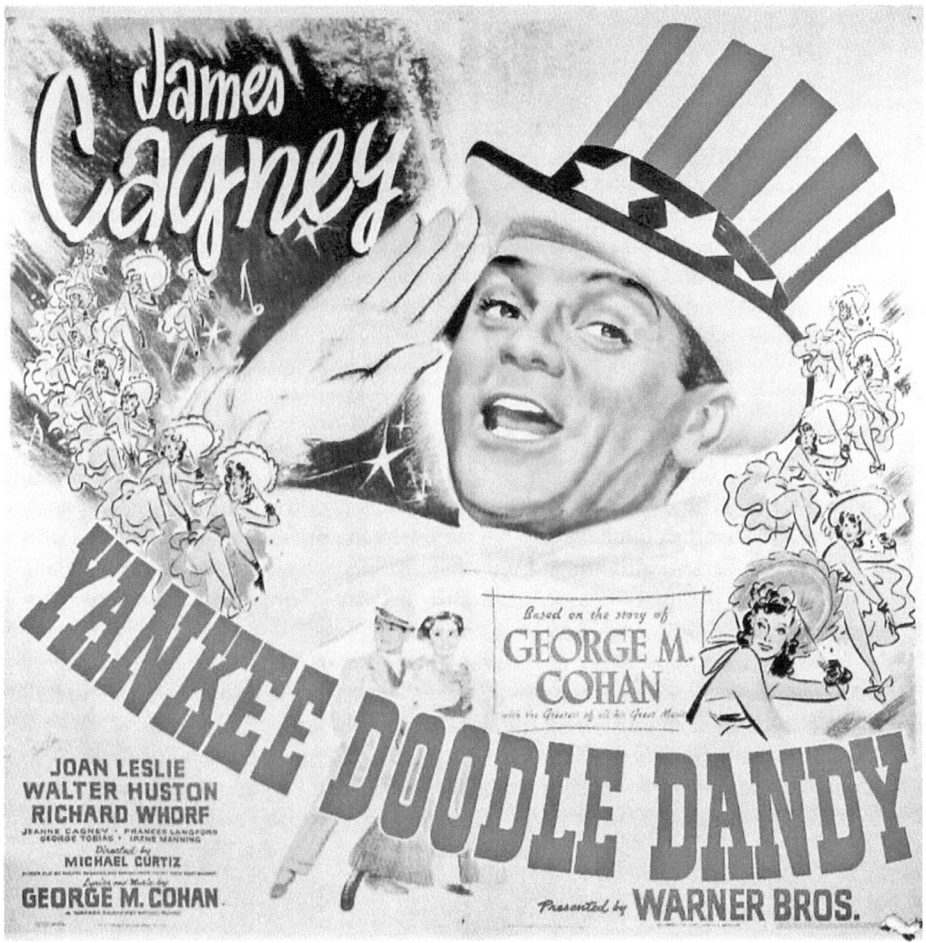

An advertisement for the Warner Brothers film *Yankee Doodle Dandy* (courtesy Center for the Study of the Korean War, Independence, Missouri).

Yankee Doodle in Berlin (1919)

Produced and distributed by Mack Sennett Comedy Films (United States). Directed by F. Richard Jones and written by Mack Sennett. Cinematography by Fred Jackman and J.R. Lockwood. This 58-minute, silent, black and white film, with English intertitles, starred Mack Sennett, Bothwell Browne, Bert Roach, Ford Sterling, Malcolm St. Clair, Eve Thatcher, Marie Prevost, Ben Turpin, Charles Murray, Heinie Conklin, Joseph Belmont, and the famous Sennett Bathing Girls.

Story: A feature-length spoof of the recently concluded war. Mark Sennett builds on the Kaiser's (Ford Sterling) well-known desire for the company of young women. The Army disguises one of their captains, Bob White (Bothwell Browne), as a young woman and sends him behind German lines. Not only is the Kaiser impressed with the young "woman" but so is the crown prince. When the Kaiser makes his move, the three of them are involved in a fracas. The captain escapes, taking a young Belgian refugee (Marie Prevost) as his bride-to-be.

Military Correlation: None

Comment: This very odd film relies totally on the slapstick nature of the comedy. Bothwell Browne was a famous vaudeville female impersonator and he does his usual act for the film. Made after the war and at a time when people were forgetting the hatred that had built up, it is a film that is spent entirely making fun of the Germans and pointing out the stupidity of their army. In this, as in all his work, Sennett had the tendency to rely on obvious slapstick rather than the more inspired sight gags.[47]

Zeppelin (1971)

Produced and distributed by Getty and Fromkess Corporation (United Kingdom). Directed by Etienne Pierier and written by Arthur Rowe and Donald Churchill based on a book by Owen Crum. Cinematography by Alan Hume. This 100-minute, Technicolor film starred Michael York, Elke Sommer, Peter Carsten, Marius Goring, Andrew Keir, Anton Diffring, Alexandra Stewart, and Michael Robbins.

Story: At the outbreak of the war, a young Scot, Geoffrey Richter-Douglas (Michael York), finds himself with mixed emotions for he is loyal to England but he is also the heir of an aristocratic Bavarian family. When the Germans ask him to spy for them, he tells the English intelligence and they, in turn, send him to Germany as a double agent. Accompanied by the beautiful daughter (Elke Sommer) of the zeppelin designer, Geoffrey ultimately finds himself aboard the Zeppelin LZ36 that is heading for Scotland to steal the Magna Carta that has been safely secured there. He prevents the theft and accepts his true identify and true love.

Military Correlation: Good

Comment: This film can boast of a remarkable staging of the zeppelin's flights. The filming was done basically with a 40-foot model of the British Rigid Airship R33 that was based on the German design of the LZ36, a famous zeppelin that flew more than 74 missions during the war. The plot wavers a bit and is a little farfetched in spots, and the proposed attack on Great Britain's national treasures was a rather consistent and well-used plot effort. During the filming a replica of a S.E.5a plane collided with a camera helicopter and several peopled were injured.

The dirigible (confused with the zeppelin) symbolized the awesomeness of German power but also showed the German weakness as it was no match for the Allied planes set to attack it.

The Zeppelin's Last Raid (1917)

Produced and distributed by Thomas H. Ince Corporation, States Rights, and Exhibitors Booking Company (United States). Directed by Irvin V. Willat. Written by C. Gardner Sullivan and Willat. Cinematography by Willat. This five-reel silent, black and white film, with English intertitle, starred Alfred Hickman, Thomas H. Ince, and Enid Markey.

Story: A young German commander (Alfred Hickman) is in command of an airship engaged in bombing raids. His sweetheart (Enid Markey) is a member of a resistance group that is working to overthrow the Kaiser. During the course of his adventure, the commander changes his mind, sinks his own ship and drowns in order to prevent additional bombings. Producer Thomas H. Ince was determined that his films convey his primary message, which was that there will be no peace until Germany's militarism is stamped out.

Military Correlation: Good

Comment: Alfred Hickman, who played the commander, was himself German and had chosen to side with the Allies. Zeppelin movies, like submarine movies, were generally popular because of the uniqueness of the craft. Popular with the few rich who had flown on them, they were also alluring and mysterious. Many still wonder how they operated. There are no copies of this film available though some still shots can still be located. The storyline of *The Zeppelin's Last Raid* parallels that of *Civilization* (1916) and some critics list this as a sequel to *Civilization*. A good deal of newsreel footage was used and did not fit the context.

An advertisement in *World* proclaimed, "For the first time the workings of a German dirigible [meaning zeppelin] are shown on the screen, and the details of a raid upon a defenseless village is reproduced."[48]

Appendix: Films by Year of Release

1909	The Invaders		Outrage
	The Peril of the Fleet		Patriot and the Spy
1913	O.M.H.S.		Pimple's Dream of Victory
1914	By the Kaiser's Orders		Remembering Belgium
	Daughter of France		The Secret of the Submarine
	England Expects		Somewhere in France
	The German Spy Peril		A Submarine Pirate
	The Heroine of the Mons		Tommy Atkins
	Huns of the North Sea		Under the German Yoke
	In the Name of the Prince of Peace		War Is Hell
	It's a Long Way to Tipperary	**1916**	As in a Looking Glass
	The Kaiser's Spies		Bugler of Algiers
	Last Volunteer		Civilization
	Lieutenant Pimple and the Stolen Submarine		The Devil at His Elbow
			Edith Cavell
	Lucille Love: The Girl of Mystery		The Hero of Submarine D-2
			Martyrdom of Nurse Cavell
	Saving the Colors		La Revanche
1915	The Battle Cry of Peace		War Brides
	Brother Officers		The War Brides Secrets
	The Coward	**1917**	Arms and the Girl
	The Crimson Wings		The Birth of Patriotism
	Doorway to Destruction		The Bond
	From Flower Girl to Red Cross Nurse		The Dark Road
			Draft 258
	The Gray Nun of Belgium		Follow the Girl
	I Didn't Raise My Boy to Be a Soldier		For France
			For Liberty
	In the Hands of the Enemy		For the Freedom of the World
	My Boy Grew Up to Be a Soldier		The Greatest Power
			The Little American
	On the Russian Frontier		Might and the Man
			Miss Jackie in the Army

My Four Years in Germany
On Dangerous Ground
Secret Game
The Showdown
Slacker
The Slacker's Heart
Spy
Treason
The Volunteer
War and the Women
Womanhood, the Glory of the Nation
My Country
The Zeppelin's Last Raid

1918
At the Front
Battling Jane
Bonnie Annie Laurie
Bud's Recruits
The Claws of the Hun
Daughters of France
The Doughboys
Every Mothers Son
Geezer of Berlin
The Great Love
The Greatest Thing in Life
Heart of Humanity
Hearts of the World
Her Boy
An Honest Man
The Hun Within
Huns and Hyphens
Hunting the U–Boats
I'll Say So
The Invasion of Britain
Joan of Plattsburg
Joining the Tanks
The Kaiser's Finish
Kaiser's New Dentist
Kaiser's Shadow
The Kaiser, the Beast of Berlin
Kiddies in the Ruins
Kulture
Landing a Spy
Lest We Forget

Little Miss Hoover
Mrs. Slacker
My Four Years in Germany
On the Jump
Our Four Days in Germany
Over the Top
Patriotism
Pot Luck in the Army
Private Peat
The Prussian Cur
The Service Star
The Seventy Mile Gun
Shoulder Arms
The Spreading Evil
Till I Come Back to You
To Hell with the Kaiser
To the Rescue
The Unbeliever
The Woman the Germans Shot

1919
Behind the Door
Comradeship
The False Face
The Girl Who Stayed Behind
J'Accuse!
The Light of Victory
The Littlest Scout
The Lost Battalion
The Profiteer
U-9 Weddigen
Unknown Love
The Unpardonable Sin
Yankee Doodle in Berlin

1920 *The Woman of Mystery*
1921 *Four Horsemen of the Apocalypse*
Love Light
1922 *Sonny*
1924 *Reveille*
1925 *The Big Parade*
The Dark Angel
Havoc
1926 *Behind the Front*
Better 'Ole
Mademoiselle from

Appendix: Films by Year of Release

	Armentieres		*Suspense*
	Mare Nostrum		*Three Faces East*
	Mons		*The W Plan*
	Three Faces East		*War Nurse*
	What Price Glory?	1931	*Dishonored*
1927	*Blighty*		*East Lynne on the Western Front*
	Face Value		
	Ham and Eggs		*Hell on Earth*
	Hotel Imperial		*Mata Hari*
	Lost at the Front		*Phantom Submarine U67*
	Motherland		*Seas Beneath*
	The Patent Leather Kid		*Tell England*
	Poppies of Flanders		*Waterloo Bridge*
	Rose of Picardy	1932	*Broken Lullaby*
	U-9 Weddigen		*Doomed Battalion*
	Wings		*A Farewell to Arms*
1928	*Captain Swagger*		*Wooden Crosses*
	Carry on Sergeant!	1933	*The Eagle and the Hawk*
	Dawn		*Ever in My Heart*
	The Enemy		*Hell Below*
	Exploits of the Emden	1934	*Brown on Resolution*
	For Valor		*Crimson Romance*
	Four Sons		*The Lost Patrol*
	The Guns of Loos	1935	*The Dark Angel*
	Legion of the Condemned		*Devil Dogs of the Air*
	Lilac Time	1936	*Boom Boom*
	Submarine		*Cafe Moscow*
	Victory		*Everything Is Thunder*
1929	*The Burgomaster of Stilemonde*		*The Road to Glory*
	The Lost Patrol		*Secret Agent*
	Lucky Star	1937	*Grand Illusion*
	Marianne		*The Road Back*
	She Goes to War		*Submarine D-1*
	Sky Hawk	1938	*Blockheads*
1930	*All Quiet on the Western Front*		*The Dawn Patrol*
	The Case Against Sergeant Grischa		*Heroes of the Marne*
			J'accuse!
	The Dawn Patrol		*Men with Wings*
	Doughboys		*Mystery Girl*
	Half Shot at Sunrise		*Submarine Patrol*
	Hell's Angels		*13 Men and a Gun*
	Journey's End		*Three Comrades*
	Mamba		*Ultimatum*
	Men Without Women	1939	*Hotel Imperial*

Appendix: Films by Year of Release

	Nurse Edith Cavell		*The Return of the Soldier*
	The Spy in Black	1983	*The Kid Who Couldn't Miss*
1940	*Forty Thousand Horsemen*	1985	*ANZACS: The War Down Under*
	The Fighting 69th		
1941	*Sergeant York*		*Mata Hari*
1942	*For Me and My Girl*	1987	*The Lighthorsemen*
	Yankee Doodle Dandy	1992	*Chunuk Bair*
1943	*The Life and Death of Colonel Blimp*		*Hedd Wyn*
1944	*Wilson*	1996	*Captain Conan*
			In Love and War
1951	*The African Queen*	1997	*Behind the Lines*
1952	*What Price Glory*	1999	*All the King's Men*
1953	*The Royal African Rifles*		*The Trench*
1955	*The Court Martial of Billy Mitchell*	2001	*The Officer's Ward*
			The Lost Battalion
1957	*A Farewell to Arms*	2004	*A Bear Named Winnie*
	Paths of Glory		*Company K*
1958	*Lafayette Escadrille*		*Letters of the Great War*
1962	*Lawrence of Arabia*		*A Very Long Engagement*
1964	*King and Country*	2005	*Merry Christmas*
1966	*The Blue Max*	2006	*Flyboys*
	King of Hearts	2007	*My Boy Jack*
1969	*Oh What a Lovely War*		*The Great War*
1970	*Darling Lili*	2008	*Johnny Got His Gun*
1971	*Johnny Got His Gun*		*Letters of the Great War*
	Von Richthofen and Brown		*Passchendaele*
	Zeppelin		*The Red Baron*
1974	*The Fall of Eagles*	2010	*Beneath Hill 60*
1975	*The Land that Time Forgot*	2011	*The Jockstrap Raiders*
1976	*Aces High*		*War Horse*
	Shout at the Devil	2012	*Private Peaceful*
1977	*Wings*	2013	*Forbidden Ground*
1979	*All Quiet on the Western Front*	2014	*The Water Diviner*
1981	*Gallipoli*	2015	*Dark Invasion*
1982	*Austeria*		*The Water Diviner*

Notes

Preface

1. Paul Fussell, *Wartime: Understanding and Behavior in the Second World War* (New York: Oxford University Press, 1989).
2. A history in which a significant event is changed to suggest a very different outcome.
3. Some film experts like Kathryn Kane have suggested there is little difference between the war film and the western as both are framed around individual and group behavior in the presence of death and are involved in the conflict between good and evil.
4. These films were lost because as the indstry became more sophisticated, and prodced so many, they simply lost track of these earlier films which, in time disappeared or were destroyed.
5. The highly respected British historian Paul Fussell had nothing good to say about the American film industry during World War I in his book *Wartime: Understanding and Behavior in the Second World* War (1989).

A Brief History of the Production of Films About World War I

1. As located in Lawrence Stuid's *Guts and Glory: The Making of the American Military Image in Film* (Lexington: University of Kentucky Press, 2002).
2. This is about the same number that have been made about the Korean War.
3. A week after America declared war, the Committee on Public Information, chaired by George Creel, was formed to sponsor films to arouse the public against Germany.
4. This topic is highly significant for those doing a serious study of the film industry and is perhaps best discussed in an interview with Thomas Sherak the head of the American Academy of Motion Pictures and found in *Thought Economics*, June 19, 2011. http//www.thogheconomics.blogspot.com.

5. This attitude was later identified with the term "pragmatic patriotism."
6. B-films were those deliberately made with less care to be shown as double-bill companions with longer feature films.
7. The most common theme was the Hun threatening the virginity of a young woman, and it is used over and over again in such movies as *Remember Belgium* (1915).
8. This comedy came late, opening on Armistice Day in Chicago. Nevertheless it was dubbed "A Great Film. with a Great Man. on a Great Day."
9. As quoted in Leslie Midkidff DeBauche, *Reel Patriotism: The Movies and World War I* (Madison: University of Wisconsin Press, 1997), 43.
10. "The Four Horsemen Ride on the Screen," *Morning Telegraph*, 7 March 1921, 29.
11. Despite the critics, this film became the paradigm for Marine Corps films and the one against which all other such films are judged.
12. When the script first became available there was an effort to produce it in Germany but no company was willing to take on the risk.
13. *The Last Train from Madrid* (1937) used the Spanish Civil War as a backdrop to discuss issues facing those involved in the military buildup in Europe.
14. The massive waste of life was first best identified in D. H. Griffith's *The Birth of a Nation* about the American Civil War.
15. Alex fon Tunzelmann, "Paths of Glory Clears a Route Through World War One's Moral Mudbath," *The Guardian*, October 9, 2013, http://www.theguardian.com/film/2013/oct/09/paths-of-glory-stanley-kubrick.
16. In Great Britain during World War I many women whose husband or lovers had been killed or wounded in action wore a white armband as a badge of honor.
17. Professor Bourke also noted that there was a difference in the pain portrayal depending on the director or producer. Joanna Bourke,

"Pain Through the Prism of War," *BBC History Magazine* Vol. 154, No. 6 (2014).

18. As times changed this changed and about 1950 the foreigner was replaced with a black character.

19. In 1901 George Méliès used a double for filming the coronation of Edward VII and showed it as news.

20. "First World War News," http://firstworldwsar.cloudworth.com/mjltimediafilms-photos.php.

21. Mike Dash, "The Early History of Faking War on Film," *Smithsonian Magazine*, November 19, 2012, http://www.smithsonianmag.com/history/the-early-history-of-faking-war-on-film-133838317/.

An Introduction to the Films

1. William K. Everson, *American Silent Films* (New York: Da Capo Press, 1998), 16.

The Films

1. *Guts and Glory*, 186.

2. An attack on the banks and industries that were belived to have gotten rich off the profits of World War I. Based on a book by H. C. Engelbrecht and F. C. Hanighen, *Merchants of Death* (New York: Dodd and Meade and Company, 1934).

3. When the number of volunteers declined during World War I, Britain advertised for men to enlist as groups that were based on their common jobs, town, professions or even sports teams. Thousands did so and in the process the nation raised thousands of troops, but whole professional or fraternal groups were wiped out. In this case the unit was the 1/5th Territorial Battalion of the Norfolk Regiment.

4. Susan Brennan, http:///movies.msn.com/movies/movie-synopsis/the-battle-cry-of-peace.

5. Peter C. Rollins and John E. O'Connor, *Hollywood's World War I: Motion Picture Images* (Bowling Green, OH: Bowling Green State University Press, 1987), 149–150.

6. James A. Farmer, "Hollywood's World War One Aviation Films." *Air Classics* Vol. 24, No. 12 (December 1988): 32.

7. Pauline Kael, *5001 Nights at the Movies* (New York: Macmillan, 2011), 86.

8. Ben Kenigsberg, "Review of *Broken Lullaby (The Man I Killed)*," *TimeOut*, August 28, 2008, http://www.timeout.com/us/film/broken-lullaby-the-man-i-killed.

9. President Wilson won by a mere 4,000 votes in California. That win put him over the top. David M. Kennedy, *Over Here: The First World War and the American Society* (New York: Oxford University Press, 1980), 12.

10. "Drama: Not Daring, Violates Good Taste," *Los Angeles Times*, April 18, 1916.

11. The film also bears a strong resemblance to A. S Long's *War Patrol* (London: John Hamilton, 1934).

12. Considered to be the first syndicated comic strip in America but that is not really the case, more likely it is the first daily-produced comic strip.

13. President Wilson decided early to call up men by conscription rather than rely on a volunteer army that would take longer. The Selective Service Act, passed in 1917, called on military service for all physiclly fit men ages 21 to 32 (later extended to 18–45) and was not all that well received.

14. Interestingly no films (or memorials, for that matter) have been made about the Belgium nurse, Gabrielle Petit, who was executed by the Germans in 1916 in the same fashion for treason.

15. Fought on November 1914, at Direction Island.

16. Brock Garland, *War Movies* (New York Facts on File, 1987), 88.

17. It is now generally agreed that Rudolph Valentino was one of the major reasons for the great success of the film and yet producers at the time did not seem to recognize this and Valentino's career lagged for a long time because of it.

18. In an interview with Katherine Lipke of the *Los Angeles Times*, Mathis said, "That scene stood out as one of the most terrific things in the picture" ("Most Responsible Job Ever Held by a Woman," *Los Angeles Times*, June 3, 1923, 13, 16).

19. This view is pretty much supported by Les A. Carlyon's excellent history *Gallipoli* (London: Bantam, 2001).

20. The movie was based on the ideas expressed by Norman Angell, a British economist, who wrote *The Great Illusion: The Study of the Relation of Military Power to the Economic and Social Advantage* (New York: G. P. Putnam and Sons, 1910), to suggest the disappearance of the aristocracy and the price that would be paid for it.

21. Paolo Cherchi Usai and Cynthia Rowell, eds. *The Griffith Project*, Volume 9, Films Produced in 1916–1918 (London: British Film Institute, 2005), 168–170.

22. Officially the 369th Infantry Regiment of the 15th New York National Guard. When the war was over and the troops of the Rainbow Division were called on to parade in New York, the mayor refused to allow the African Americans to march, remarking "There is no black in the rainbow."

23. Garland, *War Movies*, 2.

24. The Irish poet Francis Ledwidge, author of "At the Poets Grave," was killed on the same day.

25. Generally Universal Pictures is listed as the film's distributor but this is not the case. It was produced by an independent company and then sold to Univeral for distrbution.

26. Jim Beaver, Jumblejim@prodigy.net.

27. Historians have pretty well established that the famed Red Baron was shot down by a single rifle shot fired by an Australian machine gunner on the line.

28. Michael Powell, Emeric Pressburger and Ian Christie, eds., *The Life and Death of Colonel Blimp* (London: Faber & Faber, 1994).

29. In 1918 DeMille, the director, collaborated with Army intelligence in an effort to track down an industry person with pro–German sympathies. He was a member of the American Protective League—a volunteer organizaton working for the justice department. He also offered to arm and lead a 75-man home guard regiment for the protection of Los Angles, a somewhat melodramatic gesture.

30. DeBauche, *Reel Patriotism*, 59.

31. This is referring to the 1836 treaty by which several nations guaranteed the neutrality of Belgium.

32. Cecil B. DeMille lost more than one close friend from the sinking of the *Lusitania* and some critics suggest this is why he made such a point of the Germans sinking a passenger ship.

33. *Chicago Tribune*, July 3, 1917.

34. DeBauche, *Reel Patriotism*, 212*fn*.

35. Unlike many Hollywood remakes this is not the same story but rather a considerably varied account with a different slant.

36. He later sings the role of Jimmy Cricket.

37. In 1927 the USS S-4 (SS 105) was in a collision with the Coast Guard cutter USS *Paulding* and sank. All hands were lost when the diving gear, established for just this sort of rescue, did not work as designed.

38. This story of Christmas, like the story of the "Angels of Mons" simply will not go away despite the best of historical evidence that it did not happen, at least as we remember. That it would come out again in a modern movie seems unreasonable.

39. This term was self-imposed by the British to mean those serving in the regular army, and grew out of a comment made by the Kaiser when he heard the British Army was on its way.

40. Some references suggest she was charged with espionage but in fact it appears the Germans considered her actions as treason.

41. The song "Oh What a Lovely War" was written by J. P Long and Maurice Scott in 1917 and was a part of the repertoire of the well-known male impersonator Ella Shields.

42. In 1918 he published a book outlining his war experiences, *My Adventures as a German Secret Agent* (New York: R.M McBride & Company, 1917).

43. British Film Institute as quoted at www.wikipedia.org/wiki/Reveille_ (film).

44. This was a telegram supposedly sent from the German Military Chief of Staff proposing to Mexico that if they would join Germany in a war against the United States, that Germany would help Mexico regain some of the land lost in the American expansion. It later proved to be a fake.

45. Winston Churchill was relieved from his post as First Lord of the Admirality because of the fiasco at Galliopli.

46. DeBauche, *Reel Patriotism*, 131.

47. Of the diversified sources given for the term "slapstick," the best appears to come from the comic routine in which a devise, composed of two pieces of wooden slats were slapped together making a loud noise. The devise, and the comedy routines involved, were very popular in 19th century music halls and theatres.

48. *Exhibitor Trade Reviews*, November 24, 1917.

Bibliography

Baird, Robert. "Hell's Angels Above the Western Front." In *Hollywood's World War I: Motion Picture Images*, eds. Peter Rollins and John E. O'Connor. Bowling Green, OH: Bowling Green State University Press, 1997.
Bennett, Carl. "Progressive Silent Film List." Silent Era Corporation, 2014. http://www.silent-era.com/PSFL/.
Blake, Michael F. *The Films of Lon Chaney*. Lanham, MD: Madison Books, 2001.
Bordwell, David, Janet Staiger, and Kristin Thompson. *The Classical Hollywood Cinema: Film Style and Mode of Production to 1960*. New York: Colombia University Press, 1985.
Bowers, Q. David. *Thanhouser Film, 1909–1917: An Illustrated History*. Vestal, NY: Emprise Publishing, 1996.
Brock, Garland. *War Movies*. New York: Facts on File, 1987.
Brownlow, Kevin. *The Parade Gone By*. New York: Knopf, 1968.
Butler, Ivan. *The War Films*. South Brunswick: A. S. Barnes and Company, 1974.
Butters, Gerald R. *Banned in Kansas: Motion Picture Censorship, 1915–1966*. Columbia: University of Missouri Press, 2007.
Campbell, Craig. *Reel America and World War I: A Comprehensive Filmography and History of Motion Pictures in the United States, 1914–1920*. Jefferson, NC: McFarland, 1985.
Canton, S.C. *Lawrence of Arabia: A Film's Anthropology*. University of California Press, 1999.
Cawkwell, Tim, and John M. Smith. *The World Encyclopedia of the Film*. New York: Galahad Books, 1972.
Crafton, Donald. *Before Mickey: The Animated Film 1898–1928*. MIT Press, 1982.
Cunningham, James. *Hungarian Cinema: From Coffee House to Multiplex*. Wallflower Press, 2004.
DeBauche, Leslie Midkiff. *Reel Patriotism: The Movies and World War I*. Madison: University of Wisconsin Press, 1997.
Dibbets, Karel and Bert Hogenkamp (ed). *Film and the First World War*. University of Amsterdam Press, 1995.
Early, Emmett. "Johnny Got His Gun" in *The War Veteran in Film*, McFarland, 2003.
Everson, William K. *American Silent Films*. da Capo Press, 1997.
Ferguson, Niall .*The Pity of War; Explaining World War One*. Basic Books, 2000.
Fussell, Paul. *The Great War and Modern Memory*. Oxford University Press, 1975.
Gans, Herbert J. "Hollywood Films on British Screens: An Analysis of American Popular Culture Abroad." *Social Problems* Vol. 9, No. 4 (Spring 1962): 324–328.
Garland, Brock. *War Movies*. New York: Facts on File, 1987.
Gatzke, Hans W. *Germany and the United States: A "Special" Relationship*. Cambridge, MA: Harvard University Press, 1980.
Halliwell, Leslie, and John Walker, ed. *Halliwell's Film Guide*. New York: HarperPerennial, 1991.
Hanson, Peter. *Dalton Trumbo, Hollywood Rebel: A Critical Survey and Filmography*. Jefferson, NC: McFarland, 2001.
Isenberg, Michael T. *War on Film: The American Cinema and World War I, 1914–1941*. Rutherford: Farleigh Dickenson University Press, 1983.

Jung, Uli, and Walter Schatzberg. *Beyond Caligari: The Films of Robert Wiene*. New York: Berghahn Books, 1999.
Kael, Pauline. *5001 Nights at the Movies*. New York: Macmillian, 1991.
Kennedy, David M. *Over Here: The First World War and American Society*. New York: Oxford University Press, 1980.
Konzett, Delia Konzett. "War and Orientalism in Hollywood Combat Film." *Quarterly Review of Film and Video* Vol. 21, No. 4 (October–December 2004): 327.
Lamster, Frederick. *Souls Made Great Through Love and Adversity: The Film Work of Frank Borzage*. Metuchen, NJ: Scarecrow Press, 1981.
Latham, James. "*Patriotic Satire: Shoulder Arms*" in *American Cinema of the 1910s: Themes and Variations*. New Brunswick, NJ: Rutgers University Press, 2009.
Lindgren, Ernest. *The Art of the Film*. Macmillan, 1963.
Low, Rachael. *History of the British Film, 1918–1929*. London: Allen & Unwin, 1971.
Lyons, Timothy. "Hollywood and World War I, 1914–1918." *Journal of Popular Films* Vol. 1, No. 1 (January 1972): 15–30.
Murphy, David. *The Arab Revolt, 1916–18: Lawrence Sets Arabia Ablaze*. Oxford: Osprey, 2008.
Niemi, Robert. "Gallipoli." In *History and the Media: Film and Television*. Santa Barbara, CA: ABC-CLIO, 2006.
Paris, Michael, ed. *The First World War and Popular Cinema, 1914 to the Present*. New Brunswick, NJ: Rutgers University Press, 2000.
Parrish, James R. *The Great Combat Pictures: Twentieth Century Warfare on the Screen*. Metuchen, NJ: Scarecrow Press, 1990.
Perimutter, David A. *Visions of the War: Picturing Warfare from the Stone Age to the Cyber Age*. New York: St. Martin's Griffin, 1999.
Pris, Michael. "Wings." *History Today* Vol. 45, No. 7 (July 1995).
"Private Lives." *Life Magazine*, December 28, 1936.
Rollins, Peter C., and John E. O'Connor. *Hollywood's World War I: Motion Picture Images*. Bowling Green, OH: Bowling Green State University Press, 1987.
Rollins, Peter C., and John E. O'Connor. *Why We Fought: America's Wars in Film and History*. Lexington: University Press of Kentucky, 2008.
Roquemore, Joseph H. *History Goes to the Movies: A Viewer's Guide to the Best (and Some of the Worst) Historical Films Ever Made*. New York: Main Street Books, 1999.
Slater, Jay, ed. *Under Fire: A Century of War Movies*. Hersham, UK: Ian Allan Publishing, 2009.
Stewart, Philip W. *Battlefilm: U.S. Army Signal Corps Motion Pictures of the Great War*. Crestview, FL: Pms Press, 2010.
Suid, Lawrence H. *Guts & Glory: The Making of the American Military Image in Film*. Lexington: University Press of Kentucky, 2002.
Toumarkine, Doris. "Joyeux Noel." *Film Journal International* Vol. 109 (April 200): 137–138.
Tyler, Parker. *The Three Faces of the Film*. New York: T. Yoseloff, 1960,
Ward, Larry Wayne. *The Motion Picture Goes to War: The U.S. Government Film Effort During World War I*. Ann Arbor: University of Michigan Press, 1985.
Weintraub, Stanley. *Silent Night: Story of World War I Christmas Truce*. New York: Plume, 2002.
White, David Manning, and Richard Averson. *The Celluloid Weapon: Social Comment in the American Film*. Boston: Beacon Press, 1972.
Winter, J. M. *The Experience of World War I*. New York: Oxford University Press, 1989.

Index

Numbers in **bold italics** indicate pages with photographs.

A&E Home Television Networks 138
Aamechik, J.S. 208
Abbott, George 34
Abbott and Costello 70
Abby, May 184
Abdy, Harry 88
Aboukir 195
Academy Awards 75, 129
Academy of Motion Picture Arts 6, 33, 51, 75, 86, 103, 106, 129, 141, 177, 208, 210, 221n4
Ace 31, 48, 56, 119, 122, 126, 167, 177, 200
Aces High (1976) 31, 119
Achard, Paul 107
Ackroyd, Jack 44
Adair, Alice 81
Adair, Robert 118
Adams, Claire 45
Adams, Harvey 88
Adams, Michael 37
Adams, Tom 200
Adler, Felix 47
Adler, Jane 87
Adolfi, John G. 210
Adoree, Rene 45
Afghanistan 159
Afra Films 38
African-American 83, 98–100
The African Queen (1951) 33, 34
After You're Gone 86
HMS *Agamemnon* 162
Agee, James 33
Ahern, Lassie Lou 63
Ahern, Peggy 172
Aherne, Brian 200
Aherne, Patrick 172
Ahlm, Philip 173
Ainley, Anthony 126
Ainley, Henry 51, 158
Airship R33 214
Albert, Arthur 162
Albertelli, Mario 190

Alberti, Fritz 195
Albertson, Frank 76, 197
Alcoholism 133
Alden, Mary 73, 197
Alderson, Erville 176
Aled, Gruffudd 102
Alex, Shannon 201, 202
Alexander, Alec 151
Alexander, Ben 34, 135
Alexander, Clifford 162
Alexander, Ernie 187
Alexander, Frank 109
Alexander, Richard 34
Alexander, Sara 211
Alfred, Dalby 181
All Quiet on the Western Front (1930) 14, 34, 170, 179
All Quiet on the Western Front (1979) 35
All the King's Men (1999) 27, 35
Allan, Joseph, Sr. 94
Allardice, David 37
Allardt, Arthur 162
Allary, Pierre 195
Alleborn, Al 160
Allen, Alfred 84
Allen, Frank 182
Allen, Tanya 43
Allied Arabs 129
Allies 64, 77, 80, 112, 134, 145, 175, 215
Allister, Claud 64
Allnut, Charles 33
Almasy, Paul 108
Almgren, Susan 96
Alper, Murray 76, 187
Alternative history 2
Altscholer, Modest 178
Ambassado 36, 67, 127, 153, 158
Ambulance 66, 77, 80, 82, 86, 136, 153, **200**
American Ambulance Service 69, **80**, 126
American Correspondent Film Company 26

American Expeditionary Force 60
An American Home (1915) 40
American International Pictures 126
American Motion Picture Academy 141
American Pathe 39, 72, 118, 127, 158, 163, 178, 193
American Protective League 223n36
American Secret Service 20
Ames, Gerald 51, 60
Ames, Robert 204
Amiot, Paul 115
Amnesia 168
Amy, Dennis 211
Analysis (commentary): absurdity 20; authenticity 24–27; character 21–23; democratic view 19; fate 17–18; military 16–19; moral issues 16; situational 15–21; waste 18
Anatole (Gabrielle's brother) 53
Anderson, Brian 91
Anderson, C.E. 119
Anderson, Doris 146
Anderson, Frank 85
Anderson, Gilbert 168
Anderson, Herbert 83
Anderson, James 176
Anderson, Marion Clayton 34
Anderson, Mary 79, 80, 208
Anderson, Maxwell 34, 206
Anderson, Nellie 149
Anderson, Richard 160
Anderson, Robert Gordon 101, 109, 158
Andoree, Renee 45
Andra, Fern 54
Andre, Marcel 195
Andress, Ursula 48
Andrews, Julie 65, 164
Andrews, Mary Raymond Shipman 193, 196

228 INDEX

Andrews, Robert 54
Andriot, Lucien N. 157
Angels with Dirty Faces (1938) 83
Animation 116, 118, 121, 127, 158, 178, 193
Animatronics 203
Ann, Warrington 178
Ann Margret 181
The Anthill 160
Anthony, Andrews 134
Anthony, Jane 32
Anthony, Michael 147
Anti-war films: concept 4, 10, 19, 46, 51, 90, 104, 160; genre 2; movement 14, 57, 111; movies 34, 70, 90, 207
ANZACS (1985) 37
Anzacs, the War Down Under (1935) 37
Apfel, Oscar 62, 127, 144
Arboretum and Botanic Gardens 172
Archer 132
Archer, Arthur 112
Archer, Mary 77
Arditi, Catherine 155
Arenburg, Griselda von 125
Arestrup, Niels 203
Arey, Wayne 201
The Argonaut 174
Argue, David 91
Aristocracy 223n21
Arkoff, Sameul Z. 126
Arledge, John 64
Arlen, Richard 208, 210
Armetta, Henry 71, 187
Armistice 37, 55, 111, 114, 123, 138, 178, 179, 183
Arms and the Girl (1917) 38
Armstrong, John 209
Armstrong, W.M. 96
Army, U.S. 77, 113
Army Air Corps 208
Army Nurses *see* Nurses
Army Veterinary Corps 41
Arnaud, Captain 107
Arnell, David 57
Arnold, John 45
Arnold, Edward 182
Arnold, J. Gordon 168
Arnoux, Alexandre 193
Arthur, Julie 211
Arthure, Richard 123
Arundell, Dennis 132
Arundell, Teddy 60
As in a Looking Glass (1916) 38
Ash, William 35
Ashbrook, Florence 157
Asher, Irving 185
Asher, Max 138

Ashmore, Aaron 41
Ashmore Creelman, James 99
Ashton, Charles 169
Ashton, John 69
Ashton, Tom 42
Asquith, Anthony 51, 189
Asquith, Herbert H. 122
Assassination 148
Astor, Gertrude 42
Astor, Mary
At the Front (1918) 38, 99
At the front (place) 37, 44, 50, 69, 115, 123, 138, 160, 207
Atheists 58, 195
Atherton, Ted 41
Atkins, Robert 78
Atkins, Tommy 193
Atoline, France 93
Attenborough, Richard 155
Attila of Sunnybrook Farm 136
Attorícities 20, 34, 134, 206
Atwill, Lionel 170
Aubrey, Jimmy 181
Die Audere seitz 118
August, Joseph 148
Ault, Marie 142, 171, 198
Austeria (1982) 39, 113
Austin, Albert 179
Australian (Australia): armed forces 37, 44, 57, 71, 78, 91, 93, 168, 169; citizens 75; film sources 6, 37, 44, 57, 78, 87, 133, 154; heritage 6
Austrian (Austria) 39, 102, 108, 127, 190, 195
Authenticity 4, 24
Avery, Charles 188
Avric, Yola 178
Awkward Squad 179
AWOL (Absent Without Leave) 99
Axt, William 144, 146
Axzelle, Violet 105
Ayers, Lew 35
Aylesworth, Arthur 176
Azais, Paul 212
Azema, Sabine 155
Azizi, Anthony 138

Back to the Primitive (1917) 40
Bacon, Lloyd 69, 186
Badcoe, Brian 147
Baddeley, Hermione 98
Bailey, Meredith 159
Bailey, William 49, 50, 111
Baily, Raymond 125
Bainbridge, W.H. 119
Bairnsfather, Bruce 44
Baker, Betty 59
Baker, Friend F. 125
Bakers, Robert 38

Bakewell, William 62
Bako, Marta 147
Balcon, Michael 174
Baldrick, Bill 189
Baldry, Captain Chris 168
Baldry, Kitty 168
Baldwin, Earl 69
Balfour, Betty 52, 169
Balfour, Sue 72, 73
Ball, Vincent 37
Ballard, Jonathon 41
Ballin, Mable 177
Ballin the Jack 86
Bancroft, George 187
Banfiel, George 54
Banks, Monty 93
Banks, Perry 175
Banky, Vilma 68
Bantock, Leedham 91
Baranyi, Laszio 147
Barbette, Percy 56
Barbier, George 212
Bardell, Lord 184
Barkas, Geoffrey 189
Barker, Betty 79
Barker, Bradley 197
Barker, Frank 139
Barker, Howard 32
Barker, Pat 43
Barker Motion Picture Company 54, 93, 193
Barkley, Catherine 81, 82
Barlow, Reginald 57
Barnes, George S. 63
Barnes, G.H. 168
Barnett, Vince 62
Barrat, Robert 69
Barrault, Jean Louis 115
Barre, Raoul 118, 127, 163, 178, 198
Barrett, Guy 194
Barriscale, Bessie 162
Barron, Kieth 126
Barrows, Henry A. 119
Barry, Cecil 67
Barry, Wesley 197
Barry R. Cooper Productions 168
Barrymore, Ethel 97
Barrymore, Lionel 51, 146, 170
Barsony, Istvan 54
Barstar, A.H. 127
Barthelmess, Richard 67, 93, 183, 184
Bartlett, Clifford 78
Barzman, Ben 48
Bassermann, Albert 107
Bata, Janos 147
Bateman, Victory 177
Bates, Alan 124, 168
Bates, J.C. 105

Index

Bates, Louise 38
Batley, Dorothy 167
Batley, Ernest G. 167
Batley, Ethyle 168, 204
Battle 2, 3, 12, 14, 16, 18, 19, 21–24, 26, 27, 36, 37, 44, 46, 51–53, 56, 58, 60, 65, 70, 71, 84, 85, 88, 89, 95, 103, 109, 112, 114, 115, 123, 138, 142, 164, 167, 170, 181, 183, 189, 195
Battle and Fall of Przemysl (1915) 10
The Battle Cry of Peace (1915) 10, 36, 40, 55, 111
The Battle Cry of War (1915) 40, 111
Battle of Beersheba 89
Battle of Belleau Woods 27
Battle of Cocos 79
The Battle of Galliopli (1931) 15, 40, 91, 189, 205
Battle of Loos 152
The Battle of Midway (1942) 72
Battle of Passchendale 103, 159
Battle of St. Michel 114
Battle of the Mons 107, 131, 151
Battle of the Nek 91
Battle of the Somme 18
The Battle of the Somme (1916) 25
Battleground (2013) 40, 87
Battling Jane (1918) 41
Bauer, Arthur 138, 201
Baum, L. Frank 95
Baxter, George 144
Baxter, Warner 170
Bayerling, Karl von 147
Bayne, Beverly 62
Beagle Eddie 83, 84
Beal, Frank 111
A Bear Named Winnie (2004) 41, 204
The Beast of Berlin (1918) 42, 119
Beattie, Darryl 57
Beaudet, Louise 40
Beaudry, Joseph 175
Beauieu, Renee 125
Beauregard, F. 119
Becce, Giuseppe 71
Bechtel, William 105
Beck, Captain Frank 36
Beday, Eugene 73, 181
Beddard, Jamie 36
Beecher, Janet 64
Beery, Noah, Jr. 135, 170, 176
Beery, Wallace 43, 89, 157, 197
Behat, Gilles 32
Behind the Door (1919) 42
Behind the Lines (location) 75, 99, 192

Behind the Lines (1997) 43, 45, 99, 192
Behn, Harry 45, 104
Belasco, Walter 119, 167
Belgium 54, 61, 75, 101, 119, 151, 171, 172, 192, 204
Bell, Albert 122
Bell, Colin 66, 67
Bell, Francis 37
Bell, Fred 160
Bell, Geoff 203
Bell, Howard 37
Bell-Booth, Stephen 57
Bellamy, George 51, 76
Bellamy, Madge 99, 100
Bellamy, Quex 184
Bellamy, Ralph 60, 76
Bellew, Dorothy 107, 196
Bellows, Gil 41
Belmont, Joseph 214
Belvaux, Lucas 49
Beneath Hill 60 (2010) 188
Benedict, Brooks 138
Benedict, Harold 160
Benedict, Kingsley 53
Benko, Tina 59
Bennett, Alma 173
Bennett, Charles 174
Bennett, Constance 78, 191
Bennett, Edward 203
Bennett, Enid 205
Bennett, Hugh 175
Bennett, Richard Rodney 168
Benson, Lydia 180
Bent, Buena 169
Beranger, George 45
Berend, Istvan 54
Bergen, Fred von 62
Bergman, Helmer 211
Bergman, Henry 49
Bergman, Neil 69
Berkele, Reginald 51, 66, 154
Berkeley, Busy 86
Berkeley, Gertrude 201
Berkeley, Reginald 66
Berkhamsted, Hertfordshire, England 6
Berleand, Francois 55
Bernard, Albert 97
Bernard, Barry 172
Bernard, Carl 75
Bernard, Raymond 212
Bernerd, Jeffrey 59
Berry, Richard 175
Bertran, Edwin 195
Beseler, General Hans von 119
Besserer, Eugenie 134, 135
Bessy, Maurice 124
Best Actor 36, 177
Bett, Mairi 194
Bettenfield, Dominque 198

The Better 'Ole (1926) 44
Bevan, Billy 118, 181
Bevens, Clem 176
Bevington, Nancy 204
Bickel, George 51
Bickford, Charles 60
The Big Parade (1925) 12, 45, 53
The Big Shot (1930) 46, 86
Big Time (1942) 46
Bikel, Theodore 33
Bill, Tony 85
Billings, Phineas 177
Billings, Tommy 177
Billions, Bill 131
Billy Bishop Goes to War (1918) 46, 122
Bing, Hermann 81
Binge, Ronald 190
Bird, Charlotte 130
Birell, Tala 71
Birinsky, Leo 146
Birkel, John 144
Biro, Lajos 108
The Birth of a Nation (1915) 3, 10, 115, 150
The Birth of Patriotism (1917) 46
Bishop, Billy (W.A.) 47, 122
Bison, Motion Picture Company 72
Bittner, William 153
Bitzer, G.W. 95
Black, James 111
Black, Maurice 56
Black, William 166
Blackface 98, 99
Blackman, Don 172
Blackmer, Sidney 208
Blackton, J. Stuart 10, 40, 137, 211
Blackton, Paula 137
Blackton, Violet 137
Blackwell, Carlyle 47, 159, 199
Bladier, Jon 133
Blair, Henry 212
Blake, Christopher 32, 37
Blake, Joan 134
Blake, Jon 133
Blake, Larry 170
Blanchar, Pierre 212
Blanchard, Jean Francois 96
Blanche, Adele 74
Blanche, Davenport 195
Blanche Sweet Productions 197
Blanchette 161
Blancke, Kate (Cate) 130
Blandick, Clara 76, 170
Blatt, Edward 80
Blatty, William Pete 65
Bleifer John 170

Bletcher, Billy 50
Blighty (1927) 19, 47, 219
Blimp, Colonel 59, 132, 220
Blockheads (1938) 37, 219
Bloomer, Raymond 140
Blue, Ben 86
The Blue Max (1966) 32, 48
Blum, Howard 64
Blyler, James 157
Blystone, John G. 47, 181
Blythe, Betty 159
Blythe, Captain 134
Blythe, Harry 121
Blythe, Philip 134
Blyton, Jane 157
Boardman, Eleanor 81, 143, 178
Boardman, Vurtina True 179
Boasberg, Al 71
Bock, Rainer 203
Bodart, Ada 66
Boer War (1899–1902) 132
Bogarde, Dirk 123
Bogart, Humphrey 23, 33
Boggs, Benny 36, 37
Boghosian Sam 125
Boland, Eamon 35
Boland, Eddie 141
Bolsheviks 55
Bolt, Robert 127, 129
Bolte, August 143
Bolton, Guy 63, 64
Bolton, Michael 52
Bombasa Harbor, Africa 172
Bonaparte Films 194
Bonce, Charles 43
The Bond (1917) 49
Bond, James 146
Bond, Julian 210
Bond, Ward 76, 177, 187
Bonham, Joe 117
Bonner, Tony 27, 133
Bonnie Annie Laurie (1918) 49, 218
Book of Revelations 90
Booker, William 68
Boom Boom (1936) 50, 219
Boon, Dany 149
Booth, John 142
Borchard, Adolphe 195
Bordeaux, Joe 186
Borden, Eugene 73, 181
Borden, Robert 122
Borden, Walter 122
Borg, Verda Ann 186
La Borgmestre de Stilemonde 54
Borgnine, Ernest 35
Born for Glory (1934) 50, 22
Boros, Ferike 105
Borrows, Geoff 37
Borzage, Frank 29, 36, 80, 142, 190

Bosworth, Hobart 42, 45, 135
Boteler, Wade 100
Bottoms, Timothy 116, 117
Boulanger, Daniel 124
Bound for Morocco (1918) 12
Bow, Clara 208, 209
Bowell, Charles 165
Bowers, Charles 39, 72, 110, 118, 120, 127, 158, 163, 178, 193
Bowers, Frederick 197
Bowers, Jack 164
Bowman, Earl 173
Bowman, William 79
Bowser, Glen 87, 96
Boy Scouts 137
Boyce, Todd 83
Boyd, Clement 121
Boyd, Russell 91
Boyd, William 194
Boyel, Charles 143
Boylan, Malcom Stuart 69
Boyle, Charles P. 143
Boyle, Jack, Jr. 83
Bracey, Sidney 68
Bracken, Bertram 85
Bradley, Charlotte 61
Bradley, Dai 35
Bradley, Dale G 57
Bradley, Ruth 83
Bradshaw, Lionel 141
Brady, Cyrus Townsend 1, 84, 106, 211
Brady, Ed 138, 191
Brady, Joseph Ewing 106
Braham, Henry 83
Bramble, A.V. 114
Brampton, Kenneth 88
Brand, Major 68
Brande, Bill 173
Brando, Marlon 33
Brandon, Michael 138
Brantford, Mickey 54, 66, 144, 188
Brasseur, Pierre 124
Bray, Tim 57
Bray Films 194
Breakenback, Igor 88
Breese, Edmund 34, 146
Breisacher, George 163
Brendel, El 208
Brennan, Paul 35
Brennan, Wallace 53
Brennan, Walter 176
Brenner, Jules 116
Brenon, Herbert 201
Brent, George 82
Bret, Tom 92
Brewster, Florence 157
Brialy, Jean-Claude 124
Brian, Mary 43

Briant, Shane 133
Brice, Monte 43
Bridgeman, Chris 194
Bridges, Alan 168
Briese, Gerd 195
Briggs, Oscar G. 182
Brigham Young University Archives 6
Bright, Vera 109
Brighton, Robert 96
Brincken, Wilhelm von 62, 143, 191
Brinkmann, Hanne 195
British Broadcasting Company 35, 43
British Film Institute National Archives 6, 7, 143, 169
British Flying Club 74
British Government 132
British Instructional Films 150, 151, 189
British Intelligence 166, 174, 191
British War Office 102
Brochmann, Byron J. 88
Brockman, David N. 186
Brockwell, Gladys 85, 125
Brodie, Edgar 174
Brody, Estelle 142
Brody, Raymond 123
Broken Lullaby (1932) 51, 82, 143, 219, 222n8
Brook, Clive 191
Brooke, Benedict 198
Brooke, Michael 68
Brooke, Tom 201
Brooks, Rupert 26
Brooks, Sammy 157
Brooks, Thomas 211
Brophy, Edward 69, 72
Brosset, Claude 55
Brother Officers (1915) 51, 217
Brough, Mary 66
Broulard, General 20
Brown, Albert 52
Brown, Elizabeth 153
Brown, Gaye 35, 147
Brown, Halbert 153
Brown, J. Edwin 46
Brown, Karl 41
Brown, Louis Polliman 172
Brown, Lucie 46
Brown, Naaman 172
Brown, Roy 167
Brown, Judge Willis 53
Brown in Resolution (1934) 50, 52, 87, 219
Browne, Bernard 185
Browne, Bothwell 214
Browne, Derick 126
Browne, Porter Emerson 115

Index 231

Brownlow, Kevin 225
Bruce, Belle 40, 181
Bruce, Clifford 69
Bruce, David 176
Bruce, Kate 93, 97, 101
Bruce, Tony 189
Brucker, Maxmilliam 203
Bruhl, Daniel 149
Brundage, Mathilde 181
Brunel, Aorian 47
Brunelli, Peter 173
Brunswick, Earl 73
Brutality 20, 34, 131, 207; see also atrocities
Bryant, Alfred 111
Bryant, Betty 88
Bryant, Charles 201, 202
Bryna Production Company 160
Buckens, Celine 203
Buckley, Keith 123
Buckner, Robert 212
Budgett, Captain 204
Bud's Recruits (1918) 53, 218
Buel, Krenean 202
Buell, Leonce 114
Bugler of Algiers (1916) 53, 206, 217
Bujard, Marc 107, 114
Bujold, Genevieve 124
Bull, Peter 33
Bunce, Stuart 35, 43
Buquet, Jean 107
Burger, Paul 60
Burgomaster of Stilemonde (1929) 54, 219
Burke, Billie 38, 58
Burke, J. Frank 57
Burke, James 68
Burke, Joseph 94
Burke, Tom 35
Burkell, John 157
Burlingham Standard Corporation 167
Burn, Tam Dean 203
Burnett, Beatrice 37
Burnham, Julie 199
Burning of books 190
Burns, Edmund 178
Burns, Harry 157
Burns, Robert 50
Burns, William 185
Burrett, Bartine 93
Burroughs, Edgar Rice 126
Burton, Clarence 196
Burton, Ned 201
Burton, Noel 96
Burton, Peter 129
Burton, Val 205
Busch, Ernst 104
Busch, Robert 120

Bush, James 62
Bushell, Anthony 118, 191
Bushman, Ralph 90
Butler, Alexander 156
Butler, David 93, 97, 100
Butler, Jimmy 154
Butterworth, Earnest 53
Butterwortth, Frank 192
Butts, Billy 63
Buxton, Judy 32
By the Kaiser's Orders (1914) 54
Byington, Spring 170
Byrd, Anthony 105

Cabanne, Christy 173, 181
Cable, Boyd 198, 199
Caddo Corporation 104
Caesar, Arthur 191
Cafe Moscow (1936) 54, 158
Caffray, Frank 46
Cafrdiff, Jack 33
Cagney, James 69, 70, 82, 207, 212
Cagney, Jeanne 212
Cagney, William 212
Caine, Shirley 168
Cairns, Dallas 87
Calhoun, Jean-Claud 55
Calhoun, William 159
Caliendo, Christopher 142
Calil, George 138
Call to Arms Against War (1915) 40, 55
Caltagirone, Daniel 138
Calvert, Corine 207
Calvert, Elish Helm 62, 68
Cambo, Paul 107
Cameo the Dog 99
Cameron, John 162
Cameron, Robin 162
Campbell, Bruce 116
Campbell, Daisy 163
Canadian 28, 41, 42, 46, 78, 87, 101, 122, 123, 159, 165–167, 198, 205
Canal + Les Films 55
Canet, Guillaume 149
Cannes Film Festival 117
Cannon, Pomery 89
Cannon City Distributors 146
Capell, Peter 160
Capponi, Pier 124
Capra, Frank R. 42, 186
Caprona (island) 127
Captain (rank) 42, 69, 78, 105, 118, 119, 151, 185, 190, 193, 214
Captain Conan (1996) 84
Captain Swagger (1928) 22
Carabatsos, James 138
Caravaca, Eric 155

Carette, Jullian 94
Carew, James 113
Carewe, Edwin 96
Carey, Timothy 160
Carion, Christian 149
Carlisle, Peggy 60, 151
Carlton, Lewis 121
Carlyle, Rita 206
Carol, Sue 36
Carow, Leonard 203
Carpenter, Betty 119
Carr, Cameron 163
Carradine, John 187
Carroll, Frank J. 211
Carroll, John 72
Carroll, Madeleine 98, 99, 174, 200, 201
Carroll, Nancy 51
Carson, Charles 174
Carson, Nattrass 42
Carsten, Peter 214
Carter, Claude 78
Carter, Ellis W. 172
Carter, Harry 53
Carter, Louise 51
Cartmell, Charles 194
Casablanca (1942) 95
The Case of Sergeant Grischa (1930) 56
Cassinelli, Dolores 131, 197
Castle, John 110
Castleton, Barbara 89
Catlett, Walter 212
Cattrall, Kim 152
Cauterio, Robert 81
Cavell, Edith 67, 145, 154, 169, 211
The Cavell Case (1918) 56, 75, 210
Cavender, Glen 188
Cawthorn, James 126
Cazenove, Christopher 147
Cecil, Edward 121
Celebrated Players 110, 118, 120
Celi, Adolfo 124
Cendrars, Blaise 111, 115
Center for the Study of the Korean War 7, 16, 80, 81, 92, 105, 147, 209, 213
Central Powers 10
Chair of the National Eisteddfod 102
Challenger, Percy 181
Challres, Christian 94
Chamberlain, Winston 191
Chandlee, Harry 176
Chandler, Eddy 178
Chandler, Edward 121
Chandler, Helen 181
Chandler, James Robert 105
Chandler, Lane 130

232 INDEX

Chaney, Lon, Jr. 79, 80, 113, 187
Chaplain 83, 179
Chaplin, Charlie 49, 157
Chaplin, Sidney (Sydney) 44, 129, 188
Chapman, Audrey 100, 135, 191
Chappell, Dick 100
Charing Cross Roads 154
Charity, Stan 194
Charlie Chaplin Production 179
Chase, Colin 85
Chaston Fred 87
Chateau-Thierry, France 97
Chatfield-Taylor, Hobart 62
Chatterton, Ruth 81
Chatterton, Tom 175
Chaumontel, Marie 183
Chautard, Emile 134, 144
Chauvel, Charles 89
Chauvel, Elsa 88
Chauvel, Gen. Sir Harry 89
Chequer, Paul 164
Chevalier, Albert 78
The Chicago Tribune 7, 179
Chief of the Signals Office 6
Childers, Naomi 42
Chilton, Charles 155
China Sea 148
Chivalry in the air 68, 70
Choureau, Etchika 125
Christie, Julie 168
Christmas (eve) 77.119, 149
Christophe, Francoise 124
Christy, Dorothy 187
Chrystal Heart Award 42
Chunuk Bair (1992) 57
Churchill, Donald 214
Churchill, Winston 132, 189, 223n49
Cinematic Public Enemy 95
Civil War 9, 14, 21
Civilian 5, 61, 135, 146.170
Civilization (1916) 10, 58, 215
Clarendon, Hal 161
Clarendon British Film Production 107, 196
Clark, Brigette 89
Clark, Edward 119
Clark, Fred 60, 104
Clark, Harvey 100
Clark, Howard 92
Clark, John 37
Clark, Lillian 109
Clark, Marguerite 136
Clark, Neville 140
Clark, Russ 187
Clarke, Andrew 37
Clarke, Mae 205
Clarke, Redfield 96
Clary, Charles 85

The Claws of the Hun (1918) 85, 100
Clawson, Dal 57, 183
Clawson, Elliot J. 53
Clayton, Arthur 44
Clayton, Eddie 134
Clayton, Ethel 153, 199
Clayton, Lisa 126
Clayton, Marion 34
Clayton, Richard 83
Clean pictures for clean people 36
Clem, Robert 59
Clemence, Andy 155
Clements, Charlie 61
Clements, Hal 150
Clere, Paul 151
Clifford, Ruth 119
Clifton, Elmer 41
Clifton, Wallace 69
Clive 98
Clive, Colin 118
Clothier, William H. 125
Clouston, Michael 185
Cobb, Darian 207
Cobbs, Humphrey 160
Coburn, Charles 208
Coburn, Wallace 119
Cochrane, Michael 185, 210
Code book 69, 73, 104, 117, 133, 192
Code of ethics 146, 168, 200
Cody, Lew 70
Codyre, Martin 61
Coffin, Adeline Hayden 54
Cohan, George M. 212, 213
Cohan, Sammy 83
Cohen, Bennett 85
Cohen, Octavus Roy 121
Cohen Media Group 98
Cohn, Harry 186
Colbert, Claudette 81
Colboran, Harry 4
Cole, Sasche 96
College Park Maryland 6
Collier, Terence 139
Collier, William, Sr. 173
Collins, Anthony 154
Collins, Arthur 76
Collins, Cora Sue 64
Collins, G. Pat 31
Collyer, June 90
Colman, Ronald 63
Colonel Blimp (1943) 112, 159
Colonial empires 33
Colonial forces 57
Colton, John 75
Colton, U.S.N. (1916) 59, 106
Combat 2, 3
Committee on Public Information 7, 221n3

Community 2
Company K (2004) 59
Compson, Betty 56, 133
Compton, Fay 189
Compton, Joyce 181
Comradeship (1919)
Comradeship (feeling) 1, 104, 190
Conflict 3, 108, 175
Conflict (1933) 60
Congressional Medal of Honor 176
Conklin, Chester 43
Conklin, Heinie 99, 214
Conley, Lige 157
Connelly, Bobby 197, 211
Connelly, Edward 89
Connolly, Jack 137
Connor, Kevin 126
Connors, Kathleen 189
Conrad, John 97
Conscientious objector 34, 176
Conscription 74, 102, 105, 222n14
Conscription (1918) 60
Conservative 17
Constantini, Nino 195
Constantinople 205
Contemptibles 151
Conti, Albert 71, 130
Converse, Evelyn 181
Conway, Harry 39, 118, 127, 163, 179
Conway, Jack 103
Cook, Clyde 180
Cook, David 123
Cook, Elisaha, Jr. 187
Cook, Lillian 38
Cook, Warren 197
Cooke, Ray 187
Coolidge, Calvin 61
Cooper, Bradley 64
Cooper, D. P. 98
Cooper, Elliott 52
Cooper, Gary 60, 61, 71, *81*, 108, 114, 134, 176, 208
Cooper, George 134
Cooper, Melville 68
Cooper, Merian 140
Cooper, Texas 130
Cooper, William S. 87
Cooper Smith, William 142
Coote, Robert 134
Copley, Peter 123
Copping, Cecil 134
Copping, Martin 88
Corbett, Olver 202
Corbould, Neil 61
Corcoran, F. 119
Cordy, Raymond 212
Cormack, James 32

Index

Corman, Gene 199
Corman, Roger 199
Cornillac, Clovis 198
Cornwall, Dan 123
Corr, Ryan 205
Corraeau, Evelyn 32
Corrington, John William 199
Corrington, Joyce Hooper 200
Cosby, Ronnie 76
Cosgrave, Jack 101
Cosmos, Jean 55
Cossar, John John 62
Costello, Abbott 70
Cotillard, Marion 198
Cotterill, Ralph 133
Le Coucher de la Mariee 30
Coulouris, George 180
Countiss Cathleen 95
Cournoyer, Maxime 96
Court martial 55, 103, 133, 164
Court Martial of Billy Mitchell (1955) 60, 157
Courtenay, William 84
Courtnay, Tom 123
Courtney, Captain 68
Courtney, Jai 205
Courtney, Will 84
Courtot, Marquerite 196
Coury, Simon 152
Cowan, Paul 122
Cowan, Sam 176
The Coward (1915) 61
Coward, Noel 102
Cowardice 16, 22, 43, 61, 76, 83, 104, 152, 161, 164, 178, 181
Cowel, Brenden 44
Cowl, Jane 134
Cowles, Jules 177
Cox, Ernest A. 114
Cox, Jack E. 47
The Cradle of Souls (1918) 63, 97
Craig, Daniel 194
Craig, David 138
Craig, Gordon 66
Craig, Hill 207
Craig, Madge 183
Craiglockart, Scotland 43
Crandall, Howard, Jr. 79
Crane, Doc 127
Crane, Frank Hall 38
Crashing Through to Berlin (1918) 5
Craven, James 172
Crawford, Broderick 187
Crawford, Howard 52, 129
Crawford, Jack 40
Creel, George 13, 221*n*3
Crehan, Joseph 83
Cressy 195
Crews, Laura Hope 170

Crimson Romance (1934) 62
The Crimson Wing (1915) 62
Crisp, Donald 68
Croft, Douglas 212
Croix de Guerre 126
Cromelin, Paul H. 51
Crompton, Ben 36
Cromwell, Richard 170
Cronin, Jules 84
Cronin, Roy 205
Cronjager, Henry 140, 183
Crosby, Sonny 183
Cross, Gerrard 54
Crossland, Alan 196
Crossley, Syd 188
Crowder, Gen. E.H. 93
Crowe, Russell 15, 205
Crowell, Josephine 101
Crown Prince 192, 214
Crucified 20, 166
Crum, Owen 214
Cserhalmi, Erzsi 55, 147
Csortes, Gyula 55
Cuiffo, Steve 59
Cullen, Alma 35
Cullen, Robert 66
Culver, Roland 132
Cummings, Irving 127
Cummins, Christopher 137
Cunard, Grace 72, 141
Cunard, Mina 72
Cunniffe, Emma 35
Cunningham, Genevieve 157
Cunningham, James 172
Cunningham, Liam 203
Cunningham, Peggy 81
Cunnington, Cerl 103
HMS *Curacoca* 52
Curley, Pauline 105, 160
Currier, Franki 75, 96, 97
Curtis, Bob 180
Curtis, Dick 197
Curtis, Richard 203
Curtiz, Michael 212
Cutie Beautiful 94

Dailey, Dan 207
Daker, David 32
Dalberg, Camille 73
D'Albrook, Sidney 73
Dalio, Marcel 94
Dalton, Dorothy 65, 121
Daly, Mark 60, 74
Damberger Film and Cattle Company 159
D'Ambricourt, Adrienne 74
Daniels, Bebe 157
Daniels, Howard 72
Daniels, Josephus 184
Daniels, William 86
D'Archeville, George 171

D'Arcy, James 194
Darensbourg, Joe 130
Dark, John 126
The Dark Angel (1925) 63
The Dark Angel (1935) 64
Dark Invasion (2015) 64
The Dark Road (1917) 65, 171
Darling Lili (1970) 207
d'Arras, Harry 208
Darrow, John 105
Darvas, Magda 147
Dashiell, Willard 153
Da Silva, Howard 176
Daste, Jean 94
Daughter of France (1914) 66
A Daughter of France (1918) 66
Dauvray, Maryse 114
Davenport, Blanche 196
Davenport, Dorothy 194
Davey, Dahren 194
David, Agnes 147
David, Daker 32
David, William 38
David and Goliath 22, 139
Davidson, J.B. 121
Davidson, Leonard 173
Davidson, Max 109
Davidson, William B. 69, 97, 170
Davies, Escott 74
Davies, Gareth 210
Davies, Howard 184
Davies, Marion 144, 145
Davis, Alan 187
Davis, Bette 34, 205
Davis, Desmond 210
Davis, Edwards 79
Davis, George 51
Davis, Hal 56
Davis, Harry 105
Davis, J. Gunnis 134
Davis, Mildred 53
Davis, Rex 151
Davis, Rita 164
Davis, Shan 102
Davis, Virginia 62
Davison, Lawford 160
Dawn (1928) 145, 154
The Dawn of Reckoning (1918) 67
The Dawn Patrol (1930) 14, 67
The Dawn Patrol (1938) 68, 74
Dawson, Albert K. 10, 26
Days Before the Storm (1991) 195
Dazecki, Seweryn 39
Dean, Paula 137
Dean, Louis 120, 153
Deanne, Dacia 67
Dear John letter 155
Dearing, Anna 153

Death 3, 17, 21, 26, 48, 58, 59, 74, 75, 80, 84, 99, 131, 132, 141, 146, 169, 174, 189, 202, 208, 211, 221*n*3
Deauville, Myra 205
De Bauche, Leslie Midkiff 136
de Boeldieu, Captain 99
de Bornay, Rene 125
de Briac, Jean 140
de Broca, Philippe 124
De Brulier, Nigel 119, 125, 160
De Camp, Rosemary 212
de Cippico, Giuseppe 130
de Ciron, Louise 8, 66
Decker, Jennifer 83, 84
De Conde, Syn 93
de Cordova, Rudolph 97
Deering, Violet 100
Defeatism 17, 144
de Gresac, Fred 178
de Guillebon, Xavier 195
Deighton, Len 153, 156
Dekker, Albert 108
De Lacy, John 197
De Lacy, May 38
Delafield, Joe 59
Delaitre, Marchel 212
Delaney, Joe 59
Delaney, Leo 181
de la Tour, Frances 164
Delicate Situation (1917) 38
de Limur, Jean 129
De Linsky, Victor 120
Del Lord 138
Delmar, Watson 142
Delmont, Endouard 107
del Rio, Dolores 206
Del Ruth, Roy 138
Demarest, George 105
Demarest, William 207
De Mille, Cecil B. 6, 135, 191–193, 198, 223*n*30, 223*n*33
De Mille, William C. 174
Demographic 2
Dempster, Carol 98
Denet, Lieutenant 170
Denha, Maurice 180
Dennis, Amy 211
Denny, Reginald 140
Depew, Joseph 173
de Planta, Carl 94
Derangere, Gregori 155
Dermoz, Germaine
de Salvo, Brian 152
de Segurola, Andres 145
De Sica, Vittorio 82
Desjardins, Maxime 114
Desmond, William 36
de Souza, Edward 163
Despair 35, 76, 170
Desspy, Natalie 149

Detective 30, 43, 78, 158, 159, 162
de Tolignac, Gaston 102
De Turck, Lillian 182
Deuerich, Ned G. 95
Deus ex Machina 199
Devenish, Nat G. 141
De Vere, Harry 112
DeVernon, Frank 196
The Devil at His Elbow (1916) 69
Devil Dogs in the Air (1935) 69, **70**
Devillers, Renee 115
Devin, Dean 83
Devine, Andy 170
Devine, Denny 125
DeVinna, Clyde 57
de Vogt, Carl 195
Devreaux, Captain 169
Dew, Eddit 83
Dewey, Admiral 40
Dhavernas, Caroline 159
Dial, Patterson 184
Diaz, Jean 115
Dibbs, Kem 160
Dick and Doof 48
Dickinson, Desmond 98
Dietrich, Marlene 70, 71
Dietrich, Ralph 187
Different Productions Company 61
Diffring, Anton 214
Dill, Jack 84
Dillion, Basil 190
Dillion, Edward 149
Dillion, Robert 99
Dillon, John 116
Dimech, John 129
DiMonte, Anthony 116
d'Ines, Denis 107
Dingle, Charles 60
Dinicol, Joe 159
Dinosaurs 127
Dintenfass, Mark M. 153
Diplomat 78, 153
Directors (generic) 4, 5, 12, 16, 18–20, 26, 28, 54, 93, 189
Dirigible 215
The Dirigible (1931) 186, 215
Dishonored (1931)71
Disillusionment 17, 20, 35
Disney Studios 42, 203
Dix, Beulah Marie 76
Dix, Marion 78
Dixon, Campbell 174
Dixon, John 37
Dobiesz. Laurence 36
Dobtcheff, Vernon 147
Dr. Brian Pellie and the Secret Dispatch 156

Documentary films 7, 10, 25, 79, 122, 131, 150, 151
Doe, Edgar 189
Doherty, Ethel 43
Dolby mix system 129
Domanska, Ewa 39
Dominquez, Beatrice 135
Donaldson, Arthur 85, 159
Donnelly, Ruth 76
Donnelly, Terry 61
Dooley, Brian 159
Doomed Battalion (1932) 71
The Doorway of Destruction (1915) 72
Dorgeles, Roland 212
Dormer, Richard 152
Dorosh, Michael 122
Dorrington, Lucile 135
Double Cross System 72
Doughboy 45, 99, 179
The Doughboy (1918) 19, 72
Doughboys (1930) 46
Dougherty, Joe 50
Douglas, Colin 202
Douglas, Frank 109
Douglas, Hugh 104
Douglas, Kirk 160, 161
Douglas, Louis 104
Douglas, Tom 51
Dowling, Dan 134
Dowling, Joseph J. 162, 183
Downey, Gail 83
Downing, Rex 154
Downing, Terence 78
Dowst, Henry Payson 36
Doyle, Laird 103
Draft 258 (1917) 73
HMS *Drake* 162, 187
Drake, Lieutenant 188
Drewry, Mark 35
Driant, Jean 32
Dronne, Agatha 155
Drugs 48, 179
Drumier, Jack 199
Drummond, Hugh 56
du Brey, Claire 59, 84
Duckett, Luke 194
Dudicourt, Marc 124
Duff, Warren 186
Duffy, Brian 155
Duffy, Father 83
Duffy, Gerald C. 159
Dugain, Marc 155
Dukes, Alan 44
Dulac, Marie 198
Dumo, Evelyn 140
Dunkinson, Harry 62, 84
Dunlap, Grosset 130
Dunlap, Paul 172
Dunn, Emma 51
Dunn, Malcolm 38

Index

Dunn, Michael 159
Dunn, Ralph 83
Dunn, Winifred 143, 159
Dunton, Roddy 100
Dupeyron, Francois 154
Dupont, Alvert 198
Dupree, George 211
Duprez, June 185
Durante, Jimmy 103
Durham, Bill 111
Dussollier, Andre 155, 198
Duvel, Arthur C. 153
Dvorak, Ann 72
Dyall, Alentine 132
Dyer, Danny 194
Dyer, Fred 139

The Eagle and the Hawk (1933) 74
Eagler, Paul 79
Earl, John 87, 88
Earle, Edward 85
Earley, Sergeant 176
East Africa 172
East Lynne on the Western Front (1921) 74
Easter, Cindy 7
Easter Sunday 58
Eastman, Orlo 119
Eastmancolor film 147
Eastwood, Clint 125
Eaton Sidney 92
Eberhard, Lieutenant Von 101
Ebert, Roger 132
Ecksrom, Karl 80
Ecosse films 152
Edelman, Louis F. 82
Edens, Roger 86
Edeson, Arthur 69, 160, 186, 205
Edeson, Robert 144
Edison Company 196
Edith Cavell (1916) 145, 154, 168, 169
Edmonds, Elizabeth 168
Edmund, Joseph 213
Edwaqrd, Jose 165
Edwards, Blake 65
Edwards "Ukulele Ike" Cliff 72, 73
Edwards, Edgar 83
Edwards, Greg 7
Edwards, Thorton 79
Edwin, Stevens 198
Eggerth, Matha 80
Eggs 99, 100
Eldridge, Charles 38
Elinor, Vafrli 101
Elkas, Edward 116
Ellers, Sally 72
Elliott, Frank 63

Elliott, Paul 35
Elliott, Robert 116, 197
Ellis, Edwin 74
Ellis, Gwen 102
Ellis, Patricia 47, 48
Ellison, David 83
Ellsberg, Commander Edward 103
Elsie, Lily 60
Elstree Studio 189, 200
Eltz, Theodore Von 170
Elvey, Maurice 59, 114, 171
Elvidge, June 199
SMS *Emden* 78
Emerald, Charles 139
Emerson, John 94
Emerton, Roy 78
Emery, Gilbert 81, 82
Emery, John 170
Emil and the Detectives 137
Emmett, Edna 88
Emmons, Bob 133
Emmons, Marion 101
Emms, Robert 203
Empey, Guy Arthur 158
Endermann, Gernot 180
The Enemy Within (1918) 76, 79, 109
England (English): citizen 19, 26, 33, 37, 38, 43.54, 75.81, 82, 100, 104, 110, 133, 146, 151, 154, 164, 180, 188, 189, 200, 210; films 3–5, 36, 41, 52, 74, 76, 96,, 100, 110, 112, 114, 133, 139, 143, 150, 163, 166, 170, 171, 189, 212; location 6, 47, 63, 97, 116, 135, 143, 154, 155, 166, 172; military 6, 12, 14, 15, 36, 37, 47, 52, 65, 67, 68, 74, 75, 78, 84, 85, 88, 91, 92, 100, 102, 107, 108, 110, 114, 124, 125, 129, 132, 134, 138–140, 143, 151, 156, 167, 174, 185, 191, 193, 194, 196, 199, 201, 203; nation 1, 10, 26, 27, 35, 57, 76, 92, 119, 127, 132, 145, 173, 190, 189, 194
England Expects (1914) 11, 76
Englemann, Andrews 144
Ephron, Phoebe 207
Erdogan, Yilmaz 205
Erdos, Ilona 54
Ericson, Karen 200
Ernest, Marion 4
Escape 2
Essanay Film Manufacturing 62
Estabrook, Howard 104, 178
Ethier, Alphonse 161
Evans, Blake 83
Evans, Ellis Humphrey 102, 103

Evans, Fred 131, 163
Evans, Grey 102
Evans, Herbert 62, 66, 68
Evans, Jean 83
Evans, Joe 131, 163
Evans, Madge 137, 199
Evans, Reg 91
Ever in My Heart (1933) 76
Evers, Arthur 113
Everson, William K. 28
Every Mother's Son (1918) 77
Everything Is Thunder (1936) 78
Exhibitors Booking Company 215
Exotic 146
The Exploits of the Emden (1928) 78
Explosive 54, 69, 103, 104
Exposition 169
Eythe, William 208

F-Ray 54
Face Value (1927) 78
Fair, Henry 165
Fair, Joyce 211
Fairbanks, A. 58
Fairbanks, Douglas, Jr. 68, 179
Fairbanks, William 183
Fairbrother, Sidney 169
Fairfax, Lettice 51, 52
Fairfax, Marion 154
Faisel (Prince) 129
Fakes 24, 25, 131, 174, 212
Falcon, Andre 55
Falcon, Black 84
Falconer, Margaret Elizabeth 183
The False Face (1919) 79, 138
Famous Players–Lasky Studio 94, 95, 99, 121, 165
Fang, Charles 181
A Farewell to Arms (1932) 51, **80, 81**
A Farewell to Arms (1957) 82
Faris, Alexander 210
Farmer, Alan 210
Farmers 37, 103, 107, 202, 205, 2103
Farmham, Joseph 144
Farnham, Joe 204
Farnum, Dustin 185
Farrell, Charles 142
Farrell, Colin 126, 127, 151
Farrell, J. 148, 187
Fascism 90
Fashion 18, 67, 115
Fassbender, Michael 41
Fatalism 17, 68, 90, 203
Fate 17, 32, 99, 167
Faulkner, Ralph 166, 201

Faulkner, William 170
Faust, Martin 211
Fawcett, Douglas 109
Fawcett, George 83, 92–96, 101, 109
Fawkes, Guy 93
Fay, Billy 157
Fay, Jack 206
Faye, Julia 192
Faylen, Frank 83
Fazenda, Louise 170
Feature films 3, 9, 12, 13, 25, 88, 95, 176, 212n6
Feducha, Marion 179
Fellowes Juian 43, 99
Fenton, Leslie 100, 207
Fenton, Mark 89
Ferber, Hans 173
Ferdinand, Archduke Franz 195
Ferguson, William J. 40
Ferns, Alex 149
Ferraro, Matty 47
Ferrer, Jose 129
Fichman, Niv 159
Fielding, Romain 87
Fields, Kathy 46
The Fifth Commandment (1932) 51, 82
The Fighting 69th (1940) 82
Fildew, William 73
Film critics 4, 34, 75, 133
Findlater, George 87
Finlay, Frank 168
Finlay, Stephen 168
Finlayson, James 47, 67
Finley, Peter 37
Finn, Arthur 137, 173
Finney, Albert 129
First Canadian Contingency 165
First National 179
First National Pictures (films) 63, 78, 134, 138, 159, 179, 186
Firth, Peter 32
Fischbeck, Harry 74
Fischer, Marguerita 150
Fisher, George 57, 183
Fisher, Gerry 32
Fisher, Harry Conway "Bud" 12, 39, 57, 110, 118, 120, 122, 158, 164, 165, 178, 179, 193
Fisher, Millicent 181
Fitzgerald, Barry 68
Fitzgerald, F. Scott 190
Fitzgerald, Geraldine 208
Fitzmaurice, George 134, 146
Five Graves to Cairo (1943) 108
Fix, Paul 125, 142, 170
Fix Film 66
Flagg, Captain 207, 208

The Flags of Mothers (1918) 82
Flaherty, Pat 176
Flanagan, Anthony 161
Flanagan, John 200
Flanders 44, 163
Flanders House in Glasgow, Scotland 7
Flateau, Georges 131
Flavin, James 85
Fleishmann, Albert Sidney 125
Fletcher, Herman 180
Fletcher, Jerry 83
Fliakos, Ari 59
The Flight (1929) 68
Flight Commander (book) 68, 83
Flight Commander (1932) 67
Florey, Robert 79
Florian, Werner 94
Flothow, Rudolph 143
Floyd, Robert 145
Fluidity Films 168
Flyboys (2006) 83
Flynn, Errol 68
Fogwell, Reginald 98
Fokker Dr 1 tri-planes 49
Foley, Brian 200
Follow the Girl (1917) 84
Folly Films 131
Fonteney, Catherine 107
For France (1917) 84
For King and Country (1964) 85, 123
For Liberty (1917) 85
For Me and My Gal (1942) 86
For the Freedom of the World (1917) 87
For Valour (1928) 87
Foran, Dick 83
Forbes, Mary 81
Forbes, Ralph 75, 143, 169
Forbidden Ground (2013) 40, 87
Force of Arms (1951) 81
Ford, Francis 72, 141, 142, 173
Ford, Glen 90
Ford, Jack 72
Ford, John 90, 140, 141, 148, 187
Ford, Karen 83
Ford, Leon 44
Ford, Ruth 208
Ford, Wallace 141
Foreign Correspondent (1940) 14
Foreman, Grant 62
Forester, C.S. 33
Forever England (1934) 52, 87
Formula system 37, 53, 63, 71, 93, 121, 130, 133, 161, 183
Forrest, Ann 36, 46

Forsythe, Blanche 156, 193
Fortescue, Kenneth 120
Forty Thousand Horsemen (1940) 78
Forward March (1930) 89
Foster, Barry 123
Foster, J. Morris 112
Foster, Jodie 198
Foster, Maurice 114
Foster, Preston 187
Four Horsemen of the Apocalypse (1921) 13, 89, 136, 221n10
Four Sons (1928) 90
Fowler, Guy 134
Fowler, Harry 129
Fowley, Douglas 187
Fox, Lucy 181
Fox, William 77, 85, 124, 142, 147, 206
Fox Film (Company) Corporation 48, 77, 85, 90, 91, 100, 111, 121, 124, 139, 142, 166, 170, 173, 181, 184, 202, 206, 207, 208
Fox Pathe 114
Foxe, Earl 91
Frames 28
Franc, Albert 167
France, C.V. 54
Francen, Victor 82, 115
Francis, Alec B. 56
Franco, James 83
Frank, Leonhard 104
Frankau, Nicholas 168
Frankenstein 119
Franklin, John E. 166
Franklin, Sidney A. 64
Fransined, Jean 107
Fraser, James 205
Fräulein Doktor 147
Frechette, Jessie 159
Frederick Ireland 182
Freed, Arthur 86
Freed, Berl 160
Freeman, Jonathan 138
Fremont, Alfred 125
French (France): citizens 43, 45, 46, 66, 75, 77, 80, 99, 130, 135, 137, 144, 146, 165, 179, 204, 205; film 27, 53, 66, 68, 102, 104, 114, 171, 182, 205; location 51, 54, 90, 98, 100, 101, 106, 126, 133, 135, 161; military 18, 34, 44, 51, 56, 65, 69, 75, 77, 83–86, 95, 98101, 102, 107, 118, 124, 125, 129, 130, 135, 146, 148, 152, 154, 155, 161, 171, 177, 183, 184, 195, 197; nation 10, 73, 84, 85, 90, 135, 148
French, Charles K. 121

Index

French, Harold 74
French Foreign Legion 125, 130
Frenkle, Theo 112
Fresnay, Pierre 48, 94
Frey, Arno 85
Friderici, Blanche 146
Friedl, Loni von 48
Fries, Otto 108
Frift, Mike 126
From Flower Girl to Red Cross Nurse (1915) 91
Fromkess Corporation 214
Fry, Dwight 170
Fuerberg, Hans 181
Fulton, John P. 178
Furmann, Benno 149
Fusiliers 102, 140, 149
Fussell, Paul 1
Fychen, Catrin 102

Gabin, Jean 94
Gabrio, Gabriel 212
Gaby (1956) 205
Gaby, Perrie 130
Gaffney, Majoire 198
Gail, Jane 173
Gainsborough Pictures 47, 118, 174
Galafilm Productions 96
Galbraith, Alastair 43
Galland, Jean 212
Gallia, Edith 195
Gallipoli (battle) 7, 36, 40, 57, 189, 190, 205
Gallipoli (location) 6, 189, 205
Gallipoli (1981) 91, **92**
Galloway, James T. 105
Galvani, Dino 47
Gamley, Douglas 126
Gance, Abel 114, 115
Gangsters 139
Garbo, Greta **147**
Gardiner, Becky 204
Gardner, Arthur 34, 58
Gardner, Cyril 215
Gardonyi, Lajos 54
Garland, Brock 210
Garland, Judy 86
Garmon, Huw 102
Garner, James 126
Garner, Steward 75, 169
Garon, Pauline 183
Garrett, H.P. 81
Garrick, John 181
Garson, Harry 197
Gauvin, Robert 41
Gavin, Agnes 145
Gavin, Jack 145
Gaydon in Warwickshire 6
Gaye, Howard 185

Gaynor, Janet 142
Gebhardt, George 175
The Geezer of Berlin (1918) 92, 120
Geldart, Clarence 135
Gender Consciousness 21, 22
General Electric 210
Genre 2–4, 13, 28, 206
Gentlemen Prefer Blonds 94
Geoffrey Production 65
George Eastman House in Rochester, New York 6
George Klein Collection, Library of Congress 6
Georgetown University 6
Gerard, James W. 153
Gerber, David 138
Gericke, Gene 170
German, Germany: atrocities 5, 11, 20, 54, 62, 67, 77, 89, 109, 110, 127, 131, 145, 153; citizens 34, 38, 57, 62, 65–67, 73, 75, 76, 83, 84, 97, 99, 109, 111, 113, 120, 127, 130, 137, 139, 145, 163, 170, 174, 184, 185, 191, 193, 214; films 34, 35, 42, 49, 73, 79, 93, 95, 104, 109, 110, 118, 143, 145, 153, 158, 162, 179, 196, 202; location 77, 121, 138, 157, 158, 190, 192, 195; military 10, 12, 15, 20, 33, 35, 36, 38, 44, 45, 48, 52, 56, 58, 60–62, 66, 68, 69, 76, 83–85, 88, 89, 101, 102, 107, 114, 120, 122, 124, 126, 133, 135, 139, 145, 149, 150, 152, 156, 159, 163, 167, 175, 180–182, 185, 196, 200, 201, 209; nation 4, 12, 14, 20, 38, 54, 62, 67, 119, 121, 145, 171, 173, 190, 195, 196
The German Spy Peril (1914) 93
Gerrard, Charles K 44, 109, 148
Gerrard, Henry W. 130
Gerstle, Edward 130
Ghent, Derek 89
Gibbs, Robert 151
Gibney, Sheridan 187
Gibson, Mel 91
Giddy, Jack 91
Gielgud, John 174
Gilbert, Billy 48
Gilbert, John 45
Gilbert, Mrs. 48
Gilbertson, Harrison 44
Gill, Moss 196
Gillespie, William 157
Gillette Safety Razor Company 162
Gilmore, Douglas 104

Gilmore, Helen 157
Giraci, Mae 192
Girard, Joseph 193
Girardot, Etienne 170
The Girl of Mystery (1920) 141
The Girl Who Stayed at Home (1919) 93
Gish, Dorothy 41, 101, 102, 109
Gish, Lillian 25, 76, 95–98, 101
Glaum, Louise 183
Glazer, Benjamin 80, 146
Gleason, James 204
Gleason, Russell 34
Glendon, Marcia 85
Glenn, Roy 172
Glennie, Evelyn 194
Globus, Yoram 146
Glover, Edmund 83
God 1, 17, 23, 176, 195, 205
Goddard, Alf 74
Goddard, Jim 210
Godfrey, John 126
Godfrey, Philip 74
Godfrey, Robin 47
Golan, Globus 146
Golan, Menahem 146
Gold 188
Gold, John 41
Gold Jack 32
Gold Medal 156
Gold Rooster Plays 151
Goldbeck, Willis 73, 144
Goldblatt, Stephen 168
The Golden Bird 136
Goldsmith, Frank 38, 98
Goldsmith, John 41
Goldstein, Robert 10
Goldstrom, Michael 138
Goltz, H. von der 166
Goldwyn, Samuel 177, 190, 205, 206
Gombell, Minna 47
Gomer, Emlyn 102
Gone with the Wind 143
Gonzales, Myrtle 181
Goodard, Alf 142
Good-Bye Bill (1918) 84
Goodwin, Harold 34, 44
Goodwin, Richard B. 123
Gorden, Kelley 38
Gordon, B. 157
Gordon, Craig 66
Gordon, Harvey 87
Gordon, Henry 71, 146
Gordon, James 42
Gordon, Julia Swayne 40
Gordon, Kitty 199
Gordon, Leslie Howard 98
Gordon, Mary 181
Gordon, Maude Turner 177
Gordon, Pete 109

Gordon, Robert 119, 135
Goring, Marius 185, 214
Gorzano Govanni 189
Gosh Darn the Kaiser (1918) 94
Gotell, Walter 33
Gotschalk, Louis 89
Goudal, Jetta 191
Goulding, Alfred (Art) J. 157
Goulding, Edmund 68, 100
Gowen, Peter 152
Gowing, Gene 79
Gowland, Gibson 42, 71
Grace, Dick 134
Graham, Frank 85
Graham, John 73
Graham, Rau 91
Grainger, Edmund 169, 170
The Grand Illusion (1937) 94
Grandada International 152
Grant, Cary 74
Grant, Duncan 200, 201
Grant, Edwin 165
Grantley, Gyton 44
Granville, Fred LeRoy 101
Grassby, Bertram 41, 85, 100
Grattin, C. Hartly 13
Grauman Theater 136
Graves (location) 156
Graves, Peter 60
Graves, Ralph 186
Gray, Allan 132
Gray, Donald 190
Gray, Eve 163
Gray, John 122
Gray, Lawrence 144
Gray, Mary 127
Gray, Nadia 66
Gray, Robin 202
Gray, Vivean 37
The Gray Nun of Belgium (1915) 95
Grayson, Elizabeth 196
Great Britain *see* England
The Great Escape (1963) 95
The Great Love (1918) 97
Great Victory (1919) 75
The Great War (2007) 96
The Greatest Power (1917) 96, 106
The Greatest Thing in Life (1918) 62, 97
Greeley, Evelyn 199
Green, Dorothy 69
Green, Duke 187
Green Fancy 153
Greene, Angela 172
Greene, Richard 187
Greentree, Diana 37
Greenwood Hill Productions 117
Gregory, Beresford 200

Gregory, Carl 161
Gregory, Carl Louis 161
Greiner, Fritz 78
Grey, Gloria 142
Grey, John 136
Grey, Margaret 165, 168
Greyeyes, Michael 159
Griffies, Ethel 205
Griffin, Frank 138
Griffith, D.W. 3, 10, 12, 14, 25, 26, 28, 45, 93, 95, 97, 98, 101, 102, 109, 150, 221n14
Griffith, Edward H. 55
Griffith, Gordon 135
Griffith, Raymond 34
Griffiths, Richard 164
Grimes, Milton 62
Grimlaw, John 98
Grimwood, Herbert 183, 189
Grinling, Amanda 168
Gross, Paul 159
Grover, Adam 59
Groves, Fred 188
Grubb, Robert 91
Gsell, Paul 122
Guardian 155
Guardian (protector) 41, 111
Guest, John G. 130
Guest, Revel 203
Guette, Toto 130
Guggenheim, J.C.E. 196
Guinness, Alex **128**, 129
Guiomar, Julie 124
Guire, Lois 150
Guissart, Rene 200
Guldahl, Ralph 125
Gullermin, John 48
Gundrey, Gareth 118
Gunn, Charles 162
The Guns of Loos 98
Gurfinkel, David 147
Gurney, Kate 60
Guynemer, George 122
Guys, Angele 114
Gwillim, Jack 129
Gwynedd, Wales 102
Gyalog, Odon 147

Haab, Gordy 116
Hackathorne, George 100
Hackett, William 184
Haig, David 152
Hal Roach Studio 47
Haldane, Bert 93
Hale, Alan 83, 89, 140
Hale, Creighton 152
Half Shot at Sunrise (1930) 99
Hall, Brian 126
Hall, Ella 53
Hall, Evelyn 104, 178
Hall, James 104, 105, 108

Hall, Lee 203
Hall, May 41
Hall, Stuart 68
Hall, Thurston 121
Hall, Winter 119, 153
Hall-Davis, Lillian 47
Hallam, John 202
Hallan, John 210
Halliam, Henry 50
Halliday, John 64
Halliday, Lena 151
Hallier, Ernest 67
Halperin, Edward 178
Halsey, Brett 125
Halton, Charles 170
Ham and Eggs (1918) 99
Ham and Eggs at the Front (1927) 99, 100
Hamburger, Max 157
Hamilton, Charlie 162
Hamilton, Chuck 83
Hamilton, Gilvert P. 181
Hamilton, John F. 54
Hamilton, Lucie 40
Hamilton, Neil 67
Hammeras, Ralph 160
Hampton Del Ruth 53
Handley, Steve 61
The Hands of the Hun (1918) 100
Hanley, Gerald 48
Hanley, Jimmy 52
Hanlon, Alma 165, 166
Hanna, Lain 131
Hanna, Richard 57
Hansen, Stefan 167
Hansford, Roy 93
Hanson, Paul 140
Harben, Hubert 189
Harbord, Carl 189
Hard-drinking 68
Hardt, Captain Ernest 185
Hardwick, Cedric 208
Hardy, J. B 78
Hardy, Oliver 117
Hare, Lumsden 38, 180
Hargraves, Captain 123
Harker, Gordon 200
Harlan, Russell 65
Harlem Hell Fighters 100
Harlin, von 113, 156
Harlow, Jean **105**
Harrington, Curtis 146
Harris, Harry B. 133
Harris, Heath 91
Harris, Jack 171
Harris, Jamie 138
Harris, Johnny 203
Harris, Marilyn 170
Harris, Paula 121
Harris, Wadsworth 119

Index

Harrison, William 166
Harron, John 82
Harron, Robert 93, 95, 97, 101
Harronson, John Kent 41
Hart, Joy 88
Hart, Karl 71
Hart, Lew 196
Hart, Neal 46
Hartley, Richard 32
Hartman, Carl von 105
Hartman, Gretchen 178
Hartmann, Rose 200
Harton, Charles 208
Harvey, Forrester 74
Harvey, Gordon 87
Harvey, Jack 120, 161
Harvey, John Martin 54
Hastings, Baston 93
Hastings, Ian 35
"Hate-the Hun" films 12, 20
Hatfield, Hurd 200
Hathaway, James 166
Hathaway, Jean 141
Hatton, Raymond 43
Hauer, William 98
Haupt, Ulrich 56, 91, 135, 191
Hauptmann, Captain 49
Havana, Cuba 3, 10
Haver, Phyllis 206
Havoc (1925) 100
Hawkins, Jack 129
Hawks, Howard 68, 170, 176
Hawks, J.G. 64, 183
Hawtree, Frances 191
Hay, Ian 174
Hayakawsa, Sussue 175
Haydel, Dorothy 181
Hayden, Jo 86
Hayer, John 88
Hayes, Anthony 44
Hayes, Helen **81**
Hayman, David 45
Hays committee 30
Hayward, Louis 172
Hayward's Associated Film Artists, Inc. 172
Haywood, John 134
Hazell, Scott 83
Headey, Lena 167
Healey, Annesley 47
Hearn, Edward 193, 194
Hearn, Fred 120
Hearst, William Randolph 58, 175
The Heart of Humanity (1918) 67, 101
Hearts of the World (1918) 12, 45
Heath, George 88, 91
Heatherlay, Clifford 171
Hecht, Ben 82

Hedd Wyn 102, 103
Hedd Wyn (1992) 102
Hedley, Jack 129
Heilbron, Adelaide 55
Hell Below (1933) 108, 163
Hell Bent on Glory (1957) 103, 167
Hell on Earth (1931) 104
Hellman, Lillian 64
Hell's Angels (1930) 104, **105**
Hembrow, Mark 37
Hemingway, Ernest 81, 82
Hemmingway, John 177
Henderson, Grace 201
Henley, Hobart 151
Henley, Jacques 195
Henley, Paul 32
Hennecke, Clarence 135
Henson, Juanita 176
Hepburn, Katharine 33
Hepworth Production Company 158
Hepworth, Cecil M. 159
Her Boy (1918) 60
Her Greatest Power (1917) 96
Herald, Douglas 198
Herbert, A.P. 189
Herbert, Gwynne 51
Hero Fiennes-Tiffin 164
The Hero of Submarine D-2 (1916) 59, 106
Hero to Me: The Billy Bishop Story—A World One Canadian Ace 122
Heroes of the Marne (1938) 107
Heroine 21, 50, 116, 130, 136, 141, 145, 150, 169
Heroine of the Mons (1914) 107
Hesser, Edwin Bower 87
Hewitt, Rod 37
Hewland, Philip 98
Hickman, Alfred 136, 215
Hickman, Howard C. 57, 183
Hickox, Sidney 134
Hicks, James 61
Hicks, Russell 69
Hicks, Seymour 47
Hiddleston, Tom 203
Hiens, Walter 152
Higgins, Ernest 114
Higgins, John 194
Hill, Craig 207
Hill, Doris 44
Hill, George W. 45
Hill, Maude 66
Hill, Sinclair 98
Hillier, James 35
Hilton, Harland 134
Hinden-Miller, Grant 57
Hinds, Samuel 51
Hindustan 48

Hinky Dinky Parlez Vous 143
Hitchcock, Alfred 14
Hitler, Adolf 26, 34
Hobson, Valerie 185
Hodgson, Leyland 56
Hoey, Dennis 189
Hoffman, Otto 121
Hofman, Aaron 69
Hofmann, Ernest 195
Hogan, Dick 187
Hogan, Michael 37, 52, 54
HMS *Hogue* 195
Hohl, Arthur 170
Holberg, Hilda 182
Holbrook, John K. 165
Holcomb, Thomas 196
Holden, Arthur 96
Holden, William 191
Holder, Donald 56
Holder, Roy 126
Holderness, Fay 101
Holeman, Vincent 132
Holgado, Ticky 198
Hollacher, Harold 196
Hollis, Hylda 175
Hollmann, Patricia 190
Holloway, Sterling 103
Holly, Jane 35
Hollywood 177, 185, 199, 200
Hollywood Hussars 61, 71
Hollywood Reporter 206
Holm, Ian 168, 180
Holmes, Phillips 51
Holmes, Stuart 89
Holmes, William 177
Holt, Jack 135, 174.186
Holt, Jim 37
Holub, Allen 193
Homolka, Oskar 78
Homosexuality 48
An Honest Man (1918) 36, 37
Hooley, Teresa 151
Hoover, Herbert 126, 136
Hope, Gloria 95
The Hopeless Case 163
Hopkins, Clyde 150
Hopkins, T 41, 44
Hopper, Hedda 204
Hopper, William 93
Hopson, Violet 158
Horizon Pictures 127
Horne, Pliny 36
Horse 13, 34, 45, 89, 108, 134, 203, 204
Hotaling, Arthur 92
Hotaling, Louise 165
Hotel Imperial (1927) 108, 111
Hotel Imperial (1939) 108
Housman, A.E. 123
Houston, Billie 47
Houston, Renee 47

INDEX

How We Fought the Emden 79
Howard, Ben 126
Howard, David 62
Howard, E.L. 165
Howard, George Bronson 184
Howard, Leslie 107
Howard, Lionelle 158
Howard, Mary 154
Howard, Norah 200
Howard, Ray 77
Howard, Trevor 32
Howe, Betty 85
Howell, Dorothy 186
Howell, Virginia 76
Howes, Bobby 98
Hoyt, Arthur 180
Hoyt, Edward 127
Hubbel, Raymond 183
Hubert, Robert 115
Hudson, Rock 65, 82
Huemer, Dick 39, 72, 118, 127, 193
Hughes, Frederic 92
Hughes, Howard 104, 105, 178
Hughes, J. Anthony 83
Hughes, Llewellyn 181
Hughes, Lloyd 100
Hughes, Rupert 178, 197
Hugon, Andre 107
Hull, Henry 190, 199
Humberston Wright 142
Hume, Alan 214
Humphrey, William 115
Humphreys, Griffith 67, 198
Humpty Dumpty 36
Hun 11, 12, 19–21, 58, 76, 100, 109, 110, 116, 135, 185
The Hun Within (1918) 11, 109
Hungary (Hungarian) 39, 54–56, 107
Huns and Hyphens (1918) 109
Huns of the North Sea (1914) 110, 162
Hunt, Irene 46
Hunt, Jack D. 48, 49
Hunt, John 142
Hunt, Marsha 116
Hunt, Peter R. 179
Hunter, James 123
Hunter, Tab 125, 126
Hunter, Henry 170
Hunting the U-Boat (1918) 110
Hupp, Georgie 119
Hurley, Frank 88
Hurst, Brandon 140
Hurst, Veronica 172
Huston, John 33, 82, 176
Huston, Walter 103, 212
Hutcheson, David 132
Hutchins, Will 125
Hutchinson, Charles 201

Hutt, William 122
Hutton, Leona 175
Hyde, Dr. 162
Hyland, Peggy 49, 50, 149, 211
Hymer, Warren 173

I Didn't Raise My Boy to Be a Soldier (1915) 111
I Love a Soldier (1926) 108, 111
Ibanez, Vincente Blasco 144
Ibert, Jacquest 107
Icsey, Rudolf 54
Ida, Windy 159
If England Were Invaded (1909) 111, 113
Igor, Stanislaw 39
Ilfman, Haim Frank 61
I'll Say So (1918) 111
Illegitimate 52
Illidge, Fletcher 44
Illidge, Morgan 44
I'm Glad My Boy Grew Up to be a Soldier (1915) 111
Imeson, A.B. 54
Immigrant 62, 64, 113
Imperadio Pictures, Ltd. 154
Imperial German Air Service 167
Imperial War Museum, London 6
In Cold Blood (1967) 93
In the Hands of the Enemy (1915) 112
In the Name of the Prince of Peace (1914) 112
Ince, Thomas H. 121, 182, 215
Independent Film Production 132
Inescort, Frieda 64
Ingleton, Magnus 46
Ingraham, Lloyd 150
Ingram, Rex 89, 144
The Inn (1982) 113, 147
Innocent 20, 21
Insane asylum 124
Inspiration (1915) 30
Inspiration Pictures 178, 183
Intelligence officer 57, 147, 166, 185, 214
Interlenghi, Franco 82
Interventionist 9
Intolerance 95
The Invaders (1909) 9, 111, 113
The Invasion of Britain (1918) 113, 199
The Invasion of 1915 113
Inventor 137, 188, 192
Ireland 61, 200
Ireland, Layne 83
Irish Air Corps 49

Irish Guards 152
HMS *Irresistible* 162
Irvin, Emily 168
Irvine, Jeremy 202
Irving, Mary Jane 162
Irving, Penny 32
Irving, William 34, 99, 192
Irwin, Charles 103
Isenberg, Michael T. 12
Isham, Virginia 78
The Island of Adventure (1918) 114
Isolationist 9
Italy: film source 130; place 28, 81, 203
ITC Entertainment 35
Itkine, Sylvain 94
It's a Grand Old Flag 212
It's a Long Way to Tipperary (1914) 114
Izsof, Virmos 147
Izykowska, Anna 39

J. Paul Getty Jr. Conservation Centre 6
J. Stuart Blackton Productions 10
J'Accuse (1919) 115
J'Accuse (1938) 115
Jackman, Fred 214
Jackson, Barry 32
Jackson, Glenda 168
Jackson, Peaches 97
Jaffe, Carl 132
Jakab, Csaba 147
Jalabert, Berthe 123
James, Adam 138
James, Gardner 67
James, Gladden 38
James, Godfrey 126
James, Rian 187
James, Russell 114, 167, 204
James, Steven 126
James, Walter 160
James K. Keane Feature Photo Play 184
Janson, Horst 180
Janssen, David 125
Japan 175
Japrisot, Sabastien 198
Jarre, Maurice 127
Jarrett, Daniel 182
Jarrold, Julian 27, 35
Jarvis, Richard 134
Jason, David 35, 36, 116
Jean-Max 115
Jeans, Ursula 132
Jeayes, Allen 190
Jeffries, Edgar Horace 39, 59, 158, 164, 178, 193
Jenks, George Elwood 36

Index

Jennings, Deuereaux 57
Jennings, Dewitt 135
Jensen, Eulalie 100, 178
Jephcott, Dominic 35
Jeremy, Thorsen 131
Jerome, Eddy 146
Jerome, Helen 146, 204
Jerrold, Mary 200
Jesus Christ 58
Jeunet, John-Pierre 198
Jew 39, 104, 113, 133, 149, 151, 191
Jewel Productions 101
Jewson, Alex 88
Jingoistic 4
Joan of Arc (as image) 116, 137
Joan of Plattsburg (1918) 115
The Jockstrap Raiders (2011) 116
Johar, I.S. 129
John, Gottfried 147
John Ford Productions 72
Johannisthaler Filmanstalten 195
Johnny Got His Gun (1917) 116, 155
Johnny Got His Gun (2008) 117
Johnson, Adrian 35, 66
Johnson, Agnes Christine 75
Johnson, Nobel 143
Johnson, Richard 32
Johnson, Tefft 40
Johnston, Jack W. 21
Joining the Tanks (1918) 118
Jolivet, Ritan 130, 131
Jonathan Livingston Seagull (1973) 200
Jones, Billy "Red" 63
Jones, Evan 123
Jones, Hazel 143
Jones, Ian 133
Jones, J. Parks 153, 179
Jones, Jennifer 82
Jones, Nicholas 210
Jones, Richard 214
Jones, Tiny 178
Joseph, Rowan 117
Joshua, Llyr 102
Joube, Romuald 114, 115
Journey's End (1930) 118
Joy, Gloria 100
Joyce, Alice 211
Joyeux Noel (2005) 119, 149
Jozsef Timar 54
Judge, Jack 114
Juhasz, Jozsef 54
Julian, Rupert 53, 119, 120, 191
Jurado, Elena 206
Jury, W.F. 25
Jury Films 122
Juschkiewitsch, General 108
Justice, Barry 123

K rations 43
Kaa, Peter 57
Kada-abd-el-Kader 144
Kael, Pauline 49
Kahl, Rainer 159
Kahler, Wolf 138
Kahn, Florence 174
Kaiser 39, 49, 64, 72, 92, 111, 113, 119–121, 164, 166, 191, 192, 214, 215
The Kaiser, the Beast of Berlin (1918) 12, 42
The Kaiser's Finish (1918) 120
The Kaiser's Last Sequel (1912) 121
The Kaiser's New Dentist (1918) 121
The Kaiser's Shadow (1918) 121
The Kaiser's Spies (1914) 121, 163
Kaminski, Janusz 203
Kane, Kathryn 221n3
Karloff, Boris 140
Karr, Darwin 196
Kase (Kage), Bruce 57
Kasznar, Kurt 82
Katterjohn, Monte M. 191
Katz, Pitzy 72
Kauffman, Ethel 66
Kaufman, Charles 85
Kaufman, Joseph 38
Kawalerowicz, Jerzy 39
Kay, Bernard 65
Kay, Philip 121
Kay-Bee Pictures 65
Kaye, Frances 136
Kayser, Charles Willey 78
Keane, James 184
Keane, Murray 57
Kearney, Patrick 71
Keaton, Buster 72, 73
Kedrova, Lila 195
Keegin, Hilary 59
Keeley, Ed 111
Keene, George 196
Keene, Hamilton 88
Keep 'Em Flying (1941) 70
Kehoe, Fred 168
Keighley, William 82
Keir, Andrew 214
Keleti, Laszlo 54
Keller, Edgar 141
Kelly, Emma 102
Kelly, Gene 86
Kelly, Nancy 187, 188
Kelly, Paul 191, 210
Kelly, Walter C. 173
Kelly Field 45
Kelly's Heroes 117
Kelsey, Fred 133

Kelso, Mayme 153
Kemp, Jeremy 65, 168
Kemp, Jerry 48
Kendall, Meredith 117
Kennard, Victor 199
Kennedy, Adam 60
Kennedy, Arthur 129
Kennedy, Edgar 44
Kennedy, Iris 88
Kennedy, Kathleen 203
Kennedy, Madge 177
Kennedy, Patrick 203
Kennedy, Tom 43, 44, 99
Kent, Billy 75
Kent, Charles 40
Kent, Crauford 62, 191
Kent, Jean 180
Kent, Larry 173
Kenyon, Charles 170
Keogh, Agnes 75, 169
Kern, Jerome 156
Kerr, Bill 37, 91, 133
Kerr, Deborah 132
Kerr, Donald 83
Kerr, Frederick 203
Kerr, Norman 135
Kerrigan, J.M. 87
Kerwood, Colonel 150
Keysor, Leonard 87
Keystone Kops (Cops) 188
Kibbee, Guy 190
The Kid Who Couldn't Miss (1918) 46, 122
Kidd, R.B. 162
Kiddies in the Ruin (1918) 122
Kidnapped 121, 137
Kiely, Pat 96
Kilgen, George 83
Kilgour, Joseph 40, 211
Kilian, Victor 171
Kilmer, Joyce 83
Kimble, Lawrence 186
Kimbrough, Clint 200
Kinematograph Trading Company 121
King, Burton L. 69
King, Henry 178, 183, 208
King, Jack 50
King, John "Dusty" 120
King, Major 198
King, Oscar 42
King George V's 36
King of Hearts (1966) 124
Kingsley, Bob 173
Kingston, Natalie 138
Kingston, Winifred 185
Kinskey, Leonid 170
Kipling, John "Jack" 152
Kipling, Rudyard 152
Kirby, Madge 109
Kirk, Brian 27, 152

Kiss, Ferenc 54, 55
Kiss, Manyi 54
Kithnog, Mademoiselle 144
Klaffki, Roy H. 193
Kleeman, Gustave 182
Klein, Philip 90
Kleinschmidt, Franz 97, 102
Kline, Benjamin H. 118
Klingler, Warner 118
Klugermann, Gunther von 48
Knaggs, Skelton 185
Knechtel, Alvin 160
Knight, Cecil 122
Knight, James 132, 161
Knobelspiess, Roger 55
Knoles, Harley 199
Knorr, Rudolph Ernest von 66
Knott, Lydia 65
Knowles, Bernard 66, 174
Knowlton, Thomas 103
Knox, Alexander 208
Knox, Stuart 134
Koch, Howard 176
Koffler, Hanno 167
Kohner, Paul 71
Kolb, John 138, 160
Kolldehoff, Reinhold 180
Konig, Wilhem 200
Konwicki, Tadeusz 39
Korda, Alexander 185
Korff, Arnold 72
Koser, Henry 94
Kosleck, Martin 154
Koster, Otto 190
Kot, James 159
Kotz, Adam 35, 138
Koutik, Tomas 167
Krajco, Richard 167
Kramf, Gunther 78
Krapt, von 113
Kremer, Arthur 138
Kremlin, William 121
Kristel, Sylvia 147, 148
Kristen, Anna 210
Kross, David 203
Kruger, Diana 149
Kruger, Frank R. 66
Kruger, Julie 212
Kruger, Otto 76
Kruse, George 160
Krutz, Karl von 192
Ku Klux Klan 102
Kubrick, Stanley 19, 39, 160
Kull, Edward 119
Kultur (1918) 124
Kurylenko, Olga 205
Kutler, Benjamin S. 66

La Badie, Florence 201
Labine, Tyler 83
Labry, Pierre 212

Ladoux, Georges 147
Lady Liberty 135
Laemmle, Carl 205
Lafayette, Ruby 119
Lafayette Escadrille 83, 118, 125, 126, 130
Lafayette Escadrille (1958) 125
Lagorio, Alexander von 104
La Grisbi Productions 64
Lahaye, Michele 195
Laidlaw, David 98
Lake, Arthur 133
Lake, Paul 134
Lamkoff, Paul 191
Lancret, Bernard 195
Lancret, Richard 107
The Land That Time Forgot (1975) 126
Landeck, Ben 193
Landing a Spy (1918) 126
Landiscutt, Philip 193
Lane, CharlesWillis 81
Lang, June 170, 171
Lang, Matheson 113
Lange, Arthur 187
Langford, Frances 212
USS *Langley* 136, 188
Langley, Victor 147
Langsford, Robin 168
Langson, Lillian 150
Language 73
Lania, Leo 197
Lanning, Frank 157
Lanyard, Michael 79, 80
Larareff, Searge 134
Larking, John 133
La Roche, Captain 170
La Rocque, Rod 56
La Rue, Jack 81
Laskey, Jesse 135
The Last Volunteer (1914) 127
Lathalu, Charles 91
La tourneaux, Robert 200
Laughlin, Phea Catto 182
Laughlin, Tom 125
Laughton, Charles 34
Launder, Frank 200
Laurel, Mae 100
Laurel, Stan 43, 47, 109, 110
Laurenson, James 164
Laurie, John 132
Laurie, Sandy 50
Laurier, Marguerite 89
Lavant, Denis 198
Law, Burton 141.193
Law, John Phillip 200
Law, Walter 202
Lawrence H. Suid Collection, Georgetown 6
Lawrence, Edmund 66
Lawrence, T.H. 124, 129

Lawrence, Walter 166
Lawrence of Arabia (1962) 127, **128**
Lawson, Wilfred 74
Lawton, Thais 40
Lazare, Maria 114
Lazarus, Sidney 72
Leads, Susan 187
League of Nations 208
Leavitt, Sam 60
LeBaron, William 56
Lebas, Renaud 155
Le Cog, Bernard 55
Ledebur, Friedrich von 48
Lederer, Gretchen 119
Ledwidge, Francis 223n25
Lee, David 132
Lee, Dorothy 99
Lee, Frankie 119
Lee, Harry 38
Lee, John 102
Lee, Mark 90
Lee, Rowland V. 100
Lee, Seth 198
Leesher, John 64
Lefebvre, Robert 195
LeFrancois, Bernard 107
Legion of Death, Russian 138
The Legion of the Condemned (1928) 14, 129, 139
Legitimate theatre 11
Legrand, Augustin 83
LeGuere, George 211
Leigh, Frank 157
Leigh, John 57
Leighton, Lillian 192
Leimbach, Oliver 44
Lemkow, Tutte 74
Lennartz, Elisabeth 104
Lentz, General Von 85
Lenz, Gottfried 190
Leodtras, Kevin 109
Le Person, Paul 155
Le Queux, William 121
Lesk, Stan 41
Leslie, Joan 176
Lessing, Marion 174
Lest We Forget (1918) 130
Lester, Bruce 172
Lester, Kate 196, 199
Lestina, Adolph 41, 93, 96, 101, 109
Lethem, Circe 155
Letondal, Henri 204, 207
Letters of the Great War (2008) 131
Leun-Walram, Count von 62
Levantal, Francois 55
Le Vaye, Jeanne 98
Levering, Joseph 135
Levien, Sonya 142

Index

Le Vino, Albert S. 96
Levy, Avi 138
Levy, Benn 205
Lewis, Cecil 32
Lewis, Gary 149
Lewis, Harold C. 81
Lewis, Ida 161
Lewis, Idea 161
Lhomme, Pierre 124
Lianos, Theo 88
liberal 17
Liboiron, Landon 159
Library of Congress 6, 7, 58, 142
Lieutenant Pimple and the Stolen Submarine (1914) 5, 131
The Life and Death of Colonel Blimp (1943) 59
Life expectancy 32, 71
The Light of Victory (1919) 14, 133, 168
Lighthorse 68, 89, 134
The Lighthorsemen (1987) 133
Lilac Time (1928) 134, 44
Lincoln, E.K. 87, 197
Lincoln, Elmo 98, 119, 150
Lincoln, W.J. 75, 145, 168, 169
Linden, Margaret 75
Lindsay, Margaret 70
Lingard, Oswald 54
Lip readers 29, 90, 207
Lipman, Harry 138
Lirova, Katherina 35
Litel, John 83
Little, Kitty 175
The Little American (1917) 11, 135, 136
Little Bear 55
The Little Comrade (1917) 136, 157
Little Miss Hoover (1918) 136
The Little Patriot (1917) 137, 199
Littlefield, Lucien 51
The Littlest Scout (1919) 7, 138
The Littlest Volunteer (1917) 138, 198
Littlewood, Joan 135
Livesey, Roger 74, 132
Livingston, Jack 65
Livingston, Margaret 100
Lloyd, Doris 205
Lloyd, Frank 134
Lloyd, Frederick 200
Lloyd, Harold 157, 188
Llwyd, Alan 102
Loback, Marvin 93
Lockhart, Gene 108, 176
Lockney, J.P. 42
Lockwood, Harold 134
Lockwood, J.R. 214

Loder, Jona 174, 199
Lodge, Andrew 126
Logan, Phyllis 35, 36
Logue, Charles 153, 177
Lohe, Marie 113
Lombard, Miroslawa 35
London 36, 50, 51, 60, 65, 76, 89, 96, 100, 154, 162, 185, 204
London Film Production 76
The Lone Wolf 79, 138
The Lone Wolf (1919) 79
Lonergan, Phillip 201
Long, Walter 135
Looney Tunes 50
Loose, Anita 94
Lorch, Theodore 44
Lord, Jack 60
Lord, Robert 65
Loring, Hope 208
Lorraine, Harry 110
Lorraine, Leota 121
Lorre, Peter 174
Lory, Jacques 83, 170
Los Angeles Times 58
Lost at the Front (1927) 138
The Lost Battalion (2001) 27
The Lost Patrol (1929) 23, 139
The Lost Patrol (1934) 23, 140
Lotis, Kim 32
Lou, Marie 115
Loubeque, Hugo 141
Louis Hayward Production Company 172
Love, Montagu 199
Love Light (1921) 140
Love Never Dies (1928) 134, 141
Lovell, Patricia 91
Love's Strggle (1918) 101, 141
Lovewell, Jesse 96
Low, Ben 122
Lowe, Edmund 206
Lowe, Greg 164
Lowell, Helen 69
Lowery, Robert 187
Lowry, Ira M. 87, 106
Lowry, L. 101
Lowry, Morton 68, 87
Lowry, William 185
Loy, Myrna 99
Lubin, Emily 87
Lucas, George 210
Lucas, Wilfred 71, 83
Lucille Love: The Girl of Mystery (1920) 141, 142
Lucky Star (1919) 142
Lucy, Arnold 34
Ludwig of Saxe-Thunberg 127
Lukis, Adrian 194
Lukis, Danny 194
Lullaby (1932) 51, 83, 143, 222n8

Lundigan, William 83
Luranian, Throne of 153
Luther, Anna 112
Lychow, General von 56
Lye, Reg 210
Lynbook, Billy 202
Lynch, David 37
Lynch, John 164, 165
Lynn, Earl 93
Lynn, Emmy 123
Lynn, Jeffrey 82
Lyon, Ben 104, 182
Lyons, Charles 142
Lytel, Bert 79
Lytton, L. Rogers 106, 130

Ma and Pa Kettle (1940) 136
Mac, Nila 201
Macardle, Donald 98
MacDonald, Charles 135
MacDonald, Katherine 41
MacDonald, Philip 140
MacDougal, Jean 202
MacDowell, Melbourne 43
MacGil, Patrick 188
MacGregor, Norval 133
Machin, Alfred 101
Mack, Hughie 93, 144
Mack, Sean 144
Mack Sennett Comedy Film 214
MacKay, Barry 52
MacKenna, Kenneth 147, 148
Mackinnon, Gillies 43
MacLean, Douglas 109
MacLeod, Lady 48
MacPherson, Arne 41
Macpherson, Jeanie 135, 192
Macready, George 160
Maday, Georg 147
Mademoiselle from Armentieres (1926) 142, 143
Maeterlinck, Maurice 54
Magee, Virginia 183
Magg, Dan 167
Magna Carta 214
Mailly, Fernand 144
Majeroni, George 211
Making of the American Military Image 3
Malahide, Patrick 35
Malandrinos, Andreas 174
Malcangi, Greg 194
Malena, Lena 104
HMS *Marlin* 172
Malleson, Miles 200
Malone, Molly 114
Maltby, H.F. 78
Maly, Gero 54
The Man I Killed (1932) 51, 143, 222n8

Mandy, Jerry 43
Maneuvers 24
Mann, Bertha 34
Mann, Delbert 33, 159
Mann, Hank 144, 160
Mann, Margaret 90
Manning, Irene 212
Manning, Robert 74
Mannix, Roy 89
Map, Frank 72
Mapp, Neville 132
Maranne, Andre 65
March, Fredric 170
March, General 93
March, Marilyn 177
March, Marion 104
March, Moncure 118
March, Oliver T. 144
March, William 59
Marcus, James 166
Marden, Joe 183
Mare Nostrum (1926) 144, 158
Marianne (1929) 145
Marier, Captain Victor 97
Marine 13, 29, 40, 70, 165, 195, 196, 207, 221n11
Marion-Crawfrd, Howard 52
Maris, Mona 173
Maritza, Sari 62
Markey, Brian 61
Markey, Darrell Ware 187
Markey, Enid 87, 215
Markey, Fred 57
Markey, Gene 187
Marks, Fraulein 191
Marley, J. Peverell 191
Marmont, Percy 174
Marne River 88, 89, 97, 107
Marner, Richard 33
Marriott, Albert 103, 205
Marriott, Frederic 195
Marriott, Moore 198
Marsan, Eddie 203
Marsh, Marian 104, 116, 127
Marsh, Oliver 144
Marsh, William 136
Marshall, Colonel 99
Marshall, Frank 203
Marshall, Herbert 64
Marshall, John Whitney 177
Marshall, Tully 93
Marshall, William 37, 136
Marta, John 6
Martan, Nitz 138
Marthes, Paul 107
Martial, Jean Francois 212
Martin, Jacques 65
Martin, James 145
Martindel, Edward 69, 143
Martine, Mortimer 196
Martineili, Arthur 96

The Martyrdom of Nurse Cavell (1916) 145, 217
Marvin, Lee 179, 180
Marvin, Richard 130
Mary, Warren 36, 37
Mary Pickford Films 115
Mascot Pictures 82
Mason, Andrew 205
Mason, Bob 186
Mason, Charles Post 145
Mason, Haddon 67
Mason, Hilary 168
Mason, James 48
Mason, J.M. 136
Mason, Rupert 61
Mason, Shirley 94
Mason, Sidney 49, 50, 166
Massacre 36, 129
Masterson, Peter 200
Masturbate 148
Mata Hari (1931) 146, 147, 219
Mata Hari (1985) 146, 148, 220
Mata Hari films 147
Matalon, Vivian 123
Mathis, June 73, 89, 90, 192, 222
Matras, Charles 94
Matthews, A.E. 132
Matthews, Durcus 58
Maude, Arthur 163
Maudlin, Bill 45
Maugham, W. Sumerset 174
Maurice, Mary 40, 85
Maury, Jacques 32
Mawbey, Sarah 88
Maxwell, Charles 144
Maxwell, Edwin 170
Maxwell, Steve 88
Maxwelton Braes 50
May, Brian 91
Mayall, Herschel 57, 162
Mayer, Louis B. 86
Mayes, Colin 35
Mayne, F. (Freddy) 200
Mayo, Archie 91
Mayo, Frank 73
Maywell, Charles 187
McAllister, Paul 56
McAlpin, Edith 116
McAndrews, John 158
McAvoy, Mary 192
McCall, William 109
McCambridge, Mercedes 82
McCann, Martin 61, 152
McCann Rescue Chamber 187
McCarthy, Francis X. 96
McClure, Doug 127
McConnell, Mollie 58
McConnochie, Rhys 37
McCormack, Frank 55
McCormick, John 134, 138

McCrea, Jody 125
McCrea, Joel 75, 76
McCrery, Nigel 35
McCullouch, Andrew 127
McCullough, Philo 135
McCutcheon, George Barr 134
McDiarmid, Ian 35, 36
McDonald, Francis 69, 130
McDonald, Mac 83
McDowell, Claire 45
McDowell, Malcolm 32
McDowell, Nelson 134
McEnery, John 126
McEvoy, Charles 47
McEwen, Walter 166
McFarland & Company 222
McFee, Malcolm 155
McGarry, Gary 79
McGavin, Darren 60
McGill, Barney 206
McGill, Bernard 191
McGill, "Sock" 187
McGrail, Walter 100, 173, 211, 212
McGrath, Hugh 78
McGreagh, Stanley 126
McGregor, Donald 50
McGuiness, James Kevin 148
McGuire, Tom 44
McGure, Kathryn 134
McHattie, Stephen 200
McHugh, Frank 69
McIntosh, Burr 134
McKay, George 164
McKechnie, James 132
McKee, Phil 138
McKee, Raymond 196
McKee, Shorty 43
McKenna, Brian 96
McKenzie, Benjamin (Ben) 118
McKenzie, Compton 189
McKenzie, Jacqueline 205
McKenzie, Tim 91, 133
McKern, Leo 123
McKidd, Kevin 43
McKim, Robert 58
McLaglen, Cyril 139, 188
McLaglen, G. 61, 70, 71, 139, 140, 206
McLaglen, Victor 71, 139, 140
McLaughlin, Gibb 163, 190, 200
McMaster, Andrew 139
McMenamin, Ciaran 194
McNally, Stephen 86
McNeile, Herman 163
McNeilly, Paul 61
McSorley, Gerard 203
McVea, Satchel 130
McWhinnie, Donald 20, 98
medical corpsman 34

Index

Meehan, Elisabeth 56
Meeker, George 90
Meeker, Ralph 160
Meighan, Thomas 38
Mellon, William 108
Melvin, Murray 180
Men Without Women (1930) 148, 174, 219
Mendan, Willy 195
Mendoza, David 144
Menjou, Adolphe 69, 81, 160
mental illness 43
Mercanton, Jacques 195
Mercer, Beryl 34, 35
Merchant of death hearing in Congress 34
Meredith, Lois 159
Merkel, Klaus 167
Merlo, Tony 66
Merouze, Georges 123
Merrick, Fred V. 171
Merritt, George 52, 78, 201
Merritt, Tom 165
Merry Christmas (2005) 149, 219, 220, 223n40
Merwin, Bannister 52
Mescall, John J. 170
Mesopotamia 139, 140
Mestayer, Harry 112
Metcalf, Jimmy 86
Meter, Harry von 119
Metro Film Corporation 106, 181
Metro-Goldwyn-Mayer 45
Metro Pictures 89, 96
Meyer, Emile 160
Meyer, Greta 170
Meyer, Torben 143
Meyers, Carmel 150
Meyring, Fritz von 66
Mezon, Jim 159
Mickey (1918) 12
Middleton, Greg 159
Midgley, Fanny 57, 183
Miehmet, Maxim 167
Mierendorff, Hans 195
Might and the Man (1917) 149, 217
Milburn, Betty 87
Mile, Karina 91
Miles, Bernard 185, 190
Milestone, Lewis 34
Military ignorance 19
Military justice 164
Millakowsky, Herman 195
Milland, Ray 32, 108
Millarde, Harry F. 49
Miller, Arthur 187
Miller, Charles 65, 177
Miller, Ernest 62
Miller, George 37

Miller, Hugh 129
Miller, J. Lee 43
Miller, Seton I. 67, 69, 74
Miller, Victor 51
Miller, Walter 73, 181
Millhauser, Bertram 76
Millo, Mario 133
Mills, John 34, 52
Mills, Thomas 106
Milne, A.A. 42
Milne, Matt 203
Milo Films 195
Minnelli, Vincente 90
The Miracle of the Marne 89
Miranda, Isa 108
Miranda, Tom 143
Mireau, General Paul 160
Miss Jackie of the Army (1917) 150
Miss Jackie of the Navy (1916) 150
Mitchell, Dave 134
Mitchell, John 37
Mitchell, Lendrum "Billy" 60, 61
Mitchell, Thomas 208
Mizenti, Maria 78
Modot, Gaston 94
Mohyeddin, Zia 129
Moja, Hella 195
Monash, Paul 35
Mong, William V. 206
Monophonicgram Pictures 88
Monroe, Randolph 97
Mons (1926) 150, 151, 219
Montagu, Ivor 47, 74
Montana, Bull 197
Monteran, Jacques 94
Montgomery, Douglass 78, 205
Montgomery, Elisabeth 60
Montgomery, Robert 103, 204
Montis, Rene 212
USS *Moody* 103
Moorcock, Michael 126
Moore, Alice 142
Moore, Cleve 134
Moore, Colleen 134
Moore, Dennie 186
Moore, Dickie 176
Moore, Eve 151
Moore, Mary Tyler 114
Moore, Matt 197
Moore, Roger 180
Moore, Rowland 173
Moorkins, Victor Maxim 198
Moral weakness 23
Moran, Frank 188
Moran, Neil 87
Moran, Nick 61
Moran, Polly 75
Morans, Joan 178

Moreland, Michael 194
Morell, Andre 190
Moreno, Antonio 144
Morey, Harry T. 211
Morgan, Dennis 83
Morgan, J.P. 64
Morgan, Kewpie 44
Morgan, Sidney 110
Morley, Karen 146
Morley, Robert 33
Morning Telegraph 13, 221
Morpurgo, Michael 164, 203
Morris, Chester 56
Morris, Mary 185
Morris, Oswald 82
Morris, Wayne 160, 186, 187
Morrison, James 106, 211
Morrison, Mary 40
Morros, Gouverneur 42
Morse Building (Brooklyn, New York) 10
Morton, Charles 90
Moss, George 66
"Most Wanted" 169
Mother of Men 58
Mother Superior 95
Motherland (1927) 151, 219
Motion Picture Sound Editors Award 139
Motion Picture World and Official Film News 17
Mottram, Ralph H. 171
Mower, Jack 79, 150, 179
Mrs. Clark 206
Mrs. Hobbley 206
Mrs. Slacker (1918) 74, 151, 152
Mrs. Warrington 112
Mrs. Whiggs of the Cabbage Patch (1932) 137
Mucke, Kapitanleutnant von 78
Mulcahy, Russell 138
Mulheron, Danny 57
Mulholland, Declan 126
Mullan, Peter 203
Mullerschon, Nikolai 167
Mulliagan, Carey 152
Mullion, Tom 194
Mundin, Herbert 75
Munsun, Audrey 31
Muresan, Crina 55
Murfin, Jane 134
Murillo, Mary 202
Murphy, Cillian 194
Murphy, George 86
Murphy, Maurice 170
Murphy, Steve 79
Murphy, Tim 194
Murray, Charles 138
Murray, James 35
Murray, John 56

Murray, M. Gary 114
Murray, Marnie 158
Murray, Stephen 61
Museums 6, 7, 142, 149, 151
Mutt, Augustus J. 110, 158, 118
Mutt and Jeff 158, 164, 178, 179, 193
My Boy Jack ((2007) 27
My Country (1917) 152, 201
My Four Years in Germany (1918) 153, 158
My Four Years in Germany, Incorporated 153
Myles, Norbet A. 85
Mylong-Munz, Jack 78
Mysterious (mysteries) 13, 36, 39, 72, 97, 142, 153, 173
The Mystery Girl (1938) 153
Myton, Fred 84, 132

Nagata, Tetsuo 155
Nahon, Philippe 203
Nakamura, Henry 125
Napier, Niel 96
Nardella, James 59
National Archives and Records Administrations 6
National Arts Council Award 159
National Board of Review 86, 185
National Eisteddfod Chair in Black 103
National Film and Television Archives (UK) 6
National Film Board (Canada) 122
National Film Preservation Unit of the Library of Congress 6, 7
National Film Registry 6, 35, 44, 58, 90, 176
National Kinematographic Exhibit 6
National Registry of the British Film Institute 6
National War Aims Commission 113, 114
Navy, U.S. 52, 58, 66, 70, 78, 80, 103, 110, 133, 150, 162, 175
Nazi party 170, 190, 195
Nazimova, Alla 201, 202
Neagle, Anna 154
Neal, Patricia 35, 46
Neame, Gareth 35
Neilan, Marshall 104, 197
Neill, James 135, 198
Neill, Roy William 121
Nelson, Ruth 208
Nemeth, Laszio 147

Nemethy, Ferenc 147
Nesbigtt, Darrey 48
Neurotic 190
Neutrality 4, 5, 10, 12, 84, 119
Neville, John 43
The New York Observer 204
New York Times 165
New Zealand 37, 57
Newall, Guy 60
Newark, Derek 48
Newell, David 103
Newell, Jamie 194
Newlands, Anthony 147
Newman, Nanette 156
Newsreels 208
Niblack, Samuel N. 161
Niblo, Fred, Jr. 75
Nicholas, Eileen 43
Nicholls, Fred 183
Nicholls, Captain James 203
Nicholls, Paul 194
Nichols, Dudley 140, 173
Nichols, George 41, 133
Nicolson, Gerda 211
Niemeyer, Bernard 135
Nieto, Jose 82
Nieuport 28s 69
Nigh, William 153
Nihilistic 21
Niven, David 34, 68
No Man's Land (1931) 99, 104, 1545
No Man's Land (place) 99, 104
Noisom, George 63
Noland, Ciaran 152
Nomis, Leo 68
Norfolk 37
Norfolk Estate 36
Norman, Eva 10
Norman, Gertrude 196
Norman, Lucille 86
Norman Rosemont Production 35
Normand, Mable 116
Norris, William 137
North, Rupert 67
North, Wilfred 40, 158
Northrup, Harry S. 96
Norton, Barry 70, 130, 206
Nova, Alex 144
Novak, Jane 42, 58
Novarro, Ramon 133, 146
Nox, Andre 107, 115, 195
Noy, Wilfred 107, 196
Nugent, Edward J. 204
Nun 192
Nurse 20, 21, 36, 42, 50, 67, 71, 75, 81, 82, 85, 87, 89, 91, 112, 117, 134, 145, 154, 155, 160, 167, 169, 180, 183, 191, 204, 205, 211

Nurse Cavell (1916) 75, 145, 154
Nurse Edith Cavill (1939) 154
Nutt, Danny 194

Oakie, Jack 74
O'Beck, Fred 160
Ober, Robert 45
Oberon, Merle 64
O'Brien, Billy 142
O'Brien, Edmond 129
O'Brien, Eugene 136
O'Brien, George 100
O'Brien, Pat 70, 82, 186, 187
O'Brien, Tom 45
O'Connell, Jack 164
O'Connor, Di 133
O'Connor, Doreen 156
O'Connor, John E. 3, 9, 46
O'Connor, Pat 164
O'Day, Molly 160
Odd, David 35
O'Donohoe, James 206
Offenbach, Jacques 69
The Officer's Ward (2001) 154
O'Flynn, Captain 120
O'Flynn, Paddy 79
Ogan, A.C. 114
Ogle, Charles 174, 175
Oh What a Lovely War (1969) 155, 156
Oh, You Beautiful Doll 86
O'Halloran, Mark 61
Oland, Warren 70
Oldsmith, Sebastian 180
Oliver, Clarence 177
Oliver, Edna May 154
Oliver, Guy 112, 135
Oliver, Laurence 129, 132
Oliver, Roland 35, 36
O'Malley, Pat 100, 166
On Dangerous Ground (1917) 136, 157
On the Jump (1918) 157
On the Russian Frontier (1915) 157
Once on Chunuk Bair 57
One Man Mutiny (1955) 157
USS 166 174
O'Neill, Edward 67
O'Neill, Henry 186
Only One Night (1936) 138
Orientals 175
Orkney Islands 185
Ortiz, Charles R. 131
Osborne, Lieutenant 118
Osborne, Marie "Babby" 137
Osborne, Ralph 118
Oscar 56, 64, 81, 95, 103
Osen, Moroni 187
Osterloh, Robert 172

Index

Ostime, Roger 48
Ostriche, Muriel 199
O'Toole, Peter **128**, 129
Otto, Henry 76
Our Four Days in Germany (1918) 158
Our Sea (1926) 144
The Outrage (1915) 158
Over the top (action) 12, 46
Over the Top (1918) 159
Over There 29, 156, 176
Overbaugh, Roy F. 166
Overman Act of 1918 59
Overton, Evart 40
Owens, Wilfred 43
Oz Film Manufacturing 95

Pacey, Steven 32
Pacifism (pacifist) 9, 53, 58, 60, 75, 96, 111, 137
Pack Up Your Troubles 43
Page, Anita 204
Page, Paul 148
Pahe Executive 196
Pahle, Theodore J. 195
Paihas, Geraldine 155
Pain 2, 21, 23, 221n17, 222n17
Palace 86
Palau 124
Palestine 89, 133
Pallette, Eugene 103
Palmer, Harry 86
Palmer, Inda 112
Palmer, Lilli 174
Palmer, Terry 123
Pals Battalion 36
Panzer, Paul 127, 191, 211
Paquerette 144
Paquis, Gerald 180
Paquis, Gerard 32
Parakins, Leonard 56
Paralta Plays Incorporated 162
Paramore, Edward A. 190
Paramount Famous Laskey 38, 41, 42, 51, 65, 70, 75, 80, 81, 91, 95, 97, 108, 121, 129, 136, 153, 155, 165, 174, 208, 210
Parant, Forrester 195
Paris (city) 53, 79, 89, 90, 99, 115, 151
Paris, Manuel 187
Paris, Michael 226
Parker, Jack 150, 189
Parker, James, Jr. 173
Parker, Louis N. 59
Parker, William 150
Parkins, Barbara 180
Parks, Francis 93
Parle, Michael 61
Parliament 43, 93, 168
Parlo, Dita 94, 195

Parr, Bobby 126
Parr, Charles 120
Parsons, Donovan 74
Parsons, Mary 74
Parsons, Percy 188
Partlow, Shane 117
Pascale, Lucien 195
Pascale, Christophe 32
Pasch, Reinhold 51
Pasque, Ernest 79
Passchendaele 159
Passchendaele (2008) 159
Passeur, Steve 115
Pasztor, John J 182
Patch, Wally 190, 207
Pate, Michael 88, 172
The Patent Leather Kid (1925) 30, 159, 219
Pathe Exchange Film 55, 151, 157, 177
Pathe of France 127, 196, 197
Paths of Glory (1957) 18, 160, 161, 220, 222n15
Paton, Charles 200
Patria Films 54
Patriot (1917) 85, 161
The Patriot and the Spy (1915) 161, 185, 217
Patriotic fever 11, 19, 21, 23, 29, 37, 46, 71, 73, 77, 96, 106, 176, 180, 212, 220
Patriotism (1918) 162, 218
Patterson, Private 61
Paul, Fred 156
Paul, Gloria 65
Paul, Heinz 195
Paulais, Georges 107, 195
Pavan, Marissa 207
Pawle, Lennox 181
Paynter, Corona 77
Peace activist 1, 2, 10, 12, 13, 16, 20, 23, 36, 40, 45, 46, 49, 51, 53, 55, 58, 61, 71, 73, 84, 102, 112, 113, 123, 149, 199, 217, 222
Peaceful, Charlie 164
Peake, Maxine 164
Pearce, George 193
Pearce, Vera 145
Pearson, George 74, 122, 169
Pearson, Virginia 66, 202
Pearson, Welch 169
Peat, Harold 165
Peclet, George (Georges) 94, 104, 107
Peerless Productions 157
Pegge, Edmund 37
Peil, Edward, Sr. 93
Peile, Kinsey 54
Pellegraino, Roland 167
Pember, Ron 126

Pendleton, Steve 173
Penhaligon, Susan 126
Pennell, R.O. 93
Pennick, Jack 90, 142, 187
Penny, Pat 88
Peppard, George 48, 49
Percival, Lance 65
Peres, Marcel 195
Perez, Paul 56
Perfitt, Frank 67
The Peril of the Fleet (1909) 10, 162, 217
Perinal, Georges 132
Perkins, Gil 118
Perley, Poore 53
Perrett, Leonce 130, 197
Perrett Production Incorporated 197
Perrier, Gaby 130
Perry, Harry 104, 208
Perry, Ralph 87
Pertwee, Robert 185
Peterman, Tom 7
Peterson, Dane 91
Peterson, Eric 122
Petin, Laurent 154
Petin, Michele 154
Petit, Gabrielle 67, 222n15
Petrie, Hay 185, 188
Pettie, Graham 36
Pfell, Cosmos 59
Pfister, Ian 59
Phelps, Peter 133, 134
Philips, Francis Charles 38
Phillips, Dorothy 100, 101
Phillips, Guy 169
Phillips, Mary 81
Phillips, Tubby 163
Phoenix 131, 163
Pickering, Jenny 194
Pickford, Mary 135, 136, 140, 141, 179
Pieczka, Franciszek 39
Pierce, Betty 95
Pierce, Norman 78
Pierce-Roberts, Tony 194
Pierier, Etnne 214
Pierott, Frederic 55
Pierson, F.M. 149
Pierson, Leo 46, 184
Pigboat (1933) 103, 163
Piggot, Derek 49
Pigutt, Tim 32
Pimple, Lieutenant 5, 131, 217
Pimple's Dream of Victory (1915) 163, 217
The Pink Panther 65
Pinkovitch, Albert 94
Pinky (1949) 99
Pinon, Dominique 198
Piper, Frederick 78

Piro, Grant 133
Pitcairn, Jack 118
Pitts, Tom 203
Pitts, Zasu 35, 51, 97, 98, 154, 204
Plains Indians 10
Playbill 128
Pleasence, Donald 35
Plot productions 4
Plummer, Christopher 32
Plumpick, Charles 124
Plunkett, Jerry 83
Plunkett, Joseph L. 210
Pocknaill, George 163
Pocock, Tim 88
Podalydes, Denis 155
"Poetic feel" 26
Poets war 103
Pola, Negri 108
Polack 139
Poland 28, 39
Pole 39
Polito, Sol 176
Pollard, Daphne 181
Pollard, "Snub" 157
Pollick, Charles 75
Pommer, Erich 108
Pommy bashing 14
Ponder, Jack 134
Poppies of Flanders (1927) 163, 219
Porel, Jacqueline 107
Porky Pig 50
Porn 148
Portal, Jean Michael 155
Portalupi, Piero 82
Porter, Sarah 210
Porterfield, Robert 176
Portman, Rachel 164
Portus, George 145
Post, G.O. 100
Posters 5, 70, **70**, **92**, 105, 110, 151
Pot Luck with the Army (1918) 163, 218
Potel, Victor 56, 72
Pour le Merite 48
POW 56, 78, 167, 192, 201
Powell, Eline 164
Powell, Michael 132, 185, 223n29
Powell, Robert 57
Powell, Violet E. 163
Powers, Adrian 87
Powers, Francis 95
Pragmatic patriotism 4, 221n5
The Prahran Chronicle 108
Preminger, Otto 60
Preservation copy 58
President Wilson (1944) 164, 208

Presle, Micheline 124
Pressburger, Emeric 132, 185, 223n59
Preuose, Peggy 179
Prevost, Marie 204, 214
Prevost, Simone 123
Price, Ensign 148
Price, Gale 130
Price, Stanley 179
Price, Vincent 208
Priggen, Norman 123
Prikazsky, Lukas 167
Prime Minister 189
Primus, Barry 200
Prince of Peace Corporation 112
Prisco, Albert 140
Private Peaceful (2012) 164, 220
Private Peat (1918) 165, 218
Probyn, Hugh 159
Proctor, David 95
Proctor, Rupert 43
The Profiteer (1919) 165, 218
Progressive Silent Film 225
Projection time (comment) 28, 39
Propaganda 5, 10, 14, 22, 26, 67, 76, 92, 93, 112, 113, 135, 153, 166, 172, 182, 211
ProPatria 57
Prostitution (prostitutes) 69, 71, 76, 125, 146
The Prussian Cur (1918) 166, 218
Pryce, Jonathan 43
Prysor, Manon 102
Pseudonym 97
Psychological film 188
Psychologist 147
Pszoniak, Wojciech 39
Publicity 58, 177
Pursall, David 48
Purviance, Edna 49, 179

Quakers 199
Qualen, John 170
Quartermaine 148
Quayle, Anthony 129
The Queen's African Rifles (1953) 166
Quiet on the Western Front (1979) 35
Quigley, Poll 136
Quin, Barry 89
Quine, Richard 86
Quinn, Anthony **128**, 129
Quinn, Arthur T. 40
Quinn, Regina 111
Quota Quickies 125, 201

Racist 23, 99
Radcliffe, Daniel 152

Rae, John 155
Rae, Zoe 53, 119
Rafferty, Chips 88
The Raid of 1915 113
Raiders, Leeds 116
Raimu (Jules Muraire) 107
Raine, Jack 188
Raine, Norman Reilly 82
Rains, Claude 129
Ralph, Louis 78, 79
Ralston, Jobyna 208, 210
Ramirez, Rosita 144
Randolf, Anders 106
Ranevsky, Boris 142
Rankin, Arthur 186
Rape 21, 66, 102, 115, 129, 135, 150, 158, 161, 192, 197
Rapee, Erno 206
Raphaelson, Samson 51
Rath, Willy 195
Rathbone, Basil 68
Ratib, Gamil 129
Ratoff, Gregory 170
Rattenberry, Harry L 141.
Rauffestein, von 94
Ravignac, Captain Henry 183
Rawlings, Blaine 83, 84
Rawlinson, Gerald 189
Ray, Charles 58, 121
Ray, Michel 129
Ray, Rene 174
Ray, Rupert 189
Raymond, Charles 121
Raymond, Cyril 185
Raymond, Ernest 189
Raymond, Francis 43, 48
Raymond Rohauer Collection 98
Raymore, Edythe 170
Raynham, Fred 54
Read, Barbara 170
Reade, Simon 164
Ready, Paul 164
Reagan, Ronald 187
Realism 4, 28, 32, 33, 87, 209
Rearmament 14
Reciprocity Films 181
Recruiting 3 181
Red (army) 55
Red (name) 89
Red Baron (character) 48, 122, 166, 167, 200, 223n28
The Red Baron (1971) 166, 199
The Red Baron (2008) 167, 202
Red Cross 41, 42, 81, 85, 87, 91, 101, 112, 136, 137, 217
Red Cross Nurse 42, 77, 81, 91, 112, 217
Red Salute (1917) 38, 167
Redgrave, Corin 156, 200

Redgrave, Michael 174
Reed, Luther 42, 104
Reed, Michael 200
Reed, Tom 205
Reeve, Tom 138
Reeves, Alf 179
Regas, George 140
Regeneration 43
Regent Films 173
Reichardt, Dirk 167
Reicher, Frank 90, 146, 170
Reicher, Hedwigs 142
Reid, Alastair 179
Reid, Hal 136
Reiden, Karl von 143
Reiman, Eric 88
Reinhardt, John 143
Reisner, Charles 44
Reisser, Thomas 167
Reitz, Albert 161
Religion 23, 48, 176, 195
Remarque, Erich Maria 35, 190
Remember Belgium (1915) 167, 222n7
Renauld, Isabelle 155
Rendel, Robert 185
The Renegade (1914) 133, 168
Rennie, Michael 174
Renoir, Auguste 95
Renoir, Jean 94, 95
Renowned Pictures 119
Resolution 52
The Return of the Soldier (1982) 168, 220
La Revanche (1916) 75, 197
Reveille (1925) 169, 218, 223n45
Revelle, Hamilton 130, 131
Revenge 42, 144, 168, 183, 192
Reviczky, Gabor 147
Revier, Dorothy 186
Reville, Alma 41, 47
Revolutionary War 20
Reynolds, Charles 166
Reynolds, Harrington 145
Reynolds, Lynn 180
Rhind-Tutt, Julian 194
Ribault, Rene 212
Rich, Catherine 55
Rich, Claude 55
Richard, Albert 151
Richards, Mike 74
Richardson, Cliff 189
Richardson, Ian 149
Richman, Charles 40, 106
Richter, Von 68
Richter-Douglas, Geoffrey 214
Richthofen, Manfred Von 167, 200, 207
Ridell, George 153
Ridges, Stanley 176
Ridgeway, Fritzi 79
Riegel, Charles 105
Ries, Park 92
Riesenfeld, Hugo 57, 191
Rimoux, Alain 155
Risdon, Elisabeth 114
Rita Jolivet Film Corporation 130
River Marne 107
RKO Radio Pictures 56, 99, 140, 154, 200
Roach, Alexandra 164
Roach, Bert 93, 214
Roach, David 44
Roach, Hal 157
Roache, Cillian 61
The Road to Glory (1936) 70, 212
The Road to Honor (1917) 65, 171
Robards, Jason, Jr. 116
Robards, Jason, Sr. 62
Robb, David 43
Robbins, Michael 214
Roberts, Angharad 102
Roberts, Guto 102
Roberts, John (J.K.) 69
Roberts, Johnny 46
Robertson, George 126
Robertson, John S. 136
Robertson, Steven 149
Robertson, William 76
Robinson, Dorothy 121
Robinson, Forrest 136
Robinson, George 170
Robinson, Neil 147
Robinson, Sam 5
Robson, Andrew 133
Robson, E.W. 132
Robson, May 154
Robson, M.M. 132
Rock, Charles 51, 76
Rodan, Jay 138
Roddham, David 61
Rodgers, Meradith 37
Rodion, John 68
Rodwell, Stanley 150, 189
Roe, Emil 130
Roeves, Maurice 156
Rogell, Albert S. 143
Rogers, Bogart 74
Rogers, Butch 187
Rogers, Charles 47
Rogers, Charles "Buddy" 208
Rogers, Howard Emmett 86
Rogers, James E. 189
Rogers, L. 40, 106, 130
Rogers, Lela E 49, 136
Rogers, Walter Browne 34
Roitfeld, Jacques 32
Rollins, George 115
Rollins, Peter C. 3, 9, 46, 222n5
Rollmer, Frank 94
Romano, Nina 138
Romantic (idea) 3
Rombi, Philippe 149
Rome, Stewart 169
Romeo and Juliet 174
Roosevelt, Theodore 40, 212
Roosevelt Boy Scout troops 137
Rorke, J.F. 196
Rorke, Mary 87
Rose 86
Rose-Mai 104
Rosebury, Paul 32
Rosenman, Leonard 125
Rosenthal, Joe 198
Roses of Picardy (1927) 171
Rosher, Charles 140
Rosing, Bodil 62
Ross, Milton 79
Rossington, Norman 129
Rosson, Harold 103
Rostand, Maurice 51
Rothafel, S.L. 40
Rouge Bouquet 83
Rouget, Paul 88
Rounds, Stephen 53
Routh, George 85
Rouverol, Jean 170
Rowe, Arthur 214
Rowe, Lewis 57
Rowland, Robert 145
The Royal African Rifles (1953) 166, 172, 186
Royal Air Force 74
Royal Army 36
Royal Australian Navy 78
Royal Canadian Flying Club 167
Royal Council on Needlework 132
Royal Flying Corps 67, 68, 69, 105
Royal Navy 52, 162172
Royal Scot 148
Royal Welch Fusiliers 102, 149
Royalty 58, 127, 135
Royce, Lionel 154
Royce, Norman 110
Rozsa, Miklos 185
Ruanian 106
Rubens, Alma 178
Rubin, Benny 144
Rubun, Daniel 70
Rucker, Richard 208
Rudder, Michael 96
Ruddock, John 129
Ruggles, Wesley 84
Ruhbeck, Max 165

250 INDEX

Runaway Daughtter (1917) 38, 172
Running time 4
Russian 40, 55, 56, 71, 104, 108, 138, 157, 158, 190, 223*n*36
Russian front 158
Russian Legion of Death 138
Rutherford. John 99
HMS *Rutland* 52, 193
Rutland, Barbara 193
Ryan, Taylor 147
Rysson, Danick 193, 194

Sadoski, Thomas 59
Sage, Stuart 202
Sagittarius Rising 32
Sahara (1943) 23
Saillard, Georges 115
St. Clair, Malcolm 214
St. John, Al 178
St. Johns, Rogers Adela 134
St. Leger, H.P. 130
St. Magnus 185
St. Mihiel 115
St. Polis, John 89
Sakall, S.Z. 212
Salis, Abdul 83
Salisbury, Monroe 133
Samoslui, Zygmunt 39
Sampson, Teddy 38
Samuelson, G.B. 87, 151
Samuelson, Samuel 87
Samuelson-Victoria Film Productions 87
Sanders, George 154
Sandringham Company 27, 36
Sandway, Mark 69
Santell, Alfred 159
Sapper 163, 201
Sarde, Alain 55
Saretok, Zofia 39
Sarno, Hector 142
Sartov, Hendrik 98, 101
Saskatchewan 159
Sassoon, Siegfried 43
Saturday Evening Post 80
Saum, Cliff P. 120, 130
Saunders, Monk 14, 68, 69, 74, 178
Saunders, Stuart 129
Saville, Victor 142, 171, 201
Saving the Colors (1914) 173
Sawyer, Ann 187
Sawyer, Joe 176
Sawyer, Laura 113
Saxe, Tunberg 127
Sayre, Joel 170
Scaddan, Harry 156
Scapa Flow 185
Scardon, Paul 40.106
Schaefer, Billy Kent 75

Schayer, Richard 72
Schell, Carl 48, 49
Schellinger, Rial 120, 153
Schenck, Earl 120, 153, 196
Schertzinger, Victor 57
Schieffenzahn, General 56
Schiller, Von 89
Schlesinger, Leo 50
Schmauser, Thomas 149
Scholl, Ogla Linek 100
Schonemann, Hinnerk 203
Schroeder, Rick 138
Schroeder, Romain 139
Schroeder, Steffen 167
Schumann-Heink, Ferdinand 90, 143, 187
Schumm, Harry 72, 141
Schuster, Hugo 48
Schuyler, David 177
Schweiger, Til 167
Schweighofer, Matthais 167
Scot, Justin 139
Scotand (Scottish) 7, 12, 43, 50, 149, 151, 162, 202
Scott, Alex 48
Scott, Allan 43
Scott, Betty 62
Scott, Douglas 74
Scott, Dougray 43
Scott, Joseph 93
Scott, Maurice 156
Scott, William 125
Scout Week 137
Sea Wolf (1930) 174
Sealy, Lewis 73
Searle, Donald 169
Sears, Allan 119
Sears, Phil 83
Seas Beneath (1931) 173
Sebastian (Prince) 153
Second Ypres 159
Secret Agent (1936) 174
The Secret Game (1917) 174
The Secret of the Submarine (1915) 175
Secret Service (unit and agents) 151, 174, 191
Seddon, Jack 48
Seddon, Margaret 170, 178, 183
Sedgwick, Edward 72, 73
Seiter, Robert 74
Seitz, John F. 89, 144
Sekely, Steve (Istvan) 54, 55
Selander, Lesley 172
Selby, Nicholas 147
Selective Service (conscription) 60, 74, 105, 106
Selective Service Act of 1917 94
Selwyn, Edgar 204
Selznick, David O. 82, 201
Semler, Dean 133

Semon, Larry 109, 110
Sennet Bathing Girls 214
Sennett, Mark 188, 214
Serb (Serbian) 125, 195
Sergeant York (1941) 14, 123, 176, 200
Serpico, Terry 59
Serrault, Michel 124
Serret, John 32
The Service Stars (1918) 83, 177
The Seventy Mile Gun (1918) 178
Severin-Mars 114
Sex (sexual) 21, 30, 48, 71, 73, 75, 95, 116, 141, 151, 183, 205
Seyffertitz, Gustav von 56, 71, 192
Seymour, Clarine 93, 94
Seymour, Houston 47
Seymour, Jane 156
Seymour, Jonah 123
Shadbolt, Maurice 57
The Shame and Disgrace of Colonel Blimp 132
Shamroy, Leon 208
Shannon, Alex 201
Shannon, Effie 105
Shannon, Gerald 63
Sharif, Omar 129
Sharp, John 168
Shaw, C. Montague 64
Shaw, Harold M. 51
Shaw, Sabastian 185
Shdanoff, George 104
She Goes to War (1928) 178
Shean, Al 170
Sheard, Michael 35
Sheldon, Dr. 41
Shell shock 43, 123, 168, 183, 207
Shelley, Norman 74
Shelley, Paul 156
Shenton, William 142
Shepherd, James 88
Sheridan, Taylor 64
Sherman, General 204
Sherman, Richard 86
Sherman, Steward 59
Sherre, J. Barny 57
Sherriff, R.C. 31, 118, 170
Sherrill, Jack 165
Sherwood Robert 205
Shields, Ernest 46
Shilkret, Nathanel 134
Shine, Wilfred 54
Shipman, David 61
Shipwrecked 180
Shirley, Arthur 193
Shirley, Dorinea 151
Shoulder Arms (1918) 11, 93, 179, 193

Shout at the Devil (1976) 179
Showalter, Max 207
The Showdown (1917) 40, 180
Shumway, Lee 150
Sibirskaian, Nadia 47
Sidney, George 138
Sidneyan Society 132
Siegel, Bernard 211
Siegmann, George 95
Sigurdson, Chris 41
Silburn, Tom 194
Silvers, Sid 86
Simpkins, Susie 151
Simpson, Peggy 78
Sims, Jeremy 44
Sinai and Palestine campaigns 89
Sinclair, "Dude" 125
Singer, Marlow 49
Siodmak, Robert 195
Siracusa, Frank 159
Sixty Four Ninety Four 171
Skene, Robin 171
Sketchley, Leslie 118
Skeyhill, Tom 176
Ski Patrol (1940) 71
Skinner, Eugene 83
Skinner, Marian 182
Skreba Films 168
The Sky Hawk (1929) 14
Slacker (individuals) 11, 73, 106, 111
The Slacker (1917) 181
The Slacker's Heart (1917) 11, 182
Slapstick 45, 48, 99, 131, 188, 214, 225n51
Slaven, M.J. 73
Sleeper, Martha 204
Sloan, Paul 99
Slocombe, Douglas 48
Small, Izzy Meikle 164
Smiley, Joseph W. 116
Smirnova, Dina 178
Smith, Albert (Al) 163
Smith, Cyril 52
Smith, Ebell 175
Smith, Greg 7
Smith, Gunboat 208
Smith, Henry 130
Smith, Jay 119
Smith, John 207
Smith, Kim 156
Smith, Leonard 40, 72
Smith, Maggie 35
Smith, Mark Coles 44
Smith, Miriam 41
Smith, R. Cecil 58
Smith, Tim Pigott 83
Smith, Will 179
Snow, Marguerite 160

Sokoloff, Vladimir 104
Solm, Fred 195
Somerset, Pat 148
Somewhere in France (1915) 132
Sommerlad, Damian 88
Somogyi, Nusi 54
Sonny (1922) 183, 184
Sordi, Alberto 82
Sorley, Edward 67
Sose, Pedro 119
Sosko, P.J. 59
Sottong, Florence 137
The Sound of Music (1965) 195
South, Frank 57
South Africa 132, 143
South America 126
Southampton 162
Southern, Ann 72
Spaak, Charles 20
Spanish American War 1, 221n13
Spanish Civil War (1936) 14
The Spanish Farm 171
Spanish Influenza 38
Sparkuhl, Theodor 188
Special effects 1, 34, 131, 144, 207
Spell of the Waltz 86
Spencer, Norman 50
Spenser, Jeremy 123
Sperling, Milton 60
Spiegel, Sam 127, 129
Spielberg, Stephen 203
Spies (function and individual) 17, 38, 54, 64, 65, 72, 73, 77, 80, 85, 88, 93, 97, 100, 108, 110, 111, 113, 121, 127, 129, 130, 137, 141–146, 148, 150, 156, 157, 161–163, 166, 171, 173, 175, 182, 183, 185, 191, 192, 194, 201, 214
Spies of the Kaiser 121
The Spirit of '76 (1917) 10
The Spreading Evil (1918) 184
Springer, Norman 186
Sproule, Peter 126
The Spy (1917) 185
The Spy and the Patriot (1915) 167, 185
The Spy in Black (1939) 194
Squirrel Inn 157
Staffel, Charles 126
Stafford, Nick 203
Stahl, Armin Von 56
Stallings, Laurence 29, 45, 144, 145, 205–207
Stallor, Marjorie 87
Standey, Maxfield 95
Standing, Guy 74
Standing, Herbert 117
Standing, Percy 120, 153

Standing, Wyndham 63, 105
Standing Committee on Social Affairs, Science and Technology (Canada) 122
Stanhope, Captain 118
Stanley, Edwin 77
Stanley, Muriel 78
Stannard, Eliot 114
Stanton, Paul 170
Stanton, Richard 184
Stanton, Will 143
Stanwyck, Barbara 76, 77
Star Wars 210
Stark, Graham 185
Starke, Yvonne 178
Starr, James 99
Stars of Glory (1919) 186, 199
States Rights Production Company 180, 215
Stavely, Roland 145
Steele, William 72
Steerman, A. Harding 151
Steiger, Rod 60
Stein, John 160
Stein, Sammy 140
Steiner, Max 68, 176
Stephens, Harvey 83, 176
Steppings, John 150
Sterling, Arthur 79
Sterling, Ford 214
Sterling, Jefferson 192
Sterling Pictures 79
Sternberg, Erich von 29, 62, 70, 94
Stevens, Edwin 197
Stevens, Emily 181
Stevenson, Burton E. 157
Stevenson, Hayden 43
Stewart, Agnes 169
Stewart, Alexandra 214
Stewart, Athole 185
Stewart, F.W. 165
Stewart, Gareth 61
Stewart, Grant 38
Stewart, Leonora 166
Stewart, Paul 96
Stewart, Philip W. 7
Stewart, Roy 84
Stewart, Sophie 154
Stigwood, Robert 91
Stiller, Mauritz 108
Stillwell, George 113
Stobrawa, Renee 104
Stoker, H.G. 52
The Stolen Ranch (1926) 28
Stoll Film Company 54, 60, 98
Stone, Arthur 143
Stone, Frank 153
Stone, George E. 187, 192
Stone, Lewis 146
Stone-Fewings, Jo 35

Stonehouse, Ruth 63, 84
Stoney, Jack 134
Storm, Jerome 183
Storm Over Africa (1953) 172
Story, Byron 126
Story of Christmas 223n40
Stow, Perry 113
Stowell, William 100
Strachan, Anthony 194
Strategy 2, 15, 44, 94, 95, 101, 102, 109, 191, 195, 196
Stratford, Peter 37
Stricy, Eldine 82
Stroheim, Erich von 28, 29, 62, 73, 85, 94, 95, 101, 108, 191, 196
Strong, Percy 74
Strong, Pereival 169
Stroud, Don 200
Stuart, Jon 142, 171
Stuart, Kathryn 197
Stuart, Simon 169
Stuart Blackton, Charles 137
Stubven, Anna Maria von 173
Styan, Arthur 75, 169
Styles, Edwin 103
Submarine (as vessel) 5, 42, 57–59, 69, 80, 103, 106, 131, 133, 137, 144, 148, 162, 173–175, 183, 185–188, 196, 197, 215
Submarine D-1 (1937) 106, 187
USS *Submarine S13* 148
Submarine Patrol (1938) 187
A Submarine Pirate (1915) 188
Submarine Story (1915) 188
Suedo, Julie 198
Suicide 43, 57, 68, 87, 91, 202
Suid, Lawrence 3, 6
Sullivan, C. Gardner 58, 215
Sullivan, Charles 46, 160
Sullivan, Karl 61
Summers, George 155
Summers, Walter 139, 150, 151, 188
Summerville, Slim 34, 170, 187
Sunderland, John 120
Sunrise 99
Sunrise (1927) 91
Super Panavision 127
Survival 2, 12, 28
Suspense (1930) 188
Sussin, Mathirde 195
Sutherland, Donald 116
Sutherland, Edward 46
Sutherland, Grant 195
Sutton, Carios 147
Sutton, Charles 106
Swanson, Hilda 845
Swanson, Riff 43
Swayne, Marian 135

Swedish (Swede) 23
Sweet, Blanche 197
Sweet, Gary 133
Swickard, Josef 143
Switzerland 81, 174
HMS *Sydney* 78, 79
Symansky, Adam 122
Syphilis 184
Szoreghy, Guylz 54

Tabakowitsch, Nicholae 8
Talbot, Rowland 54, 95, 193, 156
Tamas, Istvan 54
Tannen, Charles 64
Tannen, Julius 170
Tapioca Films 198
Tarbell, James 183
Tarzan of the Apes (1918) 12
Tatasciore, Fred 116
Tate, Reginald 132
Tautou, Audrey 193
Tavernier, Bertram 51
Taylor, Alma 158
Taylor, E.V. 93, 95
Taylor, Grant 88
Taylor, Larry 123
Taylor, Robert 190
Tearing Down the Spanish Flag (1898) 3, 10
Technicolor 32, 131, 143, 168, 179, 205
Tedmarsh, William 175
Television 2, 6, 7, 27, 138, 163
Tell England (1931) 40
Tell It to the Marines (1926) 13
Ten Most Wanted films 120
Tencer, Golda 39
Tennyson, Walter 169
Terris, Malcolm 147
Teriss, Ellaline 47
Terry, Alice 89, 90, 144
Terry, Ellen 118
Tessier, Jack 193
Thalberg, Irving 45, 46
Thanhouser, Edwin 42
Thanhouser Film Preservation Center 112
That They Might Live (1938) 189
Theater Research, University of Wisconsin 7
Thenault, Captain 84
Therese, Countess 154
Thewlis, David 203
"They Didn't Believe Me" 156
They Were Expendable (1942) 72
Thielen, Jason 116
Third Battle of Ypres 103
Thomas, Barry 210

Thomas, Jameson A. 47, 163
Thomas, Martin 44
Thomas, Rhys Miles 138
Thomas, Richard 35
Thomas H. Ince Corporation 57, 79, 141, 183, 215
Thompson 155
Thompson, Alex 44
Thompson, Fred 141
Thompson, Hamilton 49
Thompson, Hugh 66
Thompson, Jim 160
Thornby, Robert G. 157
Thorndike, Sybil 67
Thorton, F. Martin 54
Thorton, Sigrid 134
"Three Cheers for the Yanks" 86
Three Comrades (1938) 190
"Three Episodes in the Life of Timothy Osborn" 142
Three Faces East (1926) 191
Three Faces East (1930) 191
Three Stooges 138
The Three Things 196
Throughton, David 36
Thule, Ingrid 90
Thunder Over the Desert (1940) 88, 192
Tiffany Films (Production) 143
Tilbury, Zeffie 47
Till I Come Back to You (1918) 192
Tiller Sunshine Girls 99
Time 117
The Times of London 5, 159
Timms, E.V. 88
Tin Pan Alley musical 29
Tiomkin, Dimitri 170
Tipperary 114
Tipping, Brian 123
Titus, Lydia Yeamans 46
To Hell with the Kaiser (1918) 192
To the Rescue (1918) 193
Tobias, George 176, 212
Tobias, Oliver 147
Tod, Malcolm 163
Todd, Arthur L 76
Tokes, Anna 54
Toland, Gregg 170
Toler, T.J. 103
Tolignac, Gastonde 102
Tom and Jerry 146
Tommy Atkins (1915) 193
Tonau Production Service 179
Toncray, Kate 41
Tone, Franchot 190
Tooker, William H. 73
Toomey, Regis 186
Torrence, David 64

Index 253

Torrens, Pip 203
Torreton, Philippe 55
Totheroh, Dan 67, 68
Touchstone Pictures 203
Toulout, Jean 107
Townley, Robin H. 165
Townsend, Perry, III 187
Trajkovski, Oliver 88
Trapp, Captain Von 195
Trapp, Georg Von 195
Trask, Nina 179
Travarthen, Noel 37
Travers, Roy 97
Treason (1917) 193
Treason (an act) 67, 183, 222n15
Treaty of Versailles 1
Trejan, Guy 155
Trench Warfare 2, 34, 41
Trenker, Luis 71
Trent, Captain Alan 64
Tres Hermano Productions 117
Trevelyan, H.B. 63
Trevor, Austin 200
Trevor, Spencer 132
Tribby, John E. 56
Trieste, Leopoldo 82
Triggers, Captain 210
Trimble, George S. 38
Triple Cross (1918) 121
The Tripple Cross 121
Trivas, Victor 104
Trotsky, Leon 40
Troughton, David 210
Trover, Leo 51
Trowbridge, Charles 176, 187
Truex, Ernest 94
Trumbo, Dalton 116, 117
Trump, Marshall Von 127
Trytel, W.L. 151
Tucker, George Loane 115
Tucker, Richard 56
Tunney, Tom 64
Tupper, Tristan 142
Turkel, Joe 160
Turkey (Turks, Turkish) 36, 89, 129, 133, 134, 189, 205
Turkish bath 132
Turley, Captain Tom 64
Turnbull, Hector 56
Turnen, Raymond 160
Turner, Bowditch M. 89
Turner, Florence 63
Turner, Maude 177
Turner, Paul 102
Turner, Vickery 168
Turpin, Ben 214
Turpin, Gary 155
Turton, Claude 88
TV Quick Awards. 36
Twentieth Century Fox 187, 208

Two Cities Films 190
Twohill, Pat 88
Tyler, Bowen 126
Tyrolean Pass 71

U-boat *see* submarine
U-Boat 29 (1939) 185
U-9 Weddigen (1927) 195
USS *U-172* 174
Ukrainian 39
Ulliel, Gaspard 198
Ullman, Daniel B. 172
Ullman, Ethal 57
Ulster 114
Ultimatum (1938) 194, 195
The Unbeliever (1918) 196
Uncredited 76, 90, 104, 134, 135, 141, 146, 150, 155, 174, 176, 186–188, 208.
Under the German Yoke (1915) 196
Underdog 23, 24
Underwater service 175
Underwood, Loyal 179
Unger, Gladys 144
Uni, Louis 144
Uniform 3, 73, 92, 104, 137, 161, 188, 208
United Artists 33, 104, 114, 132, 141, 160, 199
United States National Film Preservation Board 6
United States Navy 8, 58, 80, 175
Universal Film 16, 53, 70, 72, 85, 92, 100, 133, 141, 170, 189, 193, 199, 205
Universal Gold 141
Universal Pictures (Australia) 88
Universal Pictures (United States) 34, 170, 186, 205
University of California at Los Angles 6
University of Southern California Cinema-Television Library, Los Angles 7
University of Wyoming, Library Division 7
Unknown Love (1919) 186, 197
Unpardonable Sin (1919) 5, 197
Unrealistic 6, 29, 161, 197
Unsere Emden 78
Usztics, Matyas 147
Uzan, Devin 116

Vajda, Ernest 51
Val, Pierre F. 55
Val-de-Grace 155
Valbel, Marc 212

Valdar, Lovstad 191
Valente, Nathan 41
Valentino, Rudolph 13, 89, 90, 222n18
Valerie, Joan 187
Valli, Joe 71, 88
Valmour, Martin 204
Vamps 183
Vanaire, Jacques 170
Van Blerman, Amniel 73
Van Bureen, Ned 177
Van Buren, Mable 89
van den Ende, Walter 149
Vanderlynden, Madame 171
Vanderveer, Ellinor 181
van Dyck, Paul 96
Vane, Kitty 63
Vanel, Charles 212
Van Loan, Philip 120
Van Moyland, Joe 61
Van Sloan, Edward 170
Van Trees, James 138
Varconi, Victor 187
Varsi, Diana 116
Vassort, Cecile 55
Vaudeville 73–75, 86, 188, 214
Vaughan, Simon 41
Vavitch, Michael 108
Veidt, Conrad 185
Venereal diseases 184
Vengeance (1916) 169, 197
Vengeance (an action) 115, 169, 197
Veritania (read *Lusitania*) 135
Vernon, Isabel 116
Vernon, Wally 207
Vertes, Lajos 54
A Very Long Engagement (2004) 198
Veterinarian services 77
Vibart, Henry 163
Vickers machine guns 172
Victor, Henry 95
Victoria Cross 87
Victorian 1, 81
Victory (events) 5, 10, 23, 60, 86, 199
Victory (1928) 198
Victory (pictures) 124
Victory and Peace (1918) 199
Vidor, Charles 82
Vidor, Florence 174, 175, 192
Vidor, King 28, 29, 45, 53
Viertel, Peter 33
Vietnam War 9, 34
Village Roadshow (Associated) 91
Villiers, Charles 145
Villiers, James 123
Vippolis, Andre 138
Virgil, Jack 181

254 INDEX

Vitagraph Producton Company 84, 106, 159, 211
Vitray, Georges 195
Vivino, Robert 202
Vivitch, Michael 108
Vogler, Karl Michael 180
Volejnik, Ondrej 167
Volunteer 26, 73, 87, 103, 114, 129, 169, 181, 182, 205
The Volunteer (1917) 127, 137, 199
Von Richthofen and Brown (1971) 167
Vonelly, Louis 195
Vonn, Veola 125
Voss, Carl 64
Voya, George 130

The W Plan (1930) 200
Wadham, Julian 152, 203
Wagner, Billie 120
Wagner, Carolyn 184
Wagner, Hugo 121
Wagner, Robert 207
Wagstaff, Kieth 37
Walbrook, Anton 132
Walger, Sonya 35
Walker, Mrs. Allan 135
Walker, Brent 168
Walker, Charlotte 27
Walker, Craig 88
Walker, Joseph 186
Walker, June 204
Walker, Nella 76
Walker, Stuart 74
Walker, Thad 125, 126
Wall, Henry 100
Wall Street 111
Wallis, Hal B. 68, 76, 82, 175, 212
Walsh, Justin 96
Walsh, Percy 32
Walsh, Raoul A. 77, 111, 166, 206, 207
Walshe, Perry 145
Walt Disney Studios 203
Walters, Dorothy 136
Walters, Glen 178
Walthall, Henry B. 95, 96, 191
Walton, Douglas 140
Walton, John 134
Walturdaw Distribution 167
War and the Women (1917) 152, 201
War Brides (1916) 201
The War Bride's Secret (1916) 202
War film (generic) 2, 3, 4, 9, 11–15, 18, 22–25, 28, 30, 47, 68, 71, 84, 102, 109, 111, 137, 145, 151, 152, 175, 177, 184, 202

War Graves Commission 152
War Horse (2011) 203, 209
War Is Hell (1915) 204
War Nurse (1930) 204
War of 1812 96
War Pride (1917) 202
Warburton, John 172
Ward, Mary 211
Ward, Simon 203
Warde, Ernest C. 201
Warfield, Thadora 201
Warner, H.B. 154
Warner, Jack L. 68
Warner, Mariam 137
Warner Brothers 44, 50, 60, 64, 67, 68, **70**, 82, 120, 153, 167, 186, 191, 198, 212, **213**
Warnography 30
Warren, Mary 36, 37
Warrington, Ann 178
Warrington, George 112, 171
Warrington, James 112
Warrington, Kenneth 185
Warwic, Robert 170
Warwick, Virginia 89
Washburn, Bryant 62, 192
Wasrnack, Henry Christen 58
Water Diviner (2014) 9, 205
Waterloo Bridge 205
Waterloo Bridge (1931) 205
Waters, Ed 35
Watson, Delmar 142
Watson, Emily 203
Watson, Henrietta 169
Watson, Minor 212
Watts, James 139
Waybills 5
Wayne, Bert 107
Wayne, John 30, 148, 186
Wayne, Richard 42, 107
We Are French (1916) 206
We won't come back—we'll be buried over there 156
Wead, Frank "Spig" 186
Webber, Arthur 36
Weddigen, Captain 195
Weddigen, Otto 195
Weddigen, U-9 195
Weems, Walter 87
Weepers 77
Weigert, Robert Lee 195
Weimar Republic 78
Weinkauf, Gregory 210
Weir, Peter 91, **92**
Weisbarth, Michael 138
Welch 44, 103; *see also* Wales
Welchmen, Harry 132
Welles, Orson 213
Wellington Evening Post 41
Wellman, Bill 126
Wellman, William A. 14, 125,

129, 208, 209
Wells, Conrad 181
Wells, L.M. 193
Welsh, Niles 105
Welsh, T.A. 74
Welsh, William 100
Welsh-Pearson Company 123
Wending, Pete 79
Wendy Allnut 155
Wenstrom, Harold 140
Wentworth, Issac 177
Wentworth, Marion Craig 201, 202
Wessel, Dick 187
West (as place) 28, 84, 141, 158, 186
West, Charles 153
West, Raymond B. 57, 173
West, Rebecca 168
West, Tony 182
Westen, Charles 157, 173
Westfall, T.H. 182
Westminster 154
Weston, Charles 173
Weston, David 200
Weston, Doris 186, 187
Wetherell, M.A. 171
Whale, James 118
What Price Glory? (1926) 29, 30, 118, 206
What Price Glory (1952) 207
"What's the Wrong Way to Tickle Mary?" 214
Wheatcroft, Stanhope 157
Wheddon, Horace 150
Wheeler, Bert 99
"When You Wore a Tulip and I Wore a Big Red Rose" 86
Where Were You the Night I Shot Down Baron von Richthofen? (1970) 207
Whishaw, Ben 194
"Whistling the Blues Away" 99
Whitaker, Raymond 56
White, Huey 76
White, Merrill 154
White, Pearl 147
White, William 141
White Armed Joe 150
White scarves 70
Whiteley, Tom 168
Whitemore, Hugh 168
Whitman, Walt 100
Whitney, Claire 120
Whittaker, Charles E. 38
Whittington, Valerie 168
Whittlesey, Charles 138
Whitworth, Robert 201
Whorf, Richard 212
Why We Fought: America's Wars in Film and History 3

Index

Wieczorek, Izabela 39
Wiene, Robert 195
Wilby, James 43
Wilcox, Frank 89
Wilcox, Herbert 66, 67
Wilder, Gene 90
Wiley, Hugh 43
Wilk, Marek 39
Wilkerson, Billy 206
Wilkinson, Sam 139, 189
Willard, Louis 123
Willat, Edwin W. 79, 80
Willat, Irvin V. 79, 186
Willes, Peter 68
Willet, Irvin 42, 113
Willets, Gilson 111
William (Prince) 204
William, Gracie 176
William Chaudet, Louis 84
Williams, George B. 184
Williams, Guinn "Big Boy" 83, 142
Williams, John J. 136, 203
Williams, Matthew 35
Williams, Megan 35, 37
Williams, Sioned Jones 102
Williams, Tam 194
Williamson, David 91
Williamson, J.C. 75
Willie and Joe 45
Willingham, Calder 160
Wilson (1944) 161, 208
Wilson, Alec 37
Wilson, Bob 62
Wilson, Carey 134
Wilson, Fred L. 133
Wilson, Howard 140
Wilson, Jack 179
Wilson, John 123
Wilson, Jom 99
Wilson, Kevin 57
Wilson, Lois 193, 194
Wilson, Mark 116, 127
Wilson, Michael 129
Wilson, Roy 104
Wilson, Tom 99
Wilson, Woodrow 58, 106, 164, 208, 212
Wimbush, Mary 156
Wincer, Simon 133
Winch, Arden 210
Winchester, Philip 83
Wincott, Harry 143
Wing, Pat 76
Winger, Henry 109
Wings (1927) 209, 210
Wings (1977) **209**, 210
Winn, Godfrey 47
Winnie 4
Winnie the Pooh 42
Winnipeg 41

Winslow, Harry 131
Winter, George 35
Winter, Sergeant 194
Winton, Jane 104
Withey, Chester 27, 109
Witney, Michael 65
Witter, Frank 149
Witting, Mattie 84
Wohanka, Jiri 167
Wohlbold, Captain von 119
Wolbert, William 133
Wolf, Millicent 87
Wolfe, Nora 110
Wolfit, Donald 129
Wolheim, Louis 34
Woman (women, womenhood) 1, 3, 5, 13, 17, 18, 20–23, 29, 42, 45, 51, 52, 56, 57, 65–67, 75–77, 81, 89, 91, 98, 99, 131, 104, 125, 135, 138, 142, 147, 148, 151, 152, 156–160, 162, 169, 174, 177, 183, 184, 190, 196, 201, 202, 204–207, 211, 214
The Woman the Germans Shot (1918) 74, 145
The Womanhood Glory of the Nation (1917) 211
Women's International League for Peace and Freedom (WILPF) 51
Women's programmers 77
Wonderly, W. Carrey 105, 106
Wong, James 212
Wontner, Arthur 190
Wood, David 32
Wood, Freeman 130
Wood, Sam 135
Wooden Crosses (1932) 171, 212
Wooden Crosses (1936) 212
Woodruff, Eleanor 106, 127
Woods, Arthur B. 139
Woods, Chester 182
Woods, Ellen 75
Woodthorpe, Georgia 125
Woodthorpe, Peter 48
Woodward, Eugenie 153
Woodward, Harry 153
Woodward, Oliver 44
Woodward, Tim 210
Woolfe, Harry Bruce 139
Woolley, Monty
Woolsey, Robert 99
World Film Corporation 157, 199
World War II (as event) 9, 14, 15, 21, 23, 34, 44, 52, 72, 90, 96, 110, 166, 178, 206, 211
The World's Greatest Lover (1977) 90
Wormaid, S. 162

Worters, Danny 36
Worth, Richard 66
Wraight, John 57
Wray, Fay 130
Wray, John 34
Wright, Edmund 105
Wright, Heather 180
Wycherly, Margaret 176
Wyckoff, Alvin 135
Wylie, I.A.R. 46, 90
Wyllie, Daniel 205
Wynn, Keenan 86
Wynne-Candy, General Clive 132

Yankee Doodle Dandy (1942) 212, **213**
Yankee Doodle in Berlin (1919) 93, 120, 214
Yarmough county 36
Yates, Maud 193
Yelland, David 164
Yellow Peril 174
Yiddish 104
Yilmaz, Cem 205
YMCA 86
York, Alvin C. 176–177
York, Michael 214
Young, Duncan 44
Young, Freddie A. 198, 200
Young, Hal 188
Young, James 95
Young, Jerry 74
Young, Jonathon 41
Young, Loretta 205
Young, Noah 99
Young, Paul 43
Young, Robert 103, 174, 190
Young, Tammany 177
Young, Waldemar 133, 180
Young, Warwick 44
Young Indiana Jones Chronicles 27
Ypres 103
Yr Arwr (The Hero) 102
Yuma, Arizona 140

Zahler, Lee 62
Zampi, Mario 189, 190
Zanuck, Darryl F. 44, 99, 170, 187, 191, 207
Zanzibar 180
Zeller, Baron Ferdinand von 125
Zeppelin (1971)
zeppelin (airship) 95, 96, 180, 181, 214, 215
The Zeppelin's Last Raid (1917) 214, 215
Zespol Filmowy "Kadr" 39
Ziegfeld, Florenz 38

Ziegfeld Follies 5
Zielinski, Jerzy 163
Zier, H.M. 178
SMS *Ziethenr* 52

Zimmerman Telegram 182
Ziskin, Joel 147 149
Zoe, Frank 104
Zoli, Charles 88

Zollinger, William 85
Zuber, Bernadine 181
Zukor, Adolph 129
Zweig, Arnold 56

www.ingramcontent.com/pod-product-compliance
Lightning Source LLC
Chambersburg PA
CBHW051215300426
44116CB00006B/589